D1720517

Social Cognition and Metacognition in Schizophrenia

Psychopathology and Treatment Approaches

Social Cognition and Metacognition in Schizophrenia

Psychopathology and Treatment Approaches

Edited by

Paul H. Lysaker

Richard L. Roudebush VA Medical Center,
Indianapolis, IN, USA
and
Indiana University School of Medicine, Indianapolis, IN, USA

Giancarlo Dimaggio

Center for Metacognitive Interpersonal Therapy, Rome, Italy
and
University La Sapienza, Rome, Italy

Martin Brüne

LWL-University Hospital Bochum, Bochum, Germany

AMSTERDAM • BOSTON • HEIDELBERG • LONDON
NEW YORK • OXFORD • PARIS • SAN DIEGO
SAN FRANCISCO • SINGAPORE • SYDNEY • TOKYO
Academic Press is an imprint of Elsevier

Academic Press is an imprint of Elsevier
32 Jamestown Road, London NW1 7BY, UK
225 Wyman Street, Waltham, MA 02451, USA
525 B Street, Suite 1800, San Diego, CA 92101-4495, USA

Copyright © 2014 Elsevier Inc. All rights reserved

No part of this publication may be reproduced, stored in a retrieval system or
transmitted in any form or by any means electronic, mechanical, photocopying,
recording or otherwise without the prior written permission of the publisher
Permissions may be sought directly from Elsevier's Science & Technology
Rights Department in Oxford, UK: phone (+44) (0) 1865 843830;
fax (+44) (0) 1865 853333; email: permissions@elsevier.com. Alternatively,
visit the Science and Technology Books website at www.elsevierdirect.com/rights
for further information.

Notice
No responsibility is assumed by the publisher for any injury and/or damage to persons
or property as a matter of products liability, negligence or otherwise, or from any use
or operation of any methods, products, instructions or ideas contained in the material
herein. Because of rapid advances in the medical sciences, in particular, independent
verification of diagnoses and drug dosages should be made.

British Library Cataloguing-in-Publication Data
A catalogue record for this book is available from the British Library

Library of Congress Cataloging-in-Publication Data
A catalog record for this book is available from the Library of Congress

ISBN: 978-0-12-405172-0

For information on all Academic Press publications
visit our website at elsevierdirect.com

Typeset by MPS Limited, Chennai, India
www.adi-mps.com

14 15 16 17   10 9 8 7 6 5 4 3 2 1

Working together
to grow libraries in
developing countries

www.elsevier.com • www.bookaid.org

Contents

3.   Social Cognition During the Early Phase of Schizophrenia

Amanda McCleery, William P. Horan and Michael F. Green

4.   Empathy

Birgit Derntl and Christina Regenbogen

5.   Memory-Related Metacognition in Patients with Schizophrenia

Elisabeth Bacon and Marie Izaute

**6.　Metacognition in Schizophrenia Spectrum Disorders:
Methods of Assessment and Associations with Psychosocial
Function, Neurocognition, Symptoms, and Cognitive Style**

*Paul H. Lysaker, Jaclyn Hillis, Bethany L. Leonhardt,
Marina Kukla and Kelly D. Buck*

**7.　The Impact of Metacognition on the Development
and Maintenance of Negative Symptoms**

Hamish J. McLeod, Andrew Gumley and Matthias Schwannauer

**8.　Metacognition as a Framework to Understanding
the Occurrence of Aggression and Violence
in Patients with Schizophrenia**

Sune Bo, Ahmad Abu-Akel and Mickey Kongerslev

12. Metacognitively Focused Psychotherapy for People with Schizophrenia: Eight Core Elements That Define Practice

Paul H. Lysaker, Kelly D. Buck, Bethany L. Leonhardt, Benjamin Buck, Jay Hamm, Ilanit Hasson-Ohayon, Jenifer L. Vohs and Giancarlo Dimaggio

13. Adapted-Metacognitive Interpersonal Therapy Applied to Paranoid Schizophrenia: Promoting Higher Levels of Reflection on One's and Others' Minds, Awareness of Interpersonal Schemas, Differentiation, and Mastery of Social Problems

Giampaolo Salvatore, Raffaele Popolo, Paul H. Lysaker, Paolo Ottavi, Nadia Di Sturco and Giancarlo Dimaggio

Ahmad Abu-Akel   University of Birmingham, Birmingham, UK

Elisabeth Bacon   Strasbourg, France

Ryan Balzan   Flinders University, Adelaide, SA, Australia

Rebecca Bargenquast   Queensland University of Technology, Brisbane, QLD, Australia

Michael R. Basso   The University of Tulsa, Tulsa, OK, USA

Sune Bo   Psychiatric Research Unit, Region Zealand, Denmark

Benjamin K. Brent   Beth Israel Deaconess Medical Center and Massachusetts Mental Health Center, Boston, MA, USA; Massachusetts General Hospital, Harvard Medical School, Boston, MA, USA; Harvard Medical School, Boston, MA, USA

Martin Brüne   LWL-University Hospital Bochum, Bochum, Germany

Elliot C. Brown   LWL-University Hospital Bochum, Bochum, Germany; International Graduate School of Neuroscience (IGSN), Ruhr-University Bochum, Bochum, Germany

Benjamin Buck   University of North Carolina at Chapel Hill, Chapel Hill, NC, USA

Kelly D. Buck   Richard L. Roudebush VA Medical Center, Indianapolis, IN, USA

Dennis R. Combs   The University of Texas at Tyler, Tyler, TX, USA

Sarah Daniel   University of Copenhagen, Copenhagen, Denmark

Birgit Derntl   RWTH Aachen University, Aachen, Germany

Nadia Di Sturco   Center for Metacognitive Interpersonal Therapy, Rome, Italy

Giancarlo Dimaggio   Center for Metacognitive Interpersonal Therapy, Rome, Italy; University La Sapienza, Rome, Italy

Emily Drake   The University of Texas at Tyler, Tyler, TX, USA

João M. Fernandes   Centro Hospitalar de Lisboa Ocidental, EPE, Lisbon, Portugal

Peter Fonagy   University College London, London, UK

Cristina Gonzalez   LWL-University Hospital Bochum, Bochum, Germany; Ruhr-University Bochum, Bochum, Germany

Michael F. Green   David Geffen School of Medicine at UCLA, Los Angeles, CA, USA; VISN 22 Mental Illness Research Education and Clinical Center, Los Angeles, CA, USA

Andrew Gumley   University of Glasgow, Glasgow, UK

Jay Hamm   Indiana University School of Medicine, Indianapolis, IN, USA

Susanne Harder   University of Copenhagen, Copenhagen, Denmark

Ilanit Hasson-Ohayon   Bar-Ilan University, Ramat-Gan, Israel

Jaclyn Hillis   University of Indianapolis, Indianapolis, IN, USA

William P. Horan   David Geffen School of Medicine at UCLA, Los Angeles, CA, USA; VISN 22 Mental Illness Research Education and Clinical Center, Los Angeles, CA, USA

Marie Izaute   LAPSCO - UMR 6024 CNRS, Clermont-Ferrand, France

Katja Koelkebeck   University of Muenster, Muenster, Germany

Mickey Kongerslev   Psychiatric Research Unit, Region Zealand, Denmark

Marina Kukla   Richard L. Roudebush VA Medical Center, Indianapolis, IN, USA

Bethany L. Leonhardt   University of Indianapolis, Indianapolis, IN, USA

Paul H. Lysaker   Richard L Roudebush VA Medical Center Indianapolis, IN, USA; University School of Medicine, Indianapolis, IN, USA

Amanda McCleery   David Geffen School of Medicine at UCLA, Los Angeles, CA, USA

Hamish J. McLeod   University of Glasgow, Glasgow, UK

Mahesh Menon   University of British Columbia, Vancouver, BC, Canada

Steffen Moritz   Universitätsklinikum Hamburg-Eppendorf, Hamburg, Germany

Paolo Ottavi   Center for Metacognitive Interpersonal Therapy, Rome, Italy

Manuela Pasinetti   Center for Metacognitive Interpersonal Therapy, Rome, Italy

Raffaele Popolo   Center for Metacognitive Interpersonal Therapy, Rome, Italy

Christina Regenbogen   RWTH Aachen University, Aachen, Germany; Karolinska Institutet, Solna, Sweden

David L. Roberts   University of Texas Health Science Center, San Antonio, TX, USA

Giampaolo Salvatore   Center for Metacognitive Interpersonal Therapy, Rome, Italy

Matthias Schwannauer   University of Edinburgh, Edinburgh, UK

Robert D. Schweitzer   Queensland University of Technology, Brisbane, QLD, Australia

Cumhur Tas   LWL-University Hospital Bochum, Bochum, Germany; Ruhr-University Bochum, Bochum, Germany

Jenifer L. Vohs   Indiana University School of Medicine, Indianapolis, IN, USA

Christine Wilhelm   School of Medicine, University of Muenster, Muenster, Germany

Todd S. Woodward   BC Mental Health and Addictions Research Institute, Vancouver, BC, Canada; University of British Columbia, Vancouver, BC, Canada

Preface

Seemingly, as much as any subject in the field of medicine and mental health, our contemporary understanding of schizophrenia has been subject to vigorous debate and significant ongoing revision. Since the late 1990s (or the past few decades), we have witnessed fundamental changes in our ideas about the incidence and prevalence of schizophrenia, its natural course, and the validity of long-held subtypes. In our opinion, one of the most remarkable developments is the accumulation of evidence that schizophrenia may be characterized by relatively specific problems related to being aware of and reflecting upon one's own thoughts, feelings, and intentions, and the thoughts, feelings, and intentions of other people. In other words, schizophrenia, contrary in part to the direction provided by diagnostic manuals, may be more than a diffuse set of unrelated decrements in mental processes. As a disorder, it may more specifically involve difficulties in noticing and making sense of the things that allow people to experience themselves as unique beings in the world.

Different names have been used to refer to these deficits. They have been called impairments in social cognition, theory of mind, metacognition, emotional intelligence, mind-reading, and mentalization, just to name a few. While each construct emphasizes a slightly different phenomena, to have deficits in any of them suggests some form of difficulty in recognizing what one and others think, feel, and intend. In addition, each construct, whether it states it directly or just infers it, is concerned with the capacities that allow us to know and scrutinize self-experience and link our experience in the moment with some larger picture of who we, and others, are across the histories of our lives. Applied to schizophrenia, the implication is that this core element of disability interferes with a person's ability to form the types of ideas about the self and others that are needed to negotiate the demands of life itself, as well as the challenges posed by schizophrenia.

One limitation we see to date is that there has been a lack of integration of the work in this area. Many of the papers published, for instance, have been confined within their own 'silos'. One example of this is that work on social cognition has not been integrated with work on metacognition. Work on metacognition has not been integrated with social cognition, and so forth. This book thus seeks to bring together the developments on these related constructs, which often is not found in the same volume. We have included chapters on both social cognition and metacognition without waiting for an agreed-upon definition about how exactly these constructs overlap and diverge with the hope that discussing them in the same volume will speed along that process. We have chosen these two constructs given that each potentially functions as an umbrella term, with others seen as fitting under the umbrella. Social cognition, for instance, often includes constructs such as theory of mind while metacognition refers to a spectrum of activities which involves thinking about thinking and stretches from consideration of discrete psychological phenomenon to the synthesis of discrete perception into an integrated representation of self and others.

A further limitation of work in this area has been the bifurcation of clinical and academic research. Work on schizophrenia offered by clinician scholars has not been integrated with the science performed by more traditional laboratory-based scientists. To address this, this book will also include chapters by scholars who are primarily researchers and others who are clinicians and have spent years in conversations with people with schizophrenia. There are chapters that offer rich case reports and others that present statistical analyses of large and diverse samples. Finally, much work in schizophrenia can be classified as focused either on psychopathology or treatment, with the two literatures rarely informing one another. This book thus includes sections dealing with both psychopathology and treatment.

The first overall set of objectives of the book are thus integration and dialogue: the integration and dialogue of research on social cognition and metacognition, the integration and dialogue of work from primarily clinical and research settings, and the integration of work on treatment and psychopathology. Pragmatically, the book opens with chapters regarding the biologic and social roots of social cognitive and metacognitive activity. The next set of chapters then focuses on different forms of social cognitive and metacognitive deficits and their linkages with functional outcomes. Finally, a range of different treatment approaches are offered and discussed.

We imagine the readers of this book will come from many different clinical and academic backgrounds. We anticipate this book will end up in the hands of clinicians, scientists, students, and even policy makers. And for all, we hope the book accomplishes two larger goals. First, we hope for a more deeply human and nuanced portrait of schizophrenia. We believe that the chapters offered here have the potential to paint a richer picture of how schizophrenia interrupts the lives of unique human beings via alteration of the basic experience of one's own being and the being of others. We believe this picture will be richer because of the integration rather than the exclusive focus on one construct, one form of evidence, or one type of author. Second, we hope to spur the development of treatments that help people with this condition to meaningfully recover. We explicitly do not want to find 'the' new treatment or promote one universal response to deficits in social cognition or metacognition. We do not want to privilege one view or one treatment above another but instead desire to spur on the type of dialogue that will allow for the proliferation of many different treatments, which could meet the needs of many different types of people who experience schizophrenia. Finally, we hope to support the development of treatments that move beyond a symptom focus and take into account the whole person and his or her core experience as a unique being in the world.

Paul H. Lysaker
Giancarlo Dimaggio
Martin Brüne

Neurobiologic Underpinnings of Social Cognition and Metacognition in Schizophrenia Spectrum Disorders

Elliot C. Brown,[1,2] Cumhur Tas,[1,3]
Cristina Gonzalez[1,3] and Martin Brüne[1]

[1]LWL-University Hospital Bochum, Bochum, Germany, [2]International Graduate School
of Neuroscience (IGSN), Ruhr-University Bochum, Bochum, Germany, [3]Ruhr-University Bochum,
Bochum, Germany

INTRODUCTION

As the field of psychiatry is currently becoming more focused on the brain as the target organ for treatment, it is natural then to search for the neurobiologic factors that play a role in the pathologic features of mental illness and disorder. In schizophrenia, potential dysfunctions of the 'social brain' provide a tangible

Social Cognition and Metacognition in Schizophrenia.
DOI: http://dx.doi.org/10.1016/B978-0-12-405172-0.00001-6
© 2014 Elsevier Inc. All rights reserved.

starting point to explore the underlying neurobiology of deficits in social cognition. This line of inquiry is particularly pertinent due to the growing work on animal models of schizophrenia, as well as with the rise of social neuroscience as a discipline that utilizes neuroimaging and brain stimulation techniques to uncover the neural substrates of the cognitive processes underlying human social interaction.

The aim of this chapter is to present the current state of research in the neurobiology of social cognition in schizophrenia. As animal studies provide the initial steps that lead to human studies, we first focus on rodents as animal models of schizophrenia and social cognition. The translation of these findings, as well as the neurobiologic evidence on social cognition in schizophrenia, is also summarized with current limitations and future suggestion in the following sections.

ANIMAL STUDIES ON BASIC SOCIAL COGNITION AND SOCIAL BEHAVIOR WITH SCHIZOPHRENIA MODELS

In order to understand the most fundamental neural underpinnings of social behavior in humans, many scientists have opted for animal models owing to the opportunity to explore and alter and measure the brain mechanisms and the resulting behavior. Furthermore, while sociocognitive tasks for humans are usually designed in experimental settings and involve large machinery or cables (e.g., magnetic resonance imaging (MRI) or electroencephalography (EEG)), that is in non-natural circumstances, social behavior and basic social cognition assessed in animals reduces the effects of, or at least controls, laboratory influence. Lastly, neurotransmitter networks can be more easily explored in the brains of animals, while brain networks in low- and high-level social cognition are better investigated in humans.

A variety of animal models of schizophrenia, mostly in rodents, have been developed and have brought new insights into the neurobiologic underpinnings that lead to social dysfunction in this psychiatric disorder. One of the greatest challenges in neuropsychiatric animal research is to reproduce and relate the clinical characteristics observed in humans to less complex animals. Given the heterogeneity of symptoms in schizophrenia, most animal models do not recreate the whole psychopathology of the disease, but instead, present certain aspects of the disorder (Brüne, 2009). Therefore, some models embody positive symptoms, while others try to characterize some of the negative symptoms, such as social isolation.

Interestingly, some of the behavioral abnormalities common to patients with schizophrenia also occur and can be assessed in rodents, and these are thus widely used to determine face and predictive validity of the psychiatric animal models. These behaviors can be examined by using sensorimotor gating experiments and by measuring social withdrawal. Sensorimotor gating refers to the filtering of external information that is trivial or unnecessary, such as the background noise of a party. Deficits in sensorimotor gating lead to an overload of sensory and cognitive processes that have been associated with impaired social behavior in patients with schizophrenia and in rodent models of schizophrenia (Duncan *et al.*, 2004; Koh *et al.*, 2007; Lijam *et al.*, 1997). For instance, Wynn and colleagues showed that patients with schizophrenia who performed better in a sensorimotor gating test also performed better in a social perception task (Wynn *et al.*, 2005). Thus, assessing the levels of sensorimotor gating is greatly informative in terms of social cognition and social behavior in both humans and animals. Sensorimotor gating impairments have been consistently found in patients with schizophrenia as well as their first-degree relatives (Kumari *et al.*, 2005), and even though these deficits are not disease-specific, it has been repeatedly demonstrated to be a key characteristic of this group of psychiatric disorders. Moreover, most of the literature on sensorimotor gating has been addressed in schizophrenia given the reliability to replicate the results in this disease and its relationship to social cognition. However, patients diagnosed with other disorders, such as obsessive-compulsive disorder (Ahmari *et al.*, 2012), Huntington disease (Swerdlow *et al.*, 1995), or bipolar disorder with acute psychotic mania (Perry *et al.*, 2001) have also been shown to exhibit deficits in sensorimotor gating, although all of these disorders present dysfunctions in sensory, motor, and/or cognitive information processing (Geyer, 2006). The most widely used test to assess the levels of sensorimotor gating is through pre-pulse inhibition (PPI), which occurs when the startle reaction to a particular stimulus (usually auditory but also visual and tactile) is decreased by presenting a weaker pre-stimulus before. Therefore, animals or people who do not display a decrease (or inhibition) of their startle reaction when a weak tone precedes a strong tone, as compared with when only a strong tone is presented, are considered to have reduced PPI, which is related to deficits in social cognition. The benefit of this test is that it can be measured in both humans and rodents and thus offers the possibility for translational approaches. In the case of social performance, several behavioral measures are used in rodents, such as mating behavior, nest building, and playful behavior. Hence, animal models that present deficits in these behaviors may help us learn the underlying mechanisms responsible for the social cognitive deficits found in schizophrenia.

Animal studies have found that several factors, including neurodevelopment (during and after pregnancy), brain lesions, genetic predisposition, and exposure to certain substances, induce abnormalities in PPI responses. For instance, neonatal rats exposed to epidermal growth factor (EGF), rats with lesions in the ventral and caudodorsal striatum (Kodsi and Swerdlow, 1995), rats treated with the adrenoreceptor agonist ciralozine (Carasso *et al.*, 1998), and rats that are reared in isolation (Wilkinson *et al.*, 1994) present deficits in this test. Neonatal lesions to the ventral part of the hippocampus (Sams-Dodd *et al.*, 1997), basal amygdala (Decker *et al.*, 1995; Wan and Swerdlow, 1997), and prefrontal cortex (PFC) (Schneider and Koch, 2005) in rats causes social interaction abnormalities as well as other schizophrenia-related behavioral malfunctions in juvenile and adults, as occurs in people with this disorder.

Studies have shown that respiratory or immune infection of a pregnant mouse induces PPI deficits and social withdrawal in the offspring once they reach adulthood (Bitanihirwe *et al.*, 2010; Shi *et al.*, 2003; Wolff and Bilkey, 2008). Finally, several genes suggested to be partly responsible for the etiology of schizophrenia in humans (e.g., DISC 1, Neuregulin 1, ErbB4, Dysbindin) have been manipulated in animal models and have been linked to social deficits (Ehrlichman *et al.*, 2009; Feng *et al.*, 2008; Moy *et al.*, 2009; O'Tuathaigh *et al.*, 2007; Pletnikov *et al.*, 2008). These studies emphasize the importance of environmental as well as genetic factors in the modulation of the PPI startle response and the ensuing induction of sociocognitive deficits in schizophrenia.

NEUROTRANSMITTERS AND RECEPTORS RELATED TO SOCIAL COGNITION

Compatible with lesion, genetic, and immunodevelopmental manipulations, numerous animal studies have demonstrated a dysfunction in distinct neurotransmitter networks to explain the social deficits in schizophrenia. Altering the dopaminergic system by exposing rodents to direct and indirect dopamine agonists such as apomorphine, D-amphetamine, and cocaine disrupts PPI, and this effect has been suggested to be driven by the dopamine D_2-receptor family. The atypical antipsychotics clozapine, quetiapine, and olanzapine reverse the apomorphine-induced PPI deficits in both animals and humans with schizophrenia, implying the involvement of similar dopamine-dependent mechanisms for the induction of this dysfunction (Geyer and Moghaddam, 2001; Swerdlow and Geyer, 1998). Despite the evidence toward hyperactivity of the dopaminergic system, some authors have more recently suggested that the hyperdopaminergia is restricted to subcortical mesolimbic regions and mostly explains positive symptoms, while mesocortical projections to the PFC might indeed be characterized by dopamine hypofunction and may be related to the cognitive and negative symptomatology (Abi-Dargham and Moore, 2003; Kondiziella *et al.*, 2007; Laruelle *et al.*, 2003).

In addition to manipulation of the dopaminergic system, acute and chronic administration of the *N*-methyl-D-aspartate (NMDA) receptor noncompetitive antagonist phencyclidine (PCP) in rats and mice induces PPI deficits and social withdrawal (Lee *et al.*, 2005; Mansbach and Geyer, 1989; Qiao *et al.*, 2001; Sams-Dodd, 1995; Sams-Dodd, 1996). Some atypical antipsychotics, such as clozapine and olanzapine, but not typical ones, partially reverse the NMDA blocker-induced social disturbances (Qiao *et al.*, 2001; Sams-Dodd, 1996). Other NMDA antagonists such as ketamine and MK-801 are also widely used in animal research to induce PPI deficits (Bast *et al.*, 2000; Geyer and Moghaddam, 2001; Swerdlow *et al.*, 1998). Interestingly, a mouse model where the NMDAR1 (NR1) has been knocked down (i.e., expressed in lower amounts) displays disturbances in both PPI and social behavior (Mohn *et al.*, 1999). This is supported by findings showing that NMDA receptors and intracellular NMDA receptor-interacting proteins are dysregulated in patients with schizophrenia (Gao *et al.*, 2000; Kristiansen *et al.*, 2007). Finally, the connection between the influence of dopamine and glutamate on sensorimotor gating can be explained because hypoactivity of the glutamate system increases mesolimbic and inhibits mesocortical dopamine release (Gururajan *et al.*, 2010).

Other neurotransmitters, such as gamma-aminobutyric acid (GABA), acetylcholine, and serotonin (5-HT), have been suggested to influence social cognition in schizophrenia. Both GABA and acetylcholine have been repeatedly reported to be necessary for adequate PPI responses (Bosch and Schmid, 2008; Fendt *et al.*, 2001; Schreiber *et al.*, 2002; Yeomans *et al.*, 2010), and studies in patients with schizophrenia have revealed abnormalities in these neurotransmitter networks (Beasley *et al.*, 2002; Benes *et al.*, 1992; Leonard, 2002; Raedler, 2003). Moreover, dopaminergic neurons from the brainstem seem to be connected to cortical glutamatergic neurons via GABAergic interneurons, bringing the three neurotransmitter networks together (Sesack *et al.*, 2003). In the case of serotonin, it has been shown that this neurotransmitter plays a role in emotion recognition and social cognition (Canli and Lesch, 2007), and serotonin receptor abnormalities have also been reported in the brains of patients with schizophrenia (Sumiyoshi *et al.*, 1996). Finally, other neuromodulators such as oxytocin and adenosine have been proposed to be implicated in the negative symptoms of schizophrenia by affecting the dopaminergic and glutamatergic networks (Boison *et al.*, 2012).

In conclusion, animal studies give insights into the possible biochemical, anatomical, and genetic disturbances that can give rise to schizophrenia-like behavioral abnormalities. It seems that a combination of environmental factors (prenatal infections, immunoneurodevelopmental abnormalities, genetic predisposition) and neurotransmitter network aberrations (including dopaminergic, glutamatergic, serotonergic, cholinergic, and GABAergic) are at least partly responsible for the social cognitive deficits apparent in patients with schizophrenia. Furthermore, brain lesion studies suggest that abnormalities in certain areas, such as the ventral hippocampus, the amygdala, and the PFC, might account for these social disturbances as well. Given the complexity of schizophrenia and the social brain, it is challenging to assign specific neurotransmitter disturbances to precise deficits in social cognition. However, it is reasonable to suggest that, because these neurotransmitter networks are involved in processing basic social cognition in rodents, they will certainly have an effect in higher-order sociocognitive processing in patients with schizophrenia, as described in the following sections.

SOCIAL COGNITION IN SCHIZOPHRENIA: NEUROIMAGING RESEARCH

Investigating the brain at the level of neurotransmitters and cellular processes is clearly crucial in understanding the neurobiologic foundations of pathologies of social cognitive deficits in schizophrenia. Complementary to this, the study of brain structure and function at the systems level, by looking at how neural populations work together in localized brain regions and in networks across these regions, provides a conceptual bridge to understanding behavioral features of the illness. Using neuroimaging methods such as structural/functional magnetic resonance imaging (fMRI) and EEG, research in the social neuroscience of schizophrenia seeks to find malfunctions of the social brain, and link this to the pathology and impaired behaviors associated with deficits in social cognition. The outcome of past neuroimaging studies looking at functional activity in schizophrenia have generally found a reduced activation of frontal areas, also referred to as a hypofrontality (Glahn *et al.*, 2005), and an increased activation in cortical midline structures (CMS) such as the anterior cingulate cortex (ACC) (Minzenberg *et al.*, 2009). Another core outcome has revealed abnormal functional connectivity across multiple brain regions and networks (Friston, 1999; Schmitt *et al.*, 2011). Structural MRI studies have also consistently found decreased gray matter volumes in left frontal areas and limbic and paralimbic areas, including the thalamus (Ellison-Wright *et al.*, 2008; Fornito *et al.*, 2009; Glahn *et al.*, 2008). A meta-analysis of voxel-based morphometry (VBM) studies has identified white matter reductions in bilateral frontal cortices and bilateral internal capsules (Di *et al.*, 2009). It is understood that these diffuse functional and structural abnormalities seen across multiple brain regions in schizophrenia also include some areas recruited for social cognition. An increasing number of studies have been emerging to uncover more specific abnormalities in the social brain in schizophrenia, which will now be discussed in more detail in the forthcoming sections.

Neuroimaging of Emotion Processing

At the lower levels of social cognition, the processing and understanding of others' emotional states are crucial for interpreting others' behaviors in a social interaction. It is likely that the ability to understand others' emotions is also, at least partly, dependent on having awareness and understanding of one's own emotions (Mayer and Salovey, 1995; Ochsner *et al.*, 2004). In the case of schizophrenia, this therefore presents a serious problem, as negative symptoms, such as anhedonia, severely diminish the expression of one's own emotions and leads to a flattening of affect (Berenbaum and Oltmanns, 1992). A large body of work has consistently found substantial emotion perception deficits in patients with schizophrenia at the behavioral level, reporting generally large effect sizes (Kohler *et al.*, 2010). This has been further confirmed by numerous neuroimaging studies, as patients have been found to have reduced volumes and activation levels in brain areas that are central to emotion processing.

Bogerts and colleagues (1993) were one of the first to find structural differences in hippocampal and amygdala volumes in patients with schizophrenia, which was also, counterintuitively, associated with positive psychotic symptoms and not negative symptoms. Subsequently, more recent studies have largely confirmed these early findings, with larger sample sizes and more advanced imaging data analysis techniques (Rajarethinam *et al.*, 2001; Velakoulis *et al.*, 2006), also revealing a possible genetic influence (Bediou *et al.*, 2007; de Achaval *et al.*, 2012; Tian *et al.*, 2011). A meta-analysis of 17 fMRI studies looking at facial emotion perception in patients with schizophrenia revealed a robust finding of reduced activation bilaterally in the amygdala/parahippocampal gyrus, fusiform gyrus, and in the right superior frontal gyrus and right lentiform nucleus, when compared with healthy controls (Li *et al.*, 2010). One main conclusion of the meta-analysis was that the pattern of reduced activity seen in patients spread across a number of different regions of the brain, suggesting a disruption in the network associated with emotion perception at the systems level, rather than a localized dysfunction in specific brain regions. Two other meta-analyses, including a broader range of studies, also came to similar conclusions of a reduced amygdala activation and a network disruption in patients (Anticevic *et al.*, 2012; Taylor *et al.*, 2012). This conclusion is further supported by a more recent study finding abnormalities in functional connectivity between the amygdala and frontal and parietal areas (Mukherjee *et al.*, 2012; Tian *et al.*, 2011), which could also consequently impact on the cognitive processes required for higher-level mental representations of other people. Notably, Li and colleagues (2010) acknowledge the limitations of their meta-analysis, as it is not clear if the reduced activations seen in patients are of the same degree across the implicated brain areas or to the same degree across the schizophrenia population as a whole. There is also some evidence in the studies included in the meta-analysis, and from other recent fMRI studies, which contradict the final conclusion of reduced amygdala activation in patients. Escarti and colleagues (2010) presented patients with schizophrenia with emotional words and actually found greater activity in the parahippocampal gyrus and amygdala in patients with auditory hallucinations, as compared with patients without auditory hallucinations, and even in comparison to healthy controls. Other examples of a limbic hyperactivation during the perception of negative and neutral emotional stimuli also exist in the literature (Morris *et al.*, 2009). This therefore further suggests that a reduced activation in emotion-related brain areas may not be generalized across the whole schizophrenia population, but may instead be more symptom specific (Fahim *et al.*, 2005). Furthermore, some studies suggest that the abnormal neural activity associated with the perception of emotion in patients may also be specific to negative affect, and particularly, in that patients may tend to interpret and process neutral emotional stimuli as being negative (Kucharska-Pietura *et al.*, 2003; Michalopoulou *et al.*, 2008; Pinkham *et al.*, 2011; Schneider *et al.*, 1998).

One crucial issue here is whether an impairment in the experience of one's own emotions is deterministic of an impairment in the recognition of others' emotions. It seems intuitive to suggest that the link between the experience of one's own and of others' emotions would be a direct one, although the literature on schizophrenia has revealed conflicting findings. One fMRI study from Fahim and colleagues (2004) showed little difference in neural activation of emotionally centered brain regions during the perception of emotionally negative pictures, when comparing patients with schizophrenia with and without flattened affect, but argued that a difference in effective connectivity may exist between these groups of patients. A later study from the same group (Stip *et al.*, 2005) confirmed their earlier suggestion of dysfunctional neural circuitry in patients with flattened affect, and thereby falling on the side of support for blunted affect leading to impaired processing of others' emotions. However, there is more recent neuroimaging evidence to show that patients with schizophrenia do not have differences in brain activation in areas associated with emotion (Ursu *et al.*, 2011). Therefore, some have suggested that patients do not have an impairment in having rewarding and affective experiences (Cohen and Minor, 2010; Gold *et al.*, 2008), but may be more likely impaired in the ability to form goal-directed behaviors that would normally be driven by rewards and affective experience, or what is known as anticipatory pleasure (Juckel *et al.*, 2006; Wynn *et al.*, 2010).

Some EEG studies looking at the event-related potentials (ERPs) related with the perception of emotional faces have shown that the early ERPs associated with face perception were abnormal in schizophrenia. This was found in the N170, an early ERP associated with the encoding of facial features, and the N250, a slightly later ERP associated with the encoding of emotions (Johnston *et al.*, 2005; Streit *et al.*, 2001; Wynn *et al.*, 2008). These studies thus suggest a low-level encoding deficit of facial features or emotional information in patients, which occurs at the early stages of processing others' emotions. In contrast to these previous ERP studies, Horan and colleagues (2010) demonstrated that a later EEG component, at about 500–1000 ms after stimulus onset, was diminished in patients with schizophrenia, but not earlier ERPs associated with low-level sensory processing. However, this study did not use stimuli with facial emotions, but instead used pictures of emotional scenes. These contrasting findings raise another interesting issue in the previous work, in that it is not clear whether impairments in emotion perception occur at a low-level of sensory processing or at a higher level of attentional or possibly contextual processing (Kring and Elis, 2013), or if even impairments at both levels of processing exist in schizophrenia.

In summary, the results from neuroimaging studies of emotion perception in schizophrenia appear to be mixed, with some fundamental issues still unresolved. Studying emotion perception in schizophrenia presents several methodological difficulties, (1) one being due to impairments in emotional expression and emotional awareness seen in schizophrenia, (2) another in the design of emotional stimuli that are free from confounding variables and potential misinterpretation from the patient, and (3) whether behavioral differences in emotion perception may be a product of low-level sensory deficits or high-level processes requiring integration of both sensory and contextual information.

Neuroimaging of Theory of Mind

Emotion perception, in its simplest form, occurs at a low level of processing, essentially involving phylogenetically older subcortical brain structures such as the amygdala. Theory of mind (ToM), or mentalizing, is a more complex cognitive skill that involves the attribution of others' emotional and cognitive mental states through understanding that others' minds are independent from one's own (Premack and Woodruff, 1978), and thus recruits more high-level cortical areas in prefrontal and parietal regions. ToM is also critical for successful social interaction as it allows one to understand the intentions of others' behavior and to predict forthcoming behavior. A distinction between affective and cognitive ToM has been made in schizophrenia, with distinct neural activations seen in different brain regions for affective and cognitive ToM tasks (Shamay-Tsoory *et al.*, 2007). More specifically, the brain regions that have been associated with affective ToM also overlap with subcortical areas related to emotion perception, including the amygdala and ventral striatum, but also include the ventral anterior cingulate and orbitofrontal cortices. Brain areas associated with cognitive ToM tasks and self and other distinction have most consistently been found in the temporoparietal junction (TPJ), superior temporal sulcus (STS), medial prefrontal cortex (MPFC), dorsolateral prefrontal cortex (DLPFC), and posterior cingulate cortex (PCC) (Abu-Akel and Shamay-Tsoory, 2011; Amodio and Frith, 2006; Saxe and Baron-Cohen, 2006).

Behavioral impairments in ToM have consistently been found in patients with schizophrenia (Brüne, 2005), with one meta-analysis demonstrating that both first-episode and clinically remitted patients (Bora *et al.*, 2009) exhibit ToM deficits, and therefore suggesting ToM deficits to be inherent to the illness. Numerous neuroimaging studies have been done with different paradigms to look at activity in the ToM and mentalizing network in patients with schizophrenia, producing some contrasting results. Temporal areas of the ToM network, including the TPJ and STS, may be more involved in regulating the distinction made between self and other (Abu-Akel and Shamay-Tsoory, 2011), which is an intrinsic property of mental state attribution and mentalizing. Higher activations have been found in the right superior temporal gyrus in patients, for both cognitive and affective ToM (Benedetti *et al.*, 2009), whereas other research groups have found reduced activity in the right STS in patients (Brüne *et al.*, 2008). In the TPJ, greater activation has been found during performance of story-telling ToM tasks in patients (Andreasen *et al.*, 2008; Brüne *et al.*, 2008), whereas a reduced activation of the TPJ was found during the performance of ToM tasks that involve the inference of intention (Das *et al.*, 2012; Walter *et al.*, 2009). However, it is important to note here that the definition of anatomical boundaries of the TPJ may actually overlap with, or encapsulate, areas that include the inferior parietal lobule (IPL) and the caudal parts of the STS (pSTS), which have been found to be differentially activated under different types of mental state attributions, and thus may actually be responsible for different functions (Bosia *et al.*, 2012). Therefore, these mixed results may reflect the differential activations in these subregions of the TPJ and STS as a result of the different types of ToM tasks used in different studies.

In schizophrenia, frontal lobe pathology is a hallmark of the disease, with many studies demonstrating broad functional and structural frontal abnormalities across patients, which have been linked with numerous characteristics of the disease (Hill *et al.*, 2004; Ingvar and Franzen, 1974). In the case of ToM, the MPFC, orbital frontal cortex (OFC), and ACC are the main frontal areas that have been implicated in mental state attribution. Poor performance on cognitive and affective ToM tasks have been associated with reduced gray matter volumes in ventromedial PFC and ventrolateral PFC, respectively (Hirao *et al.*, 2008; Hooker *et al.*, 2011). The studies that have investigated functional activity in patients during different ToM tasks have consistently revealed aberrant activation patterns in the MPFC, but at the same time reflecting contrasting degrees of activation, with some demonstrating a hypoactivation (Brunet *et al.*, 2003; Lee *et al.*, 2006; Walter *et al.*, 2009) and others reporting hyperactivation (Andreasen *et al.*, 2008; Lee *et al.*, 2010; Lee *et al.*, 2011; Pedersen *et al.*, 2012). ToM activity in other areas of the frontal cortex have also shown inconsistent activation patterns in patients, with increased activity seen in the inferior PFC (Andreasen *et al.*, 2008; Lee *et al.*, 2010; Pedersen *et al.*, 2012), reduced activity in the inferior frontal gyrus (IFG) (Das *et al.*, 2012), and contrasting results in the OFC (Andreasen *et al.*, 2008; Brüne *et al.*, 2008). For the activity in the ACC associated with ToM tasks, the results are just as mixed as those in other frontal regions with some studies demonstrating hyperactivation (Andreasen *et al.*, 2008; Lee *et al.*, 2006) and others, a hypoactivation (Brüne *et al.*, 2008; Lee *et al.*, 2011; Walter *et al.*, 2009).

The PCC and precuneus have also been found to play a possible role in ToM impairments seen in schizophrenia. These structures fall under the category of the CMS, which also includes the MPFC, and have been implicated in numerous paradigms that involve self-referential processing in some form or another (Pfeifer and Peake, 2012). It has been suggested that the PCC may be a modulator of perspective-taking and self-evaluation. Therefore, it makes sense that these areas become activated during the performance of ToM and mentalizing tasks. The studies that have found a functional difference in the PCC and precuneus in patients have shown both a hypoactivation compared with healthy controls (Lee *et al.*, 2006; Lee *et al.*, 2011; Walter *et al.*, 2009) and a hyperactivation (Andreasen *et al.*, 2008; Pedersen *et al.*, 2012).

A wide variety of ToM and mentalizing tasks have been used in the different neuroimaging studies mentioned here, including verbal and nonverbal stimuli, some using false-belief, faux-pas, affective stimuli, nonaffective stimuli, some requiring more of a self-other distinction than others, etc. Therefore, these mixed results across the literature showing both increased and decreased activity in ToM-related brain areas in patients with schizophrenia is most likely a result of the inconsistencies in the nature of the ToM tasks used, with some tasks recruiting different cognitive processes than others. Though interestingly, one longitudinal study found an increased activation of ToM-related areas in patients following recovery from an acute psychotic episode (Lee *et al.*, 2006), suggesting that a hyperactivation seen in some patients may be a reflection of an effective compensatory neural mechanism as a way to deal with ToM impairments. Further to this, Brüne and colleagues (2011) demonstrated that an at-risk schizophrenia group exhibited greater activation of the ToM network that both manifest patients with schizophrenia and healthy controls. This may also serve as indirect evidence for a compensatory neural mechanism, as the at-risk subjects may have still had sufficient neurocognitive ability to utilize compensatory strategies for ToM deficits, whereas the manifest patients may have lacked this ability to compensate.

Action Observation and the Mirror Neuron System in Schizophrenia

As a prerequisite for understanding and interpreting others' behavior in a social interaction, one must first be able to process, decode, and understand others' actions. So far, this section has highlighted impairments in the ToM or mentalizing network in the brains of patients with schizophrenia, though there is also one other neural system thought to be crucial for successful social interaction, activated for both one's own and through the observation of others' actions. The discovery of a functionally specific mirror neuron system (MNS) in the monkey brain, which is activated during both action execution and action observation (Gallese *et al.*, 1996), has led many authors to suggest that the MNS plays a central role in action understanding, imitation, and possibly also other higher-level social cognitions such as ToM and empathy (Gallese *et al.*, 2004). Some authors have also made the proposal that a dysfunction in the MNS can been used to explain deficits in social cognition in psychiatric and developmental disorders, namely schizophrenia (Arbib and Mundhenk, 2005), autism spectrum disorders (Williams *et al.*, 2001), and Williams syndrome (Tager-Flusberg and Sullivan, 2000). This has subsequently been termed the 'broken-mirror' hypothesis (Ramachandran and Oberman, 2006). Arbib and Mundhenk (2005) propose an extension of this 'broken-mirror' hypothesis to try to account for deficits in self-monitoring in schizophrenia as well as misattributions of agency, and auditory hallucinations, and thus have some underlying causal role in the expression of deficits in social cognitive skills. In support of this hypothesis, some behavioral studies have shown that patients with schizophrenia have reduced imitation abilities. One study demonstrated that patients with schizophrenia were less able than healthy controls to imitate facial expressions from still photographs (Schwartz *et al.*, 2006). Moreover, patients with schizophrenia show reduced contagiousness to observed yawning (Haker and Rössler, 2009). Rapid mimicry-like reactions to the observation of angry and happy faces are also reduced in patients with schizophrenia compared with controls (Varcin *et al.*, 2010). Park *et al.* (2008) found that patients with schizophrenia are poor at imitating hand gestures, mouth movements, and emotional expressions. In their study, imitation errors also correlated with reduced social competence and increased negative symptoms.

Some functional imaging studies have provided further support to the suggestion of a disturbed mirror-neuron system in schizophrenia (Andreasen *et al.*, 2008), as abnormal activity has been discovered in parietal areas associated with the human MNS, in an unmedicated schizophrenia population (Kato *et al.*, 2011). Other fMRI studies have demonstrated abnormalities in the perception of biologic motion in schizophrenia, with activity in the extrastriate body and the STS; an area also implicated in the human MNS (Kim *et al.*, 2011; Takahashi *et al.*, 2010). It may be that these neuroimaging studies showing abnormalities in the neural activity related to perception of biologic motion could provide an explanation for previous findings that demonstrate impairments in understanding of nonverbal communication in schizophrenia (Toomey *et al.*, 2002). The EEG mu rhythm suppression, as an index of motor mirror neuron-related activity, has been used to investigate possible abnormalities in schizophrenia. One study from Singh and colleagues (2011) compared healthy control subjects and patients with first-episode schizophrenia while they observed videos of a moving hand, a social interactive game setting, and a point-light biologic full-body motion display. They had hypothesized that the context of the social interaction in the observation of others' actions may be the most revealing in terms of a potential abnormality in mirror neuron-related activity. However, a significant difference in the power of the mu suppression between controls and patients was only found in the point-light biologic motion condition, with substantially lower mu suppression in the patient group. Interestingly, they found that lower mu suppression was associated with greater negative symptom burden and poorer social adjustment. One other study from McCormick and colleagues (2012) investigated the mu rhythm suppression in patients with schizophrenia, comparing patients who were actively psychotic with patients who had only residual symptoms, along with a healthy control group. In contrast to the study from Singh and colleagues, the McCormick study found greater mu rhythm suppression in patients who were actively psychotic, as compared with those with residual symptoms and the healthy controls, and psychotic symptoms were also positively correlated with the mu suppression. Preliminary findings from our own group suggest that patients with schizophrenia generally have lower mu suppression than matched healthy controls, and additionally, that the magnitude of the mu suppression is positively correlated with negative symptoms, in which those with greater negative symptoms have greater mu suppression. (Brown *et al.*, personal communication).

To sum up, there does appear to be some evidence to suggest an impairment in the MNS, or action observation network in patients with schizophrenia, which is also related to the severity of psychotic symptoms. However, it is not yet clear as to whether this abnormality in the neural activation associated with the processing of others' actions may be manifested in an overactivation or underactivation. It is also still not clear as to what the specific functional specificity of this network might be, and how this has implications on higher-level social cognitive processes and overt functional social behavior.

Neuroimaging of Social Decision-Making

Although not classically discussed in the typical literature on social cognitive impairments in schizophrenia, the recent emergence of the field of neuroeconomics has stimulated more research looking into social decision-making in psychiatric disorders such as schizophrenia. Neuroeconomics combines behavioral economics and neuroscience with the use of neuroimaging during the performance of economic games, which also often include a social component. Both cognitive and affective functions are involved in making decisions, which naturally also applies to decisions made in a social context, though often with the addition of social and moral judgment, such as judgments of trust and fairness. Many of the brain areas implicated in emotion perception, ToM, and mentalizing have also been found to be activated during decision-making tasks, including the inferior and dorsolateral PFC (Paulus *et al.*, 2001), ventromedial and ventrolateral frontal cortex (Rogers *et al.*, 1999), anterior cingulate (Elliott *et al.*, 2000), insula (Critchley *et al.*, 2001), TPJ (Kahnt and Tobler *et al.*, 2013), and parietal cortex (Paulus *et al.*, 2001). Reward and punishment (i.e., positive and negative reinforcers) fundamentally guide behavior and drive motivation, and also determine the 'value' and 'utility' ascribed to stimuli in the environment, which is inclusive of social stimuli. Disturbances in the dopaminergic reward system are central to understanding of the neurobiology of schizophrenia. Therefore, the field of neuroeconomics provides a particularly salient and useful platform to explore how reward-driven decision-making in the social context may help to inform therapeutic strategies aimed at improving social cognition and social functioning. Investigating the neural substrates of decision-making in a social context will also help in understanding how impairments at the low level of neurocognition and social cognition may translate to impairments in higher-level complex social cognition and real-world social functioning.

Several authors have shown aberrant dopaminergic-mediated responses to rewarding stimuli in the reward-processing network in schizophrenia. For example, abnormalities in patients have been found in the reward centers of the ventral tegmental area and ventral striatum (Nielsen *et al.*, 2012), and in the DLPFC and OFC, which plays a critical role in the ability to represent the value of outcomes and plans (Wallis, 2007), and in the interactions between prefrontal and striatal areas (Barch and Dowd, 2010). As more work is done in this field, it is becoming more apparent that there is a selective deficit in the processing of reward in schizophrenia, that maybe more specific to the translation of hedonic experience into motivated behavior, rather than being a problem stemming from the actual degradation of hedonic experience, as was previously thought (Kraepelin, 1919). The representation of future rewards is essential in goal setting, for driving motivation to seek rewards, and for decision-making, and thus has salient implications in social functioning. Some focus has begun to be placed on the potential implications of impaired reward-processing in social functioning in autism (Dichter and Adolphs, 2012); however, little work has yet to be done to explore how the specific deficits in reward-processing seen in schizophrenia may specifically impact on social cognition, social decision-making, and social functioning.

Behavioral economics in schizophrenia has been investigated in some studies that have used a task called the Ultimatum Game (UG). In the UG, a scenario is presented in which the participant and another person, the 'proposer', find a sum of money together. The proposer then makes an offer of how they should split the money, and the participant is given the choice of accepting or rejecting the offer. If the participant accepts the offer, they each get the sum of money proposed, but if they reject the offer, both get zero. In some trials, the proposer offers a 50/50 split, and in others, offers a split of varying degrees of unfairness, such as 70/30, 80/20, whereby the participant would receive less than the proposer. Typically, healthy populations will reject some of the unfair offers, despite the fact that they would both get zero when rejecting an offer. However, patients with schizophrenia have a tendency to accept unfair offers more often, and reject fair offers less often (Csukly et al., 2011). When put in the position of the proposer, patients with schizophrenia interestingly tend to make more 'hyperfair' offers, whereby patients offer more than half the money to the other person (Agay et al., 2008). Patients also appear to be less strategic, as healthy controls will increase their offers after a rejection and decrease them after a rejection, whereas patients do not seem to follow the same pattern as the proposer in the UG. van't Wout and Sanfey (2011) also demonstrated that schizotypal traits in a nonschizophrenia student population correlated with the magnitude of the proposed offers, whereby those with greater schizotypal traits tended to offer more money than those without these traits. Taken together, these behavioral findings seem to suggest that patients have an impairment in the assessment. However, other findings using the Dictator Game, a modification of the UG in which a third player is involved, and participants have the ability to punish unfair offers by deciding how offers are split, patients appeared to punish unfair offers just as much as healthy controls (Wischniewski and Brüne, 2011). This suggests that patients do not have an impairment in the assessment of fairness *per se*, but this response pattern may instead reflect a strategy to attempt to avoid potential punishment from others, by making hyperfair offers.

Very few studies have directly sought to reveal abnormalities in neural activation during social decision-making tasks in schizophrenia. One from Baas and colleagues (2008) presented pictures of faces to participants, and they were asked to judge the trustworthiness of these faces. They found differences in activity between patients and controls in the medial OFC, amygdala, and the right insula. The authors suggested that abnormal activation in this network of brain regions may contribute to impairments in social judgment in schizophrenia. One other study used a trust game, whereby the participants are given a fixed sum of money that they can share with another player (Gromann et al., 2013). The money shared is then tripled and then the other player can choose how much they repay the participant. In this study from Gromann and colleagues, they used a modified version of the game in which there two conditions; a cooperative whereby subsequent repayments increased if the participant demonstrated an increase in trust, and a deceptive one in which subsequent repayments decreased if the participant increased trust in the other player. They found that patients with schizophrenia had lower activity in the right caudate nucleus and TPJ, which correlated with the Positive and Negative Syndrome Scale (PANSS) persecution score and PANSS positive score, respectively. A surprising result from this study was that there were no group differences in MPFC activation. Due to the differences in activation of the caudate nucleus in patients, the authors interpreted these results in terms of social rewards, suggesting that the data indicate a reduced sensitivity to social reward in psychosis. Aside from their findings, this suggestion could be a well-justified one, particularly because some authors have suggested that social interaction, in itself, is rewarding. It would be plausible to argue that patients with schizophrenia are less sensitive to the rewards associated with social stimuli and social interaction. This would thus reduce the motivation to seek social interaction. Although this raises the question of whether this is caused by a fundamental impairment in the reward system, or whether the impoverishment of the perception of social stimuli in schizophrenia consequently also diminishes their rewarding nature.

The work in social decision-making in schizophrenia is still relatively young, and little work has been done to address this topic head-on. However, the field of neuroeconomics clearly has potential for being a bridge for translation of research in low-level neurobiology to more complex high-level social cognition and social functioning.

THE NEUROBIOLOGY OF METACOGNITION

Humans are metacognitive by nature: they have a general tendency to constantly monitor and control their cognition. By definition, metacognitive capacity is not merely a high-level cognitive functioning that depends only on ToM capacities. Previous studies in metacognition argue that, in addition to ToM processes, synthetic components of metacognition require metamemory, attention, conflict resolution, error correction, and the cognitive control of cognitive processes also referred to as executive functioning (Fleming and

Dolan, 2012). Today, the brain correlates of these fundamental elements of metacognition have received greater interest in recent studies in neuroscience. Although most of this previous neuroscientific work has not been performed particularly with patients with schizophrenia, however, their findings have brought insights into understanding the neurobiologic underpinnings of meta-cognitive deficits in the illness.

In essence, metamemory refers to the reflection on one's knowledge and the monitoring of memory to gather online information about the current memory system (Cavanaugh and Perlmutter, 1982), which subsequently pre-pares the way for high-order metacognition.

Accumulating evidence has highlighted the role of activity in the medial, ventrolateral, and left dorsolateral PFC (Chua *et al.*, 2009), with the contri-bution of a top-down modulation coming from dopamine (van Schouwenburg *et al.*, 2010), in acting as biologic predictors of metamemory processes. In support of this, Rounis (2010) demonstrated that participants who underwent transcranial magnetic stimulation (TMS) over bilateral DLPFC displayed significant impairments in metacognitive visual awareness, with the authors arguing that the stimulation specifically reflected a disturbance in a critical metacognitive process. Fleming and Dolan (2012) have provided promising evidence in regards to the role of rostral PFC (Brodmann area 10) as one key brain area responsible for the self-evaluative introspection involved in meta-cognitive awareness. Interestingly, this area appeared to be related the size of the social network of nonhuman primates (Sallet *et al.*, 2011). In terms of schizophrenia, a growing body of literature has also revealed structural abnor-malities in rostral PFC in patients (Quan *et al.*, 2013; Vogeley *et al.*, 2003). In addition, rostral ACC dysfunction was related to error monitoring in schizo-phrenia in an fMRI study (Laurens *et al.*, 2003). Although metamemory deficits in schizophrenia have been studied behaviorally and appeared to be impaired (Souchay *et al.*, 2006), the role of rostral PFC in metacognitive defi-cits in schizophrenia has not yet been studied, but has potential to become one fruitful focus for future research in metacognition in schizophrenia. Though notably, many previous neuroimaging studies investigating metacognition have also underlined the role of the activity of a network of regions rather than localized areas being responsible for specific metacognitive processes, in which the network is supervised by processes of self-evaluation of current cognitive or memory units.

BIOMARKERS FOR DEFICITS IN SOCIAL COGNITION

One main goal of investigating the neurobiologic underpinnings of deficits in social cognition and metacognition is to work toward identifying potential biomarkers that are specific to the pathology of schizophrenia. The identifi-cation of biomarkers of the disease could thus ideally serve to be integrated into diagnostic criteria and could also potentially be used for manipulation to improve symptomatology and related cognitive deficits. A number of possible brain-based biomarkers of deficits in social cognition have been suggested in the previous literature, although these are still in their infancy, as their use as standardized clinical tools is still far from being established.

In general, neuroimaging tools have been applied with the aim of identifying categorical differences in brain activation and brain structure that have some direct etiologic link with the pathology of social cognitive deficits. However, there is much heterogeneity in the paradigms and concepts used across the literature on social cognition in schizophrenia. An article from Brunet-Gouet and colleagues (2011) reviews the neuroimaging literature on social cognition in schizophrenia and concludes that much of the work done so far is generally disparate, with few well-replicated and robust findings. The authors of the article suggest a need for an integrated model of social cognitive deficits in schizophrenia, with greater consensus across tasks and paradigms, to be used with larger patient populations. The Cognitive Neuroscience Treatment Research to Improve Cognition in Schizophrenia (CNTRICS) is one large-scale initiative from the National Institute of Mental Health (NIMH) that has already made much headway in forming a consensus for defining constructs and paradigms to facilitate the translation of basic neuroscientific research into practical assessment and treatment tools for the clinician (Carter et al., 2008; Carter and Barch, 2012). Two paradigms for reliably assessing emotion recognition of patients with schizophrenia have been recommended from the CNTRICS group, namely the Penn Emotion Recognition Paradigm (ER-40) and the Facial Affect Recognition with the Effects of Situational Context Tasks (Carter et al., 2009). The CNTRICS initiative presents a prime example of a step in the right direction, for promoting a consensual, collaborative, and integrative approach for understanding social cognitive deficits in schizophrenia, and for facilitating the application of basic neuroscience research into clinical use.

LIMITATIONS AND FUTURE SUGGESTIONS

Despite the large increase in interest in identifying the neurobiologic foundations of social cognition, this field is still relatively young, with the research in the neurobiology of social cognitive deficits in schizophrenia being even younger. Naturally in such a young field, there is still disparity and a lack of consensus across the concepts related to social cognition in the research. However, substantial efforts are being made to work toward addressing this issue (Green et al., 2008). For this field of research to prosper, and for basic research to be translated from the laboratory to the clinical setting, it will be important for future work to consider social cognition not in isolation, but instead with consideration of the nonsocial neurobiologic characteristics of schizophrenia that are more well established, which have been previously investigated outside of the realm of social cognition, but may likely also impact on social functioning. Rather than considering social cognition as a categorically different and independent form of cognition than nonsocial cognition, future research may benefit from looking at social cognition as an additive process that is enabled by, or connected with, underlying nonsocial cognitions. One candidate for this would be in terms of the impact of deficits in dopaminergic-mediated reward-processing on social cognition and motivation in schizophrenia. It is evident that low-level biologic processes form the foundations for more high-level complex social cognition; however, it is crucial to understand the pathway between these levels before more concrete conclusions can be made about causality.

REFERENCES

Abi-Dargham, A., & Moore, H. (2003). Prefrontal DA transmission at D1 receptors and the pathology of schizophrenia. *The Neuroscientist*, *9*(5), 404–416.

Abu-Akel, A., & Shamay-Tsoory, S. (2011). Neuroanatomical and neurochemical bases of theory of mind. *Neuropsychologia*, *49*(11), 2971–2984.

Agay, N., Kron, S., Carmel, Z., Mendlovic, S., & Levkovitz, Y. (2008). Ultimatum bargaining behavior of people affected by schizophrenia. *Psychiatry Research*, *157*(1–3), 39–46.

Ahmari, S. E., Risbrough, V. B., Geyer, M. A., & Simpson, H. B. (2012). Impaired sensorimotor gating in unmedicated adults with obsessive-compulsive disorder. *Neuropsychopharmacology*, *37*(5), 1216–1223.

Amodio, D. M., & Frith, C. D. (2006). Meeting of minds: The medial frontal cortex and social cognition. *Nature Reviews Neuroscience*, *7*(4), 268–277.

Andreasen, N. C., Calage, C. A., & O'Leary, D. S. (2008). Theory of mind and schizophrenia: A positron emission tomography study of medication-free patients. *Schizophrenia Bulletin*, *34*(4), 708–719.

Anticevic, A., Van Snellenberg, J. X., & Barch, D. M. (2012). Neurobiology of emotional dysfunction in schizophrenia: New directions revealed through meta-analyses. *Biological Psychiatry*, *71*(6), e23–e24.

Arbib, M. A., & Mundhenk, T. N. (2005). Schizophrenia and the mirror system: An essay. *Neuropsychologia*, *43*(2), 268–280.

Baas, D., Aleman, A., Vink, M., Ramsey, N. F., de Haan, E. H., & Kahn, R. S. (2008). Evidence of altered cortical and amygdala activation during social decision-making in schizophrenia. *Neuroimage*, *40*(2), 719–727.

Barch, D. M., & Dowd, E. C. (2010). Goal representations and motivational drive in schizophrenia: The role of prefrontal-striatal interactions. *Schizophrenia Bulletin*, *36*(5), 919–934.

Bast, T., Zhang, W., Feldon, J., & White, I. M. (2000). Effects of MK801 and neuroleptics on prepulse inhibition: Re-examination in two strains of rats. *Pharmacology, Biochemistry, and Behavior*, *67*(3), 647–658.

Beasley, C. L., Zhang, Z. J., Patten, I., & Reynolds, G. P. (2002). Selective deficits in prefrontal cortical GABAergic neurons in schizophrenia defined by the presence of calcium-binding proteins. *Biological Psychiatry*, *52*(7), 708–715.

Bediou, B., Asri, F., Brunelin, J., Krolak-Salmon, P., D'Amato, T., Saoud, M., et al. (2007). Emotion recognition and genetic vulnerability to schizophrenia. *British Journal of Psychiatry*, *191*, 126–130.

Benedetti, F., Bernasconi, A., Bosia, M., Cavallaro, R., Dallaspezia, S., Falini, A., et al. (2009). Functional and structural brain correlates of theory of mind and empathy deficits in schizophrenia. *Schizophrenia Research, 114*(1–3), 154–160.

Benes, F., Vincent, S., Alsterberg, G., Bird, E., & SanGiovanni, J. (1992). Increased GABAA receptor binding in superficial layers of cingulate cortex in schizophrenics. *Journal of Neuroscience, 12*(3), 924–929.

Berenbaum, H., & Oltmanns, T. F. (1992). Emotional experience and expression in schizophrenia and depression. *Journal of Abnormal Psychology, 101*(1), 37–44.

Bitanihirwe, B. K. Y., Peleg-Raibstein, D., Mouttet, F., Feldon, J., & Meyer, U. (2010). Late prenatal immune activation in mice leads to behavioral and neurochemical abnormalities relevant to the negative symptoms of schizophrenia. *Neuropsychopharmacology, 35*(12), 2462–2478.

Bogerts, B., Lieberman, J. A., Ashtari, M., Bilder, R. M., Degreef, G., Lerner, G., et al. (1993). Hippocampus amygdala volumes and psychopathology in chronic-schizophrenia. *Biological Psychiatry, 33*(4), 236–246.

Boison, D., Singer, P., Shen, H. -Y., Feldon, J., & Yee, B. K. (2012). Adenosine hypothesis of schizophrenia - opportunities for pharmacotherapy. *Neuropharmacology, 62*(3), 1527–1543.

Bora, E., Yucel, M., & Pantelis, C. (2009). Theory of mind impairment in schizophrenia: Meta-analysis. *Schizophrenia Research, 109*(1–3), 1–9.

Bosch, D., & Schmid, S. (2008). Cholinergic mechanism underlying prepulse inhibition of the startle response in rats. *Neuroscience, 155*(1), 326–335.

Bosia, M., Riccaboni, R., & Poletti, S. (2012). Neurofunctional correlates of theory of mind deficits in schizophrenia. *Current Topics in Medicinal Chemistry, 12*(21), 2284–2302.

Brunet, E., Sarfati, Y., Hardy-Bayle, M. C., & Decety, J. (2003). Abnormalities of brain function during a nonverbal theory of mind task in schizophrenia. *Neuropsychologia, 41*(12), 1574–1582.

Brunet-Gouet, E., Achim, A. M., Vistoli, D., Passerieux, C., Hardy-Bayle, M. C., & Jackson, P. L. (2011). The study of social cognition with neuroimaging methods as a means to explore future directions of deficit evaluation in schizophrenia? *Psychiatry Research, 190*(1), 23–31.

Brüne, M. (2005). "Theory of mind" in schizophrenia: A review of the literature. *Schizophrenia Bulletin, 31*(1), 21–42.

Brüne, M. (2009). Are psychiatric disorders specifically human? [Sind psychische Störungen etwas spezifisch Menschliches?]. *Nervenarzt, 80*, 252–262.

Brüne, M., Lissek, S., Fuchs, N., Witthaus, H., Peters, S., Nicolas, V., et al. (2008). An fMRI study of theory of mind in schizophrenic patients with "passivity" symptoms. *Neuropsychologia, 46*(7), 1992–2001.

Brüne, M., Özgürdal, S., Ansorge, N., von Reventlow, H. G., Peters, S., Nicolas, V., et al. (2011). An fMRI study of "theory of mind" in at-risk states of psychosis: Comparison with manifest schizophrenia and healthy controls. *Neuroimage, 55*(1), 329–337.

Canli, T., & Lesch, K. -P. (2007). Long story short: The serotonin transporter in emotion regulation and social cognition. *Nature Neuroscience, 10*(9), 1103–1109.

Carasso, B. S., Bakshi, V. P., & Geyer, M. A. (1998). Disruption in prepulse inhibition after alpha-1 adrenoceptor stimulation in rats. *Neuropharmacology, 37*(3), 401–404.

Carter, C. S., & Barch, D. M. (2012). Imaging biomarkers for treatment development for impaired cognition: Report of the sixth CNTRICS meeting: Biomarkers recommended for further development. *Schizophrenia Bulletin, 38*(1), 26–33.

Carter, C. S., Barch, D. M., Buchanan, R. W., Bullmore, E., Krystal, J. H., Cohen, J., et al. (2008). Identifying cognitive mechanisms targeted for treatment development in schizophrenia: An overview of the first meeting of the Cognitive Neuroscience Treatment Research to Improve Cognition in Schizophrenia Initiative. *Biological Psychiatry, 64*(1), 4–10.

Carter, C. S., Barch, D. M., Gur, R., Pinkham, A., & Ochsner, K. (2009). CNTRICS final task selection: Social cognitive and affective neuroscience-based measures. *Schizophrenia Bulletin, 35*(1), 153–162.

Cavanaugh, J. C., & Perlmutter, M. (1982). Metamemory – a critical examination. *Child Development, 53*(1), 11–28.

Chua, E. F., Schacter, D. L., & Sperling, R. A. (2009). Neural correlates of metamemory: A comparison of feeling-of-knowing and retrospective confidence judgments. *Journal of Cognitive Neuroscience, 21*(9), 1751–1765.

Cohen, A. S., & Minor, K. S. (2010). Emotional experience in patients with schizophrenia revisited: Meta-analysis of laboratory studies. *Schizophrenia Bulletin, 36*(1), 143–150.

Critchley, H. D., Mathias, C. J., & Dolan, R. J. (2001). Neural activity in the human brain relating to uncertainty and arousal during anticipation. *Neuron, 29*(2), 537–545.

Csukly, G., Polgar, P., Tombor, L., Rethelyi, J., & Keri, S. (2011). Are patients with schizophrenia rational maximizers? Evidence from an Ultimatum Game study. *Psychiatry Research, 187*(1–2), 11–17.

Das, P., Lagopoulos, J., Coulston, C. M., Henderson, A. F., & Malhi, G. S. (2012). Mentalizing impairment in schizophrenia: A functional MRI study. *Schizophrenia Research, 134*(2–3), 158–164.

de Achaval, D., Villarreal, M. F., Costanzo, E. Y., Douer, J., Castro, M. N., Mora, M. C., et al. (2012). Decreased activity in right-hemisphere structures involved in social cognition in siblings discordant for schizophrenia. *Schizophrenia Research, 134*(2–3), 171–179.

Decker, M. W., Curzon, P., & Brioni, J. D. (1995). Influence of separate and combined septal and amygdala lesions on memory, acoustic startle, anxiety, and locomotor activity in rats. *Neurobiology of Learning and Memory, 64*(2), 156–168.

Di, X., Chan, R. C., & Gong, Q. Y. (2009). White matter reduction in patients with schizophrenia as revealed by voxel-based morphometry: An activation likelihood estimation meta-analysis. *Progress in Neuropsychopharmacology, Biology, and Psychiatry, 33*(8), 1390–1394.

Dichter, G., & Adolphs, R. (2012). Reward processing in autism: A thematic series. *Journal of Neurodevelopmental Disorders, 4*(1), 20.

Duncan, G. E., Moy, S. S., Perez, A., Eddy, D. M., Zinzow, W. M., Lieberman, J. A., Snouwaert, J. N., et al. (2004). Deficits in sensorimotor gating and tests of social behavior in a genetic model of reduced NMDA receptor function. *Behavioural Brain Research, 153*(2), 507–519.

Ehrlichman, R. S., Luminais, S. N., White, S. L., Rudnick, N. D., Ma, N., Dow, H. C., Kreibich, A. S., et al. (2009). Neuregulin 1 transgenic mice display reduced mismatch negativity, contextual fear conditioning and social interactions. *Brain Research, 1294*, 116–127.

Elliott, R., Friston, K. J., & Dolan, R. J. (2000). Dissociable neural responses in human reward systems. *Journal of Neuroscience, 20*(16), 6159–6165.

Ellison-Wright, I., Glahn, D. C., Laird, A. R., Thelen, S. M., & Bullmore, E. (2008). The anatomy of first-episode and chronic schizophrenia: An anatomical likelihood estimation meta-analysis. *American Journal of Psychiatry, 165*(8), 1015–1023.

Escarti, M. J., de la Iglesia-Vaya, M., Marti-Bonmati, L., Robles, M., Carbonell, J., Lull, J. J., et al. (2010). Increased amygdala and parahippocampal gyrus activation in schizophrenic patients with auditory hallucinations: An fMRI study using independent component analysis. *Schizophrenia Research, 117*(1), 31–41.

Fahim, C., Stip, E., Mancini-Marie, A., Boualem, M., Malaspina, D., & Beauregard, M. (2004). Negative socio-emotional resonance in schizophrenia: A functional magnetic resonance imaging hypothesis. *Medical Hypotheses, 63*(3), 467–475.

Fahim, C., Stip, E., Mancini-Marie, A., Mensour, B., Boulay, L. J., Leroux, J. M., et al. (2005). Brain activity during emotionally negative pictures in schizophrenia with and without flat affect: An fMRI study. *Psychiatry Research, 140*(1), 1–15.

Fendt, M., Li, L., & Yeomans, J. (2001). Brain stem circuits mediating prepulse inhibition of the startle reflex. *Psychopharmacology, 156*(2–3), 216–224.

Feng, Y. -Q., Zhou, Z. -Y., He, X., Wang, H., Guo, X. -L., Hao, C. -J., Guo, Y., et al. (2008). Dysbindin deficiency in sandy mice causes reduction of snapin and displays behaviors related to schizophrenia. *Schizophrenia Research, 106*(2–3), 218–228.

Fleming, S. M., & Dolan, R. J. (2012). The neural basis of metacognitive ability. *Philosophical Transactions of the Royal Society B - Biological Sciences, 367*(1594), 1338–1349.

Fornito, A., Yucel, M., Patti, J., Wood, S. J., & Pantelis, C. (2009). Mapping grey matter reductions in schizophrenia: An anatomical likelihood estimation analysis of voxel-based morphometry studies. *Schizophrenia Research, 108*(1–3), 104–113.

Friston, K. J. (1999). Schizophrenia and the disconnection hypothesis. *Acta Psychiatrica Scandinavica. Supplementum, 395*, 68–79.

Gallese, V., Fadiga, L., Fogassi, L., & Rizzolatti, G. (1996). Action recognition in the premotor cortex. *Brain, 119*(Pt 2), 593–609.

Gallese, V., Keysers, C., & Rizzolatti, G. (2004). A unifying view of the basis of social cognition. *Trends in Cognitive Sciences, 8*(9), 396–403.

Gao, X. M., Sakai, K., Roberts, R. C., Conley, R. R., Dean, B., & Tamminga, C. A. (2000). Ionotropic glutamate receptors and expression of N-methyl-D-aspartate receptor subunits in subregions of human hippocampus: Effects of schizophrenia. *American Journal of Psychiatry, 157*(7), 1141–1149.

Geyer, M. A. (2006). The family of sensorimotor gating disorders: Comorbidities or diagnostic overlaps? *Neurotoxicity Research, 10*(3–4), 211–220.

Geyer, M. A., & Moghaddam, B. (2002). Animal models relevant to schizophrenia disorders. In K. L. Davis, D. Charney, J. T. Coyle, & C. Nemeroff (Eds.), *Psychopharmacology: The fifth generation of progress* (pp. 689–701). Philadelphia, Pennsylvania: Lippincott, Williams, & Wilkins.

Glahn, D. C., Laird, A. R., Ellison-Wright, I., Thelen, S. M., Robinson, J. L., Lancaster, J. L., et al. (2008). Meta-analysis of gray matter anomalies in schizophrenia: Application of anatomic likelihood estimation and network analysis. *Biological Psychiatry, 64*(9), 774–781.

Glahn, D. C., Ragland, J. D., Abramoff, A., Barrett, J., Laird, A. R., Bearden, C. E., et al. (2005). Beyond hypofrontality: A quantitative meta-analysis of functional neuroimaging studies of working memory in schizophrenia. *Human Brain Mapping, 25*(1), 60–69.

Gold, J. M., Waltz, J. A., Prentice, K. J., Morris, S. E., & Heerey, E. A. (2008). Reward processing in schizophrenia: A deficit in the representation of value. *Schizophrenia Bulletin, 34*(5), 835–847.

Green, M. F., Penn, D. L., Bentall, R., Carpenter, W. T., Gaebel, W., Gur, R. C., et al. (2008). Social cognition in schizophrenia: An NIMH workshop on definitions, assessment, and research opportunities. *Schizophrenia Bulletin, 34*(6), 1211–1220.

Gromann, P. M., Heslenfeld, D. J., Fett, A. K., Joyce, D. W., Shergill, S. S., & Krabbendam, L. (2013). Trust versus paranoia: Abnormal response to social reward in psychotic illness. *Brain, 136*(Pt 6), 1968–1975.

Gururajan, A., Taylor, D. A., & Malone, D. T. (2010). Current pharmacological models of social withdrawal in rats: Relevance to schizophrenia. *Behavioural Pharmacology*, 690–709.

Haker, H., & Rössler, W. (2009). Empathy in schizophrenia: Impaired resonance. *European Archives of Psychiatry and Clinical Neuroscience, 259*(6), 352–361.

Hill, K., Mann, L., Laws, K. R., Stephenson, C. M. E., Nimmo-Smith, I., & McKenna, P. J. (2004). Hypofrontality in schizophrenia: A meta-analysis of functional imaging studies. *Acta Psychiatrica Scandinavica, 110*(4), 243–256.

Hirao, K., Miyata, J., Fujiwara, H., Yamada, M., Namiki, C., Shimizu, M., et al. (2008). Theory of mind and frontal lobe pathology in schizophrenia: A voxel-based morphometry study. *Schizophrenia Research, 105*(1–3), 165–174.

Hooker, C. I., Bruce, L., Lincoln, S. H., Fisher, M., & Vinogradov, S. (2011). Theory of mind skills are related to gray matter volume in the ventromedial prefrontal cortex in schizophrenia. *Biological Psychiatry, 70*(12), 1169–1178.

Horan, W. P., Wynn, J. K., Kring, A. M., Simons, R. F., & Green, M. F. (2010). Electrophysiological correlates of emotional responding in schizophrenia. *Journal of Abnormal Psychology, 119*(1), 18–30.

Ingvar, D. H., & Franzen, G. (1974). Abnormalities of cerebral blood-flow distribution in patients with chronic schizophrenia. *Acta Psychiatrica Scandinavica, 50*(4), 425–462.

Johnston, P. J., Stojanov, W., Devir, H., & Schall, U. (2005). Functional MRI of facial emotion recognition deficits in schizophrenia and their electrophysiological correlates. *European Journal of Neuroscience, 22*(5), 1221–1232.

Juckel, G., Schlagenhauf, F., Koslowski, M., Wustenberg, T., Villringer, A., Knutson, B., et al. (2006). Dysfunction of ventral striatal reward prediction in schizophrenia. *Neuroimage, 29*(2), 409–416.

Kahnt, T., & Tobler, P. N. (2013). Salience signals in the right temporoparietal junction facilitate value-based decisions. *Journal of Neuroscience, 33*(3), 863–869.

Kato, Y., Muramatsu, T., Kato, M., Shibukawa, Y., Shintani, M., & Mimura, M. (2011). Magnetoencephalography study of right parietal lobe dysfunction of the evoked mirror neuron system in antipsychotic-free schizophrenia. *PLoS One, 6*(11), e28087.

Kim, J., Park, S., & Blake, R. (2011). Perception of biological motion in schizophrenia and healthy individuals: A behavioral and fMRI study. *PLoS One, 6*(5), e19971.

Kodsi, M. H., & Swerdlow, N. R. (1995). Prepulse inhibition in the rat is regulated by ventral and caudodorsal striato-pallidal circuitry. *Behavioral Neuroscience, 109*(5), 912–928.

Koh, H. -Y., Kim, D., Lee, J., Lee, S., & Shin, H. -S. (2007). Deficits in social behavior and sensorimotor gating in mice lacking phospholipase Cbeta1. *Genes, Brain, and Behavior, 7*(1), 120–128.

Kohler, C. G., Walker, J. B., Martin, E. A., Healey, K. M., & Moberg, P. J. (2010). Facial emotion perception in schizophrenia: A meta-analytic review. *Schizophrenia Bulletin, 36*(5), 1009–1019.

Kondziella, D., Brenner, E., Eyjolfsson, E. M., & Sonnewald, U. (2007). How do glial-neuronal interactions fit into current neurotransmitter hypotheses of schizophrenia? *Neurochemistry International, 50*(2), 291–301.

Kraepelin, E., & Robertson, G. M. (1919). *Dementia praecox and paraphrenia*. Edinburgh: Livingstone.

Kring, A. M., & Elis, O. (2013). Emotion deficits in people with schizophrenia. *Annual Review of Clinical Psychology, 9*, 409–433.

Kristiansen, L. V., Huerta, I., Beneyto, M., & Meador-Woodruff, J. H. (2007). NMDA receptors and schizophrenia. *Current Opinion in Pharmacology, 7*(1), 48–55.

Kucharska-Pietura, K., Russell, T., & Masiak, M. (2003). Perception of negative affect in schizophrenia - functional and structural changes in the amygdala. Review. Annales Universitatis Mariae Curie-Skłodowska. Sectio D. *Medicina, 58*(2), 453–458.

Kumari, V., Das, M., Zachariah, E., Ettinger, U., & Sharma, T. (2005). Reduced prepulse inhibition in unaffected siblings of schizophrenia patients. *Psychophysiology, 42*(5), 588–594.

Laruelle, M., Kegeles, L. S., & Abi-Dargham, A. (2003). Glutamate, dopamine, and schizophrenia: From pathophysiology to treatment. *Annals of the New York Academy of Sciences, 1003*, 138–158.

Laurens, K. R., Ngan, E. T., Bates, A. T., Kiehl, K. A., & Liddle, P. F. (2003). Rostral anterior cingulate cortex dysfunction during error processing in schizophrenia. *Brain*, *126*, 610–622.

Lee, J., Quintana, J., Nori, P., & Green, M. F. (2011). Theory of mind in schizophrenia: Exploring neural mechanisms of belief attribution. *Social Neuroscience*, *6*(5–6), 569–581.

Lee, K. H., Brown, W. H., Egleston, P. N., Green, R. D. J., Farrow, T. F. D., Hunter, M. D., et al. (2006). A functional magnetic resonance imaging study of social cognition in schizophrenia during an acute episode and after recovery. *American Journal of Psychiatry*, *163*(11), 1926–1933.

Lee, P. R., Brady, D. L., Shapiro, R. A., Dorsa, D. M., & Koenig, J. I. (2005). Social interaction deficits caused by chronic phencyclidine administration are reversed by oxytocin. *Neuropsychopharmacology*, *30*(10), 1883–1894.

Lee, S. J., Kang, D. H., Kim, C. W., Gu, B. M., Park, J. Y., Choi, C. H., et al. (2010). Multilevel comparison of empathy in schizophrenia: An fMRI study of a cartoon task. *Psychiatry Research - Neuroimaging*, *181*(2), 121–129.

Leonard, S. (2002). Association of promoter variants in the alpha7 nicotinic acetylcholine receptor subunit gene with an inhibitory deficit found in schizophrenia. *Archives of General Psychiatry*, *59*(12), 1085–1096.

Li, H., Chan, R. C., McAlonan, G. M., & Gong, Q. Y. (2010). Facial emotion processing in schizophrenia: A meta-analysis of functional neuroimaging data. *Schizophrenia Bulletin*, *36*(5), 1029–1039.

Lijam, N., Paylor, R., McDonald, M. P., Crawley, J. N., Deng, C. X., Herrup, K., et al. (1997). Social interaction and sensorimotor gating abnormalities in mice lacking Dvl1. *Cell*, *90*(5), 895–905.

Mansbach, R. S., & Geyer, M. A. (1989). Effects of phencyclidine and phencyclidine biologs on sensorimotor gating in the rat. *Neuropsychopharmacology*, *2*, 299–308.

Mayer, J. D., & Salovey, P. (1995). Emotional intelligence and the construction and regulation of feelings. *Applied Preventive Psychology*, *4*(3), 197–208.

McCormick, L. M., Brumm, M. C., Beadle, J. N., Paradiso, S., Yamada, T., & Andreasen, N. (2012). Mirror neuron function, psychosis, and empathy in schizophrenia. *Psychiatry Research - Neuroimaging*, *201*(3), 233–239.

Michalopoulou, P. G., Surguladze, S., Morley, L. A., Giampietro, V. P., Murray, R. M., & Shergill, S. S. (2008). Facial fear processing and psychotic symptoms in schizophrenia: Functional magnetic resonance imaging study. *British Journal of Psychiatry*, *192*(3), 191–196.

Minzenberg, M. J., Laird, A. R., Thelen, S., Carter, C. S., & Glahn, D. C. (2009). Meta-analysis of 41 functional neuroimaging studies of executive function in schizophrenia. *Archives of General Psychiatry*, *66*(8), 811–822.

Mohn, A. R., Gainetdinov, R. R., Caron, M. G., & Koller, B. H. (1999). Mice with reduced NMDA receptor expression display behaviors related to schizophrenia. *Cell*, *98*(4), 427–436.

Morris, R. W., Weickert, C. S., & Loughland, C. M. (2009). Emotional face processing in schizophrenia. *Current Opinions in Psychiatry*, *22*(2), 140–146.

Moy, S. S., Troy Ghashghaei, H., Nonneman, R. J., Weimer, J. M., Yokota, Y., Lee, D., et al. (2009). Deficient NRG1-ERBB signaling alters social approach: Relevance to genetic mouse models of schizophrenia. *Journal of Neurodevelopmental Disorders*, *1*(4), 302–312.

Mukherjee, P., Whalley, H. C., McKirdy, J. W., McIntosh, A. M., Johnstone, E. C., Lawrie, S. M., et al. (2012). Lower effective connectivity between amygdala and parietal regions in response to fearful faces in schizophrenia. *Schizophrenia Research*, *134*(2–3), 118–124.

Nielsen, M. O., Rostrup, E., Wulff, S., Bak, N., Lublin, H., Kapur, S., et al. (2012). Alterations of the brain reward system in antipsychotic naive schizophrenia patients. *Biological Psychiatry*, *71*(10), 898–905.

Ochsner, K. N., Knierim, K., Ludlow, D. H., Hanelin, J., Ramachandran, T., Glover, G., et al. (2004). Reflecting upon feelings: An fMRI study of neural systems supporting the attribution of emotion to self and other. *Journal of Cognitive Neuroscience, 16*(10), 1746–1772.

O'Tuathaigh, C. M. P., Babovic, D., O'Sullivan, G. J., Clifford, J. J., Tighe, O., Croke, D. T., et al. (2007). Phenotypic characterization of spatial cognition and social behavior in mice with "knockout" of the schizophrenia risk gene neuregulin 1. *Neuroscience, 147*(1), 18–27.

Park, S., Matthews, N., & Gibson, C. (2008). Imitation, simulation, and schizophrenia. *Schizophrenia Bulletin, 34*(4), 698–707.

Paulus, M. P., Hozack, N., Zauscher, B., McDowell, J. E., Frank, L., Brown, G. G., et al. (2001). Prefrontal, parietal, and temporal cortex networks underlie decision-making in the presence of uncertainty. *Neuroimage, 13*(1), 91–100.

Pedersen, A., Koelkebeck, K., Brandt, M., Wee, M., Kueppers, K. A., Kugel, H., et al. (2012). Theory of mind in patients with schizophrenia: Is mentalizing delayed? *Schizophrenia Research, 137*(1–3), 224–229.

Perry, W., Minassian, A., Feifel, D., & Braff, D. L. (2001). Sensorimotor gating deficits in bipolar disorder patients with acute psychotic mania. *Biological Psychiatry, 50*(6), 418–424.

Pfeifer, J. H., & Peake, S. J. (2012). Self-development: Integrating cognitive, socioemotional, and neuroimaging perspectives. *Developmental Cognitive Neuroscience, 2*(1), 55–69.

Pinkham, A. E., Brensinger, C., Kohler, C., Gur, R. E., & Gur, R. C. (2011). Actively paranoid patients with schizophrenia over attribute anger to neutral faces. *Schizophrenia Research, 125*(2–3), 174–178.

Pletnikov, M. V., Ayhan, Y., Nikolskaia, O., Xu, Y., Ovanesov, M. V., Huang, H., et al. (2008). Inducible expression of mutant human DISC1 in mice is associated with brain and behavioral abnormalities reminiscent of schizophrenia. *Molecular Psychiatry, 13*(2), 173–186.

Premack, D., & Woodruff, G. (1978). Does the chimpanzee have a theory of mind? *Behavioral and Brain Sciences, 1*(4), 515–526.

Qiao, H., Noda, Y., Kamei, H., Nagai, T., Furukawa, H., Miura, H., et al. (2001). Clozapine, but not haloperidol, reverses social behavior deficit in mice during withdrawal from chronic phencyclidine treatment. *Neuroreport, 12*(1), 11–15.

Quan, M., Lee, S. H., Kubicki, M., Kikinis, Z., Rathi, Y., Seidman, L. J., et al. (2013). White matter tract abnormalities between rostral middle frontal gyrus, inferior frontal gyrus and striatum in first-episode schizophrenia. *Schizophrenia Research, 145*(1–3), 1–10.

Raedler, T. J. (2003). In vivo determination of muscarinic acetylcholine receptor availability in schizophrenia. *American Journal of Psychiatry, 160*(1), 118–127.

Rajarethinam, R., DeQuardo, J. R., Miedler, J., Arndt, S., Kirbat, R., & Brunberg, J. A. (2001). Hippocampus and amygdala in schizophrenia: Assessment of the relationship of neuroanatomy to psychopathology. *Psychiatry Research - Neuroimaging, 108*(2), 79–87.

Ramachandran, V. S., & Oberman, L. M. (2006). Broken mirrors – a theory of autism. *Scientific American, 295*(5), 62–69.

Rogers, R. D., Everitt, B. J., Baldacchino, A., Blackshaw, A. J., Swainson, R., Wynne, K., et al. (1999). Dissociable deficits in the decision-making cognition of chronic amphetamine abusers, opiate abusers, patients with focal damage to prefrontal cortex, and tryptophan-depleted normal volunteers: Evidence for monoaminergic mechanisms. *Neuropsychopharmacology, 20*(4), 322–339.

Rounis, E., Maniscalco, B., Rothwell, J. C., Passingham, R. E., & Lau, H. (2010). Theta-burst transcranial magnetic stimulation to the prefrontal cortex impairs metacognitive visual awareness. *Cognitive Neuroscience, 1*(3), 165–175.

Sallet, J., Mars, R. B., Noonan, M. P., Andersson, J. L., O'Reilly, J. X., Jbabdi, S., et al. (2011). Social network size affects neural circuits in macaques. *Science, 334*(6056), 697–700.

Sams-Dodd, F. (1995). Distinct effects of D-amphetamine and phencyclidine on the social behavior of rats. *Behavioural Pharmacology, 6*, 55–65.

Sams-Dodd, F. (1996). Phencyclidine-induced stereotyped behaviour and social isolation in rats: A possible animal model of schizophrenia. *Behavioural Pharmacology, 7*(1), 3–23.

Sams-Dodd, F., Lipska, B. K., & Weinberger, D. R. (1997). Neonatal lesions of the rat ventral hippocampus result in hyperlocomotion and deficits in social behaviour in adulthood. *Psychopharmacology, 132*(3), 303–310.

Saxe, R., & Baron-Cohen, S. (2006). The neuroscience of theory of mind. *Social Neuroscience, 1*(3–4), I–Ix.

Schmitt, A., Hasan, A., Gruber, O., & Falkai, P. (2011). Schizophrenia as a disorder of disconnectivity. *European Archives of Psychiatry and Clinical Neuroscience, 262*(2), 150–154.

Schneider, F., Weiss, U., Kessler, C., Salloum, J. B., Posse, S., Grodd, W., et al. (1998). Differential amygdala activation in schizophrenia during sadness. *Schizophrenia Research, 34*(3), 133–142.

Schneider, M., & Koch, M. (2005). Deficient social and play behavior in juvenile and adult rats after neonatal cortical lesion: Effects of chronic pubertal cannabinoid treatment. *Neuropsychopharmacology, 30*(5), 944–957.

Schreiber, R., Dalmus, M., & De Vry, J. (2002). Effects of alpha 4/beta 2- and alpha 7-nicotine acetylcholine receptor agonists on prepulse inhibition of the acoustic startle response in rats and mice. *Psychopharmacology, 159*(3), 248–257.

Schwartz, B. L., Mastropaolo, J., Rosse, R. B., Mathis, G., & Deutsch, S. I. (2006). Imitation of facial expressions in schizophrenia. *Psychiatry Research, 145*(2–3), 87–94.

Sesack, S. R., Carr, D. B., Omelchenko, N., & Pinto, A. (2003). Anatomical substrates for glutamate-dopamine interactions: Evidence for specificity of connections and extrasynaptic actions. *Annals of the New York Academy of Sciences, 1003*, 36–52.

Shamay-Tsoory, S. G., Shur, S., Barcal-Goodman, L., Medlovich, S., Harari, H., & Levkovitz, Y. (2007). Dissociation of cognitive from affective components of theory of mind in schizophrenia. *Psychiatry Research, 149*(1–3), 11–23.

Shi, L., Fatemi, S. H., Sidwell, R. W., & Patterson, P. H. (2003). Maternal influenza infection causes marked behavioral and pharmacological changes in the offspring. *Journal of Neuroscience, 23*(1), 297–302.

Singh, F., Pineda, J., & Cadenhead, K. S. (2011). Association of impaired EEG mu wave suppression, negative symptoms and social functioning in biological motion processing in first episode of psychosis. *Schizophrenia Research, 130*(1–3), 182–186.

Souchay, C., Bacon, E., & Danion, J. M. (2006). Metamemory in schizophrenia: An exploration of the feeling-of-knowing state. *Journal of Clinical and Experimental Neuropsychology, 28*(5), 828–840.

Stip, E., Fahim, C., Liddle, P., Mancini-Marie, A., Mensour, B., Bentaleb, L. A., et al. (2005). Neural correlates of sad feelings in schizophrenia with and without blunted affect. *Canadian Journal of Psychiatry, 50*(14), 909–917.

Streit, M., Ioannides, A., Sinnemann, T., Wolwer, W., Dammers, J., Zilles, K., et al. (2001). Disturbed facial affect recognition in patients with schizophrenia associated with hypoactivity in distributed brain regions: A magnetoencephalographic study. *American Journal of Psychiatry, 158*(9), 1429–1436.

Sumiyoshi, T., Stockmeier, C. A., Overholser, J. C., Dilley, G. E., & Meltzer, H. Y. (1996). Serotonin1A receptors are increased in postmortem prefrontal cortex in schizophrenia. *Brain Research, 708*(1–2), 209–214.

Swerdlow, N. R., Paulsen, J., Braff, D. L., Butters, N., Geyer, M. A., & Swenson, M. R. (1995). Impaired prepulse inhibition of acoustic and tactile startle response in patients with Huntington's disease. *Journal of Neurology, Neurosurgery Psychiatry, 58*(2), 192–200.

Swerdlow, N. R., Bakshi, V., Waikar, M., Taaid, N., & Geyer, M. A. (1998). Seroquel, clozapine and chlorpromazine restore sensorimotor gating in ketamine-treated rats. *Psychopharmacology, 140*(1), 75–80.

Swerdlow, N. R., & Geyer, M. A. (1998). Using an animal model of deficient sensorimotor gating to study the pathophysiology and new treatments of schizophrenia. *Schizophrenia Bulletin, 24*(2), 285–301.

Tager-Flusberg, H., & Sullivan, K. (2000). A componential view of theory of mind: Evidence from Williams syndrome. *Cognition, 76*(1), 59–90.

Takahashi, H., Kato, M., Sassa, T., Shibuya, T., Koeda, M., Yahata, N., et al. (2010). Functional deficits in the extrastriate body area during observation of sports-related actions in schizophrenia. *Schizophrenia Bulletin, 36*(3), 642–647.

Taylor, S. F., Kang, J., Brege, I. S., Tso, I. F., Hosanagar, A., & Johnson, T. D. (2012). Meta-analysis of functional neuroimaging studies of emotion perception and experience in schizophrenia. *Biological Psychiatry, 71*(2), 136–145.

Tian, L., Meng, C., Yan, H., Zhao, Q., Liu, Q., Yan, J., et al. (2011). Convergent evidence from multimodal imaging reveals amygdala abnormalities in schizophrenic patients and their first-degree relatives. *PLoS One, 6*(12), e28794.

Toomey, R., Schuldberg, D., Corrigan, P., & Green, M. F. (2002). Nonverbal social perception and symptomatology in schizophrenia. *Schizophrenia Research, 53*(1–2), 83–91.

Ursu, S., Kring, A. M., Gard, M. G., Minzenberg, M. J., Yoon, J. H., Ragland, J. D., et al. (2011). Prefrontal cortical deficits and impaired cognition-emotion interactions in schizophrenia. *American Journal of Psychiatry, 168*(3), 276–285.

van Schouwenburg, M., Aarts, E., & Cools, R. (2010). Dopaminergic modulation of cognitive control: Distinct roles for the prefrontal cortex and the basal ganglia. *Current Pharmaceutical Design, 16*(18), 2026–2032.

van't Wout, M., & Sanfey, A. G. (2011). Interactive decision-making in people with schizotypal traits: A game theory approach. *Psychiatry Research, 185*(1–2), 92–96.

Varcin, K. J., Bailey, P. E., & Henry, J. D. (2010). Empathic deficits in schizophrenia: The potential role of rapid facial mimicry. *Journal of the International Neuropsychological Society, 16*(4), 621–629.

Velakoulis, D., Wood, S. J., Wong, M. T. H., McGorry, P. D., Yung, A., Phillips, L., et al. (2006). Hippocampal and amygdala volumes according to psychosis stage and diagnosis – a magnetic resonance imaging study of chronic schizophrenia, first-episode psychosis, and ultra-high-risk individuals. *Archives of General Psychiatry, 63*(2), 139–149.

Vogeley, K., Tepest, R., Schneider-Axmann, T., Hutte, H., Zilles, K., Honer, W. G., et al. (2003). Automated image analysis of disturbed cytoarchitecture in Brodmann area 10 in schizophrenia. *Schizophrenia Research, 62*(1–2), 133–140.

Wallis, J. D. (2007). Orbitofrontal cortex and its contribution to decision-making. *Annual Review of Neuroscience, 30*, 31–56.

Walter, H., Ciaramidaro, A., Adenzato, M., Vasic, N., Ardito, R. B., Erk, S., et al. (2009). Dysfunction of the social brain in schizophrenia is modulated by intention type: An fMRI study. *Social Cognitive and Affective Neuroscience, 4*(2), 166–176.

Wan, F. J., & Swerdlow, N. R. (1997). The basolateral amygdala regulates sensorimotor gating of acoustic startle in the rat. *Neuroscience, 76*(3), 715–724.

Wilkinson, L. S., Killcross, S. S., Humby, T., Hall, F. S., Geyer, M. A., & Robbins, T. W. (1994). Social isolation in the rat produces developmentally specific deficits in prepulse inhibition of the acoustic startle response without disrupting latent inhibition. *Neuropsychopharmacology, 10*(1), 61–72.

Williams, J. H., Whiten, A., Suddendorf, T., & Perrett, D. I. (2001). Imitation, mirror neurons and autism. *Neuroscience and Biobehavioral Reviews, 25*(4), 287–295.

Wischniewski, J., & Brüne, M. (2011). Moral reasoning in schizophrenia: An explorative study into economic decision making. *Cognitive Neuropsychiatry*, 1–16.

Wolff, A. R., & Bilkey, D. K. (2008). Immune activation during mid-gestation disrupts sensorimotor gating in rat offspring. *Behavioural Brain Research, 190*(1), 156–159.

Wynn, J. K., Horan, W. P., Kring, A. M., Simons, R. F., & Green, M. F. (2010). Impaired anticipatory event-related potentials in schizophrenia. *International Journal of Psychophysiology, 77*(2), 141–149.

Wynn, J. K., Lee, J., Horan, W. P., & Green, M. F. (2008). Using event related potentials to explore stages of facial affect recognition deficits in schizophrenia. *Schizophrenia Bulletin, 34*(4), 679–687.

Wynn, J. K., Sergi, M. J., Dawson, M. E., Schell, A. M., & Green, M. F. (2005). Sensorimotor gating, orienting and social perception in schizophrenia. *Schizophrenia Research, 73*(2–3), 319–325.

Yeomans, J. S., Bosch, D., Alves, N., Daros, A., Ure, R. J., & Schmid, S. (2010). GABA receptors and prepulse inhibition of acoustic startle in mice and rats. *European Journal of Neuroscience, 31*(11), 2053–2061.

Chapter 2

Cross-Cultural Aspects of Social Cognitive Abilities in Schizophrenia

Katja Koelkebeck[1] and Christine Wilhelm[2]

[1]University of Muenster, Muenster, Germany, [2]School of Medicine, University of Muenster, Muenster, Germany

Chapter Outline

INTRODUCTION

Social cognition is an intensively investigated field of research in healthy humans and in people with psychiatric disorders. Social cognitive abilities are a prerequisite of the individual's ability to interact in a social environment. They comprise a set of skills related to the recognition of emotions

Social Cognition and Metacognition in Schizophrenia.
DOI: http://dx.doi.org/10.1016/B978-0-12-405172-0.00002-8
© 2014 Elsevier Inc. All rights reserved.

and intentions in other subjects and oneself, including the ability to infer one's own and other people's mental states, called theory of mind (ToM) or mentalizing (Blakemore *et al.*, 2003), or the interpretation of facial expressions (Comparelli *et al.*, 2013).

Development of social cognitive skills varies in different cultures and throughout life. Some cultures appear to be faster in developing adequate mind reading or empathy skills than others (Liu *et al.*, 2008). Factors that depend on the sociocultural background of a person seem to play a major role, with familial interaction styles and language education forming the most important components. In recent years, the concept of sociocultural factors influencing the neuroplasticity of the brain has been adapted by psychiatric research. Genetic, brain imaging, and comparative psychiatric research approaches were joined to create modern research models of neurodevelopmental disorders. A better insight into pathologic states and functioning has been expected from the identification of sociocultural factors impacting the development of social cognitive functions in healthy individuals. Schizophrenia is a disease where patients of different nations and cultures as well as climatic zones seem to be more alike than the healthy individuals of the respective areas (Pfeiffer, 1967; Pfeiffer and Schoene, 1980). In contrast, it has been hypothesized that schizophrenic symptomatology, which is partly due to an abnormal development of brain circuits that mediate certain functions in the brain (Pearlson, 2000), might also be subject to cultural influences. In schizophrenia, the functional integrity of self-structure, which is necessary for the interpretation of cultural behavior, is compromised. Thus, abnormalities of self/other perception in schizophrenia might form a model for the functioning of culture-based social cognition and vice versa (Fabrega, 1989).

In this chapter, we will review data on physiologic development and cross-cultural differences of social cognition in healthy humans, with ToM and facial emotion recognition as core features of this ability. Moreover, we will summarize important cross-cultural differences of schizophrenic symptomatology. We will also resume recent neuroimaging approaches in cross-cultural social cognitive research. Lastly, we will link the results of recent cross-cultural research to the application of culture-related paradigms in the diagnosis of schizophrenia and the assessment of symptomatology and will give an outlook on future research directions.

DEVELOPMENTAL ASPECTS OF SOCIAL COGNITION

For an active engagement in a culture, mentalizing abilities – or the ability to hypothesize about one's own and others' intentions and reactions – are necessary (Duffy *et al.*, 2009, p. 358). The development of ToM abilities takes a complicated course and relies on the cultural background of an individual. Specifically with regard to such complex and sophisticated abilities as mentalizing, differences between cultures have repeatedly been found and are most prominent in children. Only from the age of nine years, children are able to grasp the full range of interactional maneuvers forming part of ToM, including white lies, cheating, sarcasm, and the understanding of meta-expressions (Wellman *et al.*, 2001). After learning the basic rudiments of emotion and self/other distinction, children start to acquire culture-related skills, involving, for instance, cultural practices (Callaghan *et al.*, 2011). Northern American children have been described to develop an early understanding of the fact that two individuals (with desires) might have differing beliefs regarding a situation (Wellman *et al.*, 2006). In contrast, Chinese children seem to understand early in their development that individuals may be knowledgeable or ignorant of facts and situations, irrespective of their beliefs or desires. Authors attributed these time-course differences of early ToM development to educational styles. For example, it is hypothesized that literacy of parents, status of the language, and home education account for observed differential ToM-related language use in Chinese-speaking, as compared with English-speaking, children (Li and Rao, 2000). In the Chinese language, 'to believe' can be expressed by a range of different words, resulting in a greater variety of mental state-related vocabulary (Wellman *et al.*, 2006). The use of specific ToM-related language terms might in turn affect mentalizing abilities (Lee *et al.*, 1999; Wellman *et al.*, 2006). Furthermore, Naito and Koyama (2006) found that Japanese children developed false-belief task skills later than Western children, but had a tendency to interpret situations using implicit social information without receiving explicit information. Several authors hypothesize that this tendency of Japanese children may be due to early training in social behavior, specifically to implicitly infer social meanings (also see Hendry, 1986).

Taking perspectives of self and others (Galinsky *et al.*, 2005) and recognition of contexts with regard to (social) relations are important prerequisites for mentalizing abilities. Matsuda and Nisbett (2001) found that Japanese participants made more statements about contextual information and relationships while performing a picture-viewing task than Americans did. Moreover, Kitayama and colleagues (2003) found that North Americans tended to ignore contextual information when making judgments about external objects as compared to an Asian control group. It seems that Asians pay more attention to the general emotional implication of a situation than to details, which appears to be connected to their view of personhood (Shweder *et al.*, 1998). These findings point to the notion that the perception of the self in non-Asian cultures is more self-centered, while Asian cultures are likely to perceive social information in a contextual, interpersonal way. Wellman and colleagues (2001) proposed that equality of performance levels on social cognitive tasks across cultures is ultimately reached in older age. However, other authors found performance differences on social cognitive tasks in adulthood, mostly related to self/other distinction, which will be elaborated on later in this chapter.

Taken together, previous research on cross-cultural social cognition has shown a culture-dependent development of ToM abilities as well as performance, for example, the use of ToM-related language and the contextual interpretation of social cues.

CROSS-CULTURAL PSYCHIATRY

Because ToM development is culture-dependent, it is not unlikely that pathologic states, such as for example schizophrenia, are also partly affected by the individual's sociocultural background. While the prevalence of schizophrenia across cultures has been shown at a constant rate in studies performed by the World Health Organization (WHO), which included thousands of patients in 17 countries, the course of the disorder was shown to differ (Siegert, 2001). For example, patients with schizophrenia from less developed countries displayed a tendency to recover more quickly and completely from their illness (Sass, 1997). This might be explained by the fact that developing countries have other concepts of familiar inter-dependency, which could pose a protecting factor (Singh *et al.*, 2013). Furthermore, the main characteristics of the disorder remain the same, yet symptom patterns vary according to the culture of an individual.

In the following, we will review findings of culture-specific symptomatology in schizophrenia. In doing so, we will focus on positive symptomatology, investigated by the majority of studies, with only a brief digression to negative and other symptomatology.

Delusional Symptomatology in Cross-Cultural Studies

Tateyama and colleagues (1993; 1998) compared the prevalence and contents of delusions of patients with schizophrenia in Japan to patients in Germany and Austria. The number of patients with delusional symptomatology was equal in both groups. Moreover, the number of patients with delusions about world-end scenarios and the quantity of so-called 'negative' (e.g., paranoid ideas) and 'positive' (e.g., grandiosity) delusions was the same (Tateyama, 1989). However, the quality of these delusions was different. While 20% of the German-speaking sample showed religious delusions, similar delusions could only be found in 6% of the Japanese sample. In addition, while in the German-speaking sample delusional guilt was seen often, it was rare in the Asian sample. A possible explanation is that Asian religions, such as Buddhism, do not imply apocalyptic ideation or death as penalty for, or absolution from, sin (Fujimori, 1981).

In a study by Stompe and colleagues (1999), which compared Austrian and Pakistani individuals with schizophrenia, the most frequently mentioned content of delusions in both countries was persecution. In Austrian patients, though, the frequency of delusions of grandeur, guilt, as well as religious delusions was much higher. Similar results were yielded by Veling and colleagues' (2011) study among Dutch and ethnic minorities living in the

Netherlands. They found persecutory delusions to be more common among the Dutch. Minsky *et al.* (2003) found that psychiatric patients from a European-American background had a higher frequency of persecutory delusions, nervous tension, and blunted affect than did Mexican-Americans with the same diagnosis. Persecutory delusions and ideas of one's life or personality being threatened were more common in a German-speaking sample as compared with a Japanese sample (Tateyama *et al.*, 1998). In contrast, the ideas of shaming someone or being a burden to someone, as well as being worthless formed the most common delusions in Japanese patients. These delusions, while somewhat sketchy, also included the feeling that others spoke badly behind their backs (Tateyama *et al.*, 1993; Tateyama *et al.*, 1998). To interpret these findings, it is important to stress that Asian and other island states, as well as Arabic countries are considered to be collectivistic societies (Triandis, 2001). One's own individuality is less important than the interests of one's social groups, for example, the company or the family. Own needs and wishes might be neglected in favor of the social group's well-being, as the good name of the group or the family is valued more highly. Thus, individuals in collectivistic societies are more susceptible to shameful experiences and the feeling of worthlessness (e.g., by 'losing face' or being an unworthy society member). In addition, a lower rate of delusions of being poisoned was described in the Japanese group (Tateyama *et al.*, 1993). Fujimori and colleagues (1987) even found a difference between Japanese, Korean, and Chinese patients and argued that different cultural experience with food and poisoning, for example, dining habits, medical treatment, or war experience, might shape these kinds of delusions. A study of South Korean patients with schizophrenia showed that espionage was a major topic of delusional symptoms, most probably because of their particular political background (Kim *et al.*, 1993; Kim *et al.*, 2001).

Omata (1985) found in his comparison of schizoaffective patients in Japan and Germany that the delusion of being possessed occurred in Japanese schizoaffective patients only. Furukawa and Bourgeois (1984) reported that about 20% of a sample of Japanese patients had delusions of possession. Most often, the patients were under the impression that they were possessed by a nature spirit, a divine and treacherous messenger, or by a ghost of a long-dead ancestor (Fujimori, 1981). Women and inhabitants of southern, rural parts of Japan (e.g., Okinawa) more often displayed these forms of delusions, implying not only cultural but also regional influences on delusions.

Family denial syndrome known in Japanese patients with schizophrenia implies the denial of the family name, of the family origins, and of their relatives (Kimura *et al.*, 1968). While in Western patients with schizophrenia, delusions of high-ranking lineage are quite common, it could be hypothesized that the development of the denial syndrome observed in Japan might be a way of patients coping with a rigid family system and tight social boundaries. A similar phenomenon has been described in Japanese 'hikikomori' patients (see Tateno *et al.*, 2012 for a survey). This phenomenon implies that patients withdraw from society for more than 6 months, not leaving their house during that period. It is hypothesized that this patient group might partly consist of patients with chronic schizophrenia, but also of young people who want to escape from social pressure.

Hallucinatory Symptomatology in Cross-Cultural Studies

While most cultural-comparative investigations focus on delusions, there is a small body of evidence of culture-dependency of hallucinations. In a study in a cross-cultural sample, visual as well as tactile hallucinations occurred most frequently in patients from Africa and the Near East (Ndetei and Vadher, 1984). Bauer et al. (2011) investigated patients from Austria, Poland, Lithuania, Georgia, Pakistan, Nigeria, and Ghana on psychotic symptomatology and found a high percentage of visual hallucinations in participants from European countries. However, the highest rates of visual hallucinations were reported in Nigeria and Ghana, while in European and Pakistani patients visual hallucinations were seen less frequently. Barrio et al. (2003) found in a large study on symptom expression on the Positive and Negative Syndrome Scale (PANSS) in schizophrenia spectrum disorder that African-Americans reported higher hallucinatory behavior and suspiciousness scores than European-Americans. Latin-Americans scored higher on the item of somatic concerns than both European-Americans and African-Americans. It seems, though, that the pattern of hallucinations depends on the place where a person is living rather than their original culture, as a study on Pakistani immigrants in the UK showed (Suhail and Cochrane, 2002). This interpretation was supported by Wang and colleagues (1998), who found that migrants hear voices not only in their first language, but also in their second or third languages, depending on the delusional content. Hallucinations and delusions may even vary regionally within the same country, suggesting that cultural effects may not necessarily be delineated by geopolitical boundaries (Gecici et al., 2010). Brekke and Barrio (1997) reported that patients with schizophrenia from minority groups were generally less symptomatic than were nonminority patients.

Negative and Other Schizophrenic Symptomatology

In a study on Swedish and US patients with schizophrenia, patients in Sweden lived more independently for longer periods than their US American counterparts due to differences in the cognitive challenges of the cultural context (mediated, for instance, by cultural and social support systems) (Harvey et al., 2009). Catatonic symptoms, flattening of affect, and social withdrawal can be found more frequently in Japanese patients as compared to other countries surveyed by Murphy et al. (1963). One explanation could be that social withdrawal or being in a catatonic state constitutes one way of dealing with unwanted symptomatology without shaming another person. In comparison to that, patients with states of excitement can be seen more often in Western cultures. Veling and colleagues (2011) found more affective symptoms in Moroccans and Turkish people, who also had higher psychopathology scores and more negative symptoms compared with Dutch residents.

In conclusion, there are cross-cultural differences in schizophrenic symptomatology. Contents of delusions differ in quality. The quality of symptoms such as guilt and religious delusions seem to depend rather strongly on the sociocultural background of a person (Stompe *et al.*, 2003). Nonetheless, data on cross-cultural differences in schizophrenic symptomatology are still sparse.

CROSS-CULTURAL DIFFERENCES IN THE PERCEPTION OF SOCIAL CUES IN PATIENTS WITH SCHIZOPHRENIA

While universality of facial emotional expressions (Brandt and Boucher, 1985) and the ability to judge particular emotions have been verified across cultures (Ekman and Friesen, 1971; Ekman *et al.*, 1972), differences in the perception of social cues have been found. Ratings of emotional intensity (Ekman *et al.*, 1972; Matsumoto and Ekman, 1989), for example, vary across different cultures. Cultural variations might relate to sanctions and appraisals of societies to specific emotional expressions (Markham and Wang, 1996) and the influence of language on emotional expressions (Matsumoto, 1992; Russell, 1991). Specific societies, as for example the Japanese, might perceive the open expression of certain emotions as too strong or inappropriate (Aune and Aune, 1996) and also rate displayed emotions more intensely even when displayed subtly (Matsumoto *et al.*, 2000).

While in healthy populations, there is ample research on the perception of social cues with regard to culture, few data are available on cross-cultural differences in the perception of social stimuli in schizophrenia. Lee *et al.* (2010) were able to show that deficits in emotion recognition abilities in schizophrenia are similar across cultures. However, Brekke and colleagues (2005) found that patients with schizophrenia of American-Caucasian origin were more highly skilled at the perception of emotions compared with samples of African-Americans and Latin-Americans. Habel and colleagues (2000) investigated American, German, and Indian patients with schizophrenia as well as healthy controls on an emotion discrimination and mood induction task using Caucasian emotional faces. While the results indicated that healthy controls performed significantly better than patients with schizophrenia in each of the three groups, it was also shown that in both the Indian patients and control groups performance was significantly lower on facial discrimination than in their American and German counterparts. More recently, Pinkham and colleagues (2008) used stimuli including both Caucasian-American and African-American faces in an emotion recognition task in patients with schizophrenia of Caucasian-American and African-American origin. They demonstrated that patients with schizophrenia were more likely to recognize same-race faces than other-race faces.

RECENT CROSS-CULTURAL RESEARCH ON SOCIAL COGNITION

In recent research on social cognition, neuroimaging methods have been used more frequently to investigate the neurobiologic basis of social-cognitive abilities. As brain regions have distinct but complementary functions, specific brain networks were suggested to mediate social cognitive abilities, as when recognizing others' intentions (e.g., in ToM; de Lange *et al.*, 2008). In healthy humans, brain networks involving for instance the temporal, medial prefrontal cortex (mPFC), and dorsolateral prefrontal cortex (dlPFC) as well as the amygdala have been identified as parts of a mentalizing brain network (e.g., Castelli *et al.*, 2000; Völlm *et al.*, 2006). Due to cross-cultural differences in the mode and development of social cognitive abilities, it follows that specific brain regions are activated in a culture-specific manner during performance of social cognitive tasks. Research focused on the investigation of Caucasian and Asian groups and revealed differences in brain activation patterns in response to social cues. Comparing Asian to Caucasian cultures, the concept of individualism and collectivism needs to be discussed with regard to the processing of social stimuli. Individualists perceive their selves as stable entities, autonomous from other people and their environment, while collectivists view themselves as dynamic entities, continually defined by their social context and relationships. Thus, different self-concepts have been proposed by which interdependent individuals, as from Asian societies, view and represent themselves differently from Caucasians (Han, 2013). In a behavioral study of Japanese and American participants, Matsuda and Nisbett (2001) presented participants with animated vignettes and the instruction to report the contents. Japanese participants made more statements about contextual information and relationships than Americans did and recognized previously seen objects more accurately when presented in their original rather than in novel settings. Moriguchi and colleagues (2005) found in a functional brain imaging study comparing Japanese to Caucasian participants on a task with fearful faces (Ekman and Friesen, 1976) that Japanese participants activated the right inferior frontal cortex, premotor cortex, and left insula in response to the stimuli, while Caucasians activated the posterior cingulate, supplementary motor cortex, and the amygdala during task performance. Thus, various regions may be playing a crucial role in recognizing the biologic value of visual stimuli such as fearful expressions. Several authors hypothesized that Caucasians respond to fearful faces in a more direct, emotional way, while the Japanese do not attach an emotional valence to the faces. Zhu and colleagues (2012) found differences in resting states in Caucasian and Chinese participants and related those findings to self-structure or self-representation. In a different study on the impact of individualistic and collectivistic selves on brain activation in Asians and Caucasians, its authors showed that during a self-estimation task of general and contextual judgment, Westerners activated the anterior rostral portion of the mPFC more than Asian controls, which was associated with individualistic traits (Chiao *et al.*, 2009). Another study of the same group (Chiao *et al.*, 2010) demonstrated that biculturals primed with individualistic values had increased activation within the mPFC and posterior cingulate cortex (PCC) during general relative to contextual self-judgments. Biculturals primed with collectivistic values showed increased response within the mPFC and PCC during contextual relative to general self-judgments. Moreover, the degree of cultural priming was positively correlated with the degree of mPFC and PCC activity during culturally congruent self-judgments. Harada and colleagues (2010) showed in a functional magnetic resonance imaging (fMRI) study with bicultural individuals primed with individualism that the dorsal mPFC was activated less during implicit evaluation of father-relevant information, but not self-relevant information, as compared with a control condition. The authors concluded that cultural values shape neural representations during the evaluation of self-relevant information. Furthermore, an advantage of self-recognition over other-recognition has been ascribed to an enhanced self-focused attention of Western subjects (Sui *et al.*, 2009). In an event-related potential (ERP) study, its authors showed that Chinese compared with British participants had larger N2 (component of the ERP that peaks milliseconds post-stimulus, reflecting executive cognitive control functions and emotion processing) amplitudes in response to a friend's face as compared to their own.

As mentioned above, individualism and collectivism refer to cultural values that influence how people construe their selves and their relation to the world. An fMRI study with Korean and Caucasian-American participants investigated the neural basis of intergroup empathy using scenes of racial in-group and out-group members in emotional pain (Cheon *et al.*, 2011). Koreans reported experiencing greater empathy and elicited stronger activity in the left temporoparietal junction for in-group compared to out-group members. Furthermore, preferential reactivity within this region to the pain of in-group relative to out-group members was associated with greater preference for social hierarchy and in-group biases in empathy (Cheon *et al.*, 2011). An fMRI study of Adams and colleagues (2010) used the 'reading the mind in the eyes task' in a sample of Japanese participants who were asked to judge Caucasian stimuli faces regarding the emotional contents compared with Caucasian-American participants. Results showed greater bilateral posterior superior temporal sulci recruitment during same-culture versus other-culture mental state decoding in both cultural groups.

So far, however, very few studies have explicitly addressed the impact of different cultures on ToM-related brain activation. Kobayashi and colleagues (2006) have proposed differential effects of language education on ToM-related brain activation in an fMRI study comparing adult American monolinguals and Japanese bilinguals using a second-order false-belief task: while the ventromedial PFC and precuneus were recruited in both groups, the inferior frontal gyrus was recruited in a culture-dependent manner during ToM task-performance in the Japanese only. In a study by Koelkebeck and colleagues (2011), ToM abilities were investigated in a sample of native Japanese and a group of Caucasian participants living in Japan. A ToM task depicting moving geometrical shapes acting in social patterns (Abell *et al.*, 2000) was applied in fMRI. No difference in the use of ToM-related vocabulary or correctness of descriptions in both study groups on the behavioral level could be found, indicating a relative independency of cross-cultural performance. However, fMRI results showed a higher level of activation in Caucasian participants compared with Japanese controls in the mPFC as well as in temporal parts of the brain. While no association between levels of acculturation (e.g., language abilities, cultural knowledge) or empathy could be identified, a subscale of the Toronto Alexithymia Scale (Taylor *et al.*, 1985) 'difficulties in identifying feelings' as well as the Autism Questionnaire (Baron-Cohen *et al.*, 2001) correlated with the activation pattern in the mPFC in Japanese participants. It was hypothesized that Japanese participants need to activate the mPFC to a lesser extent, because they have been taught to be in tune with unspoken social signals all around and being able to react in a socially accepted way. However, when higher autistic or alexithymic traits are present, the ToM network is utilized similarly as by Caucasians. In contrast, Caucasians were hypothesized to be constantly monitoring their selves and their surrounding and thus overly activating the ToM network.

Taken together, recent cross-cultural imaging approaches in healthy subjects suggest culturally influenced activation patterns of several brain networks involved, which might also be of importance to activation differences found in patients with schizophrenia regarding self/other distinction and mentalizing (Brüne *et al.*, 2011; Pedersen *et al.*, 2012). Moreover, the concept of individualism/collectivism might also impact patients with schizophrenia, specifically with regard to self-concepts, which might be altered. A systematic review on emotional overinvolvement in schizophrenia has postulated that there might be a culture-specific impact of mutual interdependence across cultures (Singh *et al.*, 2013). This might not only constitute a pathologic but also a protective factor that needs to be further assessed.

THE ADAPTATION OF NOVEL PARADIGMS AND APPROACHES IN SOCIAL COGNITION RESEARCH IN SCHIZOPHRENIA: ONGOING RESEARCH AND FUTURE RESEARCH DIRECTIONS

The development of early detection tools as well as specific intervention programs to overcome social cognitive deficits in patients with schizophrenia is crucial. So-called vulnerability (or disease) markers are cognitive abnormalities that are specific for one disease, present in symptom-free intervals, in first-degree relatives and early on in the development (Braff *et al.*, 1981). They can help identify people at risk for the development of schizophrenia, for instance. ToM has already been identified as a potential disease marker in schizophrenia

(Koelkebeck *et al.*, 2010). For the development of more sophisticated markers that assess social cognitive abilities in schizophrenia, the cross-cultural context, for example, the investigation of emotions in faces of out-group members, might be helpful. There are two recent lines of research involving out-group-related stimuli that will be presented in the following.

Facial Emotion Recognition Using Objects with Out-Group Features

One set of abilities forming part of social cognition is the ability to recognize emotions in the face, which is known to be compromised in schizophrenia (Lewis and Garver, 1995; Suslow *et al.*, 2003) as well as in depressed patients (Domschke *et al.*, 2010; Koschack *et al.*, 2003). However, there is only little evidence that patients with schizophrenia can be reliably distinguished from depressed patients on tasks employing recognition of explicit emotions (Walker *et al.*, 1984; Weniger *et al.*, 2004). Yet, a promising approach is the recognition of subtle emotions, which seems to be specifically compromised in patients with schizophrenia (Burch, 1995).

When it comes to the recognition of emotions, the task becomes more difficult when they are displayed on a face of a person from a different cultural background. Matsumoto (1992) showed that healthy Japanese participants performed worse in the identification of Caucasian facial emotions than healthy Caucasian-American participants in the identification of Japanese facial emotions. In addition to that, Russell (1991) hypothesized that basic emotions are easy to recognize throughout all cultures, while subtle and ambiguous emotions are easier identified in members of one's own culture.

To develop a more sensitive measure to identify specific deficits of several disease entities, Minoshita and colleagues introduced a novel paradigm for the recognition of subtle emotional expressions in the face. During the task, nine photos of a painted wooden mask showing the features of a young woman in flipped angles are presented. Due to the manner of carving, they display a rich variety of emotions beyond the basic ones (e.g., ecstasy, deference, shyness). For each mask, participants are asked to decide whether the mask shows the emotional expression in question (e.g., 'is she sad?'). In two previous studies, Minoshita *et al.* (1997; 1999) validated the task in healthy controls. Patients with schizophrenia identified emotions with less variety than healthy controls, had less sensitivity for negative emotions, and were less sensitive toward uncanny emotional expressions (Minoshita *et al.*, 2005). This pattern was not observed in depressed patients, who, in contrast, responded faster to calm expressions (Minoshita *et al.*; personal communication). The emotional ambiguity expressed by the mask, as well as the fact that it displays Asian features, makes the task a valuable instrument for application in groups of Western patients with schizophrenia. It is known that patients with schizophrenia have difficulties with the perception and interpretation of ambiguous stimuli in other domains as well (ambiguous verbal information; Ketteler *et al.*, 2012). Moreover, compared with other facial emotion recognition tasks (e.g., those utilizing Ekman and Friesen faces (1976)), this task presents a nonhuman object. This might reduce bias due to a subjective view of the face models. This approach, specifically in the early detection of patients with psychotic disorders, can be combined with other neurobiologic methods such as fMRI. Due to disease-specific activation abnormalities of the amygdala (Phillips *et al.*, 2003), this endophenotype might help to additionally categorize schizophrenia compared with patients with depression.

Facial Emotion Recognition Using In-Group Human Stimuli Including Features of Out-Group Members

Other race bias (Elfenbein and Ambady, 2003; Meissner and Brigham, 2001) suggests that own-race faces are remembered and discriminated better than other-race faces, which might contribute to an ethnical bias. Emotion, context, race, and gender influence perception unconsciously and trigger automatic affective responses (Amodio *et al.*, 2004; Fazio *et al.*, 1995; Kret and de Gelder, 2010). Studies investigating people of black skin color compared with white people showed that participants made different judgments about facial expressions when the target was a black versus a white male (Hugenberg and Bodenhausen, 2003). Additionally, emotion recognition is typically faster for positive than negative emotions, but the reverse is true when Caucasians judge black targets (Hugenberg, 2005).

A second novel approach is, therefore, to include features of out-group members to tasks that employ the recognition of facial emotions. A recently developed task by Kret and deGelder (2012) introduced faces of women that were covered by traditional Islamic veils (niqab, hijab) compared with a cap or scarf. Authors investigated whether headdress interferes with emotion recognition and whether this effect depends on the type of headdress. Fear was recognized fastest by the white European sample of healthy participants when the facial expression was partly hidden by a niqab suggesting that a niqab facilitates the fear response. The results also show that a cap and scarf were more often associated with happiness than in the niqab condition.

Theories propose that anxious individuals will form either more affect-congruent or more stereotypic impressions of out-group members. In a study by Curtis and Locke (2005), anxious white Australian participants read behavioral descriptions about an Australian Aboriginal target that were stereotypic, nonstereotypic, threatening, and nonthreatening. Anxious participants formed impressions that, while not more stereotypic than those formed by control participants, were more affect-congruent. Thus, psychiatric symptomatology might interfere with emotion recognition and is most probably influenced by the cultural background of the patient. Results of research with emotional stimuli of out-group members seem to form a promising approach for tasks used in (early) detection of schizophrenia, with specific regard to the fact that emotion recognition dysfunction in schizophrenia might be enhanced by out-group features of stimuli.

Other Research Approaches

It seems that social interaction with out-group members is modulated by oxytocin, dampening the amygdala and thus promoting trust-building in participants (De Dreu *et al.*, 2011). Oxytocin is also involved in trust-building in schizophrenia. Brüne (2012) reviewed studies on oxytocin variants in psychiatric disorders and could show different polymorphisms that might influence the susceptibility to schizophrenia. A dysbalance of oxytocin might thus enhance or attenuate the other-race bias. Mehta and colleagues (2011) suggested the use of social cognition tools specialized for cultural groups. They strongly recommend validating assessment measures across varied cultures and presented the Social Cognition Rating Tools in Indian Setting (SOCRATIS). This is a test battery to assess ToM, faux pas recognition, social perception, and attributional bias. Matsumoto and colleagues (2000) have developed a measure of perception of emotion specifically for the Japanese, and they delineate methodologic requirements for studies attempting to detect both cross-cultural similarities and differences in emotion perception. All these tools might be helpful for the assessment of schizophrenic symptomatology.

Thus, the investigation of the influence of out-group features on emotion recognition in patients with schizophrenia compared with healthy controls, as well as the investigation of oxytocin might be an interesting and promising approach to the employment of cross-cultural aspects of emotion perception. Moreover, culture-specific tools should be evaluated to gain dependable measures for social cognition abilities across cultures.

SUMMARY

Taken together, cross-cultural research aims to understand factors that influence the development, sustenance, and configuration of psychiatric disorders. With regard to patients with schizophrenia, this holds specifically true for symptom constellations and the development of the disease. While in children mentalizing abilities develop over several years, with culture having a strong impact on shaping social cognitive functions, in patients with schizophrenia culture seems to have an influence on symptomatology, onset, and course of the disease on the behavioral as well as the biologic level. While little is known about the impact of culture on social cognition in schizophrenia, recent research has determined neural patterns of reactions to social cues that depend on the sociocultural background of a person. Thus, it must be assumed that patients with schizophrenia or with a risk of developing schizophrenia will be influenced by their culture or the culture that surrounds them, too. Culture-based social cognition might have an impact on future task developments that try to assess deficits in social cognition utilizing emotional face recognition tasks in schizophrenia. Presenting objects with features of outgroup subjects might render recognition of social cues more difficult and distinguish subgroups or disease entities. Imaging techniques might be helpful to distinguish biologic from cultural factors and determine developmental deficits as well as structures and abilities in schizophrenia that deteriorate over time. Moreover, evaluations of existing social cognitive tasks with regard to the specific background of an individual need to be performed. Therefore, cultural viewpoints in psychiatric research, specifically with a focus on schizophrenia, are essential in refining our understanding of biologic and sociocultural factors influencing the development and course of diseases and to determining optimized diagnostic and intervention methods.

REFERENCES

Abell, F., Happé, F. G., & Frith, U. (2000). Do triangles play tricks? Attribution of mental states to animated shapes in normal and abnormal development. *Cognitive Development*, *15*, 1–16.

Adams, R. B., Jr., Rule, N. O., Franklin, R. G., Jr., Wang, E., Stevenson, M. T., Yoshikawa, S., et al. (2010). Cross-cultural reading the mind in the eyes: An fMRI investigation. *Journal of Cognitive Neuroscience*, *22*(1), 97–108.

Amodio, D. M., Harmon-Jones, E., Devine, P. G., Curtin, J. J., Hartley, S. L., & Covert, A. E. (2004). Neural signals for the detection of unintentional race bias. *Psychological Science*, *15*(2), 88–93.

Aune, K. S., & Aune, R. K. (1996). Cultural differences in the self-reported experience and expression of emotions in relationships. *Journal of Cross-Cultural Psychology*, *27*(1), 67–81.

Baron-Cohen, S., Wheelwright, S., Skinner, R., Martin, J., & Clubley, E. (2001). The autism-spectrum quotient (AQ): Evidence from Asperger syndrome/high-functioning autism, males and females, scientists and mathematicians. *Journal of Autism and Developmental Disorders*, *31*(1), 5–17.

Barrio, C., Yamada, A. M., Atuel, H., Hough, R. L., Yee, S., Berthot, B., et al. (2003). A tri-ethnic examination of symptom expression on the positive and negative syndrome scale in schizophrenia spectrum disorders. *Schizophrenia Research*, *60*(2–3), 259–269.

Bauer, S. M., Schanda, H., Karakula, H., Olajossy-Hilkesberger, L., Rudaleviciene, P., Okribelashvili, N., et al. (2011). Culture and the prevalence of hallucinations in schizophrenia. *Comprehensive Psychiatry*, *52*(3), 319–325.

Blakemore, S. J., Boyer, P., Pachot-Clouard, M., Meltzoff, A., Segebarth, C., & Decety, J. (2003). The detection of contingency and animacy from simple animations in the human brain. *Cerebral Cortex*, *13*(8), 837–844.

Braff, D. L., Silverton, L., Saccuzzo, D. P., & Janowsky, D. S. (1981). Impaired speed of visual information processing in marijuana intoxication. *American Journal of Psychiatry*, *138*(5), 613–617.

Brandt, M. E., & Boucher, J. D. (1985). Judgment of emotions from antecedent situations in three cultures. In I. Lagunes & Y. Poortinga (Eds.), *From a different perspective: Studies of behavior across cultures* (pp. 348–363). Lisse, the Netherlands: Swets & Zeitlinger.

Brekke, J. S., & Barrio, C. (1997). Cross-ethnic symptom differences in schizophrenia: The influence of culture and minority status. *Schizophrenia Bulletin*, *23*(2), 305–316.

Brekke, J. S., Nakagami, E., Kee, K. S., & Green, M. F. (2005). Cross-ethnic differences in perception of emotion in schizophrenia. *Schizophrenia Research, 77*(2–3), 289–298.

Brüne, M. (2012). Does the oxytocin receptor polymorphism (Rs2254298) confer "vulnerability" for psychopathology or "differential susceptibility"? Insights from evolution. *BMC Medicine, 10*, 38.

Brüne, M., Ozgurdal, S., Ansorge, N., Von Reventlow, H. G., Peters, S., Nicolas, V., et al. (2011). An fMRI study of "theory of mind" in at-risk states of psychosis: Comparison with manifest schizophrenia and healthy controls. *Neuroimage, 55*(1), 329–337.

Burch, J. W. (1995). Typicality range deficit in schizophrenics' recognition of emotion in faces. *Journal of Clinical Psychology, 51*(2), 140–152.

Callaghan, T. C., Moll, H., Rakoczy, H., Warneken, F., Liskowski, U., Behne, T., et al. (2011). Early social cognition in three cultural contexts. *Monographs of the Society for Research in Child Development, 76*(2), Vii–125.

Castelli, F., Happé, F. G., Frith, U., & Frith, C. D. (2000). Movement and mind: A functional imaging study of perception and interpretation of complex intentional movement patterns. *Neuroimage, 12*(3), 314–325.

Cheon, B. K., Im, D. M., Harada, T., Kim, J. S., Mathur, V. A., Scimeca, J. M., et al. (2011). Cultural influences on neural basis of intergroup empathy. *Neuroimage, 57*(2), 642–650.

Chiao, J. Y., Harada, T., Komeda, H., Li, Z., Mano, Y., Saito, D., et al. (2009). Neural basis of individualistic and collectivistic views of self. *Human Brain Mapping, 30*(9), 2813–2820.

Chiao, J. Y., Harada, T., Komeda, H., Li, Z., Mano, Y., Saito, D., et al. (2010). Dynamic cultural influences on neural representations of the self. *Journal of Cognitive Neurosciences, 22*(1), 1–11.

Comparelli, A., Corigliano, V., De Carolis, A., Mancinelli, I., Trovini, G., Ottavi, G., et al. (2013). Emotion recognition impairment is present early and is stable throughout the course of schizophrenia. *Schizophrenia Research, 143*(1), 65–69.

Curtis, G. J., & Locke, V. (2005). The effect of anxiety on impression formation: Affect-congruent or stereotypic biases? *British Journal of Social Psychology/The British Psychological Society, 44*(Pt), 1, 65–83.

De Dreu, C. K., Greer, L. L., Van Kleef, G. A., Shalvi, S., & Handgraaf, M. J. (2011). Oxytocin promotes human ethnocentrism. *Proceedings of the National Academy of Sciences of the United States of America, 108*(4), 1262–1266.

De Lange, F. P., Spronk, M., Willems, R. M., Toni, I., & Bekkering, H. (2008). Complementary systems for understanding action intentions. *Current Biology, 18*(6), 454–457.

Domschke, K., Dannlowski, U., Hohoff, C., Ohrmann, P., Bauer, J., Kugel, H., et al. (2010). Neuropeptide Y (NPY) gene: Impact on emotional processing and treatment response in anxious depression. *European Neuropsychopharmacology, 20*(5), 301–309.

Duffy, S., Toriyama, R., Itakura, S., & Kitayama, S. (2009). Development of cultural strategies of attention in North American and Japanese children. *Journal of Experimental Child Psychology, 102*(3), 351–359.

Ekman, P., & Friesen, W. V. (1971). Constants across cultures in the face and emotion. *Journal of Personality and Social Psychology, 17*(2), 124–129.

Ekman, P., & Friesen, W. V. (1976). *Pictures of facial affect*. Palo Alto, CA: Consulting Psychologists.

Ekman, P., Friesen, W. V., & Ellsworth, P. (1972). *Emotion in the human face: Guidelines for research and an interaction of findings*. New York: Pergamon Press.

Elfenbein, H. A., & Ambady, N. (2003). When familiarity breeds accuracy: Cultural exposure and facial emotion recognition. *Journal of Personality and Social Psychology, 85*(2), 276–290.

Fabrega, H., Jr. (1989). The self and schizophrenia: A cultural perspective. *Schizophrenia Bulletin*, *15*(2), 277–290.

Fazio, R. H., Jackson, J. R., Dunton, B. C., & Williams, C. J. (1995). Variability in automatic activation as an unobtrusive measure of racial attitudes: A bona fide pipeline? *Journal of Personality and Social Psychology*, *69*(6), 1013–1027.

Fujimori, H. (1981). Special features or peculiarities of schizophrenic psychosis topics in Japan with changing times – a transcultural comparative study (author's translation). *Fortschritte der Neurologie-Psychiatrie*, *49*(8), 313–330.

Fujimori, H., Pei, Z. Z., Kizaki, Y., & Zheng-Ji, C. (1987). Delusions and society in Japan and China from a transcultural-psychiatric viewpoint. *Fortschritte der Neurologie-Psychiatrie*, *55*(11), 323–334.

Furukawa, F., & Bourgeois, M. (1984). Delusions of possession by the fox in Japan (or Kitsune-Tsuki delusion). *Annales Medico-Psychologiques*, *142*(5), 677–687.

Galinsky, A. D., Ku, G., & Wang, C. S. (2005). Perspective-taking and self–other overlap: Fostering social bonds and facilitating social coordination. *Group Processes & Intergroup Relations*, *8*(2), 109–124.

Gecici, O., Kuloglu, M., Guler, O., Ozbulut, O., Kurt, E., Onen, S., et al. (2010). Phenomenology of delusions and hallucinations in patients with schizophrenia. *Bulletin of Clinical Psychopharmacology*, *20*, 204–212.

Habel, U., Gur, R. C., Mandal, M. K., Salloum, J. B., Gur, R. E., & Schneider, F. (2000). Emotional processing in schizophrenia across cultures: Standardized measures of discrimination and experience. *Schizophrenia Research*, *42*(1), 57–66.

Han, S. (2013). Cross-cultural variation in social cognition in the social brain. In D. L. Roberts & D. L. Penn (Eds.), *Social cognition in schizophrenia: From evidence to treatment* (pp. 69–92). New York: Oxford University Press.

Harada, T., Li, Z., & Chiao, J. Y. (2010). Differential dorsal and ventral medial prefrontal representations of the implicit self modulated by individualism and collectivism: An fMRI Study. *Social Neuroscience*, *5*(3), 1–15.

Harvey, P. D., Helldin, L., Bowie, C. R., Heaton, R. K., Olsson, A. K., Hjarthag, F., et al. (2009). Performance-based measurement of functional disability in schizophrenia: A cross-national study in the United States and Sweden. *American Journal of Psychiatry*, *166*(7), 821–827.

Hendry, J. (1986). *Becoming Japanese: The World of the Pre-School Child*. Manchester, UK: Manchester University Press.

Hugenberg, K. (2005). Social categorization and the perception of facial affect: Target race moderates the response latency advantage for happy faces. *Emotion (Washington, D.C.)*, *5*(3), 267–276.

Hugenberg, K., & Bodenhausen, G. V. (2003). Facing prejudice: Implicit prejudice and the perception of facial threat. *Psychological Science*, *14*(6), 640–643.

Ketteler, D., Theodoridou, A., Ketteler, S., & Jager, M. (2012). High order linguistic features such as ambiguity processing as relevant diagnostic markers for schizophrenia. *Schizophrenia Research and Treatment*, *2012*, ID825050.

Kim, K., Hwu, H., Zhang, L. D., Lu, M. K., Park, K. K., Hwang, T. J., et al. (2001). Schizophrenic delusions in Seoul, Shanghai and Taipei: A transcultural study. *Journal of Korean Medical Science*, *16*(1), 88–94.

Kim, K. I., Li, D., Jiang, Z., Cui, X., Lin, L., Kang, J. J., et al. (1993). Schizophrenic delusions among Koreans, Korean-Chinese and Chinese: A transcultural study. *International Journal of Social Psychiatry*, *39*(3), 190–199.

Kimura, B., Saka, K., Yamamura, O., Asami, T., & Yoshikawa, Y. (1968). Zum Familienverneinungssyndrom. *Psychiatria et Neurologia Japonica*, *70*, 1085–1109.

Kitayama, S., Duffy, S., Kawamura, T., & Larsen, J. T. (2003). Perceiving an object and its context in different cultures: A cultural look at new look. *Psychological Science*, *14*(3), 201–206.

Kobayashi, F. C., Glover, G. H., & Temple, E. (2006). Cultural and linguistic influence on neural bases of "theory of mind": An fMRI study with Japanese Bilinguals. *Brain and Language*, *98*(2), 210–220.

Koelkebeck, K., Hirao, K., Kawada, R., Miyata, J., Saze, T., Ubukata, S., et al. (2011). Transcultural differences in brain activation patterns during theory of mind (TOM) task performance in Japanese and Caucasian participants. *Social Neuroscience*, *6*(5–6), 615–626.

Koelkebeck, K., Pedersen, A., Suslow, T., Kueppers, K. A., Arolt, V., & Ohrmann, P. (2010). Theory of mind in first-episode schizophrenia patients: Correlations with cognition and personality traits. *Schizophrenia Research*, *119*(1–3), 115–123.

Koschack, J., Hoschel, K., & Irle, E. (2003). Differential impairments of facial affect priming in subjects with acute or partially remitted major depressive episodes. *Journal of Nervous and Mental Disease*, *191*(3), 175–181.

Kret, M. E., & De Gelder, B. (2010). Social context influences recognition of bodily expressions. *Experimental Brain Research*, *203*(1), 169–180.

Kret, M. E., & De Gelder, B. (2012). Islamic headdress influences how emotion is recognized from the eyes. *Frontiers in Psychology*, *3*, 110.

Lee, K., Olson, D. R., & Torrance, N. (1999). Chinese children's understanding of false beliefs: The role of language. *Journal of Child Language*, *26*(1), 1–21.

Lee, S. J., Lee, H. K., Kweon, Y. S., Lee, C. T., & Lee, K. U. (2010). Deficits in facial emotion recognition in schizophrenia: A replication study with Korean subjects. *Psychiatry Investigation*, *7*(4), 291–297.

Lewis, S. F., & Garver, D. L. (1995). Treatment and diagnostic subtype in facial affect recognition in schizophrenia. *Journal of Psychiatric Research*, *29*(1), 5–11.

Li, H., & Rao, N. (2000). Parental influences on Chinese literacy development: A comparison of preschoolers in Beijing, Hong Kong and Singapore. *International Journal of Behavioral Development*, *24*, 82–90.

Liu, D., Wellman, H. M., Tardif, T., & Sabbagh, M. A. (2008). Theory of mind development in Chinese children: A meta-analysis of false-belief understanding across cultures and languages. *Developmental Psychology*, *44*(2), 523–531.

Markham, R., & Wang, L. (1996). Recognition of emotion by Chinese and Australian children. *Journal of Cross-Cultural Psychology*, *27*(5), 616–643.

Matsuda, T., & Nisbett, R. E. (2001). Attending holistically versus analytically: Comparing the context sensitivity of Japanese and Americans. *Journal of Personality and Social Psychology*, *81*(5), 922–934.

Matsumoto, D. (1992). American-Japanese cultural differences in the recognition of universal facial expressions. *Journal of Cross Cultural Psychology*, *23*, 72–84.

Matsumoto, D., & Ekman, P. (1989). American–Japanese cultural differences in intensity ratings of facial expressions of emotion. *Motivation and Emotion*, *13*(2), 143–157.

Matsumoto, D., Leroux, J., Wilson-Cohn, C., Raroque, J., Kooken, K., Ekman, P., et al. (2000). A new test to measure emotion recognition ability: Matsumoto and Ekman's Japanese and Caucasian Brief Affect Recognition Test (JACBART). *Journal of Nonverbal Behavior*, *24*(3), 179–209.

Mehta, U. M., Thirthalli, J., Gangadhar, B. N., & Keshavan, M. S. (2011). Need for culture specific tools to assess social cognition in schizophrenia. *Schizophrenia Research*, *133*(1–3), 255–256.

Meissner, C. A., & Brigham, J. C. (2001). Thirty years of investigating the own-race bias in memory for faces: A meta-analytic review. *Psychology, Public Policy, and Law*, *7*(1), 3–35.

Minoshita, S., Morita, N., Yamashita, T., Yoshikawa, M., Kikuchi, T., & Satoh, S. (2005). Recognition of affect in facial expression using the Noh Mask Test: Comparison of individuals with schizophrenia and normal controls. *Psychiatry and Clinical Neurosciences, 59*(1), 4–10.

Minoshita, S., Satoh, S., Morita, N., Tagawa, A., & Kikuchi, T. (1997). Assessing recognition of affects in facial expression through the use of nohmen. *Japanese Journal of Ergonomics, 33,* 79–86.

Minoshita, S., Satoh, S., Morita, N., Tagawa, A., & Kikuchi, T. (1999). The Noh Mask Test for analysis of recognition of facial expression. *Psychiatry and Clinical Neurosciences, 53*(1), 83–89.

Minsky, S., Vega, W., Miskimen, T., Gara, M., & Escobar, J. (2003). Diagnostic patterns in Latino, African American, and European American psychiatric patients. *Archives of General Psychiatry, 60*(6), 637–644.

Moriguchi, Y., Ohnishi, T., Kawachi, T., Mori, T., Hirakata, M., Yamada, M., et al. (2005). Specific brain activation in Japanese and Caucasian people to fearful faces. *Neuroreport, 16*(2), 133–136.

Murphy, H. B., Wittkower, E. D., Fried, J., & Ellenberger, H. (1963). A cross-cultural survey of schizophrenic symptomatology. *International Journal of Social Psychiatry, 9,* 237–249.

Naito, M., & Koyama, K. (2006). The development of false-belief understanding in Japanese children: Delay and difference? *International Journal of Behavioral Development, 30*(4), 290–304.

Ndetei, D. M., & Vadher, A. (1984). A comparative cross-cultural study of the frequencies of hallucination in schizophrenia. *Acta Psychiatrica Scandinavica, 70*(6), 545–549.

Omata, W. (1985). [Schizoaffective psychoses in Germany and Japan – a transcultural psychiatric study]. *Fortschritte der Neurologie-Psychiatrie, 53*(5), 168–176.

Pearlson, G. D. (2000). Neurobiology of schizophrenia. *Annals of Neurology, 48*(4), 556–566.

Pedersen, A., Koelkebeck, K., Brandt, M., Wee, M., Kueppers, K. A., Kugel, H., et al. (2012). Theory of mind in patients with schizophrenia: Is mentalizing delayed? *Schizophrenia Research, 137*(1–3), 224–229.

Pfeiffer, M., & Schoene, W. (1980). *Psychopathologie im Kulturvergleich.* Stuttgart, Germany: F. Enke Verlag.

Pfeiffer, W. M. (1967). *Psychiatrische Besonderheiten in Indonesien. Beiträge zur vergleichenden Psychiatrie (Bibliotheca Psychiatrica et Neurologica 132 Ed.).* Switzerland: Karger-Verlag, Basel.

Phillips, M. L., Drevets, W. C., Rauch, S. L., & Lane, R. (2003). Neurobiology of emotion perception. II: Implications for major psychiatric disorders. *Biological Psychiatry, 54*(5), 515–528.

Pinkham, A. E., Sasson, N. J., Calkins, M. E., Richard, J., Hughett, P., Gur, R. E., et al. (2008). The other-race effect in face processing among African American and Caucasian individuals with schizophrenia. *American Journal of Psychiatry, 165*(5), 639–645.

Russell, J. A. (1991). Culture and the categorization of emotions. *Psychological Bulletin, 110*(3), 426–450.

Sass, L. A. (1997). The consciousness machine: Self and subjectivity and schizophrenia and modern culture. In U. Neisser & D. A. Jopling (Eds.), *The conceptual self in context: Culture, experience, self-understanding* (pp. 203–230). Cambridge, UK: Cambridge University Press.

Shweder, R. A., Goodnow, J., Hatano, G., Levine, R. A., Markus, H., & Miller, P. (1998). The cultural psychology of development: One mind, many mentalities. In W. Damon & R. M. Lerner (Eds.), *Handbook of child psychology: Theoretical models of human development* (pp. 865–937) (5th Ed.). New York: John Wiley & Sons.

Siegert, R. J. (2001). Culture, cognition, and schizophrenia. In J. S. Schumaker & T. Ward (Eds.), *Cultural cognition and psychopathology* (pp. 171–189). Westport, CT: Praeger.

Singh, S. P., Harley, K., & Suhail, K. (2013). Cultural specificity of emotional overinvolvement: A systematic review. *Schizophrenia Bulletin*, *39*(2), 449–463.

Stompe, T., Friedman, A., Ortwein, G., Strobl, R., Chaudhry, H. R., Najam, N., et al. (1999). Comparison of delusions among schizophrenics in Austria and in Pakistan. *Psychopathology*, *32*(5), 225–234.

Stompe, T., Ortwein-Swoboda, G., Ritter, K., & Schanda, H. (2003). Old wine in new bottles? Stability and plasticity of the contents of schizophrenic delusions. *Psychopathology*, *36*(1), 6–12.

Suhail, K., & Cochrane, R. (2002). Effect of culture and environment on the phenomenology of delusions and hallucinations. *International Journal of Social Psychiatry*, *48*(2), 126–138.

Sui, J., Liu, C. H., Wang, L., & Han, S. (2009). Attentional orientation induced by temporarily established self-referential cues. *Quarterly Journal of Experimental Psychology*, *62*(5), 844–849.

Suslow, T., Roestel, C., Ohrmann, P., & Arolt, V. (2003). Detection of facial expressions of emotions in schizophrenia. *Schizophrenia Research*, *64*(2–3), 137–145.

Tateno, M., Park, T. W., Kato, T. A., Umene-Nakano, W., & Saito, T. (2012). Hikikomori as a possible clinical term in psychiatry: A questionnaire survey. *BMC Psychiatry*, *12*, 169–244.

Tateyama, M. (1989). Delusion of world destruction (Wetzel). Comparative study between Japan and West Germany. *Psychopathology*, *22*(6), 289–294.

Tateyama, M., Asai, M., Hashimoto, M., Bartels, M., & Kasper, S. (1998). Transcultural study of schizophrenic delusions. Tokyo versus Vienna and Tübingen (Germany). *Psychopathology*, *31*(2), 59–68.

Tateyama, M., Asai, M., Kamisada, M., Hashimoto, M., Bartels, M., & Heimann, H. (1993). Comparison of schizophrenic delusions between Japan and Germany. *Psychopathology*, *26*(3–4), 151–158.

Taylor, G. J., Ryan, D., & Bagby, R. M. (1985). Toward the development of a new self-report alexithymia scale. *Psychotherapy and Psychosomatics*, *44*(4), 191–199.

Triandis, H. C. (2001). Individualism-collectivism and personality. *Journal of Personality*, *69*(6), 907–924.

Veling, W., Hoek, H. W., Selten, J. P., & Susser, E. (2011). Age at migration and future risk of psychotic disorders among immigrants in the Netherlands: A 7-year incidence study. *American Journal of Psychiatry*, *168*(12), 1278–1285.

Völlm, B. A., Taylor, A. N., Richardson, P., Corcoran, R., Stirling, J., Mckie, S., et al. (2006). Neuronal correlates of theory of mind and empathy: A functional magnetic resonance imaging study in a nonverbal task. *Neuroimage*, *29*(1), 90–98.

Walker, E., Mcguire, M., & Bettes, B. (1984). Recognition and identification of facial stimuli by schizophrenics and patients with affective disorders. *British Journal of Clinical Psychology/ The British Psychological Society*, *23*(Pt), *1*, 37–44.

Wang, J. H., Morales, O., & Hsu, L. K. (1998). Auditory hallucinations in bilingual immigrants. *Journal of Nervous and Mental Disease*, *186*(8), 501–503.

Wellman, H. M., Cross, D., & Watson, J. (2001). Meta-analysis of theory-of-mind development: The truth about false belief. *Child Development*, *72*(3), 655–684.

Wellman, H. M., Fang, F., Liu, D., Zhu, L., & Liu, G. (2006). Scaling of theory-of-mind understandings in Chinese children. *Psychological Science*, *17*(12), 1075–1081.

Weniger, G., Lange, C., Ruther, E., & Irle, E. (2004). Differential impairments of facial affect recognition in schizophrenia subtypes and major depression. *Psychiatry Research*, *128*(2), 135–146.

Zhu, X., Wang, X., Xiao, J., Liao, J., Zhong, M., Wang, W., & Yao, S. (2012). Evidence of a dissociation pattern in resting-state default mode network connectivity in first-episode, treatment-naive major depression patients. *Biological Psychiatry*, *71*(7), 611–617.

Chapter 3

Social Cognition During the Early Phase of Schizophrenia

Amanda McCleery,[1] **William P. Horan**[1,2] **and Michael F. Green**[1,2]
[1]David Geffen School of Medicine at UCLA, Los Angeles, CA, USA, [2]VISN 22 Mental Illness Research Education and Clinical Center, Los Angeles, CA, USA

Chapter Outline

Social Cognition and Metacognition in Schizophrenia.
DOI: http://dx.doi.org/10.1016/B978-0-12-405172-0.00003-X
© 2014 Elsevier Inc. All rights reserved.

INTRODUCTION

Social cognition, the mental operations that underlie social interactions (Green *et al.*, 2008), is an area of research that has undergone tremendous growth since the 2000s and is now a mainstay of the schizophrenia literature (Green and Leitman, 2008). A rapid accumulation of evidence indicates that chronically ill individuals with schizophrenia exhibit marked deficits in social cognition across a range of domains (Salva *et al.*, 2013). In addition, social cognition impairments appear to make a unique contribution to functioning in people with chronic schizophrenia (e.g., Fett *et al.* 2011; Green *et al.*, 2012b).

Given the robust deficits observed in chronic schizophrenia samples, researchers have begun to investigate the scope and magnitude of social cognitive impairment early in the illness (i.e., among recent-onset or first-episode schizophrenia samples) and, to a lesser degree, among populations deemed vulnerable for schizophrenia, such as clinical high-risk (i.e., putatively prodromal) samples and unaffected relatives of schizophrenia probands. Research during the early phase has the advantage of minimizing confounds associated with chronicity (e.g., exposure to antipsychotic medication, environmental deprivation, acquired patterns of adaptation to a chronic mental illness) and can provide insights into factors associated with vulnerability to developing this disorder and its associated functional disability. The purpose of this chapter is to summarize the literature surrounding social cognition in the early phase of schizophrenia.

Research on social cognition in chronically ill people with schizophrenia has focused on four main domains: (1) emotion processing, (2) theory of mind (ToM), (3) social perception, and (4) attributional style (Pinkham *et al.*, in press). The current review is organized in terms of these same four domains since they also cover the main areas of social cognition that have been considered in the early phase of schizophrenia. For each domain, we briefly describe the construct and common assessment methods and review relevant research comparing recent-onset patients, clinical high-risk samples, and unaffected relatives to matched healthy control subjects. We then summarize studies that address the issue of the progression of social cognitive impairments across the early to the chronic phases of schizophrenia. We conclude with a summary of the current status of research in the early phase of schizophrenia, discuss limitations and implications of existing studies, and identify important areas for further research.

DOMAINS OF SOCIAL COGNITION IN EARLY-PHASE SCHIZOPHRENIA

Emotion Processing

Emotion processing refers to emotion perception and utilization of emotion information. An influential model of emotion perception proposed by Salovey and Sluyter (1997) consists of four components: (1) identifying emotions (e.g., via facial affect or vocal prosody), (2) facilitating emotions (i.e., understanding how certain emotions can assist performance on different tasks), (3) understanding emotions (i.e., understanding emotional blends and transitions), and (4) managing emotions (i.e., regulation of emotional states of self and others). These four domains are assessed in the Mayer-Salovey-Caruso Emotional Intelligence Test (MSCEIT; Mayer *et al.*, 2001). Other emotional processing tasks commonly used in the recent-onset schizophrenia literature include emotion identification or discrimination paradigms using standardized photographs of faces (e.g., Ekman stimuli; Ekman and Friesen, 1976) or vocal recordings.

Recent-Onset Schizophrenia

Over 10 studies have examined emotion processing in recent-onset samples. The operational definition of recent-onset varies across research groups, but it is typically based on one of the following: (1) a recent initial contact with psychiatric services for treatment of psychosis, (2) recent initiation of antipsychotic medications for treatment of psychosis that falls within a specified time range (e.g., within the past 3 months), or (3) recent emergence and duration of psychosis that falls within a specified time range (e.g., onset of psychosis within the past 24 months; Breitborde *et al.*, 2009). Breitborde and colleagues (2009) note that although duration of psychosis is the most direct way to assess onset of illness, it is the least frequently used of the three approaches.

The vast majority of studies in emotion processing have focused on emotion identification. Nearly all of the studies found that recent-onset patients exhibited significant impairment on tasks of facial and vocal emotion identification compared with healthy controls (Addington *et al.*, 2006a; Amminger *et al.*, 2012a; Amminger *et al.*, 2012b; Comparelli *et al.*, 2011; Comparelli *et al.*, 2013; Edwards *et al.*, 2001; Kucharska-Pietrura et al., 2005; Pinkham *et al.*, 2007; Thompson *et al.*, 2012). Comparelli and colleagues (2013) report large effect sizes for facial affect identification ($d = -1.27$) and recognition ($d = -1.26$). Similarly, Thompson *et al.* (2012) reported large effect size for a combined test of facial affect and vocal prosody identification ($d = 0.91$). The one study that found no significant group differences on a task of facial affect identification used an unusually small number of trials, which may have limited that task's sensitivity ($d = 0.26$; Achim *et al.*, 2012). Two studies have examined other aspects of emotion processing. Green and colleagues (2012a) found that recent-onset patients demonstrated impaired performance across the four subtests of the MSCEIT compared with matched controls, and the magnitude of the between-group difference for the MSCEIT total score was moderately large ($d = 0.76$). Similarly, Eack and colleagues (2010) reported marked impairment across all branches of the MSCEIT for a recent-onset sample compared with normative data for the measure. A few studies have examined the profile and correlates of emotion identification impairments in recent-onset patients. For example, similar to findings with chronic samples (e.g., Edwards *et al.*, 2002), recent-onset patients are sometimes found to have greater difficulty identifying negative than positive emotions (e.g., Amminger *et al.*, 2012a; Comparelli *et al.*, 2013; Edwards *et al.* 2001; Kucharska-Pietura *et al.*, 2005), though this remains an open question. Regarding relations to nonsocial neurocognitive and perceptual disturbances, the presence of statistically significant deficits in facial affect identification after controlling for general (i.e., nonemotional) face processing suggests that a specific deficit for processing emotional stimuli may be superimposed upon the broad cognitive processing deficits associated with schizophrenia (Kucharska-Pietura *et al.*, 2005).

Clinical High-Risk

Since 2007, emotion processing has been evaluated in clinical high-risk or putatively prodromal samples. The criteria used to define clinical high-risk vary across research groups, but are typically based on features such as: (1) presence of transient psychotic symptoms that resolve spontaneously (i.e., 'brief limited intermittent psychotic symptoms'), (2) subthreshold positive symptoms of psychosis present for a specified period of time and frequency (e.g., onset within the past 12 months, occurring at least once per week, 'attenuated psychotic symptoms'), or (3) genetic high-risk (e.g., presence of schizotypal personality disorder or first-degree relative of a schizophrenia proband) accompanied by recent deterioration in functioning ('genetic risk plus functional decline'; reviewed in Tandon *et al.*, 2012). It has become clear that only a portion of individuals identified by these clinical high-risk criteria go on to develop a psychotic illness. One meta-analysis indicated that transition rates to psychosis in clinical high-risk samples range from approximately 18% at 6-month follow-up to 36% at 36-month follow-up (Fusar-Poli *et al.*, 2012).

Among the eight studies that examined emotion processing in clinical high-risk, the findings are mixed. For emotion identification, two studies report no significant differences between clinical high-risk and control groups on facial emotion identification tests (Pinkham *et al.*, 2007; Thompson *et al.*, 2012). In contrast, other studies report impaired performance on tasks of facial emotion identification (Addington *et al.*, 2008; Addington *et al.*, 2012; Amminger *et al.*, 2012a; Amminger *et al.*, 2012b; Comparelli *et al.*, 2013). Amminger and colleagues reported that their sample of clinical high-risk participants and patients with schizophrenia differed from controls on facial affect (Amminger *et al.*, 2012a; Amminger *et al.*, 2012b) and vocal prosody identification tasks (Amminger *et al.*, 2012b).

A few studies have reported effect sizes to convey the magnitude of impairment in clinical high-risk. Comparelli and colleagues (2013) report moderately large effect size for facial affect identification ($d = -0.74$) and recognition ($d = -0.71$), with the effects largely attributable to difficulty with the specific emotions of sadness ($d = -1.02$) and disgust ($d = -0.67$). On the MSCEIT, one study reported clinical high-risk subjects were impaired on the MSCEIT total score ($d = 0.73$; Green *et al.*, 2012a), while another reported no significant differences from nonpsychiatric controls on the MSCEIT Managing Emotions subtest ($d = 0.29$; Thompson *et al.*, 2012). Discrepant findings across studies may be attributable, at least in part, to methodologic issues such as differing emotion processing paradigms and the inherent heterogeneity of clinical high-risk samples (i.e., the proportion of false vs. true positives for risk of future psychosis in any given sample). Moreover, the mixed findings may reflect insufficient power; the two studies reviewed above with null findings employed smaller sample sizes than the studies reporting significant group differences.

Unaffected Relatives

Another vulnerable group that has been studied is unaffected relatives. Research on unaffected relatives of schizophrenia probands is informative for understanding social cognitive impairment in schizophrenia due to shared genetic risk (Gottesman and Erlenmeyer-Kimling, 2001). Unaffected relatives show subtle, though reliable, deficits in nonsocial cognition and other domains impacted by schizophrenia (e.g., neurologic and motor functions) at higher rates than the general population (Erlenmeyer-Kimling, 2000). A number of studies have also evaluated whether emotion processing is detectable in unaffected relatives. Similar to the clinical high-risk research, results of individual studies have been somewhat mixed. However, one meta-analysis of 20 studies suggests the presence of moderate impairment ($d = 0.41$) in emotion processing in relatives (Lavoie *et al.*, 2013), with larger effect sizes observed for tasks of affect identification ($d = 0.52$) than for affect discrimination ($d = 0.21$). Individual studies comparing unaffected relatives to patients with schizophrenia and controls show intermediate performance in unaffected relatives, indicative of subtle emotion processing impairment (de Achaval *et al.*, 2010; Kee *et al.*, 2004).

Theory of Mind

ToM refers to the ability to make inferences about the thoughts, beliefs, and intentions of others. Also referred to as mentalizing, mind reading, or perspective taking, interest in ToM emerged from the developmental psychology and autism literature. Examples of ToM tasks used with schizophrenia samples include making mental state attributions via decoding complex emotional states from pictures of the eye region of faces (Eyes Task, Baron-Cohen *et al.*, 2001), and mental state reasoning paradigms such as picture sequencing tasks (e.g., Brune, 2005) and brief vignettes of social interactions that require the reader to make inferences about the beliefs and intentions of story characters through devices such as deception, sarcasm, double-entendres, or hinting (e.g., Faux Pas Test, Stone *et al.*, 1998; Hinting Task, Corcoran *et al.*, 1995). These tasks may assess first-order (i.e., inferring mental state of a story character) or second-order ToM (i.e., inferring beliefs one story character holds about the beliefs of another story character).

Recent-Onset Schizophrenia

One meta-analysis of eight studies demonstrated significant differences between recent-onset patients and nonpsychiatric controls on ToM tasks with a large effect size ($d = 1.00$; Bora and Pantelis, 2013). Impairment was observed across visual and verbal ToM tasks, although there is mixed evidence for sparing of first-order ToM in recent-onset patients (e.g., Achim *et al.*, 2012; Inoue *et al.*, 2006; Kettle *et al.*, 2008). To date, no clear pattern clinical correlates of ToM impairment has emerged; Koekelbeck and colleagues (2010) reported a significant association between positive symptoms and performance on a ToM task; however, Inoue *et al.* (2006) and Couture *et al.* (2008) reported no associations between symptoms and ToM.

Clinical High-Risk

Most studies of clinical high-risk samples report impaired performance on ToM tasks compared with nonpsychiatric controls (Chung *et al.*, 2008; Green *et al.*, 2012a; Kim *et al.*, 2011; Thompson *et al.*, 2012). One meta-analysis of seven studies reported that this impairment reflected a moderate effect size ($d = 0.45$; Bora and Pantelis, 2013). Similar to studies with patients with recent-onset schizophrenia, first-order ToM often appears to be spared in high-risk samples (Chung *et al.*, 2008; Couture *et al.*, 2008).

Unaffected Relatives

Studies of unaffected relatives also indicate reduced performance on ToM tasks. Two meta-analyses (evaluating 10 and 11 studies, respectively) report a moderate effect size for ToM impairment in unaffected relatives ($d = 0.37$, Bora and Pantelis, 2013; $d = 0.48$, Lavoie *et al.*, 2013), with larger effect sizes observed for tasks of mental state reasoning (e.g., Hinting Task) than for mental state decoding (e.g., Eyes Task). Similar to findings for emotion processing, when unaffected relatives have been directly compared with patients with schizophrenia in the same study, relatives tend to show attenuated impairment compared with the patients (Irani *et al.*, 2006; Janssen *et al.*, 2003).

Social Perception

Social perception refers to identifying and utilizing social cues to make judgments about social roles, rules, relationships, context, or the characteristics (e.g., trustworthiness) of others. This domain also includes social knowledge, which refers to one's knowledge of social roles, norms, and schemas surrounding social situations and interactions. Tests of social perception include videotaped scenes that require the viewer to make inferences and judgments about ambiguous social situations based on limited verbal and nonverbal social cues (e.g., Profile of Nonverbal Sensitivity (PONS); Rosenthal *et al.*, 1979; Social Cue Recognition Test (SCRT); Corrigan, 1997). The Relationships across

Domains task (RAD; Sergi *et al.*, 2009) requires participants to make inferences about the nature of relationships between people based on short written vignettes.

Recent-Onset Schizophrenia

Five studies of social perception have been conducted in recent-onset schizophrenia. Based on the available data, recent-onset patients exhibit impaired performance on social perception tasks compared with non-psychiatric controls (Addington *et al.*, 2006b; Bertrand *et al.*, 2007; Bertrand *et al.*, 2008; Green *et al.*, 2012a), with Green and colleagues (2012a) reporting a large effect size on the RAD ($d = 1.02$). Research surrounding social knowledge is also sparse, and few formal measures of the construct exist (Achim *et al.*, 2012). Using a social knowledge task that asked participants to predict how 'people in general' would feel about various hypothetical situations, Achim and colleagues (2012) found no significant differences between recent-onset patients and controls. In contrast, using the Situational Features Recognition Task (SFRT; Corrigan *et al.*, 1996a; Corrigan *et al.*, 1996b), Addington and colleagues (2006b) reported significant differences between recent-onset patients and controls.

Clinical High-Risk

To our knowledge, only two studies have examined social perception in clinical high-risk samples and both reported impairments. In one study, the clinical high-risk group performed significantly worse than a matched nonpsychiatric comparison sample on the RAD with a moderate effect size ($d = 0.47$; Green *et al.*, 2012a). On a social judgment task, Couture and colleagues (2008) reported that a clinical high-risk group rated untrustworthy faces more positively (i.e., abnormally) than the control group.

Unaffected Relatives

Two studies of social perception have been carried out with unaffected relatives and these were reviewed in a meta-analysis (Lavoie *et al.*, 2013). One sudy required participants to make judgments about the trustworthiness of faces (Baas *et al.*, 2008), while the other used the PONS (Toomey *et al.*, 1999). These studies suggest presence of moderate social perception impairment in unaffected relatives ($d = 0.42$, Lavoie *et al.*, 2013).

Attributional Style

Attributional style refers to the causal explanations one makes for outcomes of life events. Attributions are classified as internal (i.e., due to oneself) or external (i.e., not due to oneself). External attributions are further classified as either personal (i.e., due to a specific person) or situational (i.e., due to chance or situational factors). In the schizophrenia literature, research has focused on associations between attributional style and symptoms. Specifically, there is evidence that individuals prone to persecutory delusions tend to show a 'personalizing bias' (i.e., a tendency to attribute negative outcomes to others rather than situational factors) (Bentall *et al.*, 2001; Garety and Freeman, 1999). Attributional style is assessed via questionnaires that ask subjects to make causal attributions about hypothetical events (e.g., Internal, Personal, and Situational Attributions Questionnaire (IPSAQ), Kinderman and Bentall, 1997; Ambiguous Intentions Hostility Questionnaire (AIHQ), Combs *et al.*, 2007), or attributions derived from natural speech (e.g., Leeds Attributional Coding System (LACS), Munton *et al.*, 1999).

Recent-Onset Schizophrenia

Only two studies have examined attributional bias in recent-onset patients. Fornells-Ambrojo and Garety (2009) found that a recent-onset sample with 'poor me' paranoid ideation (i.e., views oneself as an innocent victim of persecution) showed preference for personal-external attributions for negative events, and showed an 'other person bias' (i.e., preference for blaming others for negative events rather than oneself) that was, not surprisingly, associated with higher levels of anger. On the AIHQ, recent-onset patients were more likely to attribute hostile intentions to others in ambiguous situations (i.e., 'hostility bias') than controls, and hostility bias was associated with ratings of suspiciousness (An *et al.*, 2010).

Clinical High-Risk

The four studies that have examined attributional style in clinical high-risk samples have been evenly mixed. Two studies found that high-risk subjects exhibited greater 'externalizing bias' (blame others rather than circumstances; An *et al.*, 2010) or externalized locus of control (Thompson *et al.*, 2013) than healthy subjects, and higher levels of these biases were associated with elevated suspiciousness. In contrast, two studies using the IPSAQ found no significant group differences (DeVylder *et al.*, 2013; Janssen *et al.*, 2006).

Unaffected Relatives

Only one study of attributional style in unaffected relatives was identified. Janssen *et al.* (2006) found no evidence for an externalizing bias on the IPSAQ among unaffected relatives.

Summary of Social Cognition in the Early Phase of Schizophrenia

As noted above, the most extensively studied areas of social cognition in the early phase of schizophrenia are emotion processing and ToM. There is consistent evidence for impairment in these domains in recent-onset patients and unaffected relatives compared with healthy controls. Evidence for impairment is also found in clinical high-risk samples though these results are somewhat variable, possibly a reflection of methodologic issues such as insufficient power. Moreover, given that a large proportion of clinical high-risk subjects do not go on to develop schizophrenia, inconsistent findings may be partly attributable to the presence of false-positive cases, that is, individuals who are erroneously identified as being at-risk for schizophrenia and thus may not exhibit social cognitive impairment. Although social perception is less extensively studied, results consistently demonstrate impairment across recent-onset, clinical high-risk, and unaffected relatives. Notably, impairments in these three social cognitive domains have shown good 12-month longitudinal stability in recent-onset patients (Addington *et al.*, 2006a; Addington *et al.*, 2006b; Horan *et al.*, 2012).

Attributional bias is the least studied domain. The available data suggest recent-onset patients exhibit attributional biases similar to those observed in chronic patients. However, the findings for clinical high-risk subjects are inconsistent, and the results of one study did not support the presence of an externalizing bias in unaffected relatives. Thus, with the exception of attributional bias, abnormality across multiple social cognitive domains appears to be present during the early course of schizophrenia and even to predate onset.

PROGRESSION OF SOCIAL COGNITIVE IMPAIRMENT

Another key question about the nature of social cognitive impairment in schizophrenia concerns its course across phases of illness – that is, whether these impairments improve, remain stable, or progressively deteriorate. This question would ideally be addressed in longitudinal studies that track social cognition from at-risk through recent-onset and chronic phases of illness. This type of research is very difficult to implement and no studies have directly examined the progression of social cognitive impairment across all phases of illness. However, other sources of information do bear upon this question, albeit indirectly, such as cross-sectional studies that compare the magnitude of deficits between groups of participants in different illness phases. For each of the four main social cognitive domains, we summarize available data for two types of comparisons between groups in different phases of illness: recent-onset compared with chronically ill patients with schizophrenia, and clinical high-risk compared with recent-onset or chronically ill patients with schizophrenia.

Emotion Processing

Recent-Onset versus Chronic Schizophrenia

One meta-analysis reports large effect size for impairment in emotion processing ($g = 0.88$) and emotion perception ($g = 0.89$) in chronic schizophrenia

(Salva *et al.*, 2013). Several cross-sectional studies have directly compared recent-onset and chronic schizophrenia samples to each other on tests of emotion identification. Fewer studies have compared separate matched control groups for each clinical sample (i.e., rather than a single control sample), a methodologic strategy that allows for stronger inference as it takes age differences into account and guards against spurious findings from cohort effects. Five of the six studies reported comparable performance levels across these phases of illness (Addington *et al.*, 2006a; Addington *et al.*, 2008; Comparelli *et al.*, 2011; Comparelli *et al.*, 2013; Pinkham *et al.*, 2007, but see Kucharska-Pietura *et al.*, 2005). On the MSCEIT, recent-onset patients showed a similar pattern and magnitude of impairment across subscales compared with a chronically ill sample recruited through the same research site (recent-onset $d = 0.76$, chronic $d = 0.72$; Green *et al.*, 2012a). Thus, the bulk of the evidence suggests the magnitude of emotion processing impairment is comparable across first-episode and chronic patients.

Clinical High-Risk versus Schizophrenia

When clinical high-risk samples are directly compared with patients with schizophrenia, the results have been somewhat mixed. For emotion perception, three studies reported no significant differences between clinical high-risk and patient groups compared with healthy controls, though the mean scores (and corresponding effect sizes) for the high-risk group tended to fall below those of patients (Addington *et al.*, 2008; Amminger *et al.*, 2012b; Comparelli *et al.*, 2013). Consistent with this pattern, Thompson *et al.* (2012) reported their clinical high-risk sample showed intermediate performance between healthy controls and recent-onset patients on tasks of facial affect and vocal prosody identification (clinical high-risk $d = 0.48$, recent-onset $d = 0.91$). However, Pinkham *et al.* (2007) found that clinical high-risk subjects did not differ from controls on tests of facial affect discrimination and identification, whereas their patient groups did.

On the MSCEIT, Green *et al.* (2012a) reported no significant differences between their clinical high-risk, recent-onset schizophrenia, and chronic schizophrenia groups on MSCEIT total score; all clinical groups differed significantly from their respective matched healthy control samples (clinical high-risk $d = 0.73$, recent-onset $d = 0.76$, chronic $d = 0.72$). In contrast, Thompson *et al.* (2012) reported their clinical high-risk sample was intermediate between recent-onset patients and healthy controls on the Managing Emotions subtest of the MSCEIT (i.e., the clinical high-risk group did not differ significantly from controls or patients; $d = 0.29$). Overall, these results suggest that when emotion processing impairments are found in clinical high-risk samples, they tend to be somewhat smaller than those seen in patients with schizophrenia.

Theory of Mind

Recent-Onset versus Chronic Schizophrenia

One meta-analysis of 36 ToM studies demonstrated large effect size ($d = 1.10$) for chronic patients with schizophrenia (Bora et al., 2009). Likewise, the meta-analysis of eight studies of ToM in recent-onset patients reports large effect size ($d = 1.00$), suggesting a similar magnitude of ToM impairment in chronic and recent-onset schizophrenia (Bora and Pantelis, 2013). Consistent with these meta-analytic findings, one study that directly compared recent-onset and chronic patients found comparable ToM deficits across these phases of illness (Green et al., 2012a).

Clinical High-Risk versus Schizophrenia

A meta-analysis of seven clinical high-risk studies demonstrated a moderate effect size ($d = 0.45$), suggesting that ToM impairment is attenuated in prodromal subjects (Bora and Pantelis, 2013). When clinical high-risk and recent-onset groups have been directly compared in the same study, the results have been mixed. One study reported no ToM impairment in the clinical high-risk group (Couture et al., 2008), another reported attenuated impairment in the clinical high-risk group (clinical high-risk $d = 0.64$, recent-onset $d = 0.93$; Thompson et al., 2012), and a third reported similar levels of impairment in the clinical high-risk and recent-onset and chronic schizophrenia groups (clinical high-risk $d = 0.86$, recent-onset $d = 1.06$, chronic $d = 0.96$; Green et al., 2012a). Thus, there appears to be a tendency for smaller ToM impairment in clinical high-risk subjects than in patients with schizophrenia.

Social Perception

Recent-Onset versus Chronic Schizophrenia

Individuals with chronic schizophrenia exhibit marked impairment in social perception ($g = 1.04$; Salva et al., 2013). Two studies directly compared recent-onset patients with patients with chronic schizophrenia on social perception tasks, and both found no differences between these phases of illness (Addington et al., 2006b; Green et al., 2012a).

Clinical High-Risk versus Schizophrenia

Only two studies have directly compared clinical high-risk and recent-onset patients on tasks of social perception. In one study, the clinical high-risk group, while differing significantly from their respective matched non-psychiatric comparison sample, exhibited less impairment on the RAD compared with recent-onset and chronic patients (clinical high-risk $d = 0.47$, recent-onset $d = 1.02$, chronic $d = 0.76$; Green et al., 2012a). In the other study, the clinical high-risk group rated untrustworthy faces more positively (i.e., abnormally) than both a recent-onset group and healthy controls on a social judgment task (i.e., recent-onset group intermediate between controls and clinical high-risk; Couture *et al.*, 2008).

Attributional Style

Recent-Onset versus Chronic Schizophrenia

We are unaware of any studies have directly compared the attributional style of recent-onset and chronic schizophrenia samples. The available limited data reviewed above suggest that recent-onset patients exhibit similar types of attributional biases as reported in chronic samples (e.g., externalizing bias, hostility bias). However, it is unclear whether the chronic and recent-onset patient groups differ in terms of relative strength of the biases or the proportion of patients who exhibit these biases.

Clinical High-Risk versus Schizophrenia

As noted above, attributional style in the clinical high-risk phase is not well studied, and the two studies to date that compared clinical high-risk versus patient groups have yielded inconsistent findings. Using the AIHQ, An *et al.* (2010) found that clinical high-risk and recent-onset patients both exhibited a higher hostility bias than controls; the clinical high-risk group also demonstrated a higher blame bias and lower aggression bias than recent-onset patients and controls. However, using the IPSAQ, Janssen *et al.* (2006) reported that patients exhibited an externalizing bias whereas clinical high-risk subjects did not.

Summary of Studies Relating to Progression Across Phase of Illness

For emotion processing and ToM, most studies suggest that there are comparable impairments across recent-onset and chronically ill patients, whereas impairments tend to be smaller and less consistent in clinical high-risk subjects. Although the knowledge base is much smaller for social perception, there appears to be a similar cross-phase pattern for this domain. Thus, large impairments in these domains appear to remain relatively stable during the postonset period rather than showing improvement or progressive decline, while attenuated impairments are usually present in clinical high-risk samples. The relatively variable magnitude of impairments in emotion processing, ToM, and social perception seen in clinical high-risk samples may reflect variations in the progression of the premorbid illness process and/or heterogeneity among subjects in terms of whether they are genuinely vulnerable or a false positive. Thus, the studies reviewed in this section, while based in indirect data, shed some initial light on the developmental course of social cognition in schizophrenia.

Regarding attributional bias, the issue of progression has been considered in only a very small number of studies. At this point, the findings are ambiguous. Thus, the small and contradictory evidence base does not permit any conclusions to be drawn about the course of attributional biases.

SUMMARY AND FUTURE DIRECTIONS

In summary, our review has demonstrated that social cognitive deficits seen in chronically ill patients with schizophrenia are also clearly detectable in the early phase of illness. There is consistent evidence for marked impairment in emotion processing, ToM, and social perception in recent-onset patients and the magnitude of impairment is comparable to that seen in chronic schizophrenia. Impairments in these domains are also evident in clinical high-risk and unaffected relative samples. However, the magnitude of impairment is more variable across these groups and, in general, appears to be smaller than impairments seen in the postonset period. Regarding attributional biases, there is some evidence for externalizing and hostility biases in recent-onset patients. However, the few studies in this domain do not yet provide a clear picture of whether such biases are present prior to illness onset or their course across illness phases.

A number of methodologic factors and limitations of this burgeoning area of research should be considered. First, operational definitions of recent-onset schizophrenia are inconsistent across studies, with some studies including individuals several years after the onset of illness (e.g., Achim et al., 2012; Eack et al., 2010). Wide variability of duration of illness across studies can make it difficult to determine whether degree of impairment differs between recent-onset and other phases of illness. Second, most studies that evaluated differences between groups in different illness phases used a single healthy comparison sample that was not optimally matched. Utilization of carefully matched healthy comparison samples is important for determining magnitude of impairment at each phase of illness. Third, the vast majority of the studies reviewed were cross-sectional, and longitudinal studies following patients across the course of illness are needed to assess the course of social cognitive impairment directly.

Another factor that makes it challenging to integrate findings in this literature is the inconsistency of social cognitive tests used across studies. The psychometric properties of commonly used tests are often suboptimal or unknown (Couture et al., 2006; Green et al., 2008). Development of a multidimensional, co-normed social cognitive battery, akin to the MATRICS Consensus Cognitive Battery (Nuechterlein and Green, 2006), would permit direct comparison of findings between studies and between groups in different phases of illness. Two ongoing National Institute of Mental Health (NIMH)-funded projects, the Social Cognition Psychometric Evaluation (SCOPE; Pinkham et al., in press) and the Social Cognition and Functioning (SCAF) projects (Green and Penn, 2013), are attempting to address these measurement limitations.

The findings reviewed above have several implications for future research surrounding social cognition in the early phase of schizophrenia. Given the presence of subtle deficits in emotional processing, ToM, and social perception in unaffected relatives, as well as impairment in these domains in clinical high-risk and schizophrenia patients, social cognition shows promise as a possible 'biomarker' or endophenotype for schizophrenia according to several of the criteria outlined by Gottesman and Gould (2003): (1) association of social cognitive impairment with the illness, (2) social cognitive impairment is found in unaffected relatives at a higher rate than the general population, (3) social cognitive impairment manifests regardless of whether illness is active or not, and (4) heritability of social cognitive impairment (e.g., Greenwood et al., 2007; Gur et al., 2007). Further research is needed to determine whether social cognition fulfills the remaining criterion of an endophenotype (i.e., co-segregation with illness within families). This line of investigation could provide novel insights into neurobiologic and genetic factors that contribute to vulnerability for schizophrenia.

Although research has consistently demonstrated a robust association between social cognitive impairments and poor functional outcome in the chronic phase of schizophrenia (e.g., Fett et al., 2011), surprisingly few studies have examined this relationship in the early phases of illness. Research in this area could be particularly informative in prodromal samples in light of emerging evidence for an association between poor functioning and increased risk for conversion to psychosis in clinical high-risk samples (Cornblatt et al., 2012). The poor social functioning in this phase might be driven in large part by social cognitive impairments. The sparse available data do not yet show an association between severity of social cognitive impairment at baseline and eventual transition to psychosis (Addington et al., 2012; DeVylder et al., 2013; Pinkham et al., 2007), and further research is warranted on the predictive utility of deficits and/or declines in social cognition for conversion to psychosis. In recent-onset patients, a few studies reported significant cross-sectional associations between social cognitive impairment and functional outcomes (Achim et al., 2012; Addington et al., 2006a; Addington et al., 2006b; Addington et al., 2010), and one study found baseline social cognitive impairments predicted functional outcomes at 12-month follow-up (Horan et al., 2012). Further investigation of this topic may clarify the factors that contribute to the poor long-term functional outcomes associated with schizophrenia.

Finally, given the evidence that social cognitive impairment is responsive to psychosocial intervention among chronic patients (Combs et al. 2007; Horan et al. 2011), future research may also investigate the impact of interventions in the early phase of schizophrenia. Interventions designed to compensate for, or remediate, social cognitive impairment may have positive effects on outcomes such as psychosocial functioning and conversion rates to psychosis in clinical high-risk samples, and psychosocial functioning and relapse rates in recent-onset patients.

REFERENCES

Achim, A. M., Ouellet, R., Roy, M., & Jackson, P. L. (2012). Mentalizing in first-episode psychosis. *Psychiatry Research, 196*, 207–213.

Addington, J., Girard, T. A., Christensen, B. K., & Addington, D. (2010). Social cognition mediates illness-related and cognitive influences on social function in patients with schizophrenia-spectrum disorders. *Journal of Psychiatry and Neuroscience, 35*, 49–54.

Addington, J., Penn, D., Woods, S. W., Addington, D., & Perkins, D. O. (2008). Facial affect recognition in individuals at clinical high risk for psychosis. *British Journal of Psychiatry, 192*, 67–68.

Addington, J., Piskulic, D., Perkins, D., Woods, S. W., Liu, L., & Penn, D. L. (2012). Affect recognition in people at clinical high risk of psychosis. *Schizophrenia Research, 140*, 87–92.

Addington, J., Saeedi, H., & Addington, D. (2006a). Facial affect recognition: A mediator between cognitive and social functioning in psychosis? *Schizophrenia Research, 85*, 142–150.

Addington, J., Saeedi, H., & Addington, D. (2006b). Influence of social perception and social knowledge on cognitive and social functioning in early psychosis. *British Journal of Psychiatry, 189*, 373–378.

Amminger, G. P., Schafer, M. R., Klier, C. M., Schlogelhofer, M., Mossaheb, N., Thompson, A., et al. (2012b). Facial and vocal affect perception in people at ultra-high risk of psychosis, first-episode schizophrenia and healthy controls. *Early Intervention in Psychiatry, 6*, 450–454.

Amminger, G. P., Schafer, M. R., Papgeorgiou, K., Klier, C. M., Schlogerhofer, M., Mossaheb, N., et al. (2012a). Emotion recognition in individuals at clinical high-risk for schizophrenia. *Schizophrenia Bulletin, 38*, 1030–1039.

An, S. K., Kang, J. I., Park, J. Y., Kim, K. R., Lee, S. Y., & Lee, E. (2010). Attribution bias in ultra-high risk for psychosis and first-episode schizophrenia. *Schizophrenia Research, 118*, 54–61.

Baas, D., van't Wout, M., Aleman, A., & Kahn, R. S. (2008). Social judgment in clinically stable patients with schizophrenia and healthy relatives: Behavioral evidence of social brain dysfunction. *Psychological Medicine, 38*, 747–754.

Baron-Cohen, S., Wheelwright, S., Hill, J., Raste, Y., & Plumb, I. (2001). The "reading the mind in the eyes" test revised version: A study with normal adults, and adults with Asperger syndrome or high-functioning autism. *Journal of Child Psychology and Psychiatry, 42*, 241–251.

Bentall, R. P., Corcoran, R., Howard, R., Blackwood, N., & Kinderman, P. (2001). Persecutory delusions: A review and theoretical integration. *Clinical Psychology Review, 21*, 1143–1192.

Bertrand, M., Achim, A. M., Harvey, P., Sutton, H., Malla, A. K., & Lepage, M. (2008). Structural neural correlates of impairment in social cognition in first episode psychosis. *Social Neuroscience, 3*, 79–88.

Bertrand, M., Sutton, H., Achim, A. M., Malla, A. K., & Lepage, M. (2007). Social cognitive impairments in first episode psychosis. *Schizophrenia Research, 95*, 124–133.

Bora, E., & Pantelis, C. (2013). Theory of mind impairments in first-episode psychosis, individuals at ultra-high risk for psychosis and in first-degree relatives of schizophrenia: Systematic review and meta-analysis. *Schizophrenia Research, 144*, 31–36.

Bora, E., Yucel, M., & Pantelis, C. (2009). Theory of mind impairment in schizophrenia: Meta-analysis. *Schizophrenia Research, 109*, 1–9.

Breitborde, N. J., Srihari, V. H., & Woods, S. W. (2009). Review of the operational definition of first-episode psychosis. *Early Intervention in Psychiatry, 3*, 259–265.

Brüne, M. (2005). Emotion recognition, 'theory of mind', and social behavior in schizophrenia. *Psychiatry Research, 133*, 135–147.

Chung, Y. S., Kang, D., Shin, N. Y., Yoo, S. Y., & Kwon, J. S. (2008). Deficit of theory of mind in individuals at ultra-high-risk for schizophrenia. *Schizophrenia Research, 99*, 111–118.

Combs, D. R., Penn, D. L., Wicher, M., & Waldheter, E. (2007). The ambiguous intentions hostility questionnaire (AIHQ): A new measure for evaluating hostile social-cognitive biases in paranoia. *Cognitive Neuropsychiatry, 12*, 128–143.

Comparelli, A., Corigliano, V., De Carolis, A., Mancinelli, I., Trovini, G., Ottavi, G., et al. (2013). Emotion recognition impairment is present early and is stable throughout the course of schizophrenia. *Schizophrenia Research, 143*, 65–69.

Comparelli, A., De Carolis, A., Corigliano, V., Romano, S., Kotzalidis, G. D., Campana, C., et al. (2011). Subjective disturbance of perception is related to facial affect recognition in schizophrenia. *Journal of Nervous and Mental Disease, 199*, 802–806.

Corcoran, R., Mercer, G., & Frith, C. D. (1995). Schizophrenia, symptomatology, and social inference: Investigating "theory of mind" in people with schizophrenia. *Schizophrenia Research, 17*, 5–13.

Cornblatt, B. A., Carrion, R. E., Addington, J., Seidman, L., Walker, E. F., Cannon, T. D., et al. (2012). Risk factors for psychosis: Impaired social and role functioning. *Schizophrenia Bulletin, 38*, 1247–1257.

Corrigan, P. (1997). The social perceptual deficits of schizophrenia. *Psychiatry, 60*, 309–326.

Corrigan, P., Buican, B., & Toomey, R. (1996a). Construct validity of two tests of social cognition in schizophrenia. *Psychiatry Research, 63*, 77–82.

Corrigan, P., Garman, A., & Nelson, D. (1996b). Situational feature recognition in schizophrenic outpatients. *Psychiatry Research, 62*, 251–257.

Couture, S. M., Penn, D. L., Addington, J., Woods, S. W., & Perkins, D. O. (2008). Assessment of social judgments and complex mental states in the early phases of psychosis. *Schizophrenia Research, 100*, 237–241.

Couture, S. M., Penn, S. L., & Roberts, D. L. (2006). The functional significance of social cognition in schizophrenia: A review. *Schizophrenia Bulletin, 32*, S44–S63.

de Achaval, D., Costanzo, E., Villarreal, M., Jauregui, I. O., Chiodi, A., Castro, M. N., et al. (2010). Emotion processing and theory of mind in schizophrenia patients and their unaffected first-degree relatives. *Neuropsychologica, 48*, 1209–1215.

DeVylder, J. E., Ben-David, S., & Corcoran, C. M. (2013). Attributional style among youth at clinical risk for psychosis. *Early Intervention in Psychiatry, 7*, 84–88.

Eack, S. M., Greeno, C. G., Pogue-Geile, M. F., Newhill, C. E., Hogarty, G. E., & Keshavan, M. S. (2010). Assessing social-cognitive deficits in schizophrenia with the Mayer-Salovey-Caruso Emotional Intelligence Test. *Schizophrenia Bulletin, 36*, 370–380.

Edwards, J., Jackson, H. J., & Pattison, P. E. (2002). Emotion recognition via facial expression and affective prosody in schizophrenia: A methodological review. *Clinical Psychology Review, 22*, 789–832.

Edwards, J., Pattison, P. E., Jackson, H. J., & Wales, R. J. (2001). Facial affect and affective prosody recognition in first-episode schizophrenia. *Schizophrenia Research, 48*, 235–253.

Ekman, P., & Friesen, W. V. (1976). Measuring facial movement. *Journal of Environmental Psychology, 1*, 56–75.

Erlenmeyer-Kimling, L. (2000). Neurobehavioral deficits in offspring of schizophrenia parents: Liability indicators and predictors of illness. *American Journal of Medical Genetics, 97*, 65–71.

Fett, A. K., Viechtbauer, W., Dominguez, M. D., Penn, D. L., van Os, J., & Krabbendam, L. (2011). The relationship between neurocognition and social cognition with functional outcomes in schizophrenia: A meta-analysis. *Neuroscience and Biobehavioral Reviews, 35*, 573–588.

Fornells-Ambrojo, M., & Garety, P. A. (2009). Understanding attributional biases, emotions, and self-esteem in 'poor me' paranoia: Findings from an early psychosis sample. *British Journal of Clinical Psychology, 48*, 141–162.

Fusar-Poli, P., Bonoldi, I., Yung, A. R., Borgwardt, S., Kempton, M. J., Valmaggia, L., et al. (2012). Predicting psychosis: Meta-analysis of transition outcomes in individuals at high clinical risk. *Archives of General Psychiatry, 69*, 220–229.

Garety, P. A., & Freeman, D. (1999). Cognitive approaches to delusions: A critical review of theories and evidence. *British Journal of Clinical Psychology, 38*, 113–154.

Gottesman, I. I., & Erlenmeyer-Kimling, L. (2001). Family and twin strategies as a head start in defining prodromes and endophenotypes for hypothetical early-interventions in schizophrenia. *Schizophrenia Research, 51*, 93–102.

Gottesman, I. I., & Gould, T. D. (2003). The endophenotype concept in psychiatry: Etymology and strategic intentions. *American Journal of Psychiatry, 160*, 636–645.

Green, M. F., Bearden, C. E., Cannon, T. D., Fiske, A. P., Hellemann, G. S., Horan, W. P., et al. (2012a). Social cognition in schizophrenia, part 1: Performance across phase of illness. *Schizophrenia Bulletin, 38*, 854–864.

Green, M. F., Hellemann, G., Horan, W. P., Lee, J., & Wynn, J. K. (2012b). From perception to functional outcome in schizophrenia: Modeling the role of ability and motivation. *Archives of General Psychiatry, 69*, 1216–1224.

Green, M. F., & Leitman, D. I. (2008). Social cognition in schizophrenia. *Schizophrenia Bulletin, 34*, 670–672.

Green, M. F., & Penn, D. L. (2013). Going from social neuroscience to schizophrenia clinical trials. *Schizophrenia Bulletin, 39*, 1189–1191.

Green, M. F., Penn, D. L., Bentall, R., Carpenter, W. T., Gaebel, W., Gur, R., et al. (2008). Social cognition in schizophrenia: An NIMH workshop on definitions, assessment, and research opportunities. *Schizophrenia Bulletin, 34*, 1211–1220.

Greenwood, T. A., Braff, D. L., Light, G. L., Cadenhead, K. S., Calkins, M. E., Dobie, D. J., et al. (2007). Initial heritability analyses of endophenotypic measures for schizophrenia. *Archives of General Psychiatry, 64*, 1242–1250.

Gur, R. E., Nimgaonkar, V. L., Almasy, L., Calkins, M. E., Ragland, J. D., Pogue-Geile, M. F., et al. (2007). Neurocognitive endophenotypes in a multiplex multigenerational family study of schizophrenia. *American Journal of Psychiatry, 164*, 813–819.

Horan, W. P., Green, M. F., DeGroot, M., Fiske, A., Hellemnn, G., Kee, K., et al. (2012). Social cognition in schizophrenia, part 2: 12-month stability and prediction of functional outcome in first-episode patients. *Schizophrenia Bulletin, 38*, 865–872.

Horan, W. P., Kern, R. S., Tripp, C., Hellemann, G., Wynn, J. K., Bell, M., et al. (2011). Efficacy and specificity of social cognitive skills training for outpatients with psychotic disorders. *Journal of Psychiatric Research, 45*, 1113–1122.

Inoue, Y., Yamada, K., Hitano, M., Shinohara, M., Tamoki, T., Iguchi, H., et al. (2006). Impairment of theory of mind in patients in remission following first episode of schizophrenia. *European Archives of Psychiatry and Clinical Neuroscience, 256*, 326–328.

Irani, F., Platek, S. M., Panyavin, I. S., Calkins, M. E., Kohler, C., Siegel, S. J., et al. (2006). Self-face recognition and theory of mind in patients with schizophrenia and first-degree relatives. *Schizophrenia Research, 88*, 151–160.

Janssen, I., Krabbendam, L., Jolle, J., & van Os, J. (2003). Alterations in theory of mind in patients with schizophrenia and non-psychotic relatives. *Acta Psychiatrica Scandinavica, 108*, 110–117.

Janssen, I., Versmissen, D., Campo, J., Myin-Germeys, I., van Os, J., & Krabbendam, L. (2006). Attribution style and psychosis: Evidence for an externalizing bias in patients, but not in individuals at high risk. *Psychological Medicine, 36*, 771–778.

Kee, K. S., Horan, W. P., Mintz, J., & Green, M. F. (2004). Do the siblings of schizophrenia patients demonstrate affect perception deficits? *Schizophrenia Research, 67*, 87–94.

Kettle, J. W. L., O'Brien-Simpson, L., & Allen, N. B. (2008). Impaired theory of mind in first-episode schizophrenia: Comparison with community, university, and depressed controls. *Schizophrenia Research, 99*, 96–102.

Kim, H. S., Shin, N. Y., Jang, J. H., Kim, E., Shim, G., Park, H. Y., et al. (2011). Social cognition and neurocognition as predictors of conversion to psychosis in individuals at ultra-high risk. *Schizophrenia Research, 130*, 170–175.

Kinderman, P., & Bentall, R. P. (1997). Causal attributions in paranoia and depression: Internal, personal, and situational attributions for negative events. *Journal of Abnormal Psychology, 106*, 341–345.

Koelkebeck, K., Pedersen, A., Suslow, T., Kueppers, K. A., Arolt, V., & Ohrmann, P. (2010). Theory of mind in first-episode schizophrenia patients: Correlations with cognition and personality traits. *Schizophrenia Research, 119*, 115–123.

Kucharska-Pietura, K., David, A. S., Masiakm, M., & Phillips, M. L. (2005). Perception of facial and vocal affect by people with schizophrenia in early and late stages of illness. *British Journal of Psychiatry, 187*, 523–528.

Lavoie, M., Plana, I., Lacroix, J. B., Godmaire-Duhaime, F., Jackson, P., & Achim, A. M. (2013). Social cognition in first-degree relatives of people with schizophrenia: A meta-analysis. *Psychiatry Research, 209*, 129–135.

Mayer, J. D., Salovey, P., Caruso, D. R., & Sitarenios, G. (2001). Emotional intelligence as a standard intelligence. *Emotion, 1*, 232–242.

Munton, A. G., Silvester, J., Stratton, P., & Hanks, H. (1999). *Attributions in action: A practical approach to coding qualitative data*. Chichester: Wiley.

Nuechterlein, K. H., & Green, M. F. (2006). *MATRICS consensus cognitive battery manual*. Los Angeles, CA: MATRICS Assessment, Inc..

Pinkham, A. E., Penn, D. L., Green, M. F., Buck, B., Healey, K., & Harvey, P. D. (in press). The social cognition psychometric evaluation study: Results of the expert survey and RAND panel. Schizophrenia Bulletin.

Pinkham, A. E., Penn, D. L., Perkins, D. O., Graham, K. A., & Siegel, M. (2007). Emotion perception and social skill over the course of psychosis: A comparison of individuals "at-risk" for psychosis and individuals with early and chronic schizophrenia spectrum illness. *Cognitive Neuropsychiatry, 12*, 198–212.

Rapoport, J. L., Addington, A., Frangou, S., & Psych, M. R. (2005). The neurodevelopmental model of schizophrenia: Update 2005. *Molecular Psychiatry, 10*, 434–449.

Rosenthal, R., Hall, J. A., Archer, D., DiMatteo, M. R., & Rogers, P. L. (1979). *The PONS test manual*. New York: Irvington Publishers, Inc..

Salovey, P., & Sluyter, D. J. (1997). *Emotional development and emotional intelligence*. New York: Basic Books.

Salva, G. N., Vella, L., Armstrong, C. C., Penn, D. L., & Twamley, E. W. (2013). Deficits in domains of social cognition in schizophrenia: A meta-analysis of the empirical evidence. *Schizophrenia Bulletin, 39*, 979–992.

Sergi, M. J., Fiske, A. P., Horan, W. P., Kern, R. S., Subotnik, K. L., Nuechterlein, K. H., et al. (2009). Development of a measure of relationship perception in schizophrenia. *Psychiatry Research, 166*, 54–62.

Stone, V. E., Baron-Cohen, S., & Knight, R. T. (1998). Frontal lobe contributions to theory of mind. *Journal of Cognitive Neuroscience, 10*, 640–656.

Tandon, N., Shah, J., Keshavan, M. D., & Tandon, R. (2012). Attenuated psychosis and the schizophrenia prodrome: Current status of risk identification and psychosis prevention. *Neuropsychiatry, 2*, 345–353.

Thompson, A., Papas, A., Bartholomeusz, C., Allott, K., Amminger, G. P., Nelson, B., et al. (2012). Social cognition in clinical "at risk" for psychosis and first episode psychosis populations. *Schizophrenia Research, 141*, 204–209.

Thompson, A., Papas, A., Bartholomeusz, C., Nelson, B., & Yung, A. (2013). Externalized attributional bias in the ultra high risk (UHR) for psychosis population. *Psychiatry Research, 206*, 200–205.

Toomey, R., Seidman, L. J., Lyons, M. J., Faraone, S. V., & Tsuang, M. T. (1999). Poor perception of nonverbal social-emotional cues in relatives of schizophrenic patients. *Schizophrenia Research, 40*, 121–130.

Chapter 4

Empathy

Birgit Derntl[1] and Christina Regenbogen[1,2]

[1]RWTH Aachen University, Aachen, Germany, [2]Karolinska Institutet, Solna, Sweden

Chapter Outline

INTRODUCTION

Emotions are salient and effective transmitters of information; they serve adaptive behavior and have a close relationship to social functioning level. The meaning of emotions becomes conspicuous when they either reach an overwhelming state and cause uncontrollable reactions or when pathologic processes alter or interfere with their normal expression and function.

The advent of neuroimaging techniques now poses an option to map the cerebral processes underlying emotional behavior. This is an important milestone, given the influence of emotions on psychological variables (such as memory, attention, learning, perception, etc.). Despite these obvious advances, due to a lack of homogeneous operationability across studies and (conscious) accessibility in an experimental setting, emotion research remains a field that can hardly be examined using objective experimental methods.

In this chapter we will present an overview of the current state of emotion research with a strong focus on the social-cognitive ability of empathy. The emotional components of human experience and behavior will be characterized in detail on their neurobiological underpinnings based on previously published behavioral, psychophysiological, and neuroimaging data.

Social Cognition and Metacognition in Schizophrenia.
DOI: http://dx.doi.org/10.1016/B978-0-12-405172-0.00004-1
© 2014 Elsevier Inc. All rights reserved.

We will present background knowledge as well as introduce our own approaches to target multiple dimensions of empathy, simultaneously, as well as assess them on various measurement levels while using dynamic and naturalistic stimulus material. Basic research will be combined with studies carried out on psychiatric populations with aberrant social cognitive abilities such as autism, major depression, and borderline personality disorder with the strongest focus on schizophrenia.

DEFINITION OF EMPATHY

Relying on accurate emotion recognition, the ability to show empathic behavior plays a critical role within social communities, particularly regarding the complexity of structures and networks in our society today. Being able to communicate about environmental events as well as perceptions of emotional states concerning others and the self thus seems critical. Empathy and empathic behavior have various definitions probably due to the complexity of the construct (see de Vignemont and Singer, 2006; Preston and de Waal, 2002); however, according to most models one can derive at least three core components (cf. Decety and Jackson, 2004): (1) the ability to recognize emotions in oneself and others via facial expressions, speech, or behavior (gestures, body language); (2) an affective responsiveness, meaning sharing of emotional states with others or the ability to experience similar emotions as others; and (3) a cognitive component, also referred to as perspective taking, describing the competency to take over the perspective of another person, though the distinction between self and other remains intact (Fig. 4.1).

Observing others and inferring their emotional state and behavioral motivation are beneficial for the feeling of social coherence and can be regarded as a prerequisite for social interaction (de Vignemont and Singer, 2006).

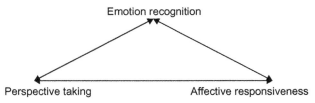

FIGURE 4.1 Illustration of the three core components of empathy according to Decety and Jackson (2004).

BEHAVIORAL EMPATHY DEFICITS IN SCHIZOPHRENIA

Deficits in social interaction and emotional competencies are described as a central characteristic of schizophrenia (Brüne, 2005). Patients with schizophrenia show substantial deficits in several aspects of emotional behavior, including emotion recognition (e.g., Schneider et al., 2006; van't Wout et al., 2007) and empathy (Bora et al., 2008; Langdon et al., 2006; Langdon and Ward, 2009; Montag et al., 2007; Shamay-Tsoory et al., 2007). However, all of the mentioned studies focused on one component according to the model by Decety and Jackson (2004) or relied on self-reported data. Therefore, it was unknown whether these deficits would be prominent for all empathy components or whether deficits in one component influenced those in the other domains.

Hence, in a study from our laboratory, we aimed at assessing the three defining components of empathy in patients with schizophrenia and matched healthy controls, enabling a more detailed and exact analysis of these emotional competencies, their interactions, and possible dysfunctions in patients (Derntl et al., 2009a).

The results showed all components of empathy to be impaired in patients with schizophrenia, which reflected severe emotional deficits not only for emotion recognition, but also affective responsiveness and perspective taking. Impairments in affective responsiveness and perspective taking remained even after controlling for emotion recognition deficits. Further, none of the three components was solely responsible for driving the empathic deficits, which suggests that they represent independent functionalities within the shared underlying theoretical construct of empathy (cf. Derntl et al., 2009a). Moreover, the results suggest that patients with schizophrenia are impaired in their capacity to simulate another person's subjective world spontaneously, that is, they cannot empathetically appreciate the likely content of another person's mind in order to take appropriate account of that other person's feelings (cf. Langdon and Ward, 2009).

SPECIFICITY OF EMPATHIC DEFICITS

While several studies compared neurocognitive functioning between patients with schizophrenia, bipolar disorder, or major depression (e.g., Tuulio-Henriksson et al., 2011; Simonsen et al., 2011; Simonsen et al., 2010; Zanelli et al., 2010), little is known about the specificity of emotional competencies in these major psychiatric disorders. This is astonishing given the high clinical relevance for planning of disorder-specific treatment and psychotherapeutic intervention. Addington and Addington (1998) compared emotion recognition performance of schizophrenia and bipolar disorder patients and observed significantly poorer performance in patients with schizophrenia; however, patient groups were not matched for age, gender, and education. Little is known about disorder-specific deficits in other emotional competencies constituting empathic abilities, despite their relevance for successful social interaction.

Behavioral deficits in specific empathy components, such as emotion recognition, have been reported for all three patient groups (schizophrenia: Kohler *et al.*, 2010; Schneider *et al.*, 2006; bipolar disorder: Derntl *et al.*, 2009b; Kohler *et al.*, 2011; major depression: Bourke *et al.*, 2010; Kohler *et al.*, 2011; Schneider *et al.*, 2012). Regarding empathy, we reported a more general emotional deficit comprising all core components in schizophrenia (Derntl *et al.*, 2009a) and major depression (Schneider *et al.*, 2012) and a specific deficit in emotion recognition and affective responsiveness in bipolar disorder (Seidel *et al.*, 2012). However, in these previous studies, we compared patients with matched healthy controls. Only the comparison with other clinical samples who are also medicated, hospitalized, and have a comparable duration of illness can delineate which deficits are specific for which disorder and what may be a general dysfunction in all major psychiatric conditions.

Therefore, we assessed empathic performance in schizophrenia, bipolar disorder, and depressed patients as well as matched healthy controls (Derntl *et al.*, 2012a). Our results indicate that patients with schizophrenia are characterized by a pronounced impairment in all tasks including general face processing and thus extend previous findings comparing facial affect recognition in schizophrenia and bipolar disorder (Addington and Addington, 1998). When compared with the two other clinical groups, schizophrenia patients show a particular deficit in emotional perspective taking and affective responsiveness. Hence, the ability to quickly infer an emotional state of another person by taking the social context and people's behavior into account (here emotional perspective taking) as well as the ability to put oneself in a certain extrinsic emotional condition (here affective responsiveness) seem specifically dysfunctional in schizophrenia. Another interesting aspect is that these empathy difficulties were not reflected in the patients' reaction times, as the reaction times of patients with schizophrenia were similar to those of the healthy controls. We speculate that schizophrenia patients are probably indicating that they are not fully aware of their deficit and thus might feel as confident in choosing an answer as controls. Simonsen *et al.* (2010) reported a significant discrepancy between clinician- versus patient-rated psychosocial functioning and when choosing answers. Moreover, this assumption is further supported by the self-reported data of schizophrenia patients, indicating that schizophrenia patients have poorer insight into their functional level than do other patients, resulting in higher self-ratings of perspective taking and empathic concern than those of controls.

Hence, the finding of worse performance in schizophrenia parallels those from studies on neurocognitive deficits. Concluding, this supports the notion that schizophrenia has the most severe impact on general human abilities, including cognition and emotional functioning. However, patients are not fully aware of their impairments, as reflected in self-report data and reaction times.

NEURAL CORRELATES OF EMPATHY

The neural correlates of empathy have attracted much attention in recent years, and evidence from functional neuroimaging studies points to the existence of specific brain regions responsible for empathy in healthy subjects. Most studies rely on the so-called 'Perception Action Model' by Preston and de Waal (2002), who proclaim that observation as well as imagination of another person in a particular emotional state automatically activates a representation of that state in the observer, along with its associated automatic and somatic responses. In other words, when we try to understand how someone is feeling in a certain situation, we simulate the feelings by activating our own affective program prompting shared neural representations (cf. Singer and Lamm, 2009). Moreover, Preston and de Waal (2002) suggest two functional networks serving empathic functions. One network comprises the amygdala, cingulate, and orbitofrontal cortex involved in emotion perception and emotion regulation. The second network relies on dorsolateral and ventromedial prefrontal regions and is engaged in holding and manipulating the afferent information. Taking into account that we are able to inhibit and control some of the empathic processes, Lamm and Decety (2006) proposed a model in which bottom-up and top-down information processes are intertwined in the generation and modulation of empathy. Bottom-up processes are mainly responsible for affect generation and automatic responses and are associated with limbic and temporal activation, while top-down regulation and evaluation are related to prefrontal and cingulate cortices. This is in accordance with the more general model of social cognition by Ochsner (2008), in which bottom-up processes of recognition of social and emotional cues, and top-down processes to draw mental state inferences, are proposed.

Some results support the assumption that the contextual appraisal of a situation rather than its sensory input alone determines the empathizer's neural and behavioral response (e.g., Lamm *et al.*, 2007; Lamm *et al.*, 2008; Ruby and Decety, 2004); thus top-down processes shape empathic responses and social understanding. According to this model, emotional cues profit from a contextual embedding so they can be interpreted correctly and justify empathy by the receiver.

Previous neuroimaging studies on empathy have covered a wide range of emotions – from pain to disgust and happiness – and tasks – from passive viewing to imagination and evaluation. Due to this diversity in study design, a heterogeneity of regions was found to be activated during empathic behavior. This leaves the question open as to which brain areas form the true 'empathy network' and whether such a core network really exists (cf. Derntl *et al.*, 2012c). Evidence showed that both the prefrontal and the temporal cortices are implicated in empathic behavior, but patterns of associations are different depending upon various factors, such as whether cognitive or affective empathy was investigated (Lee *et al.*, 2004). According to one meta-analysis on 40

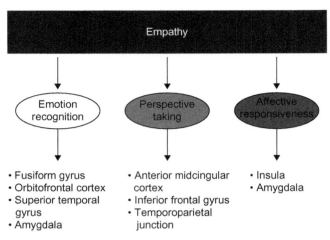

FIGURE 4.2 Results of two meta-analyses on the neural correlates of empathy (Fan *et al.* 2011; Lamm *et al.* 2011).

functional magnetic resonance imaging (fMRI) studies on empathy, Fan *et al.* (2011) assigned a key role in cognitive empathy to the left dorsal anterior midcingulate cortex (aMCC) and to the anterior insula bilaterally in affective empathy irrespective of emotional category. Focusing on empathy for pain, Lamm *et al.* (2011) reported activation of the anterior insula bilaterally, the anterior medial cingulate cortex, and the posterior cingulate cortex, partly supporting findings from Fan *et al.* (2011). Figure 4.2 shows the neural correlates of the three core components of empathy.

NEURAL DYSFUNCTIONS IN SCHIZOPHRENIA

Most neuroimaging studies that have investigated empathy in schizophrenia have put their main focus on investigating neural correlates of single components (cf. Derntl *et al.*, 2012b). For example, emotion recognition tasks were associated with lower activation in fusiform gyri, insular cortices, and amygdalar nuclei (e.g., Fakra *et al.*, 2008; Gur *et al.*, 2007; Habel *et al.*, 2010) when comparing patients to healthy controls, indicating impaired processing of facial emotion processing. This was also present in juvenile patient groups and clinically at-risk individuals (Seifert *et al.*, 2008, 2009). On the other hand, patients processing neutral faces showed hyperactivation, compared to healthy participants, in regions processing emotions (e.g., Habel *et al.*, 2010; Holt *et al.*, 2006; Mier *et al.*, 2010; Seiferth *et al.*, 2008), a finding which has been discussed as a potential correlate of misinterpretations and, potentially, delusions (Gur, 2002; Phillips, 2003), a core factor of the diagnostic criteria of schizophrenia.

Contrary to this, studies investigating cognitive empathy have mainly reported hypoactivation of prefrontal cortices in patients compared to controls (e.g., Brunet *et al.*, 2003; Lee *et al.*, 2006; Marjoram *et al.*, 2006; Russell *et al.*, 2000).

Two studies interested in empathy impairments in schizophrenia have applied similar cartoon tasks in order to target processing of more complex scenes, measuring cognitive and affective empathy (Benedetti *et al.*, 2009; Lee *et al.*, 2010). Schizophrenia patients showed higher activation compared to healthy comparison participants in the right superior temporal gyrus (STG) during affective empathy, and higher activation of right transverse gyrus and right posterior STG during cognitive empathy, while comparison subjects showed the opposite pattern (Benedetti *et al.*, 2009). Lee and colleagues (2010) partly supported these findings by showing higher activation in the right STG during cognitive empathy, but also higher activation in the left insula during affective empathy. Both studies suggested a double dissociation of neural networks serving affective and cognitive task empathy. However, neither of the two studies showed associations between psychopathology parameters and BOLD activation.

While these studies brought the field forward by focusing on more complex scenes and tapping into perspective taking aspects, the question remains whether cartoons would raise affections that were attributed to the presentations; in other words, would emotions between the viewer and the cartoon figure be shared. Further, emotion recognition abilities were not controlled for, and it remains unknown what part potential impairments in these basic prerequisites of empathy may have played in the observable social cognition deficits.

In addition to a behavioral assessment, we also aimed at characterizing empathic dysfunctions in greater detail by identifying the neural substrates of subcomponents of empathic abilities in schizophrenia. Patients performed the three tasks mentioned before (Derntl *et al.*, 2009a) in the scanner and thus were confronted with diverse socioemotional demands (Derntl *et al.*, 2012b).

As hypothesized, patients with schizophrenia showed significantly impaired performance in all three paradigms, supporting the assumption of a broader emotional deficit (Derntl *et al.*, 2009a). Moreover, in comparison to age-, gender-, and education-matched controls, we observed significant impairments in empathic behavior in the patient sample that was accompanied by dysfunctional activation in a widespread neural network, particularly in regions known to be associated with emotion processing, such as the inferior frontal gyrus, the anterior and middle cingulate cortex, the precuneus, and the amygdala.

Task performance requires salience attribution (e.g., amygdala), top-down modulation of affective responsiveness (e.g., anterior cingulate), and the ability to simulate another person's world (e.g., inferior frontal gyri) spontaneously, all of which were shown to be impaired in patients. Moreover, behavioral and neural performance correlated significantly with negative symptom severity, supporting recent assumptions that negative symptoms are particularly associated with dysfunctions in emotion processing (Strauss *et al.*, 2010). The exact influence of psychopathology on the different emotional functions is far from being elucidated and needs further research.

MULTIMODAL EMPATHY IN SCHIZOPHRENIA

Apart from the multiple levels into which empathy can be subdivided (i.e., emotion recognition, affective responsiveness, and perspective taking), empathic contents are transmitted via different communication channels. These include facial expression, emotional speech, or body language.

We have developed an approach to study the specific and combined influence of these channels simultaneously, using naturalistic stimulus material (dynamic video clips of ~11 seconds' duration). While multimodal emotionality was associated with integration processes in thalamus and precuneus, emotional facial expressions, prosody, and speech content were associated with bilateral activation patterns in the respective channel-processing areas (i.e., fusiform gyri, auditory cortices, and left angular gyrus) (Regenbogen *et al.*, 2012b). Neutral speech content presented with emotional facial expression and prosody led to the strongest behavioral empathy (which was defined as a congruence between own and other's emotion) decreases and was complemented by low physiologic arousal, which led us to claim speech content to be central in empathic contextual appraisal (Regenbogen *et al.*, 2012a).

The studies set the basis for us to move on to study patients with schizophrenia and depression with a multimodal and multidimensional approach. As stated above, many studies show large deficits when assessing emotion recognition abilities, which even remain present when combining two channels in schizophrenia (de Gelder *et al.*, 2002; Pearl *et al.*, 2009) and major depression (Müller *et al.*, 2013). However, it has been suggested that patients may profit from a more realistic and natural depiction of social cues and that this would enable targeting those aspects of empathic deficits that are beyond the temporally initial phases of an empathic response (Garrido-Vasquez *et al.*, 2011). Our study was, therefore, a novel attempt to study social cognition dynamically, multimodally, and in an ecologically valid fashion in psychiatric patients.

The results of a behavioral/psychophysiologic study (Schneider *et al.*, personal communication) replicated well-known deficits in patients with schizophrenia and depression. The performance of patients with schizophrenia deteriorated most when speech content was not understandable whereas patients with major depression performed worse when the face lacked emotionality. Affective responses, however, were behaviorally unaffected and showed the importance of an encompassing assessment of empathy, including the affective response component. The autonomous arousal completed the pattern of dysfunctions by indicating hyporesponsiveness of patients with schizophrenia and hyper-responsiveness of patients with major depression, yielding a more complex pattern of affective responses in the patients.

On a neural level, the dynamic and ecologically valid presentation of emotions resulted in robust activations in the respective processing areas of prosody, facial expression, and speech content (Regenbogen *et al.*, personal communication). However, disorder-specific impairments appeared in evaluative stages of emotion processing, namely when evaluating neutral and emotional speech content in schizophrenia (hippocampus–caudate nucleus complex, intraparietal sulcus, and middle temporal gyrus), and when balancing out more internal versus external processing styles in major depression (supplementary motor area, posterior cingulate cortex, temporoparietal junction).

Using a multimodal and naturalistic design, it was, therefore, possible to assess several communication channels and empathy components at the same time and thereby advance the studies of empathy that regard emotional construct formation and theory-of-mind aspects.

CONCLUSION

Schizophrenia patients are impaired in all components involved in the process of building an empathic response. They show decreased emotion recognition performance, affective responsiveness, and perspective taking abilities. Therapeutic interventions targeting these broad emotional dysfunctions might help to improve patients' everyday lives and social interactions as well as help to establish healthier socio-occupational lives. This is especially important given the findings that social impairments in schizophrenia worsen over time and may be involved in relapse rate (e.g., Pinkham *et al.*, 2003). This has made social cognition one of seven core domains that should be included in the context of clinical trials (NIMH Measurement and Treatment Research to Improve Cognition in Schizophrenia, MATRICS, Green *et al.*, 2004), a finding which is also supported by a study using structural equation modeling to show that social cognition can be seen as a separate construct, yet social cognition is more strongly associated with neurocognition than with negative symptoms (Sergi *et al.*, 2007).

Since empathy is related to psychosocial functioning (Smith *et al.*, 2012) and hence of high clinical relevance in schizophrenia, a more detailed understanding of the exact nature of these impairments is mandatory. In light of this significant empathic deficit, a therapy approach dealing with this impairment is mandatory for improving patient x' socioemotional functioning. Based on the results described above (e.g., Derntl *et al.*, 2009a, 2012b; Smith *et al.*, 2012), interventions aimed at improving the functioning of neural substrates supporting empathy may possess the potential to remediate these empathic deficits. Particularly IFG activation can be used as a neuroimaging marker to individualize treatment or to monitor the effects of treatment. In this regard, training of regulation of the IFG via neurofeedback might constitute a valuable tool.

Notably, there is a lack of studies investigating cognitive and affective empathy in people clinically at risk for psychosis. This seems particularly surprising given consistent findings on social interaction difficulties acting as a precursor of schizophrenia (Cannon, 2008). Hence, future studies might also want to investigate whether this precursor function is also true for empathic dysfunctions, that is, if empathic deficits develop before or after onset of the disorder (or its first symptoms in the prodromal stage).

REFERENCES

Addington, J., & Addington, D. (1998). Facial affect recognition and information processing in schizophrenia and bipolar disorder. *Schizophrenia Research, 32,* 171–181.

Benedetti, F., Bernasconi, A., Bosia, M., Cavallaro, R., Dallaspezia, S., Falini, A., et al. (2009). Functional and structural brain correlates of theory of mind and empathy deficits in schizophrenia. *Schizophrenia Research, 114,* 154–160.

Bora, E., Gokcen, S., & Veznedaroglu, B. (2008). Empathic abilities in people with schizophrenia. *Psychiatry Research, 160,* 23–29.

Bourke, C., Douglas, K., & Porter, R. (2010). Processing of facial emotion expression in major depression: A review. *Australian and New Zealand Journal of Psychiatry, 44,* 681–696.

Brunet, E., Sarfati, Y., Hardy-Baylé, M.-C., & Decety, J. (2003). Abnormalities of brain function during a nonverbal theory of mind task in schizophrenia. *Neuropsychologia, 41,* 1574–1582.

Brüne, M. (2005). Emotion recognition, 'theory of mind,' and social behavior in schizophrenia. *Psychiatry Research, 133,* 135–147.

Cannon, T. D. (2008). Neurodevelopment and the transition from schizophrenia prodrome to schizophrenia: Research imperatives. *Biological Psychiatry, 64,* 737–738.

de Gelder, B., Vroomen, J., Annen, L., Masthof, E., & Hodiamont, P. (2002). Audio-visual integration in schizophrenia. *Schizophrenia Research, 59,* 211–218.

de Vignemont, F., & Singer, T. (2006). The empathic brain: How, when and why? *Trends in Cognitive Sciences, 10,* 435–441.

Decety, J., & Jackson, P. L. (2004). The functional architecture of human empathy. *Behavioral and Cognitive Neuroscience Reviews, 3,* 71–100.

Derntl, B. (2012c). Neuronale korrelate der empathie. In F. Schneider (Ed.), *Positionen der psychiatrie* (pp. 83–89). Berlin: Springer.

Derntl, B., Finkelmeyer, A., Toygar, T. K., Hulsmann, A., Schneider, F., Falkenberg, D. I., et al. (2009a). Generalized deficit in all core components of empathy in schizophrenia. *Schizophrenia Research, 108,* 197–206.

Derntl, B., Finkelmeyer, A., Voss, B., Eickhoff, S. B., Kellermann, T., Schneider, F., et al. (2012b). Neural correlates of the core facets of empathy in schizophrenia. *Schizophrenia Research, 136,* 70–81.

Derntl, B., Seidel, E. M., Kryspin-Exner, I., Hasmann, A., & Dobmeier, M. (2009b). Facial emotion recognition in patients with bipolar I and bipolar II disorder. *British Journal of Clinical Psychology, 48,* 363–375.

Derntl, B., Seidel, E. M., Schneider, F., & Habel, U. (2012a). How specific are emotional deficits? A comparison of empathic abilities in schizophrenia, bipolar and depressed patients. *Schizophrenia Research, 142,* 58–64.

Fakra, E., Salgado-Pineda, P., Delaveau, P., Hariri, A. R., & Blin, O. (2008). Neural bases of different cognitive strategies for facial affect processing in schizophrenia. *Schizophrenia Research, 100,* 191–205.

Fan, Y., Duncan, N. W., de Greck, M., & Northoff, G. (2011). Is there a core neural network in empathy? An fMRI based quantitative meta-analysis. *Neuroscience and Biobehavioral Reviews, 35,* 903–911.

Garrido-Vasquez, P., Jessen, S., & Kotz, S. A. (2011). Perception of emotion in psychiatric disorders: On the possible role of task, dynamics, and multimodality. *Social Neuroscience, 6,* 515–536.

Green, M. F., Nuechterlein, K. H., Gold, J. M., Barch, D. M., Cohen, J., Essock, S., et al. (2004). Approaching a consensus cognitive battery for clinical trials in schizophrenia: The NIMH-MATRICS conference to select cognitive domains and test criteria. *Biological Psychiatry, 56,* 301–307.

Gur, R. C., Sara, R., Hagendoorn, M., Marom, O., Hughett, P., Macy, L., et al. (2002). A method for obtaining 3-dimensional facial expressions and its standardization for use in neurocognitive studies. *Journal of Neuroscience Methods, 115,* 137–143.

Gur, R. E., Loughead, J., Kohler, C. G., Elliott, M. A., Lesko, K., Ruparel, K., et al. (2007). Limbic activation associated with misidentification of fearful faces and flat affect in schizophrenia. *Archives of General Psychiatry, 64,* 1356–1366.

Habel, U., Chechko, N., Pauly, K., Koch, K., Backes, V., Seiferth, N., et al. (2010). Neural correlates of emotion recognition in schizophrenia. *Schizophrenia Research, 122,* 113–123.

Holt, D. J., Kunkel, L., Weiss, A. P., Goff, D. C., Wright, C. I., Shin, L. M., et al. (2006). Increased medial temporal lobe activation during the passive viewing of emotional and neutral facial expressions in schizophrenia. *Schizophrenia Research, 82,* 153–162.

Kohler, C. G., Hoffman, L. J., Eastman, L. B., Healey, K., & Moberg, P. J. (2011). Facial emotion perception in depression and bipolar disorder: A quantitative review. *Psychiatry Research, 188,* 303–309.

Kohler, C. G., Walker, J. B., Martin, E. A., Healey, K. M., & Moberg, P. J. (2010). Facial emotion perception in schizophrenia: A meta-analytic review. *Schizophrenia Bulletin, 36,* 1009–1019.

Lamm, C., Batson, C. D., & Decety, J. (2007). The neural substrate of human empathy: Effects of perspective-taking and cognitive appraisal. *Journal of Cognitive Neuroscience, 19,* 42–58.

Lamm, C., & Decety, J. (2006). Human empathy through the lens of social neuroscience. *Scientific World Journal, 6,* 1146–1163.

Lamm, C., Decety, J., & Singer, T. (2011). Meta-analytic evidence for common and distinct neural networks associated with directly experienced pain and empathy for pain. *Neuroimage, 54,* 2492–2502.

Lamm, C., Porges, E. C., Cacioppo, J. T., & Decety, J. (2008). Perspective taking is associated with specific facial responses during empathy for pain. *Brain Research, 1227,* 153–161.

Langdon, R., Coltheart, M., & Ward, P. B. (2006). Empathetic perspective-taking is impaired in schizophrenia: Evidence from a study of emotion attribution and theory of mind. *Cognitive Neuropsychiatry, 11,* 133–155.

Langdon, R., & Ward, P. (2009). Taking the perspective of the other contributes to awareness of illness in schizophrenia. *Schizophrenia Bulletin, 35,* 1003–1011.

Lee, K. H., Brown, W. H., Egleston, P. N., Green, R. D., Farrow, T. F., Hunter, M. C., et al. (2006). A functional magnetic resonance imaging study of social cognition in schizophrenia during an acute episode and after recovery. *American Journal of Psychiatry, 163,* 1926–1933.

Lee, K. H., Farrow, T. F., Spence, S. A., & Woodruff, P. W. (2004). Social cognition, brain networks and schizophrenia. *Psychological Medicine, 34,* 391–400.

Lee, S. J., Kang, D. H., Kim, C.-W., Gu, B. M., Park, J.-Y., Choi, C.-H., et al. (2010). Multilevel comparison of empathy in schizophrenia: An fMRI study of a cartoon task. *Psychiatry Research: Neuroimaging, 181*, 121–129.

Marjoram, D., Job, D. E., Whalley, H. C., Gountouna, V.-E., McIntosh, A. M., Simonotto, E., et al. (2006). A visual joke fMRI investigation into theory of mind and enhanced risk of schizophrenia. *Neuroimage, 31*, 1850–1858.

Mier, D., Sauer, C., Lis, S., Esslinger, C., Wilhelm, J., Gallhofer, B., et al. (2010). Neuronal correlates of affective theory of mind in schizophrenia out-patients: Evidence for a baseline deficit. *Psychological Medicine, 40*, 1607–1617.

Montag, C., Heinz, A., Kunz, D., & Gallinat, J. (2007). Self-reported empathic abilities in schizophrenia. *Schizophrenia Research, 92*, 85–89.

Müller, V. I., Cieslik, E. C., Kellermann, T. S., & Eickhoff, S. B. (2013). Crossmodal emotional integration in major depression. *Social Cognitive and Affective Neuroscience* in press.

Ochsner, K. N. (2008). The social-emotional processing stream: Five core constructs and their translational potential for schizophrenia and beyond. *Biological Psychiatry, 64*, 48–61.

Pearl, D., Yodashkin-Porat, D., Katz, N., Valevski, A., Aizenberg, D., Sigler, M., et al. (2009). Differences in audiovisual integration, as measured by McGurk phenomenon, among adult and adolescent patients with schizophrenia and age-matched healthy control groups. *Comprehensive Psychiatry, 50*, 186–192.

Phillips, M. L., Drevets, W. C., Rauch, S. L., & Lane, R. (2003). Neurobiology of emotion perception. II: Implications for major psychiatric disorders. *Biological Psychiatry, 54*, 515–528.

Pinkham, A. E., Penn, D. L., Perkins, D. O., & Lieberman, J. (2003). Implications for the neural basis of social cognition for the study of schizophrenia. *American Journal of Psychiatry, 160*, 815–824.

Preston, S. D., & de Waal, F. B. (2002). Empathy: Its ultimate and proximate bases. *Behavioral and Brain Sciences, 25*, 1–20. Discussion 20–71.

Regenbogen, C., Schneider, D. A., Finkelmeyer, A., Kohn, N., Derntl, B., Kellermann, T., et al. (2012a). The differential contribution of facial expressions, prosody, and speech content to empathy. *Cognition & Emotion, 26*, 995–1014.

Regenbogen, C., Schneider, D. A., Gur, R. E., Schneider, F., Habel, U., & Kellermann, T. (2012b). Multimodal human communication – targeting facial expressions, speech content and prosody. *Neuroimage, 60*, 2346–2356.

Ruby, P., & Decety, J. (2004). How would you feel versus how do you think she would feel? A neuroimaging study of perspective-taking with social emotions. *Journal of Cognitive Neuroscience, 16*, 988–999.

Russell, T. A., Rubia, K., Bullmore, E. T., Soni, W., Suckling, J., Brammer, M. J., et al. (2000). Exploring the social brain in schizophrenia: Left prefrontal underactivation during mental state attribution. *American Journal of Psychiatry, 157*, 2040–2042.

Schneider, D., Regenbogen, C., Kellermann, T., Finkelmeyer, A., Kohn, N., Derntl, B., et al. (2012). Empathic behavioral and physiological responses to dynamic stimuli in depression. *Psychiatry Research, 200*, 294–305.

Schneider, F., Gur, R. C., Koch, K., Backes, V., Amunts, K., Shah, N. J., et al. (2006). Impairment in the specificity of emotion processing in schizophrenia. *American Journal of Psychiatry, 163*, 442–447.

Seidel, E. M., Habel, U., Finkelmeyer, A., Hasmann, A., Dobmeier, M., & Derntl, B. (2012). Risk or resilience? Empathic abilities in patients with bipolar disorders and their first-degree relatives. *Journal of Psychiatric Research, 46*, 382–388.

Seiferth, N. Y., Pauly, K., Habel, U., Kellermann, T., Shah, N. J., Ruhrmann, S., et al. (2008). Increased neural response related to neutral faces in individuals at risk for psychosis. *Neuroimage, 40*, 289–297.

Seiferth, N. Y., Pauly, K., Kellermann, T., Shah, N. J., Ott, G., Herpertz-Dahlmann, B., et al. (2009). Neuronal correlates of facial emotion discrimination in early onset schizophrenia. *Neuropsychopharmacology, 34*, 477–487.

Sergi, M. J., Rassovsky, Y., Widmark, C., Reist, C., Erhart, S., Braff, D. L., et al. (2007). Social cognition in schizophrenia: Relationships with neurocognition and negative symptoms. *Schizophrenia Research, 90*, 316–324.

Shamay-Tsoory, S. G., Shur, S., Barcai-Goodman, L., Medlovich, S., Harari, H., & Levkovitz, Y. (2007). Dissociation of cognitive from affective components of theory of mind in schizophrenia. *Psychiatry Research, 149*, 11–23.

Simonsen, C., Sundet, K., Vaskinn, A., Birkenaes, A. B., Engh, J. A., Faerden, A., et al. (2011). Neurocognitive dysfunction in bipolar and schizophrenia spectrum disorders depends on history of psychosis rather than diagnostic group. *Schizophrenia Bulletin, 37*, 73–83.

Simonsen, C., Sundet, K., Vaskinn, A., Ueland, T., Romm, K. L., Hellvin, T., et al. (2010). Psychosocial function in schizophrenia and bipolar disorder: Relationship to neurocognition and clinical symptoms. *Journal of the International Neuropsychological Society, 16*, 771–783.

Singer, T., Critchley, H. D., & Preuschoff, K. (2009). A common role of insula in feelings, empathy and uncertainty. *Trends in Cognitive Science, 13*, 334–340.

Singer, T., & Lamm, C. (2009). The social neuroscience of empathy. *Annals of the New York Academy of Science, 1156*, 81–96.

Smith, M. J., Horan, W. P., Karpouzian, T. M., Abram, S. V., Cobia, D. J., & Csernansky, J. G. (2012). Self-reported empathy deficits are uniquely associated with poor functioning in schizophrenia. *Schizophrenia Research, 137*, 196–202.

Strauss, G. P., Jetha, S. S., Ross, S. A., Duke, L. A., & Allen, D. N. (2010). Impaired facial affect labeling and discrimination in patients with deficit syndrome schizophrenia. *Schizophrenia Research, 118*, 146–153.

Tuulio-Henriksson, A., Perälä, J., Saarni, S., Isometsä, E., Koskinen, S., Lönnqvist, J., et al. (2011). Cognitive functioning in severe psychiatric disorders: A general population study. *European Archives of Psychiatry and Clinical Neuroscience, 261*, 447–456.

van't Wout, M., van Dijke, A., Aleman, A., Kessels, R. P. C., Pijpers, W., & Kahn, R. S. (2007). Fearful faces in schizophrenia: The relationship between patient characteristics and facial affect recognition. *Journal of Nervous and Mental Disease, 195*, 758–764.

Zanelli, J., Reichenberg, A., Morgan, K., Fearon, P., Kravariti, E., Dazzan, P., et al. (2010). Specific and generalized neuropsychological deficits: A comparison of patients with various first-episode psychosis presentations. *American Journal of Psychiatry, 167*, 78–85.

Chapter 5

Memory-Related Metacognition in Patients with Schizophrenia

Elisabeth Bacon[1] and Marie Izaute[2]

[1]Strasbourg, France, [2]LAPSCO - UMR 6024 CNRS, Clermont-Ferrand, France

CONSCIOUSNESS AND COGNITIVE IMPAIRMENTS AS CORE SYMPTOMS OF SCHIZOPHRENIA

Schizophrenia is a common and disabling condition that limits patients' social and professional integration. Based on current findings, disturbances of consciousness and cognition are at the very basis of schizophrenia. The notion of consciousness is central to understanding this disease characterized by a loss of psychic unity. Current experimental psychology approaches highlight the

Social Cognition and Metacognition in Schizophrenia.
DOI: http://dx.doi.org/10.1016/B978-0-12-405172-0.00005-3
© 2014 Elsevier Inc. All rights reserved.

existence of different states of consciousness disturbance in schizophrenia (Raffard *et al.*, 2008). According to various studies, an estimated 50% to 80% of patients do not feel as if they have a mental disorder (Amador *et al.*, 1994; Beck *et al.*, 2004; Pini *et al.*, 2004), resulting sometimes in poor prognosis (David *et al.*, 1995) and behavioral abnormalities (Danion *et al.*, 2007; Kazes *et al.*, 1999; McGlynn, 1998; Monteiro *et al.*, 2008; Sonntag *et al.*, 2003). As early as 1992, Frith suggested that the productive symptoms of schizophrenia (e.g., hallucinations, delusions) can be interpreted as the result of a central disorder of self-consciousness, and, again according to Frith, it is reasonable to think that a central mechanism can account for the variety of deficits experienced by patients with schizophrenia (Frith, 1992). This self-consciousness would come into play for achieving voluntary action as well as for controlling one's own actions and understanding one's own intentions. In addition, a possible explanation for the failure of consciousness may be the inability to assign a meaning to external events. Patients fail to distinguish between elements emerging from their own memory and elements stemming from their environment. They have difficulty differentiating their own thoughts from intentions resulting from external stimuli.

In addition, schizophrenia is accompanied by a wide range of cognitive deficits (Addington and Addington, 2000; Aleman *et al.*, 1999; Fioravanti *et al.*, 2005; Green, 1996; Stone and Hsi, 2011), which also constitute core symptoms of the pathology (Lewis, 2004) and are predictive of patients' income, satisfaction with daily activities, and difficulties in everyday life (Green, 1996; Mohamed *et al.*, 2008) and general health (Fujii *et al.*, 2004). Virtually all cognitive functions are impaired in patients with schizophrenia (Aleman *et al.*, 1999; Heinrichs and Zakzanis, 1998), including executive functions (Bryson *et al.*, 2001), as well as attention and memory (Dickinson *et al.*, 2004; Moritz *et al.*, 2006b). However, not all cognitive functions are impaired to the same degree, and several studies have shown that memory functions are disproportionately impaired (Aleman *et al.*, 1999; Driesen *et al.*, 2008; Kraus and Keefe 2007; Ranganath *et al.*, 2008).

Moreover, explicit, declarative memory appears to be more impaired than implicit, nondeclarative memory (Cirillo and Seidman, 2003; Danion *et al.*, 2001b; Kern *et al.*, 2011; Sponheim *et al.*, 2004). Several authors have attributed this dissociation to the fact that during an explicit/declarative memory task subjects are asked to retrieve the information consciously, whereas in implicit nondeclarative cognitive tasks, information can be recalled without conscious effort (Cirillo and Seidman, 2003; Danion *et al.*, 1999; Gras-Vincendon *et al.*, 1994; Huron *et al.*, 1995).

The lack of recovery of awareness of source memory is another specific feature of patients with schizophrenia. A classic source-monitoring paradigm consists of asking participants to learn word pairs that have been paired either by the experimenter or the participant (Kern *et al.*, 2011). Then, at retrieval, participants are requested to say who paired the words and to assess their confidence about their response (Moritz *et al.*, 2003). The literature regarding such tasks is consistent in finding that patients with schizophrenia have a deficit when it comes to identifying the source of information, whether they are matching objects (Danion *et al.*, 1999) or words (Moritz *et al.*, 2003; Moritz *et al.*, 2006a; Moritz *et al.*, 2006b; Woodward *et al.*, 2007). This attribution bias has also been observed in actions (e.g., folding a sheet) by Mammarella *et al.* (2010), who asked patients and their healthy counterparts to imagine they were performing certain actions or actually to perform them. Then 24 hours later, the experimenter asked the participants whether certain actions were imagined, already actually carried out, or new. The results replicated by Gaweda *et al.* (2012) confirmed that the patients made more source monitoring errors than the healthy participants, in particular because they had difficulty classifying the imagined actions. These studies suggest that patients' recall bias could be related to a source memory deficit, which would increase the risk of producing false memories. However, according to Woodward *et al.* (2007), the source memory deficit would be associated with delusions. They observed that patients with delusions were more likely to attribute word associations to an external source.

During a recognition memory task, the process of conscious recollection that characterizes autonoetic awareness (defined as the ability mentally to relive a past event) is disrupted in patients with schizophrenia. However, another form of memory-related awareness, based on the feeling of familiarity or noetic awareness (without conscious recall) seems to be preserved (Danion *et al.*, 2007; Huron *et al.*, 1995). Some authors hypothesize that autonoetic consciousness is what renders possible the process known as 'cognitive binding' (the ability to make connections between different elements of an event) necessary for forming a coherent overall representation of the world around us and is deficient in patients with schizophrenia (Danion *et al.*, 2007).

Therefore, disturbances of patients' consciousness also affect their knowledge of their own memory abilities and own cognitive processes. It is now recognized as a subject of consensus that schizophrenia is a disease of cognition and consciousness (Izaute and Bacon, 2010; Monteiro *et al.*, 2008; Pegoraro *et al.*, 2013). In addition, a key feature of schizophrenia is the dissociation between thought and action, as observed by Bleuler back in 1911. We can therefore also suspect that these patients present a dissociation between their memory-related awareness and their behavior when engaged in a memory task.

FROM CONSCIOUSNESS TO METACOGNITION

There is only one step from consciousness to metacognition. Humans possess certain introspective abilities in respect of their own thoughts and behavior. Autoreflexion and self-awareness constitute the basis of human consciousness. In 1970, Tulving and Madigan pondered the following thought: 'Why not start looking for ways of experimentally studying and incorporating into theories and models of memory one of the truly unique characteristics of human: its knowledge of its own knowledge' (Tulving and Madigan, 1970, p. 477). The prefix 'meta' means something that encompasses the term with which it is associated. For example, metadata are data about data. As far as we know, the first person to have coined the term 'metacognition' was John Flavell in 1976. He described it as cognition about cognition, or knowing about knowing: *'Metacognition refers to one's knowledge concerning one's own cognitive processes or anything related to them, e.g., the learning-relevant properties of information or data. For example, I am engaging in metacognition if I notice that I am having more trouble learning A than B; if it strikes me that I should double check C before accepting it as fact'* (cited in Perfect and Schwartz, 2002, p. 16); and also: '(Metacognition) *refers, among other things, to the active monitoring and consequent regulation and orchestration of these processes in relation to the cognitive objects or objective'*. Since then, research in this field has flourished and has involved studying what people know about their own cognition, including cognitive experiments, neuroimaging, educational applications, and computational modeling.

Today, 'metacognition' is also a term used in the field of psychopathologic research, but more in terms of thinking about thinking, as in: 'the capacity to adopt a reflexive stance over one's own thoughts and feelings via a dialogue with oneself or with another person (that) reinforces one's subjective sense of being a self and allows for becoming aware that some of one's thoughts and feelings are symptoms of an illness' (Lysaker *et al.*, 2011), or 'Metacognition reflects a spectrum of activities that includes discrete acts in which persons form ideas about specific thoughts and feelings, and synthetic acts in which persons integrate discrete thoughts and feelings into complex representations of themselves and others' (Lysaker *et al.*, 2013, p. 103). For example, the metacognitive training presented in this book by Woodward *et al.* (Chapter 11; *Metacognitive Training and Therapy: An Individualized and Group Intervention for Psychosis*) is a cognitive approach to the treatment of positive symptoms in schizophrenia. However, in the present chapter, we shall focus on metacognition as knowing about knowing in patients with schizophrenia.

FROM METACOGNITION TO METAMEMORY

Saint Augustine wrote: 'When I remember forgetfulness there are present both memory and forgetfulness, memory, whereby I remember, forgetfulness, which I remember. Then is forgetfulness retained by Memory.' [St Augustine, Confessions]. Metamemory is a type of metacognition that refers to our awareness of our own memory processes. Flavell (1971) was also the first to introduce the term 'metamemory': 'intelligent structuring and storage of input, (. . .) intelligent search and retrieval operations, and (. . .) intelligent monitoring and knowledge of theses storage and retrieval operations – a kind of "metamemory"' (Flavell, 1971). Therefore, metamemory refers to our experiences and our knowledge of our cognitive processes.

As early as 1979, Flavell highlighted two categories of metamemory, knowledge and awareness, each with its corresponding experimental approach. Metamemory knowledge is the general knowledge and beliefs about memory processes. It can be expressed without being engaged in a memory task ('I'm good at remembering names', 'It's easier to remember things we are interested in', etc.), and concerns, for example, the knowledge and use of mnemonic strategies, knowledge of the effects of ageing on memory, knowledge about one's own memory skills, etc. It is usually explored by questionnaires. The literature shows both impairment and preservation of metamemory knowledge in patients with schizophrenia, with patients' subjective feelings of memory performance poorly correlated with objective measures (e.g., see Bacon *et al.*, 2011; Cella *et al.*, 2014; Medalia and Thyssen, 2010; Medalia *et al.*, 2008).

In this chapter, we shall be focusing more on metamemory awareness, which refers, for its part, to the monitoring and control of memory tasks in progress (Perfect and Schwartz, 2002). Experimental studies of metamemory awareness involve asking patients to predict some aspect of their memory performance during a given memory task and to register their strategic control over the task. Metamemory awareness refers to the ability to monitor and control how relevant information is processed depending on the goals and requirements of the task at hand. It can be thought of as a regulatory system influencing both memory encoding and retrieval. The memory-related metacognitive approach allows for direct and experimental quantification of metacognitive accuracy, that is, the correspondence between the subjective (metacognitive judgments) and objective (actual memory performance) measures of performance. It is this aspect of metacognition we shall be focusing on here. We shall present the main theoretical framework of metamemory awareness. We shall also concentrate on the dynamic relationships between metamemory awareness and the control of a memory task, and how patients with schizophrenia monitor and control their memory, or how they handle the relationship between thought and action during a memory task.

METAMEMORY MONITORING AND CONTROL

Two processes, metamemory monitoring and control, are involved in adjusting memory performance (Nelson and Narens, 1990). Monitoring refers to an individual's subjective assessment of his or her own memory capacity and knowledge. He or she is able to estimate the contents of his or her memory or the difficulty of a task. Monitoring is expressed as metamemory judgments, such as a judgment of learning (JOL) during or at the end of the acquisition phase (Nelson and Dunlosky, 1991), and a feeling of knowing (FOK) or confidence level (CL) at retrieval. Metamemory judgments reflect the degree of confidence, for example, from 0% (I am not at all sure my response is correct) to 100% (I am totally sure it is accurate). In typical metamemory experiments designed to study episodic memory encoding, participants are usually told to memorize pairs of words with a view to recalling the target word when they are subsequently presented with the cue word (Nelson and Narens, 1990). They are then asked to make JOL predictions about the likelihood of recalling the target word during the subsequent test. At the time of retrieval, if subjects have provided an answer, they may express a CL about its correctness. If they fail to retrieve a target answer, they can at least say whether they have a more or less strong FOK for the missing answer, that is, that they can recognize it when they come across it. The assessments provide information about underestimations or overestimations of the participants' actual knowledge. Examining what is known as 'relative accuracy' is a way of completing these data. Typically, relative accuracy is based on the computation of a correspondence between the accuracy of an answer and its metamemory rating. Monitoring will be accurate or concordant if subjects assign high judgment ratings to correct answers and low judgment ratings to incorrect answers. The relative accuracy of the metamemory judgments indicates how well people can discriminate between their correct or incorrect answers. To compute it, the most widely used correlation is the Goodman-Kruskal gamma coefficient, which indicates a participant's ability to discriminate between correct and incorrect answers, following item-by-item judgments, and provides a way of comparing correct and incorrect predictions. Nelson (1984) compared eight quantitative measures of the accuracy of estimate predictions and concluded that the Goodman-Kruskal gamma coefficient seemed the best measure of association. The values of the gamma coefficient range from 1.0 (total agreement concordance between the metamemory rating and the answer provided) to −1.0 (total discordance between the metamemory rating and the answer). The relative accuracy of healthy subjects is generally good, in other words their gamma is generally close to +1 (Perfect and Schwartz, 2002).

Metacognitive control refers to the processes regulating participants' behavior during a memory task, in other words, to anything that modifies their behavior. For example, it could be selecting a strategy, allocating a given amount of study time, spending more time searching for information or terminating a search, volunteering, or withholding an answer, etc. According to Perfect and Schwartz (2002, p. 4): 'Metacognitive control is the conscious and non conscious decisions that we make (. . .). (. . .) If control processes exist and influence human behavior and cognition, it may be possible to improve or alter control processes in ways which will improve human learning' (pp. 4–5). How participants have controlled a memory task may be ascertained by measuring study time allocation, the selection of items to be relearned, the latency of answering, and the decision to provide or withhold an answer, etc.

METAMEMORY MONITORING IN PATIENTS WITH SCHIZOPHRENIA

The literature shows that patients do not display generalized monitoring deficits but present specific disruptions and selective preservation of metamemory processes. Different patterns can be observed, depending on the type of memory (semantic or episodic), processing step (learning or retrieval), nature of the task (more or less demanding), and type of metamemory judgment involved (prospective or retrospective) (Izaute and Bacon, 2010; Schwartz and Bacon, 2008).

It has repeatedly been observed that the retrospective confidence judgments for incorrect answers expressed by patients with schizophrenia are higher than those of matched healthy participants (Danion *et al.*, 2001a; Moritz and Woodward, 2006; Moritz *et al.*, 2003; Moritz *et al.*, 2005). In the meantime, the prospective metamemory judgments of patients with schizophrenia are lower than those of healthy participants (Bacon *et al.*, 2001; Bacon *et al.*, 2007; Souchay *et al.*, 2006; Thuaire *et al.*, 2012. However, most of the time they are still able to discriminate between what they know and what they do not know, and their gamma correlations are usually higher than zero (Bacon and Izaute, 2009; Bacon *et al.*, 2001; Bacon *et al.*, 2007; Moritz and Woodward, 2006; Souchay *et al.*, 2006; Thuaire *et al.*, 2012). In addition, the mechanisms underlying the prospective FOK judgments for short-term memory and semantic memory seem to be grounded, as in healthy subjects (Koriat 1993; Koriat 1995), in the accessibility of partial information, products of memory recovery (Bacon and Izaute, 2008; Bacon and Izaute, 2009).

METAMEMORY CONTROL IN SCHIZOPHRENIA

It would seem that spontaneous control of a memory task (how to handle a memory task at hand) is sometimes impaired in patients with schizophrenia. Patients with schizophrenia present a deficit as regards the self-initiation of strategy use (Bonner-Jackson *et al.*, 2005; Christensen *et al.*, 2006). They have difficulty organizing the information in memory (Brebion et al., 2004; Landgraf *et al.*, 2011). Moreover, Bacon *et al.* (2007) observed that their spontaneous study time allocation as a function of repetition of learning was inadequate. In this study, participants were instructed to memorize pairs of words with a view to recalling the target word when presented with the first word of the pair (Nelson and Narens, 1990). One-third of the pairs were presented once, one-third twice, and one-third three times during the learning session. The results showed that patients allocated similar learning times the second and the third time they saw an item to be learned. Their behavior in the task could not be considered strategic, insofar as they did not use the maximum time available for learning (some results of this study will be presented under the heading 'When control affects monitoring').

THE DYNAMIC RELATIONSHIP BETWEEN METAMEMORY MONITORING AND CONTROL

Nelson and Narens (1990) proposed a theoretical framework to describe the relationships between monitoring and control, and their model is still largely used to organize and integrate the current research relating to metamemory. The model

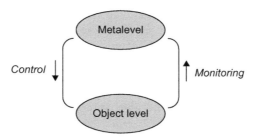

FIGURE 5.1 Representation of the model designed by Nelson and Narens (1990; 1994) to depict the relationship between metamemory monitoring and control.

consists of two inter-related levels: the metalevel and an object level. The metalevel is dynamic and assesses the current situation, step by step, and is guided by introspection (e.g., the difficulty of a task). The object level includes a subject's actions and behaviors (e.g., the time allocated to learning) and describes the external situation (e.g., the experimenter-guided repetition of learning). The system is regarded as amounting to constant feedback from one process to the other. Monitoring is the flow of information (metamemory judgments) from the object level to the metalevel. Thus, the metalevel is *informed* by the object level of the given situation (quality of learning). In contrast, the metalevel will modify the object level through metamemory control (allocation of study time, strategies, etc.) (Fig. 5.1).

The metalevel affects object level in that it can be used to direct ongoing behavior. For example, after a first study session, if, according to monitoring, we are highly confident we shall be able to recall the information later, there is no point learning it any more. Moreover, in the absence of time pressure, we spend more time studying difficult items than easy ones (Son and Metcalfe, 2000). If we feel we have not yet retained the information, an adequate form of control would be to learn it again.

In contrast, control affects monitoring. For example, metamemory control will inform the metalevel that a piece of information has been learned twice, and it will be associated with a higher JOL than items that have been learned only once. Therefore, depending on the situation, monitoring affects control and/or control affects monitoring, and they both influence memory performance (Koriat *et al.*, 2006).

THE RELATIONSHIPS BETWEEN METAMEMORY MONITORING AND CONTROL IN PATIENTS WITH SCHIZOPHRENIA

When Control Precedes Monitoring: On Control-Affects-Monitoring in Patients with Schizophrenia

A critical feature of patients' memory effectiveness may be the way they use the information provided by the external situation (the object level), which may help with strategically regulating memorization during the learning phase. The study by Bacon *et al.* (2007) set out to assess the respective contributions of control and monitoring processes towards the strategic regulation of episodic memory function. Participants had to learn 30 pairs of words. One-third of the pairs were presented once, one-third twice, and one-third three times during the learning session. After the learning session, they were asked to express their JOL ('How confident are you that in a few minutes from now you will be able to recall the second word of the pair when prompted with the first?') to predict the likelihood of ultimately recalling the target word during the final test. Then the first word of the pair is presented and participants have to try to provide the second word. The results showed that patients' JOLs were sensitive to learning repetition, in other words the JOLs increased with the repetition of learning sessions. This means the metalevel was correctly informed of the output of the object level (the number of learning sessions). However, as previously evoked, regarding the control process, it should be stressed that the spontaneous control of study time with repetition of learning was impaired in patients taking part in this study. In that particular study, patients failed to adjust the study time allocated to each item to the frequency of its presentation. These results argue in favor of impaired strategic regulation of episodic memory encoding in schizophrenia when patients are not offered the opportunity to ground their behavior in monitoring. Therefore, this study also shows that schizophrenia induces a dissociation between the preserved monitoring and impaired control processes involved in the encoding phase of a memory task.

When Control Follows Monitoring, or the Monitoring-Affects-Control Relationship in Patients with Schizophrenia

As monitoring accuracy is relatively preserved in patients, theoretically they could efficiently ground their subsequent control of the memory task in their accurate judgments. However, as patients are subject to a dissociation between thought and action, it could be that they do not follow the output of monitoring (thought) to control their behavior (action) of an ongoing task. This relationship has been explored in studies exploring episodic (Thuaire *et al.*, 2012) and semantic memory (Danion *et al.*, 2001a).

The aim of the Thuaire *et al.* (2012) study was to establish whether patients can take account of their monitoring to adapt their eventual learning behavior efficiently. After a first learning session of 40 word pairs, participants had to express a JOL reflecting their feeling of being able to retrieve the information subsequently and forming the basis for their decision to carry on learning or not. After this judgment, there was a recall phase. The same 40 word pairs were then presented a second time, and participants themselves had to control how long each pair remained on the screen for relearning purposes. After this second learning phase, there was a final recall phase. The results show that in spite of their memory impairment, patients were able to adapt their learning time appropriately (metamemory control) in the second learning session to the output of their monitoring. In other words, they spent more time relearning items that had received low judgments of learning than those that had received high judgments. So initial monitoring of patients' knowledge helped them to adapt their subsequent metamemory control (relearning time) efficiently.

Monitoring-affects-control has also been explored at the time of memory retrieval in a task assessing semantic memory, which required patients to use their previous judgments. Danion *et al.* (2001a) presented their participants (schizophrenia and healthy participants) with a general knowledge task in which they had to answer under forced-report instructions (i.e., they had to answer each question) and then rate their confidence in the correctness of the response. They were then asked to answer the same question under free-report instructions (i.e., they could refrain from answering some questions), with or without a monetary incentive. How control is grounded on the output of monitoring at the time of memory retrieval may be ascertained by computing a gamma correlation known as *control sensitivity*. It is calculated between the metamemory judgment and the decision whether or not to provide an answer. A value close to one would mean participants were likely to provide items accompanied by a high judgment and to refrain from volunteering information with a low judgment rating (Koriat and Goldsmith, 1996a). The results revealed some degree of impaired control sensitivity in patients with schizophrenia, whose confidence judgments were seen to be somewhat less consistent with their decision criteria for producing an answer. Their control sensitivity was relatively high but remained significantly lower than that of the healthy participants ($P < 0.03$). Therefore, some dissociation between metamemory assessment and subsequent control of a memory task may be observed in patients. It reflects the characteristic thought/action dissociation observed in the clinical schizophrenia environment and may, thus, also have deleterious effects on patients' memory.

CONCLUSION

Patients with schizophrenia are sometimes impaired in terms of subjectively assessing the correctness of their knowledge, but most of the time their discriminative ability and the predictive value of their metamemory monitoring are relatively preserved. Spontaneous control of learning seems to be impaired in patients with schizophrenia (references), but procedures based on 'monitoring-affects-control' seem promising, insofar as patients' control abilities may be enhanced in response to monitoring support at the encoding phase. At retrieval, patients' behavior has been shown to be less determined by subjective experience than that of normal subjects (Danion *et al.*, 2001a). Research into memory-related metacognition in patients with schizophrenia provides some rather optimistic data regarding the ability of patients with schizophrenia to improve their memory efficiency. Future research into ways of supporting metamemory monitoring and control might be useful to patients by guiding them in their learning and retrieval procedures and thus contributing to memory rehabilitation.

The metacognitive approach to memory functioning focuses more on quality than on the ensuing quantity of memory processes. It is closer to the everyday conditions of memory use and focuses on the importance of having a *'Memory as something that can be counted on* (rather than) *a memory as something that can be counted'* (Koriat and Goldsmith, 1996b). Therefore, the subjective states of memory-related consciousness studied in this research field, which currently occupy an important place among the promising new conceptualizations of memory, may not only explain why patients with schizophrenia have behavioral disorders and operation in the daily life, but also open up some original paths for cognitive remediation (Akdogan *et al.*, 2013).

ACKNOWLEDGMENT

The authors would like to thank Estelle Koning for her technical assistance with preparing the manuscript, and Gillian Wakenhut for her careful correction of our English. The authors report no biomedical financial interests or potential conflicts of interest. This research was supported by INSERM.

REFERENCES

Addington, J., & Addington, D. (2000). Neurocognitive and social functioning in schizophrenia: A 2.5 year follow-up study. *Schizophrenia Research*, 7, 47–56.

Akdogan, E., Izaute, M., & Bacon, E. (2013). Preserved strategic grain-size regulation in memory reporting in patients with schizophrenia. *Biological Psychiatry* in press.

Aleman, A., Hijman, R., de Haan, E. H., & Kahn, R. S. (1999). Memory impairment in schizophrenia: A meta-analysis. *American Journal of Psychiatry*, 156, 1358–1366.

Amador, X. F., Flaum, M., Andreasen, N. C., Strauss, D. H., Yale, S. A., Clark, S. C., et al. (1994). Awareness of illness in schizophrenia and schizoaffective and mood disorders. *Archives of General Psychiatry*, 51, 826–836.

Bacon, E., Danion, J. M., Kauffmann-Muller, F., & Bruant, A. (2001). Consciousness in schizophrenia: A metacognitive approach to semantic memory. *Consciousness and Cognition*, 10, 473–484.

Bacon, E., Huet, N., & Danion, J. M. (2011). Metamemory knowledge and beliefs in patients with schizophrenia and how these relate to objective cognitive abilities. *Consciousness and Cognition*, 4, 1315–1326.

Bacon, E., & Izaute, M. (2008). What do patients with schizophrenia know when they cannot remember? *Schizophrenia Bulletin*, 98, 23–24.

Bacon, E., & Izaute, M. (2009). Metacognition in schizophrenia: Processes underlying patients' reflections on their own episodic memory. *Biological Psychiatry*, 66, 1031–1037.

Bacon, E., Izaute, M., & Danion, J. M. (2007). Preserved memory monitoring but impaired memory control during episodic encoding in patients with schizophrenia. *Journal of the International Neuropsychological Society*, 2, 219–227.

Beck, A. T., Baruch, E., Balter, J. M., Steer, R. A., & Warman, D. M. (2004). A new instrument for measuring insight: The Beck Cognitive Insight Scale. *Schizophrenia Research*, 68, 319–329.

Bleuler, E. (1911). Dementia praecox oder gruppe der schizophrenien. In G. Aschaffenburg (Ed.), *Handbuch der Psychiatrie*. Leipzig, Germany: Hälfte.

Bonner-Jackson, A., Haut, K., Csernansky, J. G., & Barch, D. M. (2005). The influence of encoding strategy on episodic memory and cortical activity in schizophrenia. *Biological Psychiatry, 58*, 47–55.

Brébion, G., David, A. S., Jones, H., & Pilowsky, L. S. (2004). Semantic organization and verbal memory efficiency in patients with schizophrenia. *Neuropsychology, 18*, 378–383.

Bryson, G., Whelahan, H. A., & Bell, M. (2001). Memory and executive function impairments in deficit syndrome schizophrenia. *Psychiatry Research, 101*, 247–255.

Cella, M., Swan, S., Medin, E., Reeder, C., & Wykes, T. (2014). Metacognitive awareness of cognitive problems in schizophrenia: Exploring the role of symptoms and self-esteem. *Psychological Medicine, 44*, 469–476.

Christensen, B. K., Girard, T. A., Benjamin, A. S., & Vidailhet, P. (2006). Evidence for impaired mnemonic strategy use among patients with schizophrenia using the part-list cuing paradigm. *Schizophrenia Research, 85*, 1–11.

Cirillo, M. A., & Seidman, L. J. (2003). Verbal declarative memory dysfunction in schizophrenia: From clinical assessment to genetics and brain mechanisms. *Neuropsychology Review, 13*, 43–77.

Danion, J. M., Gokalsing, E., Robert, P., Massin-Krauss, M., & Bacon, E. (2001a). Defective relationship between subjective experience and behavior in schizophrenia. *American Journal of Psychiatry, 158*, 2064–2066.

Danion, J. M., Huron, C., Vidailhet, P., & Berna, F. (2007). Functional mechanisms of episodic memory impairment in schizophrenia. *Canadian Journal of Psychiatry, 52*, 693–701.

Danion, J. M., Rizzo, L., & Bruant, A. (1999). Functional mechanisms underlying impaired recognition memory and conscious awareness in patients with schizophrenia. *Archives of General Psychiatry, 56*, 639–644.

David, A., van Os, J., Jones, P., Harvey, I., Foerster, A., & Fahy, T. (1995). Insight and psychotic illness. Cross-sectional and longitudinal associations. *British Journal of Psychiatry, 167*, 621–628.

Dickinson, D., Iannone, V. N., Wilk, C. M., & Gold, J. M. (2004). General and specific cognitive deficits in schizophrenia. *Biological Psychiatry, 55*, 826–833.

Driesen, N. R., Leung, H. G., Calhoun, V. D., Constable, R. T., Gueorguieva, R., Hoffman, R., et al. (2008). Impairment of working memory maintenance and response in schizophrenia: Functional magnetic resonance imaging evidence. *Biological Psychiatry, 64*, 1026–1034.

Fioravanti, M., Carlone, O., Vitale, B., Cinti, M. E., & Clare, L. (2005). A meta-analysis of cognitive deficits in adults with a diagnosis of schizophrenia. *Neuropsychological Review, 15*, 73–95.

Flavell, J. H. (1971). First discussant's comments: What is memory development the development of? *Human Development, 14*, 272–278.

Flavell, J. H. (1976). Metacognitive aspects of problem solving. In L. B. Resnick (Ed.), *The nature of intelligence* (pp. 231–235). Cambridge, UK: Cambridge University Press. Lawrence Erlbaum Associates, Hillsdale, NJ. Cited in Perfect, T., Schwartz, B., eds. (2002). Applied Metacognition.

Frith, C. D. (1992). *The cognitive neuropsychology of schizophrenia*. London: Psychology Press.

Fujii, D. E., Wylie, A. M., & Nathan, J. H. (2004). Neurocognition and long-term prediction of quality of life in outpatients with severe and persistent mental illness. *Schizophrenia Research, 69*, 67–73.

Gaweda, L., Moritz, S., & Kokoszka, A. (2012). Impaired discrimination between imagined and performed actions in schizophrenia. *Psychiatry Research, 195*, 1–8.

Gras-Vincendon, A., Danion, J. M., Grangé, D., Bilik, M., Willard-Schroeder, D., Sichel, J. P., et al. (1994). Explicit memory, repetition priming and cognitive skill learning in schizophrenia. *Schizophrenia Research*, *13*, 117–126.

Green, M. F. (1996). What are the functional consequences of neurocognitive deficits in schizophrenia? *American Journal of Psychiatry*, *153*, 321–330.

Heinrichs, R. W., & Zakzanis, K. K. (1998). Neurocognitive deficit in schizophrenia: A quantitative review of the evidence. *Neuropsychology*, *12*, 426–445.

Huron, C., Danion, J. M., Giacomoni, F., Grange, D., Robert, P., & Rizzo, L. (1995). Impairment of recognition memory with, but not without, conscious recollection in schizophrenia. *American Journal of Psychiatry*, *152*, 1737–1742.

Izaute, M., & Bacon, E. (2010). Metamemory in schizophrenia: Monitoring or control deficit?. In A. Eckflides & P. Misailidi (Eds.), *Trends and prospects in metacognition research* (pp. 127–148). New York: Springer.

Kazes, M., Berthet, L., Danion, J. M., Amado, I., Willard, D., Robert, P., et al. (1999). Impairment of consciously controlled use of memory in schizophrenia. *Neuropsychology*, *13*, 54–61.

Kern, R. S., Gold, J. M., Dickinson, D., Green, M. F., Nuechterlein, K. H., Baade, L. E., et al. (2011). The MCCB impairment profile for schizophrenia outpatients: Results from the MATRICS psychometric and standardization study. *Schizophrenia Research*, *126*, 124–131.

Koriat, A. (1993). How do we know that we know? The accessibility account of the feeling of knowing. *Psychological Review*, *100*, 609–639.

Koriat, A. (1995). Dissociating knowing and the feeling of knowing: Further evidence for the accessibility model. *Journal of Experimental Psychology: General*, *124*, 311–333.

Koriat, A., & Goldsmith, M. (1996a). Monitoring and control processes in the strategic regulation of memory accuracy. *Psychological Review*, *103*, 490–517.

Koriat, A., & Goldsmith, M. (1996b). Memory as something that can be counted vs. memory as something that can be counted on. In D. J. Herrmann, C. McEvoy, C. Hertzog, P. Hertel, & M. K. Johnson (Eds.), *Basic and applied memory research: Practical application* (vol. 2, pp. 3–18). Hillsdale, NJ: Erlbaum.

Koriat, A., Ma'ayan, H., & Nussinson, R. (2006). The intricate relationships between monitoring and control in metacognition: Lessons for the cause-and-effect relation between subjective experience and behavior. *Journal of Experimental Psychology: General*, *135*, 36–69.

Kraus, M. S., & Keefe, R. S. (2007). Cognition as an outcome measure in schizophrenia. *British Journal of Psychiatry*, *50*(Suppl), 46–51.

Landgraf, S., Steingen, J., Eppert, Y., Niedermeyer, U., van der Meer, E., & Krueger, F. (2011). Temporal information processing in short- and long-term memory of patients with schizophrenia. *PLoS One*, *6*, e26140.

Lewis, R. (2004). Should cognitive deficit be a diagnostic criterion for schizophrenia? *Journal of Psychiatry and Neurosciences*, *29*, 102–113.

Lysaker, P. H., Dimaggio, G., Buck, K. D., Callaway, S. S., Salvatore, G., Carcione, A., et al. (2011). Poor insight in schizophrenia: Links between different forms of metacognition with awareness of symptoms, treatment needed, and consequences of illness. *Comprehensive Psychiatry*, *52*, 253–260.

Lysaker, P. H., Vohs, J. L., Ballard, R., Fogley, R., Salvatore, G., Popolo, R., et al. (2013). Metacognition, self-reflection and recovery in schizophrenia. *Future Neurology*, *8*, 103–115.

Mammarella, N., Altamura, M., Padalino, F. A., Petito, A., Fairfield, B., & Bellomo, A. (2010). False memories in schizophrenia? An imagination inflation study. *Psychiatry Research*, *179*, 267–273.

McGlynn, S. M. (1998). Impaired awareness of deficits in a psychiatric context: Implications for rehabilitation. *Metacognition in Educational Theory and Practice*, 221–248.

Medalia, A., & Thysen, J. (2010). A comparison of insight into clinical symptoms versus insight into neuro-cognitive symptoms in schizophrenia. *Schizophrenia Research, 118*, 134–139.

Medalia, A., Thysen, J., & Freilich, B. (2008). Do people with schizophrenia who have objective cognitive impairment identify cognitive deficits on a self report measure? *Schizophrenia Research, 105*, 156–164.

Mohamed, S., Rosenheck, R., Swartz, M., Stroup, S., Lieberman, J. A., & Keefe, R. S. E. (2008). Relationship of cognition and psychopathology to functional impairment in schizophrenia. *American Journal of Psychiatry, 165*, 978–987.

Monteiro, L. C., Silva, V. A., & Louzã, M. R. (2008). Insight, cognitive dysfunction and symptomatology in schizophrenia. *European Archives of Psychiatry and Clinical Neurosciences, 258*, 402–405.

Moritz, S., & Woodward, T. S. (2006). The contribution of metamemory deficits to schizophrenia. *Journal of Abnormal Psychology, 115*, 15–25.

Moritz, S., Woodward, T. S., & Chen, E. (2006a). Investigation of metamemory dysfunctions in first-episode schizophrenia. *Schizophrenia Research, 81*, 247–252.

Moritz, S., Woodward, T. S., & Rodriguez-Raecke, R. (2006b). Patients with schizophrenia do not produce more false memories than controls but are more confident in them. *Psychological Medicine, 36*, 659–667.

Moritz, S., Woodward, T. S., & Ruff, C. C. (2003). Source monitoring and memory confidence in schizophrenia. *Psychological Medicine, 33*, 131–139.

Moritz, S., Woodward, T. S., Withman, C., & Cuttler, C. (2005). Confidence in errors as a possible basis for delusions in schizophrenia. *Journal of Nervous and Mental Diseases, 193*, 9–16.

Nelson, T., & Narens, T. O. (1994). Why investigate metacognition?. In J. Metcalfe & A. P. Shimamura (Eds.), *Metacognition: Knowing about knowing* (pp. 1–25). Cambridge, MA: The MIT Press.

Nelson, T. O. (1984). A comparison of current measures of the accuracy of feeling-of-knowing predictions. *Psychological Bulletin, 95*, 109–133.

Nelson, T. O., & Dunlosky, J. (1991). When people's judgments of learning (JOLs) are extremely accurate at predicting subsequent recall: The "delayed-JOL effect". *Psychological Science, 2*, 267–270.

Nelson, T. O., & Narens, L. (1990). Metamemory: A theoretical framework and new findings. *Psychology of Learning and Motivation, 25*, 125–173.

Pegoraro, L. F., Dantas, C. R., Banzato, C. E., & Fuentes, D. (2013). Correlation between insight dimensions and cognitive functions in patients with deficit and nondeficit schizophrenia. *Schizophrenia Research, 147*, 91–94.

Perfect, T., & Schwartz, B. (Eds.). (2002). *Applied metacognition*. Cambridge, UK: Cambridge University Press.

Pini, S., de Queiroz, V., Dell'Osso, L., Abelli, M., Mastrocinque, C., Saettoni, M., et al. (2004). Cross-sectional similarities and differences between schizophrenia, schizoaffective disorder and mania or mixed mania with mood-incongruent psychotic features. *European Psychiatry, 19*, 8–14.

Raffard, S., Bayard, S., Capdevielle, D., Garcia, F., Boulenger, J. P., & Gely-Nargeot, M. C. (2008). Lack of insight in schizophrenia: A review. *Encephale, 34*, 511–516.

Ranganath, C., Minzenberg, M. J., & Ragland, D. J. (2008). The cognitive neuroscience of memory function and dysfunction in schizophrenia. *Biological Psychiatry, 64*, 18–25.

Schwartz, B. L., & Bacon, E. (2008). Metacognitive neuroscience. In J. Dunlosky & R. A. Bjork (Eds.), *Handbook of memory and metamemory: Essays in honor of Thomas O. Nelson* (pp. 355–371). New York: Psychology Press.

Son, L. K., & Metcalfe, J. (2000). Metacognitive and control strategies in study-time allocation. *Journal of Experimental Psychology: Learning, Memory and Cognition, 26*, 204–221.

Sonntag, P., Gokalsing, E., Olivier, C., Robert, P., Burglen, F., Kauffmann-Muller, F., et al. (2003). Impaired strategic regulation of contents of conscious awareness in schizophrenia. *Consciousness and Cognition, 12*, 190–200.

Souchay, C., Bacon, E., & Danion, J. M. (2006). Episodic feeling-of-knowing in schizophrenia. *Journal of Clinical and Experimental Neuropsychology, 28*, 828–840.

Sponheim, S. R., Steele, V. R., & McGuire, K. A. (2004). Verbal memory processes in schizophrenia patients and biological relatives of schizophrenia patients: Intact implicit memory, impaired explicit recollection. *Schizophrenia Research, 71*, 339–348.

Stone, W. S., & His, X. (2011). Declarative memory deficits and schizophrenia: Problems and prospects. *Neurobiology of Learning and Memory, 96*, 544–552.

Thuaire, F., Izaute, M., & Bacon, E. (2012). Evidence of some strategic preservation of episodic learning in patients with schizophrenia. *Psychiatry Research, 195*, 27–31.

Tulving, E., & Madigan, S. A. (1970). Memory and verbal learning. *Annual Review of Psychology, 21*, 4437–4485.

Woodward, T. S., Menon, M., & Whitman, J. C. (2007). Source monitoring biases and auditory hallucinations. *Cognitive Neuropsychiatry, 12*, 477–494.

Chapter 6

Metacognition in Schizophrenia Spectrum Disorders: Methods of Assessment and Associations with Psychosocial Function, Neurocognition, Symptoms, and Cognitive Style

Paul H. Lysaker,[1,2] Jaclyn Hillis,[3] Bethany L. Leonhardt,[3] Marina Kukla[1] and Kelly D. Buck[1]

[1]*Richard L. Roudebush VA Medical Center, Indianapolis, IN, USA*
[2]*Indiana University School of Medicine, Indianapolis, IN, USA*
[3]*University of Indianapolis, Indianapolis, IN, USA*

INTRODUCTION

Dysfunction found in schizophrenia is now widely thought to result from an array of biologically based psychopathologic processes often manifest as symptoms and neurocognitive deficits, and social factors such as trauma, poverty, and stigma (e.g., Braff *et al.*, 2007; Light and Braff, 2005; van Os *et al.*,

Social Cognition and Metacognition in Schizophrenia.
DOI: http://dx.doi.org/10.1016/B978-0-12-405172-0.00006-5
© 2014 Elsevier Inc. All rights reserved.

2010). More recent work, however, has stressed that the picture is incomplete without a full consideration of the core psychological processes that help or hinder the efforts of people with schizophrenia to make sense of and live with their condition (Brüne *et al.*, 2011; Lysaker *et al.*, 2010a; Lysaker *et al.*, 2010). Metacognition is one set of psychological processes that may directly affect the degree to which the lives of individuals with schizophrenia are interrupted. Originally used within the educational literature to refer to the ability to think about thinking when learning (Flavell, 1979), metacognition, as illustrated throughout this book, has come to take on a range of meanings including broader processes in which information is integrated into complex and evolving representations of the self and others. Metacognition can be referred to as a spectrum of activities that range from thinking about discrete psychological phenomenon to the synthesis of discrete perceptions into integrated representations of self and others that interact and influence one another, and allow people to evolve ideas of themselves and others in the flow of daily life (Lysaker *et al.*, 2013; Semerari *et al.*, 2003).

In this chapter, we will focus on research concerned with the more synthetic elements of metacognition, namely the complexities of representations of self and others within the personal narrative of schizophrenia. This form of metacognition may intuitively have unique links with function, as it is part of the basis for an evolving, nuanced personal understanding of immediate and long-standing challenges in any human life. However, this type of cognitive activity is naturally difficult to assess, given that at issue is the complexity and richness of a representation or metacognitive act, instead of merely whether a specific thought is accurate or not. In this chapter, we will discuss the use of the Metacognitive Assessment Scale – Abbreviated (MAS-A) as a means to solve this problem and allow for quantitatively assessing synthetic aspects of metacognition. We will present information about the methods to use the scale and its psychometric properties. We will next summarize research on the associations of metacognition in schizophrenia with psychopathology, including neurocognitive deficits and symptoms, psychosocial outcomes, and other factors closely related to outcome including cognitive style, insight, and intrinsic motivation. It is hoped this research can inform the understanding of person-centered psychological processes directly related to recovery and point to potential ways to develop and refine treatment.

ASSESSING SYNTHETIC ASPECTS OF METACOGNITION IN SCHIZOPHRENIA

Many methods exist for assessing more discrete metacognitive and/or social cognitive abilities. These include tasks in which participants are asked to detect when they make an error, determine whether movements on a computer screen mimic their own movements, or they recognize knowing something (Bacon and Izaute, 2009; Fourneret *et al.*, 2002; Koren *et al.*, 2004). While these procedures may assess the accuracy of perceptions, they do not necessarily tap the extent to which larger and integrated ideas are formed about the self and others. Additionally, these tasks are cued in affectively neutral contexts, and may not speak to how people think about thinking in emotion-laden contexts without explicit cues for metacognitive activity.

To measure synthetic metacognitive processes we have developed an interview method that elicits a sample of how people think about themselves and others in an integrated manner and then sought to rate metacognition within that speech sample. The interview is the Indiana Psychiatric Illness Interview (IPII; Lysaker *et al.*, 2002). First, rapport is established and participants are asked to tell the story of their lives. Second, participants are asked if they think they have a mental illness and if so what in their lives has been and not been affected by their condition. Third, they are asked how their condition 'controls' their life and how they 'control' their condition, and fourth, whether it is affected by others and how much others have been affected by it. They are finally asked what they expect to stay the same versus change in the future. The IPII procedures differ from other psychiatric interviews in that they do not introduce content. As a result, a narrative is produced that can be analyzed in terms of the extent to which participants engage or do not engage in synthetic metacognitive activities while thinking about matters of emotional significance.

To quantify synthetic metacognitive capacity within IPII narratives, we have used a modified version of the MAS-A (Lysaker *et al.*, 2005). The MAS-A contains four scales that reflect different forms of metacognitive activity: 'Self-reflectivity', the comprehension of one's own mental states; 'Awareness of the Mind of the Other', the comprehension of other individuals' mental states; 'Decentration', which is the ability to see the world as existing with others having independent motives; and 'Mastery', which is the ability to use knowledge of one's mental states to respond to social and psychological dilemmas. The MAS-A is an adaptation of the Metacognition Assessment Scale (Semerari *et al.*, 2003) made in 2004 in collaboration with the original authors for the study of narrative samples. The primary way in which the MAS-A deviates from the original MAS is that all scales are considered to be dimensional and the Self-reflectivity, Awareness of the Mind of the Other, and Decentration scales are conceptualized as hierarchical in nature.

Most simply, to produce a MAS-A rating, a rater determines the highest level on each subscale that the participant is capable of performing and then that level is the score that is assigned (somewhat more complex rules are involved in scoring and those rules are available in the form of a codebook from the first authors). For instance, if a participant is judged as capable of performing metacognitive acts in the fourth level of the Self-reflectivity scale (having nuanced awareness of one's own emotions) but not the fifth (knowing one's conclusions are fallible) then a score of '4' is assigned for self-reflectivity. For convenience sake, we have listed the abbreviated levels of each of these scales in Table 6.1. As can be seen in Table 6.1, higher scores on each of the

TABLE 6.1 Abbreviated Subscale Presentation.

Level	Self-Reflectivity (S)	Awareness of the Mind of the Other (O)	Decentration (D)	Mastery (M)
0	Unaware of any mental activity	Unaware others have mental activity	One is at center of all events	Unaware of psychological problem
1	Aware of thoughts, unsure thoughts are own	Aware others have mental activity	Others have separate lives outside individual	Aware of implausible problem
2	Aware thoughts are own	Others have mental activity that is their own	Different ways to understand one event	Plausible problem with no response
3	Distinguishes different cognitive operations	Others have different cognitive operations	Events unfold as result of larger, complex factors	Passive response
4	Distinguishes different affective states	Others have different affective states	–	Response seeking support
5	Recognizes thoughts are fallible	Plausible guesses about internal states of others	–	Response with specific action
6	Recognizes wishes are not reality	Complete life description thinking of others across moments	–	Response by altering
7	Integrates thoughts, emotions within narrative	Complete description of others, across larger life story	–	Response based on knowledge of self
8	Integrates several narratives, recognizes patterns over time	–	–	Response based on knowledge of others
9	Recognizes thoughts and emotions connected across larger life story	–	–	Response based on knowledge of large life understanding

MAS-A subscales reflect abilities to perform increasingly complex acts. For instance, higher scores on Self-reflectivity would suggest a capacity to form more complex representations of oneself and higher scores on Mastery would suggest the capacity to use more complex forms of metacognitive knowledge about oneself and others to respond to psychosocial challenges.

THE MAS-A: PSYCHOMETRICS AND ABILITY TO DETECT METACOGNITIVE DEFICITS IN SCHIZOPHRENIA

Since 2004, we have been gathering IPII transcripts and scoring them with the MAS-A. Table 6.2 presents the mean and standard deviations for MAS-A scores obtained for 183 adults with a Structured Clinical Interview for *Diagnostic and Statistical Manual of Mental Disorders*, Fourth Edition (DSM-IV) (SCID), confirmed diagnosis of schizophrenia collected by researchers in Indianapolis, IN. All participants were adults in a nonacute phase of illness. Regarding reliability, across a range of published studies trained raters have produced acceptable to excellent levels of inter-rater reliability. For example, as reported by Lysaker *et al.* (2008), there were significant intraclass correlations for all MAS-A subscales which ranged from $r = 0.61$ (P < 0.05) for Decentration to $r = 0.93$ (P < 0.0001) for the total score. Examination of the stability of 48 cases assessed three points in times over a period of 1 year similarly revealed a significant degree of test–retest stability with the following intraclass correlations: Self-reflectivity: 0.88; Awareness of the Mind of the Other: 0.70 Decentration: 0.68; Mastery: 0.73; and Total: 0.85.

Regarding validity, MAS-A scores in varying studies have been linked with independent assessments of awareness of illness (Lysaker *et al.*, 2005; Nicolo *et al.*, 2012), cognitive insight (Lysaker *et al.*, 2008), complexity of social schema as assessed on the Thematic Apperception Test (Lysaker *et al.*, 2010b), and self-reported coping preference (Lysaker *et al.*, 2011c). Deficits in Self-reflectivity has also been shown to be related to decrements in memory accuracy (Fridberg *et al.*, 2010), and accurate appraisal of one's own work performance (Luedtke *et al.*, 2012).

To examine whether the MAS-A, however, can detect unique forms of metacognitive deficits in schizophrenia, we have gathered a number of comparison samples. These include two groups with psychiatric conditions: one with post-traumatic stress disorder (PTSD) in standard outpatient treatment and one with substance abuse disorders in a residential treatment center. We also have obtained a third comparison group of people with human immunodeficiency virus (HIV)-positive status. The methods for obtaining the IPII and rating it with the MAS-A were identical for the PTSD and substance abuse disorder psychiatric comparison groups. For the HIV-positive group, we modified the IPII to ask about medical illness instead of psychiatric illness. We chose HIV as a comparison group given that it is a condition associated with significant psychosocial adversity and hence any differences found between

TABLE 6.2 Background Information and Analysis of Covariance Comparing Metacognition Scores Controlling for Age and Education.

Score	Schizophrenia (n =183) Group 1	Substance Abuse (n = 59) Group 2	PTSD (n = 26) Group 3	HIV-Positive (n = 51) Group 4	F	Post-Hoc Tests
Age	45.64 (11.85)	43.95 (10.34)	41.13 (11.51)	48.29 (10.93)	3.32*	1,4 > 3; 4 > 2
Education	12.64 (2.18)	13.04 (1.98)	14.41 (1.76)	13.55 (2.24	8.66*	1 < 3,4; 3 > 2
Gender M/F	155/26	55/4	22/4	45/6	–	
Race: African-American/ Caucasian/Latino	73/108/2	44/15	23/2/1	20/29/1	–	
MAS-A						
Self-reflectivity	4.23 (1.37)	6.01 (1.73)	6.19 (1.59)	6.36 (1.62)	38.39**	1 < 2,3,4
Awareness of the Mind of the Other	2.99 (0.98)	3.96 (1.02)	4.32 (1.07)	4.35 (1.25)	30.40**	1 < 2,3,4
Decentration	0.83 (0.86)	1.24 (1.10)	1.48 (0.64)	1.60 (0.87)	11.12**	1 < 2,3,4
Mastery	3.57 (1.73)	3.99 (1.35)	4.75 (1.66)	5.96 (1.46)	28.0**	<3,4; 4 > 2,34
Total	11.59 (4.17)	15.19 (3.70)	16.75 (4.12)	18.27 (4.31)	38.6**	1 < 3,4; 4 > 2,34

PTSD: post-traumatic stress disorder.
*P < 0.05; **P < 0.001.

schizophrenia and HIV-positive participants could not be explained by an absence of psychosocial adversity in the comparison condition.

In a preliminary examination of these data, we have reported that participants with schizophrenia indeed were rated as having significantly poorer metacognitive capacity relative to participants with HIV-positive after controlling for verbal memory (Lysaker *et al.*, 2012a). Comparisons of MAS-A of HIV and schizophrenia samples, now more than doubled in size, along with the PTSD and substance abuse samples are reported in Table 6.2. As Table 6.2 reveals, the schizophrenia group continues to have significantly poorer metacognitive function than the HIV-positive group on all domains. The schizophrenia group also demonstrates poorer metacognitive capacity in the domains of Self-reflectivity, Awareness of the Mind of the Other, and Decentration than the psychiatric comparisons groups. No differences between the three psychiatric groups were found for Mastery, though all three had Mastery scores significantly lower than those of the HIV-positive group. Taken as a whole, these data suggest that the MAS-A may reliably and validly assess synthetic metacognition in schizophrenia and, as a tool, it can identify a pattern of unique metacognitive deficits in schizophrenia relative to at least one prolonged nonpsychiatric medical condition and two nonpsychotic psychiatric conditions (PTSD and substance abuse).

A related question concerns whether the MAS-A can detect metacognitive deficits in people in earlier or later phases of illness. To explore this, Vohs *et al.* (2014) has compared the MAS-A scores of 26 participants with first-episode psychosis, 72 participants with prolonged psychosis, and 14 participants chosen from the substance abuse group if their age was roughly equivalent to those of the first episode group. First episode was defined as the onset of psychosis for a period of 5 years or fewer and prolonged psychosis as a documented onset of illness more than 5 years. Results revealed that participants with first-episode psychosis and prolonged schizophrenia demonstrated lower levels of metacognitive capacity than participants in the control group on all MAS-A subscales except Mastery. In addition, the first-episode group demonstrated a poorer capacity for Awareness of the Mind of the Others and Decentration than the prolonged schizophrenia group. These results suggest that the MAS-A may be sensitive to some forms of especially grave deficits uniquely present early in the illness. Of note, research using somewhat different methods for assessing synthetic metacognition has similarly reported finding deficits in first-episode patients (MacBeth *et al.*, 2014).

ASSOCIATIONS OF METACOGNITION WITH SYMPTOMS AND NEUROCOGNITION

Turning to the issue of the association of metacognition with aspects of illness typically considered to be more biologic in origin, several studies have examined whether having more severe symptoms and neurocognitive deficits is linked with poorer synthetic metacognitive function. The first of these examined whether symptom ratings and performance on neurocognitive testing were correlated with MAS-A scores among 61 men with schizophrenia in a nonacute phase of illness enrolled in outpatient treatment in a vocational rehabilitation program (Lysaker *et al.*, 2005). Greater capacity for Self-reflectivity was linked with better verbal and visual memory, processing speed, and premorbid intelligence. Greater capacities for Awareness of the Mind of the Other and Mastery were related to better verbal memory. Concerning symptoms, greater levels of emotional withdrawal were linked with greater deficits in Self-reflectivity, Awareness of the Mind of the Other, and Mastery. A second study compared assessments of neurocognition and symptoms among a new sample of 68 adults in a nonacute phase of schizophrenia with three different metacognitive profiles: (1) basic Self-reflectivity and Decentration (n = 11); (2) Self-reflectivity but without Decentration (n = 25); and (3) basic Self-reflectivity and Decentration (n = 25). Participants with basic Self-reflectivity had significantly better performances on multiple neurocognitive assessments and fewer negative and disorganized symptoms. Those people with Decentration had better visual memory.

To explore the links between synthetic aspects of metacognition and executive function, MAS-A scores were correlated with selected subtests of the Delis Kaplan Executive Function System (DKEFS; Delis *et al.*, 2001), which includes tests that measure inhibition, set shifting, and mental flexibility (Lysaker *et al.*, 2008). Drawn from the two studies described above, the sample consisted of 49 participants, who completed the DKEFS as part of another study. Results revealed that Self-reflectivity was more closely linked to mental flexibility compared with the other domains of the MAS-A. The ability to inhibit a response was more closely linked to Decentration, Awareness of the Mind of the Other, and Mastery.

Finally, research has explored the links between metacognition and positive and negative symptoms over time in a group of 49 adults with schizophrenia in a stable phase of illness (Hamm *et al.*, 2012). This study found that the total score of the MAS-A was correlated with concurrent and prospective assessments of positive, negative, and disorganization symptoms on the Positive and Negative Symptom Scale (PANSS; Kay *et al.*, 1987). In a multiple regression analysis, the MAS-A total score predicted prospective ratings of negative symptoms, even after covarying for baseline negative symptoms scores. Links between MAS-A scores and negative symptoms have been replicated in an Italian (Nicolò *et al.*, 2012) and Israeli sample (Rabin *et al.*, in press).

As a whole, results suggest that metacognitive ability is associated with symptom expression and neurocognitive impairments in schizophrenia. Possible interpretations include that metacognition may be a risk factor for the emergence of negative symptoms in the future and that as people with schizophrenia are less able to define complex matters in multiple ways, they may have difficulties in sustaining awareness of internal complexities. Similarly, without an ability to inhibit thoughts about events in the world, some may find it difficult to call to mind the perspectives of others and to detect a range of possible reactions others are having in rapidly evolving situations.

ASSOCIATIONS OF METACOGNITION WITH REASONING, AWARENESS, AND LEARNING

Focusing on the issue of the relationship of metacognition to other forms of cognition, other studies have examined whether synthetic aspects of metacognition are related to reasoning style, learning potential, motivation, and the general ability to make sense of psychiatric challenges regardless of clinical status. One of these studies compared assessments of Mastery using the MAS-A with assessments of symptoms, neurocognition, and performance in a probabilistic reasoning task among 40 adults with a schizophrenia spectrum disorder (Buck et al., 2012). Partial correlations controlling for memory, executive function, and symptoms revealed that lower levels of Mastery were associated with a greater propensity to jump to conclusions or to request less information before rendering a judgment.

Tas and colleagues (2012) examined MAS-A scores and found that they were related to learning potential in cognitive remediation experimental training among 32 adults with schizophrenia in a state of symptom remission. Results revealed that initially greater metacognitive capacity was significantly related to higher levels of intrinsic motivation. Patients with higher intrinsic motivation and preserved metacognition also improved more in the learning paradigm. Consistent with the findings of Buck et al. (2012), Mastery was found to be the best independent predictor of learning potential. Vohs and Lysaker (2014) have also examined whether Mastery assessed with the MAS-A predicts prospective levels of intrinsic motivation over a period of 6 months. Seventy-five participants with prolonged schizophrenia were administered the MAS-A, PANSS, and the Quality of Life Scale (QLS; Henrichs et al., 1984). The QLS is a clinician-administered instrument that examines an individual's drive, purpose, curiosity, and engagement in a number of domains. Results indicated that participants with high levels of Mastery demonstrated higher levels of intrinsic motivation across the 6-month period compared with participants with immediate and low levels of Mastery (Vohs et al., 2014).

Finally, Lysaker et al. (2011a) have also investigated the relationship of metacognition with awareness of the symptoms of schizophrenia, treatment need, and consequences of illness. Participants were 65 adults with a schizophrenia spectrum disorder in a nonacute phase of illness. After controlling for neurocognition, regressions revealed that Self-reflectivity was most closely linked to awareness of symptoms of psychosis while Mastery was most closely linked to awareness of treatment and consequence of illness.

Taken as a whole, these studies suggest metacognition is linked to a range of cognitive processes in schizophrenia independent of the effects of psychopathology and neurocognition. Possible interpretations of the data include not being able to use psychological knowledge to solve problems may incline some individuals to give up in the face of uncertainty and accept initial impressions rather than reason more deeply about the issue. Metacognitive capacities, especially Mastery may also increase the potential for learning as well as the potential to experience a range of tasks as intrinsically motivating. Individuals with higher levels of Mastery may also be better able to recognize challenges faced throughout daily activities, and therefore, be able to better solve problems and cope with psychological difficulties.

METACOGNITION AND FUNCTIONAL OUTCOMES

Turning to the issue of functional outcome, several studies have also suggested that metacognition may play a role in the ability to function successfully in both social and work settings. Concerning work function, Lysaker *et al.* (2010a) examined whether self-reflectivity predicted work performance measured every other week for 6 months for 56 participants with schizophrenia enrolled in a vocational rehabilitation program. Participants were divided into three groups on the basis of their Self-reflectivity score: high (n = 13), intermediate (n = 21), and low (n = 22). A repeated measures analysis of variance comparing work performance scores revealed that the high Self-reflectivity group had significantly better work performance than the other two groups. Significant group differences persisted after controlling for executive function.

Lysaker *et al.* (2010c) investigated whether the impact of neurocognition upon social function was mediated by Mastery among 102 adults with schizophrenia. Neurocognition was assessed using a small battery, which was reduced to a single index using a Principal Components Analysis. Subsequently, structural equation modeling techniques were used to test the model that the capacity for Mastery mediated the impact of neurocognition upon the quality and quantity of social relationships, controlling for symptoms. Results revealed that an acceptable level of goodness of fit was observed between the model and data. In a follow-up to this study, a second path analysis was conducted to determine whether the cross-sectional relationships observed above persisted when considering assessments of the same variables gathered 5 months later (Lysaker *et al.*, 2011b). The model tests specified that Mastery predicted concurrent social function, and affected Mastery 5 months later, which similarly affected social function 5 months later. Acceptable levels of fit were found for the proposed model.

Concerning relationships that form within treatment, Davis *et al.* (2011) examined the link between metacognitive Mastery and a therapeutic alliance in individual cognitive therapy. Participants were 63 adults in a nonacute phase of schizophrenia who engaged in cognitive therapy and completed assessments of therapeutic alliance using the Working Alliance Inventory – Short Form (Milne *et al.*, 2001). A repeated measures analysis of variance revealed that participants with initially high levels of Mastery (n = 8) reported greater levels of therapeutic alliance when compared with others rated as having intermediate (n = 38) and minimal (n = 17) Mastery. Regarding functional competence in terms of community function, Lysaker *et al.* (2011d) examined the relationship between metacognition and performance on an assessment of functional skills, the University of California, San Diego (UCSD) Performance-Based Skills Assessment Battery (UPSA; Patterson *et al.*, 2001) among 45 adults in a postacute phase of schizophrenia. The UPSA is a measure that assesses competence with everyday living skills. Correlational analyses revealed that scores on greater levels of Mastery on the MAS-A were linked with the comprehension/planning subscale of the UPSA, after controlling for symptoms and executive function.

Regarding adherence to social mores and criminality, Bo *et al.* (2013) have examined whether metacognition among 108 forensic patients with schizophrenia with histories of premeditated versus impulsive aggression. MAS-A total scores were found to be linked with histories of premeditated forms of aggression. Reanalysis of these data revealed that Awareness of the Mind of the Other moderated the effects of personality factors on aggression (Bo *et al.*, 2014). Specifically, participants with lesser capacities for Awareness of the Mind of the Other and increased psychopathy were more likely to report engagement in premeditated aggression.

Concerning subjective aspects of recovery Kukla *et al.* (2013) examined the association of the MAS-A and Recovery Assessment Scale (RAS; Corrigan *et al.*, 2004) among 45 adults with schizophrenia. Results revealed that, after controlling for symptoms, Self-reflectivity was linked with less domination by symptoms and greater Decentration with the experience of being able to seek support from others. Nabors *et al.* (2014) has similarly examined the association of metacognition with internalized stigma as measured using the Internalized Stigma of Mental Illness Scale (Ritsher *et al.*, 2003) among 65 adults with schizophrenia. Results indicated that greater levels of metacognitive capacity were linked with greater abilities to resist stigma after controlling for symptoms and stereotyped endorsement.

Taken together, results are consistent with initial speculations that metacognition plays a role in the functional outcomes in schizophrenia. Results suggest that with lesser metacognitive capacities, people with schizophrenia are less able to function over time in work settings and to form and sustain connections with others. They may also play a role in expressions of criminality as well as the self-perception of wellness.

SUMMARY

This chapter has reviewed research on the use of the MAS-A to investigate links between synthetic forms of metacognition in schizophrenia. Results supporting the reliability and validity of the MAS-A were provided along with evidence that these deficits are detectable in patients with schizophrenia, and that deficits are related to symptoms, and neurocognition, and to a range of other outcomes independent of the effects of symptom severity and poorer neurocognitive function. As such, evidence was reported that suggests these deficits may represent a unique impediment to the recovery nonacute phase of schizophrenia.

There were important issues not discussed. In particular, the issue of etiology has not been discussed. Indeed, it is unclear whether these are phenomena that predate the illness and/or whether they can result from a number of different causal influences, including atrophy, loss of cognitive functioning, attachment style, or exposure, and response to trauma. It was also not discussed how the construct of metacognition converges and diverges with related constructs, including social cognition, mentalization, and emotional intelligence. We also explored one method for assessing metacognitive activities and future work is needed considering other methods for assessing autobiographical memory (Bennouna-Greene et al., 2011; Raffard et al., 2010), as well as other methods for rating synthetic metacognitive function (Mitchell et al., 2012). Given space considerations, we have not explored a range of other important developments using the MAS-A. For instance, Ladegaard et al. (2014; personal communication) has reported evidence of significant metacognitive deficits in patients with first-episode and prolonged depression. Jansen et al. (in press) have also found that greater levels of metacognitive capacity in caretakers of first-episode patients was linked with more positive experiences of caretaking while Lysaker et al. (2014) have found that Mastery moderates the relationship of alexithymia with severity of cluster C traits among adults with substance abuse disorders.

Regarding the research to date, there are several limitations. Participants have tended to be males in a later stage of illness enrolled in treatment. Replication is needed with broader samples including women, and people who reject treatment. Consideration of gender is important given some findings that women with schizophrenia may have greater metacognitive capacities then men (Abu-Akel and Bo, 2013). Long-term longitudinal work is also needed to understand the relationships suggested above better.

REFERENCES

Abu-Akel, A., & Bo, S. (2013). Superior mentalizing abilities of female patients with schizophrenia. *Psychiatry Research, 210*(3), 794–799.

Bacon, E., & Izaute, M. (2009). Metacognition in schizophrenia: Processes underlying patients' reflections on their own episodic memory. *Biological Psychiatry, 66*(11), 1031–1037.

Bo, S., Abu-Akel, A., Bertelsen, P., Kongerslev, M., & Haahr, U. H. (2013). Attachment, mentalizing and personality pathology severity in premeditated and impulsive aggression in schizophrenia. *International Journal of Forensic Mental Health, 12,* 126–138.

Bo, S., Abu-Akel, A., Kongerslev, M., Haahr, U. H., & Batemann, A. (2014). Mentalizing mediates the relationship between psychopathy and type of aggression in schizophrenia. *Journal of Nervous and Mental Disease, 202*(1), 55–63.

Braff, D., Freedman, R., Schork, N., & Gottesman, I. (2007). Deconstructing schizophrenia: An overview of the use of endophenotypes in order to understand a complex disorder. *Schizophrenia Bulletin*, *33*(1), 21–32.

Brüne, M., Dimaggio, G., & Lysaker, P. H. (2011). Metacognition and social functioning in schizophrenia: Evidence, mechanisms of influence and treatment implications. *Current Psychiatry Reviews*, *7*(3), 239–247.

Buck, K. D., Warman, D. M., Huddy, V., & Lysaker, P. H. (2012). The relationship of metacognition with jumping to conclusions among persons with schizophrenia spectrum disorders. *Psychopathology*, *45*(5), 271–275.

Corrigan, P. W., Salzer, M., Ralph, R. O., Sangster, Y., & Keck, L. (2004). Examining the factor structure of the Recovery Assessment Scale. *Schizophrenia Bulletin*, *30*(4), 1035–1041.

Davis, L. W., Eicher, A. C., & Lysaker, P. H. (2011). Metacognition as a predictor of therapeutic alliance over 26 weeks of psychotherapy in schizophrenia. *Schizophrenia Research*, *129*(1), 85–90.

Delis, D. C., Kaplan, E., & Kramer, J. H. (2001). *Delis-Kaplan executive function system: Technical manual*. San Antonio, TX: The Psychological Corporation.

Flavell, J. H. (1979). Metacognition and cognitive monitoring: A new area of cognitive-developmental inquiry. *American Psychologist*, *34*(10), 906–911.

Fourneret, P., de Vignemont, F., Franck, N., Slachevsky, A., Dubois, B., & Jeannerod, M. (2002). Perception of self-generated action in schizophrenia. *Cognitive Neuropsychiatry*, *7*(2), 139–156.

Fridberg, D. J., Brenner, A., & Lysaker, P. H. (2010). Verbal memory intrusions in schizophrenia: Associations with self-reflectivity, symptomatology, and neurocognition. *Psychiatry Research*, *179*(1), 6–11.

Hamm, J. A., Renard, S. B., Fogley, R. L., Leonhardt, B. L., Dimaggio, G., Buck, K. D., et al. (2012). Metacognition and social cognition in schizophrenia: Stability and relationship to concurrent and prospective symptom assessments. *Journal of Clinical Psychology*, *68*(12), 1303–1312.

Henrichs, D. W., Hanlon, T. E., & Carpenter, W. T. (1984). The quality of life scale: An instrument for assessing the schizophrenic deficit syndrome. *Schizophrenia Bulletin*, *10*, 388–396.

Jansen, J. E., Lysaker, P. H., Harder, S., Haahr, U., Lyse, H. G., Pedersen, M. B., et al. (in press). Predictions of positive and negative experiences of caregiving in adults with first-episode psychosis: Emotional overinvolvement, wellbeing and metacognition. *Psychology and Psychotherapy*.

Kay, S., Fiszbein, A., & Opler, L. (1987). The positive and negative syndrome scale (PANSS) for schizophrenia. *Schizophrenia Bulletin*, *13*(2), 261–276.

Koren, D., Seidman, L. J., Poyurovsky, M., Goldsmith, M., Viksman, P., Zichel, S., et al. (2004). The neuropsychological basis of insight in first-episode schizophrenia: A pilot metacognitive study. *Schizophrenia Research*, *70*(2/3), 195–202.

Kukla, M., Lysaker, P. H., & Salyers, M. (2013). Do persons with schizophrenia who have better metacognitive capacity also have a stronger subjective experience of recovery? *Psychiatry Research*, *209*(3), 381–385.

Ladegaard, N., Larsen, E. R., Videbech, P., & Lysaker, P. H. (2014). Higher-order social cognition in first-episode major depression. *Psychiatry Research*, *216*(1), 37–43.

Light, G. A., & Braff, D. L. (2005). Mismatch negativity deficits are associated with poor functioning in schizophrenia patients. *Archives of General Psychiatry*, *62*(2), 127–136.

Luedtke, B. L., Kukla, M., Renard, S., Dimaggio, G., Buck, K. D., & Lysaker, P. H. (2012a). Metacognitive functioning and social cognition as predictors of accuracy of self-appraisals of vocational function in schizophrenia. *Schizophrenia Research*, *137*(1–3), 260–261.

Lysaker, P. H., Carcione, A. A., Dimaggio, G. G., Johannesen, J. K., Nicol, G. G., Procacci, M. M., et al. (2005). Metacognition amidst narratives of self and illness in schizophrenia: Associations with neurocognition, symptoms, insight and quality of life. *Acta Psychiatrica Scandinavica, 112*(1), 64–71.

Lysaker, P. H., Clements, C. A., Plascak-Hallberg, C. D., Knipscheer, S. J., & Wright, D. E. (2002). Insight and personal narratives of illness in schizophrenia. *Psychiatry: Interpersonal and Biological Processes, 65*(3), 197–206.

Lysaker, P. H., Dimaggio, G., Buck, K. D., Callaway, S. S., Salvatore, G., Carcione, A., et al. (2011a). Poor insight in schizophrenia: Links between different forms of metacognition with awareness of symptoms, treatment need, and consequences of illness. *Comprehensive Psychiatry, 52*(3), 253–260.

Lysaker, P. H., Dimaggio, G., Carcione, A., Procacci, M., Buck, K. D., Davis, L. W., et al. (2010a). Metacognition and schizophrenia: The capacity for self-reflectivity as a predictor for prospective assessments of work performance over six months. *Schizophrenia Research, 122*(1–3), 124–130.

Lysaker, P. H., Dimaggio, G., Daroyanni, P., Buck, K. D., LaRocco, V. A., Carcione, A., et al. (2010b). Assessing metacognition in schizophrenia with the Metacognition Assessment Scale: Associations with the Social Cognition and Object Relations Scale. *Psychology and Psychotherapy: Theory, Research and Practice, 83*(3), 303–315.

Lysaker, P. H., Erickson, M. A., Buck, B., Buck, K. D., Olesek, K., Grant, M. A., et al. (2011b). Metacognition and social function in schizophrenia: Associations over a period of five months. *Cognitive Neuropsychiatry, 16*(3), 241–255.

Lysaker, P. H., Erickson, M. A., Ringer, J. M., Buck, K. D., Semerari, A., Carcione, A., et al. (2011c). Metacognition in schizophrenia: The relationship of mastery to coping, insight, self-esteem, social anxiety, and various facets of neurocognition. *British Journal of Clinical Psychology, 50*(4), 412–424.

Lysaker, P. H., Glynn, S. M., Wilkniss, S. M., & Silverstein, S. M. (2010). Psychotherapy and recovery from schizophrenia: A review of potential applications and need for future study. *Psychological Services, 7*(2), 75–91.

Lysaker, P. H., McCormick, B. P., Snethen, G., Buck, K. D., Hamm, J. A., Grant, M., et al. (2011d). Metacognition and social function in schizophrenia: Associations of mastery with functional skills competence. *Schizophrenia Research, 131*(1–3), 214–218.

Lysaker, P. H., Olesek, K., Buck, K. D., Leonhardt, B. L., Vohs, J., Ringer, J., et al. (2014). Metacognitive mastery moderates the relationship of alexithymia with cluster C personality disorder traits in adults with substance use disorders. *Addictive Behaviors, 39*(3), 558–561.

Lysaker, P. H., Ringer, J. M., Buck, K. D., Grant, M. L. A., Olesek, K., Leudtke, B., et al. (2012a). Metacognitive and social cognition deficits in patients with significant psychiatric and medical adversity: A comparison between participants with schizophrenia and a sample of participants who are HIV-positive. *Journal of Nervous & Mental Disease, 200*(2), 130–134.

Lysaker, P. H., Shea, A. M., Buck, K. D., Dimaggio, G. G., Nicolò, G. G., Procacci, M. M., et al. (2010c). Metacognition as a mediator of the effects of impairments in neurocognition on social function in schizophrenia spectrum disorders. *Acta Psychiatrica Scandinavica, 122*(5), 405–413.

Lysaker, P. H., Vohs, J., Ballard, R., Fogley, R., Salvatore, R., Salvatore, G., et al. (2013). Metacognition, self reflection and recovery in schizophrenia: Review of the literature. *Future Neurology, 8*, 103–115.

Lysaker, P. H., Warman, D. M., Dimaggio, G., Procacci, M., LaRocco, V. A., Clark, L. K., et al. (2008). Metacognition in schizophrenia: Associations with multiple assessments of executive function. *Journal of Nervous and Mental Disease, 196*(5), 384–389.

Macbeth, A., Gumley, A., Schwannauer, M., Carcione, A., Fisher, R., McLeod, H. J., et al. (2014). Metacognition, symptoms and premorbid functioning in a first episode psychosis sample. *Comprehensive Psychiatry*, *55*(2), 268–273.

Milne, D., Claydon, T., Blackburn, I., James, I., & Sheikh, A. (2001). Rationale for a new measure of competence in therapy. *Behavioural and Cognitive Psychotherapy*, *29*(1), 21–33.

Mitchell, L. J., Gumley, A. I., Reilly, E. S., Macbeth, A., Lysaker, P. H., Carcione, A., et al. (2012). Metacognition in forensic patients with schizophrenia and a past history of interpersonal violence: An exploratory study. *Psychosis*, *4*(1), 42–51.

Nabors, L. M., Yanos, P. T., Roe, D., Hasson-Ohayon, I., Leonhardt, B. L., Buck, K. D. et al. (2014). Stereotype endorsement, metacognitive capacity, and self-esteem as predictors of stigma resistance in persons with schizophrenia. *Comprehensive Psychiatry*, *55*(4), 792–798.

Nicolò, G., Dimaggio, G., Popolo, R., Carcione, A., Procacci, M., Hamm, J., et al. (2012). Associations of metacognition with symptoms, insight, and neurocognition in clinically stable outpatients with schizophrenia. *Journal of Nervous and Mental Disease*, *200*(7), 644–647.

Patterson, T., Goldman, S., McKibbin, C., Hughs, T., & Jeste, D. (2001). UCSD Performance-Based Skills Assessment: Development of a new measure of everyday functioning for severely mentally ill adults. *Schizophrenia Bulletin*, *27*(2), 235–245.

Rabin, S. J., Hasson-Ohayon, I., Avidan, M., Rozencwaig, S., Shalev, H., & Kravetz, S. (in press). Metacognition in schizophrenia and schizotypy: Relations to symptoms and social quality of life, Israeli. *Journal of Psychiatry*.

Raffard, S., D'Argembeau, A., Bayard, S., Boulenger, J., & Van der Linden, M. (2010). Scene construction in schizophrenia. *Neuropsychology*, *24*(5), 608–615.

Ritsher, J., Otilingam, P. G., & Grajales, M. (2003). Internalized stigma of mental illness: Psychometric properties of a new measure. *Psychiatry Resarch*, *121*, 31–49.

Semerari, A., Carcione, A., Dimaggio, G., Falcone, M., Nicolo, G., Procacci, M., et al. (2003). How to evaluate metacognitive functioning in psychotherapy? The Metacognition Assessment Scale and its applications. *Clinical Psychology & Psychotherapy*, *10*(4), 238–261.

Tas, C., Brown, E. C., Esen-Danaci, A., Lysaker, P. H., & Brüne, M. (2012). Intrinsic motivation and metacognition as predictors of learning potential in patients with remitted schizophrenia. *Journal of Psychiatric Research*, *46*(8), 1086–1092.

van Os, J., Kenis, G., & Rutten, B. F. (2010). The environment of schizophrenia. *Nature*, *468*(7321), 203–212.

Vohs, J., & Lysaker, P. H. (2014). Metacognitive mastery and intrinsic motivation in schizophrenia. *Journal of Nervous and Mental Disease*, *202*(1), 74–77.

Vohs, J. L, Lysaker, P. H., Francis, M., Hamm, J., Buck, K. D., Olesek, K., et al. (2014). Metacognition, social cognition, and symptoms in patients with first episode and prolonged psychosis. *Schizophrenia Research*, *153*(1–3), 54–59.

Chapter 7

The Impact of Metacognition on the Development and Maintenance of Negative Symptoms

Hamish J. McLeod,[1] Andrew Gumley[1] and Matthias Schwannauer[2]

[1]*University of Glasgow, Glasgow, UK,*
[2]*University of Edinburgh, Edinburgh, UK*

Chapter Outline

INTRODUCTION

'The mind is not a vessel to be filled but a fire to be kindled'

Plutarch, Greek Essayist, AD 46–120

Classical views of the negative symptoms of schizophrenia include phenomena such as loss of motivational drive, a reduced capacity for experiencing pleasure, disengagement from social interaction, and a dramatic reduction of the normal flow of mental experience. These symptoms are a major source of reduced quality of life (Ho *et al.*, 1998) and caregiver burden (Provencher and Mueser, 1997) and are often a harbinger of poor clinical outcome and arrested recovery (Milev *et al.*, 2005). For many, the response of these symptoms to

Social Cognition and Metacognition in Schizophrenia.
DOI: http://dx.doi.org/10.1016/B978-0-12-405172-0.00007-7
© 2014 Elsevier Inc. All rights reserved.

pharmacologic treatment is modest at best (Barnes and Paton, 2011), and so there is a major need for the development of other viable treatments. At present, there is promising preliminary evidence that psychological thera- pies for negative symptoms may be of some therapeutic benefit but the over- all results to date leave substantial room for improvement. In this chapter, we will review how the conceptualization of negative symptoms had evolved over time and the possible implications of this for targeted psychological thera- pies. Current psychological treatment approaches will then be examined with a view to identifying theoretical gaps and opportunities for therapeutic inno- vation and improvement. The final sections will explore how taking a meta- cognitive approach to therapeutic formulation and treatment has the potential to expand our options for rekindling the fire of recovery in people who have experienced a severe loss of the capacity to engage with the challenges and joys that life has to offer.

NEGATIVE SYMPTOMS: AN OVERVIEW OF KEY CONCEPTS AND DISTINCTIONS

The distinction between positive and negative symptoms of psychiatric and neurologic diseases can be traced to 19th century accounts of how cerebral pathology can both create new symptoms (e.g., hallucinations, tremor) as well as abolishing or diminishing normal functioning (Carpenter *et al.*, 1988; Mäkinen *et al.*, 2008; Messinger *et al.*, 2011). Hence, symptoms such as apa- thy and anhedonia are abnormal because of what is missing in the behavio- ral and experiential repertoire of the patient. Such negative symptoms are not exclusive to schizophrenia; they can feature in both neurologic illnesses, such as Parkinson disease, and psychiatric conditions, such as melancholic depres- sion (Mäkinen *et al.*, 2008; Messinger *et al.*, 2011; Winograd-Gurvich *et al.*, 2006). Although prototypical negative symptoms such as 'indifference' were evident in the early descriptions provided by Kraepelin and Bleuler, it was the late 1960s before the modern distinction between positive and negative symptoms began to gain traction in the schizophrenia literature (Messinger *et al.*, 2011). By 1978, the publication of a scale for rating emotional blunt- ing saw the emergence of modern attempts to subject negative symptoms to structured assessment and quantification (Abrams and Taylor, 1978). The pub- lication of the Scale for the Assessment of Positive Symptoms (SAPS)/Scale for the Assessment of Negative Symptoms (SANS) and Positive and Negative Syndrome Scale (PANSS) in the 1980s further helped make the negative symptoms of schizophrenia spectrum disorders a viable target for research. Crow's (1985) conceptual paper arguing that positive and negative syndromes of schizophrenia have different neuropathologic origins, course, and progno- ses brought this distinction into sharper focus and helped promote the view that careful analysis of the subtypes of symptoms of schizophrenia would be a more productive way forward.

NEGATIVE SYMPTOM SUBTYPES

The subtypes of negative symptoms are often summarized as the 'five A's': affective flattening, alogia, anhedonia, asociality, and avolition (Kirkpatrick *et al.*, 2006; Messinger *et al.*, 2011). However, the content of negative symptom assessment scales over time reflects an evolving view of how negative symptoms should be conceptualized and subtyped. Table 7.1 portrays the progression of negative symptom measures from the Emotional Blunting Scale (Abrams and Taylor, 1978) through to the Clinical Assessment Interview for Negative Symptoms (CAINS) (Kring *et al.*, 2013). Although there is heterogeneity at the level of scale items, some themes are readily apparent. Abnormalities of emotional expression (e.g., restricted facial displays, reduced emotional signaling in voice tone) and diminished drive and motivation (e.g., reduced spontaneity) feature prominently. This is consistent with the accumulating evidence that the negative symptom syndrome is comprised of two main factors encompassing diminished emotional expression and disturbed motivation/volition (Blanchard *et al.*, 2005; Kring *et al.*, 2013; Messinger *et al.*, 2011).

More refined methods for subtyping and characterizing negative symptoms should help to address a number of anomalies in the literature, such as the wide variation in estimates of prevalence (ranging from 30% to 90% across studies). There is also clinical and theoretical value of distinguishing patients who experience negative symptoms as a *predominant* symptom (e.g., type II schizophrenia or deficit syndrome) (Carpenter *et al.*, 1988; Crow, 1985) versus those whose negative symptoms present alongside positive symptoms (*prominent* negative symptoms). This predominant versus prominent distinction is sometimes framed as a difference between primary versus secondary negative symptoms (Carpenter *et al.*, 1988) where the same observed behavior may be mediated by very different psychological processes. For example, social withdrawal can arise from a fundamental loss of drive to seek out normal social contact (a *primary* negative symptom) or may be a coping response to deal with paranoid and persecutory thoughts (a *secondary* negative symptom). Hence, secondary negative symptoms will diminish when any associated positive symptoms remit while, in contrast, any change in primary negative symptoms will be unrelated to positive symptoms. The existence of this deficit syndrome subgroup is borne out by latent taxon analysis that indicates that about one-third of people with schizophrenia fall into a discrete subgroup characterized by the presence of primary negative symptoms (Blanchard *et al.*, 2005).

To summarize, the research discussed above indicates that the negative symptoms of schizophrenia can be divided into an avolition-apathy (AA) and diminished expression (DE) subtypes (Foussias *et al.*, 2011) and this two-factor formulation is now echoed in newer negative symptom measures (Kring *et al.*, 2013). In addition, there is now robust evidence that the profile of negative symptoms varies across patients with about one-third presenting with predominant negative symptoms consistent with the concept of a discrete deficit

TABLE 7.1 Content of Common Clinician-Administered Negative Symptom Rating Scales (1978–2013).

Emotional Blunting Scale[1]	SANS[2]	Original PANSS Negative Symptom Subscale[3]	PANSS Five-Factor Model Negative Symptom Subscale[4]	CAINS[5]
1. Absent, shallow, incongruous mood	1. Affective flattening or blunting	N1 Blunted affect	N1 Blunted affect	**Experience/Pleasure Subscale**
2. Constricted affect	2. Alogia	N2 Emotional withdrawal	N2 Emotional withdrawal	1. Social: family relationships
3. Unvarying affect	3. Avolition-apathy	N3 Poor rapport	N3 Poor rapport	2. Social: friendships
4. Unrelated affect	4. Anhedonia-asociality	N4 Apathetic social withdrawal	N4 Apathetic social withdrawal	3. Social: past-week pleasure
5. Expressionless face	5. Attention	N5 Difficulty in abstract thinking	N6 Lack of spontaneity	4. Social: expected pleasure
6. Unvarying monotonous voice		N6 Lack of spontaneity	G7 Motor retardation	5. Vocational: motivation
7. Seclusive/withdrawn, avoids social contact		N7 Stereotyped thinking	G16 Active social avoidance	6. Vocational: expected pleasure
8. Lacks social graces				7. Recreation: motivation
9. Difficult to excite emotions/unresponsive				8. Recreation: past-week pleasure
10. Lacks spontaneity				9. Recreation: expected pleasure
11. Causeless/silly laughter, silly disposition				**Expression Subscale**
12. Indifferent to surroundings				10. Expression: facial
13. Indifference/lack of affection for family/friends				11. Expression: vocal prosody
14. Indifference/unconcern for own present situation				12. Expression: gestures
15. Indifference/unconcern for own future				13. Expression: speech
16. Paucity of thought				

[1]*Emotional Blunting Scale (Abrams and Taylor, 1978)*;
[2]*Scale for the Assessment of Negative Symptoms (SANS) (Andreasen, 1984)*;
[3]*Positive and Negative Symptom Scale (PANSS) (Kay et al., 1987)*;
[4]*Positive and Negative Symptom Scale – Five Factor Model (van der Gaag et al., 2006)*;
[5]*Clinical Assessment Interview for Negative Symptoms (CAINS) (Kring et al., 2013)*.

syndrome (Blanchard and Cohen, 2006; Carpenter *et al.*, 1988). In other patient subgroups, the presence of co-occurring positive and negative symptoms may give rise to both primary and secondary negative symptom expression. The next section examines the potential implications of these distinctions for understanding the emergence and course of negative symptom expression.

FACTORS AFFECTING THE DEVELOPMENT AND COURSE OF NEGATIVE SYMPTOMS

Negative symptoms are evident from the earliest stages of schizophrenia, including in people at ultra-high risk (Piskulic *et al.*, 2012) and those in their first episode of psychosis (Chang *et al.*, 2011; Lyne *et al.*, 2012). Over the longer term course of schizophrenia the presence of negative symptoms is associated with a poorer prognosis than either positive or disorganization symptoms (Pogue-Geile and Harrow, 1985; Rabinowitz *et al.*, 2012). Because negative symptoms are generally a poor prognostic factor, there is considerable interest in determining what may affect their emergence and diminish their negative impact over time.

At the general symptom level, the risk factors for negative symptom development include longer duration of untreated psychosis (DUP; Boonstra *et al.*, 2012), male gender (Esterberg *et al.*, 2010), a family history of psychosis (Esterberg and Compton, 2012; Esterberg *et al.*, 2010), and poor premorbid functioning in social and academic domains (Cannon-Spoor *et al.*, 1982). However, closer analysis of specific negative symptom clusters indicates that the subtype of negative symptoms that are exhibited exerts a differential effect on outcome. For example, deficit syndrome patients presenting with DE negative symptoms may have relatively better outcomes than those exhibiting the AA subtype (Strauss *et al.*, 2013). Hence, fundamental problems with drive and motivation appear to exert a more pernicious and disabling effect than deficits of expressive deficits.

Given that negative symptoms are a bad prognostic sign, it is also relevant to examine the rates of symptom recovery and remission. The original formulation of the deficit syndrome presented primary negative symptoms as enduring, recalcitrant, and treatment resistant (Carpenter *et al.*, 1988). This presents a relatively bleak and pessimistic picture that is partly borne out by the limited available longitudinal data. One 20-year repeated measures study that included patients with deficit syndrome found that that only 13% experienced at least one episode of symptom remission lasting more than 1 year (Strauss *et al.*, 2010). Although this indicates that periods of recovery are possible for a small proportion of these patients, this recovery profile was significantly poorer than that seen for comparison patients with nondeficit schizophrenia (63%) or depression (77%). Although there is some evidence that negative symptoms may be equally responsive to pharmacologic intervention in deficit versus nondeficit syndrome presentations (Stauffer *et al.*, 2012), it is also apparent that the course of negative symptoms is generally resistant to pharmacologic intervention (Barnes and Paton, 2011). This generally modest response to standard medical treatments has stimulated some interest in determining whether the course of negative symptoms can be modified through psychosocial therapies. As discussed in the following section, some of the preliminary data suggest that there may be scope to make a meaningful impact on negative symptom expression through psychological interventions.

PSYCHOLOGICAL THERAPIES FOR NEGATIVE SYMPTOMS

A number of targeted psychological interventions have shown promise in the treatment of negative symptoms. A diverse range of approaches now have some empirical support including cognitive therapy (Grant et al., 2012; Klingberg et al., 2011; Staring et al., 2013), body-oriented psychotherapy (BPT) (Priebe et al., 2013; Röhricht and Priebe, 2006), cognitive remediation therapy (CRT) (Klingberg et al., 2011), and loving kindness meditation (Johnson et al., 2011). Overall, the results of the main trials presented in Table 7.2 provide preliminary evidence that the prospect of therapeutic change for negative symptoms may be better than previously assumed. All of the interventions show at least within subject pre–post treatment effects in relevant domains such as general functioning (Grant et al., 2012), overall negative symptoms (Staring et al., 2013), or specific negative symptoms such as affective blunting (Röhricht and Priebe, 2006). However, closer scrutiny of the results suggests that there is considerable scope for refinement of the treatment models and understanding the mechanisms of therapeutic improvement.

One striking pattern evident in the results is that therapeutic gains appear possible with quite different treatments targeting very different therapeutic mechanisms of change. In the case of BPT, the argument is that the nonverbal nature of negative symptoms such as emotional withdrawal and psychomotor retardation make them most amenable to therapy approaches that are nonverbal in nature. BPT emphasizes increasing physical movement as a way of promoting sensory awareness and re-engagement with the environment. In contrast, the cognitive model of negative symptoms proposes that negative symptoms are attributable to specific cognitive processes, namely negative appraisals about personal abilities, personal resources, likelihood of success, and likelihood of enjoyment (Rector et al., 2005). Such 'defeatist cognitions' are argued to mediate the expression of diminished drive, social withdrawal, and disengagement from goal pursuit (Grant and Beck, 2009; Grant and Beck, 2010). All of the three trials that applied this cognitive model showed pre–post treatment within subject improvement in either general functioning or negative symptom ratings (see Table 7.2). However, only one study tested the mediating role of defeatist cognitions on negative symptom outcome and this analysis showed only partial evidence of mediation (Staring et al., 2013). Furthermore, the control treatment in one trial, cognitive remediation therapy (CRT), also

TABLE 7.2 Summary of Psychological Therapy Treatment Trials Specifically Targeting Negative Symptoms.

Study	Sample Characteristics	Active Intervention(s)	Primary and Secondary Outcomes	Main Findings
Röhricht and Priebe (2006)	45 patients with schizophrenia and prominent negative symptoms operationalized as PANSS Negative Scale total score of 20 or above or 'severe' baseline ratings for either emotional withdrawal, motor retardation, or blunted affect.	Participants were randomized to either group delivered BPT or supportive counselling. Up to 20 sessions (60–90 minutes) were offered over a period of 10 weeks.	Primary outcome was PANSS negative symptom score, especially subscale scores for affective blunting and psychomotor retardation. Secondary outcomes were PANSS Positive and General scale scores, and quality of life measures.	PANSS total negative symptoms, blunted affect, and psychomotor retardation were all significantly different for BPT-treated patients immediately post treatment and at 4-month follow-up. No between-group effects were seen for other PANSS scores.
Klingberg et al. (2011)	198 patients with schizophrenia and predominant negative symptoms operationalized as at least one moderate severity negative symptom on the PANSS and, no severe depressive symptoms, and no positive symptoms of greater than moderate severity at baseline.	CT for negative symptoms utilizing the Rector et al. (2005) formulation focusing on the identification and challenging of defeatist cognitions. The control condition was CRT. Up to 20 sessions were offered in both conditions over 9 months.	Primary outcome was the PANSS-MNS. Secondary outcomes included the SANS, CDSS, CGI, and SCL-90.	No between-groups effect was observed but both CBT and CRT were associated with within subject improvements on total MNS negative symptom scores (ESs: −0.49 and −0.53).
Grant et al. (2012)	60 patients with schizophrenia or schizoaffective disorder marked by prominent negative symptoms operationalized as at least two SANS symptoms of moderate severity or one of marked severity.	CT for negative symptoms utilizing the Rector et al. (2005) formulation focusing on the identification and challenging of defeatist cognitions. A mean of 51 individual sessions (range 16–81) was offered within an 18-month treatment window.	Primary outcome was the Global Assessment Scale. Secondary outcomes were the four global subscale scores of the SANS and the total SAPS score.	The CT group showed a greater within subjects CGI score improvement across the trial compared to ST (ES: 1.36 vs. 0.06). For between-group effects, the CT group had significantly greater CGI scores at 18 months (ES = 0.56).

(Continued)

TABLE 7.2 Continued

Study	Sample Characteristics	Active Intervention(s)	Primary and Secondary Outcomes	Main Findings
				Secondary outcomes indicated a significant effect of CT on SANS avolition-apathy (ES = −0.66) but no effects on other negative symptoms. Total SAPS score was significantly improved for the CT group at 18 months (ES = −0.46).
Staring et al. (2013)	21 outpatients with schizophrenia spectrum disorder with prominent negative symptoms operationalized as at least three PANSS Negative Symptom scores of mild severity or above that the patient was dissatisfied with. Patients with secondary negative symptoms were excluded.	A modified form of CT for defeatist beliefs based on an individualized formulation of the patients' goals and aspirations was used.	The primary outcome was PANSS Negative Symptom Scale total score. Secondary outcomes included mediator analyses of the role of change in defeatist beliefs on symptom change.	A significant reduction in total PANSS-N score was seen post treatment (ES = 1.26). Bootstrap analysis of the mediator relationship indicated that change in defeatist beliefs partially mediated the reduction in negative symptoms.

BPT: body-oriented psychotherapy; CAINS: Clinical Assessment Interview for Negative Symptoms; CBT: cognitive behavioral therapy; CDSS: Calgary Depression Scale for Schizophrenia; CGI: Clinical Global Impression Scale; CRT: cognitive remediation therapy; CT: cognitive therapy; ES: effect size; PANSS: Positive and Negative Syndrome Scale; PANSS-MNS: Positive and Negative Syndrome Scale Modified Negative Syndrome Factor; SAPS: Scale for the Assessment of Positive Symptoms; SANS: Scale for the Assessment of Negative Symptoms; SCL-90: Symptom Checklist-90; ST: standard treatment.

showed a significant within-subjects improvements on negative symptom ratings (Klingberg *et al.*, 2011) suggesting that targeting defeatist cognitions is not required to achieve therapeutic gains. In summary, current trial data support the possibility that negative symptoms are treatable with psychological therapies but there is no clear evidence of a single critical mechanism of change.

Given that subtypes of negative symptom presentations may have different prognostic implications (Carpenter *et al.*, 1988; Strauss *et al.*, 2010), it is potentially informative to analyze the negative symptom trials for indications that outcome varies due to negative symptom profile. The first point to note is that the current data relate to patients with either *predominant/primary* or *prominent/secondary* negative symptoms. The two studies using patients with predominant symptoms either actively excluded those who showed high levels of positive symptom comorbidity (Klingberg *et al.*, 2011) or asked supplementary questions to rule out patients whose negative symptoms were secondary to positive symptoms (Staring *et al.*, 2013). The remaining two studies included patients with prominent negative symptoms but did not exclude participants who presented with comorbid positive symptoms.

The treatment effects on specific subtypes of negative symptoms are also mixed. BPT has an effect on both total PANSS Negative scale ratings and on individual items for blunted affect and psychomotor retardation. For the cognitive behavioral therapy (CBT) trials, within subject improvements were seen on total negative symptom scores for two studies (Klingberg *et al.*, 2011; Staring *et al.*, 2013) but not the third (Grant *et al.*, 2012). The secondary outcome analysis of the SANS in the study of Grant *et al.* suggested an impact of CBT on AA but not other SANS subscale items.

These effects of various psychological therapies on negative symptoms are consistent with meta-analytic data on the outcome of general CBT approaches for psychosis (CBTp) (Wykes *et al.*, 2007). The pooled effects seen across CBTp studies where negative symptoms have been measured as an outcome variable show that improvement in negative symptoms can occur even when the primary therapeutic target is positive symptoms (mean weighted effect size (ES) = −0.437, 95% confidence interval (CI) 0.171 to 0.704). This raises questions about processes that may be active in psychological therapies that stimulate negative symptom improvement but are inadequately measured in current trial designs. A simple explanation such as a nonspecific effect of interpersonal contact is contradicted by the findings from controlled studies. For example, the trial of body psychotherapy for negative symptoms included supportive counselling as a control treatment and patients randomized to this condition showed no change in negative symptoms (Röhricht and Priebe, 2006). In further evidence against a nonspecific therapeutic relationship explanation, an earlier randomized controlled trial of CBTp versus befriending reported improvement in total SANS negative symptom scores over follow-up periods of 9 months and 5 years post therapy for CBTp-treated patients (Sensky *et al.*, 2000; Turkington *et al.*, 2008). In contrast, symptoms for patients randomized to befriending deteriorated following the withdrawal of contact. It was hypothesized that the durable effects of CBTp on negative symptoms could be attributable to various factors such as the rekindling of motivational drive, a reduction in social withdrawal due to self-stigma, or diminished use of avoidance behaviors (Turkington *et al.*, 2008). Overall, it appears that despite some promising treatment outcome studies, there is still considerable work to be done to specify models of negative symptoms that maximize treatment effectiveness and efficiency. The next sections examine the potential benefits of developing a metacognitive approach to understanding and treating negative symptoms.

APPLYING A METACOGNITIVE PERSPECTIVE TO NEGATIVE SYMPTOMS

Modern conceptualizations of metacognition can be traced to earlier work examining the capacity to reflect on and observe one's own mental processes (Flavell, 1979) and infer the mental states of others (Premack and Woodruff, 1978). Understanding this ability to 'think about thinking' and its impact on healthy functioning and psychopathology has become a major research focus in recent years. With the proliferation of empirical studies and theoretical work there has been recognition that metacognitive abilities can range from relatively discrete functions (e.g., noticing when one has made a cognitive error) through to more complex mental processes (e.g., being able to make sense of one's life experiences to produce a coherent life story). Hence, metacognitive functioning is increasingly viewed as a hierarchically organized set of competences that unfold developmentally and can be deployed flexibly to cope with social interactions (Dimaggio *et al.*, 2009; Semerari *et al.*, 2003).

Studies of metacognition in relation to negative symptoms have focused on both the discrete and more synthetic ends of this hierarchy. Frith's (1992) cognitive neuropsychological model of schizophrenia proposed that discrete problems with theory of mind (e.g., monitoring one's own willed intentions) are a major contributor to the development of negative symptoms. This view is supported by studies showing that patients with primary negative symptoms perform more poorly on second-order false-belief tasks (Pickup and Frith, 2001), have greater difficulty picking up hints in social speech (Corcoran *et al.*, 1995), and are poorer at deciphering visual jokes that require inferences about mental state (Corcoran *et al.*, 1997). These discrete competences provide the building blocks of social interaction and it can be seen how their disruption could lead to some negative symptoms such as avolition. However, the manifestation of metacognitive deficits in real world settings is typically more complex, recursive, and dynamic. Recognition of the importance of subjecting this complex processing to systematic analysis has stimulated the development of methods for describing metacognition as it unfolds in naturalistic narratives (Lysaker *et al.*, 2005a; Lysaker *et al.*, 2005b; Semerari *et al.*, 2003). Characterizing the dynamics of metacognition as seen in interpersonal dialogues is particularly relevant in the context of understanding psychological therapy for negative symptoms given that most psychotherapies rely heavily on discussions about the personal meaning of life experiences (Dimaggio *et al.*, 2012; Etkin *et al.*, 2005).

As summarized in Table 7.3, several published studies have examined the relationship between negative symptoms and the range of metacognitive functioning that can be detected in narrative speech samples (Hamm *et al.*, 2012; Lysaker *et al.*, 2005a; Lysaker *et al.*, 2007; Lysaker *et al.*, 2010b; MacBeth *et al.*, 2014; Mitchell *et al.*, 2012; Nicolo *et al.*, 2012). All of these studies assessed metacognition with the original Metacognition Assessment Scale (MAS) (Semerari *et al.*, 2003) or its derivatives that have been adapted for use with people with psychosis (Lysaker *et al.*, 2005a). These different variants of the MAS provide scores encompassing four main subscales. First, the *Self-reflectivity* or *Understanding one's own mind* score indexes the subject's ability to recognize and differentiate one's own mental functions and integrate these into a coherent narrative. Second, *Understanding the Mind of Others* conveys the ability to think about the mental states of others and distinguish these from one's own thoughts and feelings. Third, the *Decentration* subscale captures the ability to take a nonegocentric view of the mind of others and recognize that other's mental states are influenced by a multitude of experiential, developmental, and contextual factors. Fourth, the final subscale, *Mastery*, reflects the ability to use metacognitive awareness to identify, confront, and solve real world social problems in context. For each subscale, higher ratings reflect greater metacognitive capacity and more complex synthetic metacognitive processing. The source material for MAS ratings is a naturalistic speech sample elicited through a semistructured interview, such as the Indiana Psychiatric Illness Interview (IPII; Lysaker *et al.*, 2002). The IPII differs from conventional psychiatric interviews in that the interviewer provides very little content and does not inquire directly about symptoms. Instead, the aim is to create circumstances that allow the patient to provide a narrative about their experiences that can then be used to code metacognitive functioning using the MAS. Other studies have used speech samples generated from other measures such as the Adult Attachment Interview (AAI) (MacBeth *et al.*, 2014) or the Narrative Interview for Compassion and Recovery (NICR) (Mitchell *et al.*, 2012). Table 7.3 provides a summary of studies that provide data on the relationship between negative symptoms and metacognition assessed with the MAS and its variants.

The majority of participants across the studies described in Table 7.3 presented with negative symptoms alongside positive and disorganization symptoms rather than the deficit syndrome. The PANSS was used for symptom ratings across all studies and generally the group means suggest that symptom severity was in the mild–moderate range for both positive and negative

TABLE 7.3 Summary of Studies That Examine the Relationship Between MAS or MAS-A Metacognition Scores and Negative Symptom Ratings.

Study	Sample	Methods and Design	Main Findings
Lysaker et al. (2005)	61 men (schizophrenia: n = 40; schizoaffective disorder: n = 21). All in postpsychotic phase of illness receiving outpatient mental health care.	Cross-sectional design. Metacognition assessed with the MAS-A based on IPII transcripts. Negative symptoms were assessed with PANSS items N1 affective blunting, N2 emotional withdrawal, and G13 disturbance of volition.	Emotional withdrawal was negatively correlated with Understanding the Mind of Others ($r = -0.43$), Self-reflectivity ($r = -0.38$), and Mastery ($r = -0.31$).
Lysaker et al. (2007)	61 men and 8 women (schizophrenia: n = 43; schizoaffective disorder: n = 26). All were clinically stable outpatients.	Cross-sectional design. Metacognition was assessed using the MAS based on IPII transcripts. Negative symptoms were indexed with five-factor PANSS subscale score.	PANSS negative symptom subscale total score was negatively correlated with understanding one's own mind ($\rho = -0.27$) alone.
Lysaker et al. (2010b)	35 men and 2 women (schizophrenia: n = 21; schizoaffective disorder: n = 16) receiving outpatient care. All were clinically stable.	Cross-sectional design with metacognition assessed with the MAS based on IPII scores and negative symptoms assessed with the PANSS.	No correlations were observed between MAS subscale scores and PANSS negative symptoms (Self reflectivity $r = -0.10$, Mastery $r = -0.08$, and Understanding the Mind of Others $r = -0.01$).
Nicolo et al. (2012)	27 men and 18 women (schizophrenia: n = 32; schizoaffective disorder: n = 13) receiving outpatient mental health care.	A replication of Lysaker et al. (2005) using the same design and methods (see above).	Understanding one's own mind was associated with all measured negative symptoms ($r = -0.30$ to -0.33). Understanding the Mind of Others was associated with blunted affect ($r = -0.31$). Mastery was associated with disturbances of volition ($r = -0.39$).

Study	Sample	Method	Findings
Hamm et al. (2012)	44 men and 5 women with schizophrenia or schizoaffective disorder in a stable phase of illness.	Repeated measures design with positive, negative, and disorganization symptoms; metacognition; and emotion recognition measured at baseline and 6 months later.	Negative symptoms remained stable across both assessments. Overall MAS-A metacognition score was associated with total negative symptoms at baseline ($r = -0.42$) and 6 months ($r = -0.44$). Stepwise linear regression showed that baseline MAS-A scores predicted a significant proportion of the variance in negative symptoms at 6 months.
Mitchell et al. (2012)	29 people with schizophrenia spectrum disorders. 18 were assessed to have a history of interpersonal violence and were cared for by specialist forensic mental health services, the remaining 11 were receiving generic community mental health care.	A cross-sectional between-groups comparison focusing on the role of metacognitive capacity and interpersonal violence. Metacognition was assessed using the MAS-R based on transcripts of the NICR.	Planned analyses using Kendall's tau show moderate to strong correlations between PANSS total negative symptoms and understanding one's own mind ($\tau = -0.53$), understanding others' minds ($\tau = -0.51$), and mastery ($\tau = -0.44$).
MacBeth et al. (2014)	20 men and 14 women presenting to early intervention psychosis services in two urban centers. Diagnoses included schizophrenia ($n = 11$), schizophreniform disorder ($n = 3$), schizoaffective disorder ($n = 4$), persistent delusional disorder ($n = 2$), bipolar disorder ($n = 11$), mania with psychotic symptoms ($n = 1$), and recurrent depression with psychotic symptoms ($n = 2$).	Cross-sectional design with negative symptoms assessed using the PANSS negative symptom subscale score and metacognition measure using the MAS-R based on transcripts derived from the AAI.	Understanding the Mind of Others was significantly correlated with PANSS negative symptom score ($r = -0.44$). No other associations were seen between PANSS symptoms or metacognition scores.

AAI: Adult Attachment Inventory; IPII: Indiana Psychiatric Illness Inventory; MAS: Metacognition Assessment Scale; MAS-A: Metacognition Assessment Scale-Abbreviated; NICR: Narrative Interview for Compassion and Recovery; PANSS: Positive and Negative Symptom Scale.

symptoms. Five studies analyzed negative symptoms at the subscale level (i.e., total PANSS negative symptom score) and two tested the link between metacognition and specific negative symptom items such as affective blunting, emotional withdrawal, and avolition (Lysaker et al., 2005a; Nicolo et al., 2012). Only one study found no relationship between MAS ratings and negative symptoms (Lysaker et al., 2010a). The remainder of the studies provided some evidence that metacognitive functioning is related to both overall negative symptom ratings and specific symptom subtypes.

The studies that analyzed the interaction between metacognition and specific negative symptoms show somewhat mixed results. The data from Lysaker et al. (2005a) showed an association between emotional withdrawal and difficulties understanding one's own mind, the mind of others, and the ability to deploy this information to solve social problems (mastery). In the replication study of Nicolo et al. (2012), emotional withdrawal was significantly correlated with understanding one's own mind ($r = -0.30$) but not the other dimensions of the MAS.[1] However, Nicolo's data also suggest links between other negative symptoms (affective blunting, volitional disturbance) and understanding one's own mind (see Table 7.3). These multiple correlations point to the possibility of a more general relationship between metacognitive functioning and overall negative symptoms. Examination of the other results presented in Table 7.3 suggest a general link between overall negative symptoms and deficits in understanding one's own mind (Lysaker et al., 2007; Mitchell et al., 2012), problems with understanding the mind of others (MacBeth et al., 2014; Mitchell et al., 2012), and problems with mastery (Mitchell et al., 2012). What is not yet clear from the available data is the impact of third variables on the link between metacognition and negative symptoms. For example, it is possible that the mixed pattern of correlations is due to patient symptom profile differences (e.g., some experimental samples may have predominant versus prominent negative symptoms). One implication of this might be that more pervasive problems with metacognitive functioning could result in more severe overall negative symptom presentations.

Although the present data do not provide information about the causal direction of the metacognition-negative symptom link, one of the studies indicates that the relationship is robust over time. Hamm et al. (2012) report repeated measures data for patients with negative symptoms assessed twice over a 6-month period. The negative symptom data reported were restricted to the total PANSS Negative subscale score so inferences about specific relationships between metacognition and symptom subtypes is not possible. However, the results do indicate that the relationship between overall metacognitive functioning (MAS-A total score) and overall negative symptoms

---

[1] Although not statistically significant, the coefficients for the other associations are in the expected direction (Understanding the Mind of Others: $r = -0.26$; Mastery: $r = -0.27$).

is stable over time (see Table 7.3). Furthermore, metacognition scores along with executive functioning (Wisconsin Card Sorting Test (WCST) score) were unique predictors of variance in negative symptoms but not positive symptoms or disorganization symptoms at 6-month follow-up. This raises the possibility that difficulties with forming complex and integrated representations of the self and others contribute to the maintenance of negative symptoms and could, therefore, be an important treatment target. The following sections consider in more detail how these maintenance processes may operate and examines the possible implications for targeted psychological interventions.

POTENTIAL TREATMENT IMPLICATIONS OF THE METACOGNITIVE PERSPECTIVE

Viewing metacognition as a hierarchically organized set of competences that are deployed dynamically in interactions with one's own mind and the minds of others provides an important extension to existing cognitive therapy treatment models for negative symptoms. The standard cognitive model (Rector *et al.*, 2005) is predicated on the notion that, with the help of the therapist, patients can identify their defeatist thoughts and beliefs and then challenge those thoughts either through logical reasoning or via behavior change strategies (e.g., activity scheduling). However, understanding one's own mind to the extent that one can recognize one's thoughts and beliefs can be mistaken and requires a level of metacognitive functioning that may not be reliably achievable for many people with negative symptoms. We propose that therapists who are sensitive to the fluctuating levels of metacognition displayed by their patient will be in a better position to deploy appropriately targeted therapy techniques. Consequently, challenging defeatist cognitions may be entirely appropriate when the patient is capable of recognizing that the thoughts and beliefs in their mind may be mistaken and are open to appraisal and challenge. However, for someone who is struggling to understand their own mind and finds the minds of others to be confusing, opaque, or even dangerous, it will be counter-productive to attempt to engage in standard belief modification strategies. When presented with signs that the patient is experiencing difficulty engaging in even low levels of metacognitive processing (e.g., they are finding it difficult to identify thoughts, wishes, and goals), the most effective therapeutic response may be to help them to describe and label that experience. With repeated and gently titrated practice, such strategies will help shape the capacity for taking an observer perspective that is necessary for more complex operations, such as questioning or changing ones beliefs about the self, the world, or the future.

Incorporating a metacognitive perspective into the understanding and treatment of negative symptoms also provides a more nuanced view of the different functional mechanisms that may underpin the same overt behavioral sign. For example, social withdrawal and avoidance may arise because of fears about the mental state of others (e.g., 'Others wish to harm me'), defeatist cognitions (e.g., 'There is no point in engaging socially, I never enjoy it'), and confusion about one's own mental state (e.g., 'I cannot make sense of how to be with other people so I won't try'). At a more basic processing level, difficulty filtering out and selecting viable inferences about the intentions of others may lead to hyperarousal in social interactions that the patient learns to cope with by withdrawal (Salvatore *et al.*, 2007).

The proposition that some negative symptoms are directly due to problems with forming and reflecting on mental representations about the world is also supported by studies of anhedonia. Evidence indicates that anhedonia is dissociable into anticipatory and consummatory components and that it is the ability to form a representation of potential appetitive stimuli that is disturbed in people with schizophrenia (Gard *et al.*, 2006). Contrary to the historical view, it is now evident that hedonic responding typically remains intact and many patients can experience consummatory pleasure 'in the moment'. However, incentive motivation (Ward *et al.*, 2012) is impaired such that patients with pronounced negative symptoms display deficits in representing positive outcomes and/or using this information to guide and sustain goal-directed behavior (Gold *et al.*, 2012). This difficulty also extends to the ability to represent and judge any noncurrent pleasurable experience accurately, not just those that are anticipated (Strauss and Gold, 2012). When asked to report the intensity of previous pleasurable experiences as well as the prospect of pleasure in future experiences, people with schizophrenia tend to reliably make an underestimate whereas healthy comparison subjects reliably overestimate the intensity of noncurrent pleasurable experiences (Robinson and Clore, 2002). One explanation for this pattern is because patients have greater difficulty with recalling specific autobiographical memories (Wood *et al.*, 2006) they rely instead on semantic knowledge to guide the judgment (Robinson and Clore, 2002; Strauss and Gold, 2012). Hence, judgments about noncurrent pleasure may be based on negatively toned and over-rehearsed beliefs about the self and the world that are relatively impervious to modification. Using therapeutic encounters to support patients in recalling and reflecting on specific episodic memories could help decrease reliance on overgeneralized semantic knowledge and beliefs (e.g., 'Nothing gives me pleasure') and build up greater awareness and accurate monitoring of actual consummatory pleasure, both as it happens, and retrospectively.

This leads to a final point about how taking a metacognitive perspective can direct therapeutic attention to ultimately helping patients generate meaning and make sense of their experiences in a way that supports a synthesized, integrated, and coherent self-narrative. There is now preliminary evidence to suggest that people with schizophrenia marked by negative symptoms have particular difficulty with spontaneously generating meaning from self-defining memories of experiences in their past (Berna *et al.*, 2011). The rate of spontaneous meaning making in patients was half the rate seen in healthy comparison subjects, but crucially, providing a simple question[2] prompt increased the meaning making displayed by patients by over 50% from baseline and to a level comparable with the normal range for spontaneous meaning making. Although these are unreplicated preliminary data, they suggest that it is possible to induce a reflective stance on one's own mental content with relatively simple procedures that are easily deployed in the context of a standard therapeutic interaction.

In conclusion, three main messages can be extracted from material covered in this chapter. First, the conceptualization of negative symptoms in the context of schizophrenia has evolved to reflect modern data and careful analysis. In the short term, this provides a mandate to focus on trying to understand the factors underpinning DE and amotivation as key subtypes of negative symptoms (Foussias et al., 2011). It seems that in the near future we will be less concerned with developing treatments for negative symptoms as a whole but instead will focus on more targeted interventions. The second message is that developing psychosocial interventions is a viable and important enterprise, especially given the limited impact of drugs on negative symptoms (Barnes and Paton, 2011). However, the final message is that the next generation of psychological treatments will almost certainly need to be based on a more subtle and dynamic model of negative symptoms. The content-based cognitive therapy model that targets defeatist cognitions has helped to propel the field forward but, as described above, there is a clearly scope for translating the findings of research on cognitive processes such as metacognition into scientifically informed and effective treatment protocols.

REFERENCES

Abrams, R., & Taylor, M. A. (1978). A rating scale for emotional blunting. *American Journal of Psychiatry, 135*(2), 226–229.

Andreasen, N. C. (1984). *Scale for the assessment of negative symptoms.* Iowa City: University of Iowa.

Barnes, T. R., & Paton, C. (2011). Do antidepressants improve negative symptoms in schizophrenia? *British Medical Journal, 342*, d3371.

Berna, F., Bennouna-Greene, M., Potheegadoo, J., Verry, P., Conway, M. A., & Danion, J. -M. (2011). Impaired ability to give a meaning to personally significant events in patients with schizophrenia. *Consciousness and Cognition, 20*(3), 703–711.

Blanchard, J. J., & Cohen, A. S. (2006). The structure of negative symptoms within schizophrenia: implications for assessment. *Schizophrenia Bulletin, 32*(2), 238–245.

Blanchard, J. J., Horan, W. P., & Collins, L. M. (2005). Examining the latent structure of negative symptoms: is there a distinct subtype of negative symptom schizophrenia? *Schizophrenia Research, 77*(2–3), 151–165.

---

[2] The standard question prompt was: 'To what extent was this event important for you and in what ways does it help you to describe who you are?'

Boonstra, N., Klaassen, R., Sytema, S., Marshall, M., De Haan, L., Wunderink, L., et al. (2012). Duration of untreated psychosis and negative symptoms – a systematic review and meta-analysis of individual patient data. *Schizophrenia Research, 142*(1–3), 12–19.

Cannon-Spoor, H. E., Potkin, S. G., & Wyatt, R. J. (1982). Measurement of premorbid adjustment in chronic schizophrenia. *Schizophrenia Bulletin, 8*(3), 470.

Carpenter, W. T., Jr, Heinrichs, D. W., & Wagman, A. M. (1988). Deficit and nondeficit forms of schizophrenia: the concept. *American Journal of Psychiatry, 145*, 578–583.

Chang, W. C., Hui, C. L. M., Tang, J. Y. M., Wong, G. H. Y., Lam, M. M. L., Chan, S. K. W., et al. (2011). Persistent negative symptoms in first-episode schizophrenia: a prospective three-year follow-up study. *Schizophrenia Research, 133*(1–3), 22–28.

Corcoran, R., Cahill, C., & Frith, C. D. (1997). The appreciation of visual jokes in people with schizophrenia: a study of "mentalizing" ability. *Schizophrenia Research, 24*(3), 319–327.

Corcoran, R., Mercer, G., & Frith, C. D. (1995). Schizophrenia, symptomatology and social inference: investigating "theory of mind" in people with schizophrenia. *Schizophrenia Research, 17*(1), 5–13.

Crow, T. J. (1985). The two-syndrome concept: origins and current status. *Schizophrenia Bulletin, 11*(3), 471.

Dimaggio, G., Salvatore, G., Popolo, R., & Lysaker, P. H. (2012). Autobiographical memory and mentalizing impairment in personality disorders and schizophrenia: clinical and research implications. *Frontiers in Psychology, 3*, 529.

Dimaggio, G., Vanheule, S., Lysaker, P. H., Carcione, A., & Nicolò, G. (2009). Impaired self-reflection in psychiatric disorders among adults: a proposal for the existence of a network of semi independent functions. *Consciousness and Cognition, 18*(3), 653–664.

Esterberg, M., & Compton, M. (2012). Family history of psychosis negatively impacts age at onset, negative symptoms, and duration of untreated illness and psychosis in first-episode psychosis patients. *Psychiatry Research, 197*(1–2), 23–28.

Esterberg, M. L., Trotman, H. D., Holtzman, C., Compton, M. T., & Walker, E. F. (2010). The impact of a family history of psychosis on age-at-onset and positive and negative symptoms of schizophrenia: a meta-analysis. *Schizophrenia Research, 120*(1–3), 121–130.

Etkin, A., Phil, M., Pittenger, C., Polan, H., & Kandel, E. (2005). Toward a neurobiology of psychotherapy: basic science and clinical applications. *Journal of Neuropsychiatry and Clinical Neurosciences, 17*(2), 145–158.

Flavell, J. H. (1979). Metacognition and cognitive monitoring. *American Psychologist, 34*(10), 906–911.

Foussias, G., Agid, O., & Remington, G. (2011). Negative symptoms across the schizophrenia spectrum: phenomenological and neurobiological perspectives. In M. Ritsner (Ed.), *Handbook of Schizophrenia Spectrum Disorders* (vol. II, pp. 1–32). Netherlands, Dordrecht: Springer.

Frith, C. D. (1992). *The Cognitive Neuropsychology of Schizophrenia*. New Jersey: Lawrence Erlbaum Associates, Inc.

Gard, D., Gard, M., Kring, A., & John, O. (2006). Anticipatory and consummatory components of the experience of pleasure: a scale development study. *Journal of Research in Personality, 40*, 1086–1102.

Gold, J. M., Waltz, J. A., Matveeva, T. M., Kasanova, Z., Strauss, G. P., Herbener, E. S., et al. (2012). Negative symptoms and the failure to represent the expected reward value of actions: behavioral and computational modeling evidence. *Archives of General Psychiatry, 69*(2), 129.

Grant, P. M., & Beck, A. T. (2009). Defeatist beliefs as a mediator of cognitive impairment, negative symptoms, and functioning in schizophrenia. *Schizophrenia Bulletin, 35*(4), 798–806.

Grant, P. M., & Beck, A. T. (2010). Asocial beliefs as predictors of asocial behavior in schizophrenia. *Psychiatry Research*, *177*(1), 65–70.

Grant, P. M., Huh, G. A., Perivoliotis, D., Stolar, N. M., & Beck, A. T. (2012). Randomized trial to evaluate the efficacy of cognitive therapy for low-functioning patients with schizophrenia. *Archives of General Psychiatry*, *69*(2), 121.

Hamm, J. A., Renard, S. B., Fogley, R. L., Leonhardt, B. L., Dimaggio, G., Buck, K. D., et al. (2012). Metacognition and social cognition in schizophrenia: stability and relationship to concurrent and prospective symptom assessments. *Journal of Clinical Psychology*, *68*(12), 1303–1312.

Ho, B. C., Nopoulos, P., Flaum, M., Arndt, S., & Andreasen, N. C. (1998). Two-year outcome in first-episode schizophrenia: predictive value of symptoms for quality of life. *American Journal of Psychiatry*, *155*(9), 1196–1201.

Johnson, D. P., Penn, D. L., Fredrickson, B. L., Kring, A. M., Meyer, P. S., Catalino, L. I., et al. (2011). A pilot study of loving-kindness meditation for the negative symptoms of schizophrenia. *Schizophrenia Research*, *129*(2–3), 137–140.

Kay, S. R., Fiszbein, A., & Opler, L. A. (1987). The Positive and Negative Syndrome Scale (PANSS) for schizophrenia. *Schizophrenia Bulletin*, *13*(2), 261–276.

Kirkpatrick, B., Fenton, W. S., Carpenter, W. T., & Marder, S. R. (2006). The NIMH-MATRICS Consensus Statement on Negative Symptoms. *Schizophrenia Bulletin*, *32*(2), 214–219.

Klingberg, S., Wolwer, W., Engel, C., Wittorf, A., Herrlich, J., Meisner, C., et al. (2011). Negative symptoms of schizophrenia as primary target of cognitive behavioral therapy: results of the randomized clinical TONES study. *Schizophrenia Bulletin*, *37*(Suppl. 2), S98–S110.

Kring, A. M., Gur, R. E., Blanchard, J. J., Horan, W. P., & Reise, S. P. (2013). The Clinical Assessment Interview for Negative Symptoms (CAINS): final development and validation. *American Journal of Psychiatry*, *170*(2), 165–172.

Lyne, J., O'Donoghue, B., Owens, E., Renwick, L., Madigan, K., Kinsella, A., et al. (2012). Prevalence of item level negative symptoms in first episode psychosis diagnoses. *Schizophrenia Research*, *135*(1–3), 128–133.

Lysaker, P. H., Carcione, A., Dimaggio, G., Johannesen, J. K., Nicolo, G., Procacci, M., et al. (2005a). Metacognition amidst narratives of self and illness in schizophrenia: associations with neurocognition, symptoms, insight and quality of life. *Acta Psychiatrica Scandinavica*, *112*(1), 64–71.

Lysaker, P. H., Clements, C. A., Plascak-Hallberg, C. D., Knipscheer, S. J., & Wright, D. E. (2002). Insight and personal narratives of illness in schizophrenia. *Psychiatry: Interpersonal and Biological Processes*, *65*(3), 197–206.

Lysaker, P. H., Dimaggio, G., Buck, K. D., Carcione, A., & Nicolò, G. (2007). Metacognition within narratives of schizophrenia: associations with multiple domains of neurocognition. *Schizophrenia Research*, *93*(1–3), 278–287.

Lysaker, P. H., Dimaggio, G., Carcione, A., Procacci, M., Buck, K. D., Davis, L. W., et al. (2010a). Metacognition and schizophrenia: the capacity for self-reflectivity as a predictor for prospective assessments of work performance over six months. *Schizophrenia Research*, *122*(1–3), 124–130.

Lysaker, P. H., Dimaggio, G., Daroyanni, P., Buck, K. D., LaRocco, V. A., Carcione, A., et al. (2010b). Assessing metacognition in schizophrenia with the Metacognition Assessment Scale: associations with the Social Cognition and Object Relations Scale. *Psychology and Psychotherapy: Theory, Research and Practice*, *83*(3), 303–315.

Lysaker, P. H., Wickett, A., & Davis, L. W. (2005b). Narrative qualities in schizophrenia. *Journal of Nervous and Mental Disease*, *193*(4), 244–249.

MacBeth, A., Gumley, A., Schwannauer, M., Carcione, A., Fisher, R., McLeod, H. J., et al. (2014). Metacognition, symptoms and premorbid functioning in a first episode psychosis sample. *Comprehensive Psychiatry*, *55*(2), 268–273.

Mäkinen, J., Miettunen, J., Isohanni, M., & Koponen, H. (2008). Negative symptoms in schizophrenia – a review. *Nordic Journal of Psychiatry*, *62*(5), 334–341.

Messinger, J. W., Trémeau, F., Antonius, D., Mendelsohn, E., Prudent, V., Stanford, A. D., et al. (2011). Avolition and expressive deficits capture negative symptom phenomenology: implications for DSM-5 and schizophrenia research. *Clinical Psychology Review*, *31*(1), 161–168.

Milev, P., Ho, B. C., Arndt, S., & Andreasen, N. C. (2005). Predictive values of neurocognition and negative symptoms on functional outcome in schizophrenia: a longitudinal first-episode study with 7-year follow-up. *American Journal of Psychiatry*, *162*(3), 495–506.

Mitchell, L. J., Gumley, A., Reilly, E. S., MacBeth, A., Lysaker, P., Carcione, A., et al. (2012). Metacognition in forensic patients with schizophrenia and a past history of interpersonal violence: an exploratory study. *Psychosis*, *4*(1), 42–51.

Nicolo, G., Dimaggio, G., Popolo, R., Carcione, A., Procacci, M., Hamm, J., et al. (2012). Associations of metacognition with symptoms, insight, and neurocognition in clinically stable outpatients with schizophrenia. *Journal of Nervous and Mental Disease*, *200*(7), 644–647.

Pickup, G. J., & Frith, C. D. (2001). Theory of mind impairments in schizophrenia: symptomatology, severity and specificity. *Psychological Medicine*, *31*(2), 207–220.

Piskulic, D., Addington, J., Cadenhead, K. S., Cannon, T. D., Cornblatt, B. A., Heinssen, R., et al. (2012). Negative symptoms in individuals at clinical high risk of psychosis. *Psychiatry Research; Psychiatry Research*, *196*(2–3), 220–224.

Pogue-Geile, M. F., & Harrow, M. (1985). Negative symptoms in schizophrenia: their longitudinal course and prognostic importance. *Schizophrenia Bulletin*, *11*(3), 427.

Premack, D., & Woodruff, G. (1978). Does the chimpanzee have a theory of mind? *Behavioral and Brain Sciences*, *1*(4), 515–526.

Priebe, S., Savill, M., Reininghaus, U., Wykes, T., Bentall, R., Lauber, C., et al. (2013). Effectiveness and cost-effectiveness of body psychotherapy in the treatment of negative symptoms of schizophrenia – a multi-centre randomised controlled trial. *BMC Psychiatry*, *13*(1), 26.

Provencher, H. L., & Mueser, K. T. (1997). Positive and negative symptom behaviors and caregiver burden in the relatives of persons with schizophrenia. *Schizophrenia Research*, *26*(1), 71–80.

Rabinowitz, J., Levine, S. Z., Garibaldi, G., Bugarski-Kirola, D., Berardo, C. G., & Kapur, S. (2012). Negative symptoms have greater impact on functioning than positive symptoms in schizophrenia: analysis of CATIE data. *Schizophrenia Research*, *137*(1–3), 147–150.

Rector, N. A., Beck, A. T., & Stolar, N. (2005). The negative symptoms of schizophrenia: a cognitive perspective. *Canadian Journal of Psychiatry*, *50*(5), 247–257.

Robinson, M. D., & Clore, G. L. (2002). Episodic and semantic knowledge in emotional self-report: evidence for two judgment processes. *Journal of Personality and Social Psychology*, *83*(1), 198–215.

Röhricht, F., & Proebe, S. (2006). Effect of body-oriented psychological therapy on negative symptoms in schizophrenia: a randomized controlled trial. *Psychological Medicine*, *36*(05), 669–678.

Salvatore, G., Dimaggio, G., & Lysaker, P. H. (2007). An intersubjective perspective on negative symptoms of schizophrenia: implications of simulation theory. *Cognitive Neuropsychiatry*, *12*(2), 144–164.

Semerari, A., Carcione, A., Dimaggio, G., Falcone, M., Nicol, G., Procacci, M., et al. (2003). How to evaluate metacognitive functioning in psychotherapy? The metacognition assessment scale and its applications. *Clinical Psychology & Psychotherapy*, *10*(4), 238–261.

Sensky, T., Turkington, D., Kingdon, D., Scott, J. L., Scott, J., Siddle, R., et al. (2000). A random-ized controlled trial of cognitive-behavioral therapy for persistent symptoms in schizophrenia resistant to medication. *Archives of General Psychiatry, 57*(2), 165.

Staring, A. B. P., Ter Huurne, M. A., & van der Gaag, M. (2013). Cognitive behavioral therapy for negative symptoms (CBT-n) in psychotic disorders: a pilot study. *Journal of Behavior Therapy and Experimental Psychiatry, 44*(3), 300–306.

Stauffer, V. L., Song, G., Kinon, B. J., Ascher-Svanum, H., Chen, L., Feldman, P. D., et al. (2012). Responses to antipsychotic therapy among patients with schizophrenia or schizoaffective disorder and either predominant or prominent negative symptoms. *Schizophrenia Research, 134*(2–3), 195–201.

Strauss, G. P., & Gold, J. M. (2012). A new perspective on anhedonia in schizophrenia. *American Journal of Psychiatry, 169*(4), 364–373.

Strauss, G. P., Harrow, M., Grossman, L. S., & Rosen, C. (2010). Periods of recovery in defi-cit syndrome schizophrenia: a 20-year multi-follow-up longitudinal study. *Schizophrenia Bulletin, 36*(4), 788–799.

Strauss, G. P., Horan, W. P., Kirkpatrick, B., Fischer, B. A., Keller, W. R., Miski, P., et al. (2013). Deconstructing negative symptoms of schizophrenia: avolition–apathy and diminished expres-sion clusters predict clinical presentation and functional outcome. *Journal of Psychiatric Research, 47*(6), 783–790.

Turkington, D., Sensky, T., Scott, J., Barnes, T. R., Nur, U., Siddle, R., et al. (2008). A randomized controlled trial of cognitive-behavior therapy for persistent symptoms in schizophrenia: a five-year follow-up. *Schizophrenia Research, 98*(1–3), 1–7.

van der Gaag, M., Hoffman, T., Remijsen, M., Hijman, R., Dehaan, L., Vanmeijel, B., et al. (2006). The five-factor model of the Positive and Negative Syndrome Scale II: a ten-fold cross-validation of a revised model. *Schizophrenia Research, 85*(1–3), 280–287.

Ward, R. D., Simpson, E. H., Richards, V. L., Deo, G., Taylor, K., Glendinning, J. I., et al. (2012). Dissociation of hedonic reaction to reward and incentive motivation in an animal model of the negative symptoms of schizophrenia. *Neuropsychopharmacology, 37*(7), 1699–1707.

Winograd-Gurvich, C., Fitzgerald, P. B., Georgiou-Karistianis, N., Bradshaw, J. L., & White, O. B. (2006). Negative symptoms: a review of schizophrenia, melancholic depression and Parkinson's disease. *Brain Research Bulletin, 70*(4–6), 312–321.

Wood, N., Brewin, C. R., & McLeod, H. J. (2006). Autobiographical memory deficits in schizo-phrenia. *Cognition & Emotion, 20*(3–4), 536–547.

Wykes, T., Steel, C., Everitt, B., & Tarrier, N. (2007). Cognitive behavior therapy for schizophre-nia: effect sizes, clinical models, and methodological rigor. *Schizophrenia Bulletin, 34*(3), 523–537.

Chapter 8

Metacognition as a Framework to Understanding the Occurrence of Aggression and Violence in Patients with Schizophrenia

Sune Bo,[1] Ahmad Abu-Akel[2] and Mickey Kongerslev[1]

[1]*Psychiatric Research Unit, Region Zealand, Denmark,*
[2]*University of Birmingham, Birmingham, UK*

Chapter Outline

INTRODUCTION

Schizophrenia is described as 'the worst disease affecting mankind' (Editorial, 1988), and it affects approximately 1% of the world's population during the course of their lifetime (Jablensky *et al.*, 1995). It is one of the most mysterious and severe mental disorders that inflicts a broad range of human and psychological functioning (Dickerson *et al.*, 1999). Schizophrenia is a heterogeneous syndrome characterized by the presence of various symptoms with different pathogenesis and etiology. However, consensus exist that phenotypic characteristics include hallucinations and delusional thoughts (positive symptoms); apathy; lack of emotions and poor or absent social functioning (negative

Social Cognition and Metacognition in Schizophrenia.
DOI: http://dx.doi.org/10.1016/B978-0-12-405172-0.00008-9
© 2014 Elsevier Inc. All rights reserved.

symptoms); bizarre behavior; and a range of cognitive dysfunctions including disorganized thoughts, difficulty with concentration and completing tasks, reduced memory, and deficits in processing information. In addition to its association with a wide range of cognitive impairments, social functioning, including interpersonal and pro-social behavior, is largely impoverished in patients with schizophrenia (Lysaker *et al.*, 2005). Thus, difficulties in these areas may increase the risk of these patients to engage in more aggression and delinquent behavior including violence (Fazel and Grann, 2006; Witt *et al.*, 2013).

Individuals with schizophrenia have long been stigmatized by the media (Vahabzadeh *et al.*, 2011) and health professionals (Hori *et al.*, 2011; Serafini *et al.*, 2011) as being dangerous and prone to engage in acts of violence and aggression (Serafini *et al.*, 2011). While the majority of patients with schizophrenia never engage in violence (Walsh *et al.*, 2002), and that patients with schizophrenia are responsible for only a small portion of the overall violence committed, epidemiologic, prospective, cohort, and cross-sectional studies confirm that there is an interrelationship between schizophrenia and the occurrence of violence (Bo *et al.*, 2011; Dack *et al.*, 2013; Hodgins, 2008; Soyka *et al.*, 2007; Volavka, 2013; Witt *et al.*, 2013). This association has been demonstrated in various populations including the general population (Brennan *et al.*, 2000), criminal offenders (Etherington, 1993), forensic patients (Erb *et al.*, 2001), and civil patients (Aarsland *et al.*, 1996).

While these studies confirm that there is a relationship between schizophrenia and violence, explaining the inter-relationship between schizophrenia and aggression, however, remains a major challenge. Over the years, several models have been proposed. Earlier models have suggested that schizophrenia itself is a risk factor for violence (Tiihonen *et al.*, 1997). Others have proposed that violence in schizophrenia can be explained in terms of the patients' demographics and substance abuse (Bonta, 1998; Fazel *et al.*, 2009; Grann *et al.*, 2008). Later models, however, constituted a paradigmatic shift whereby psychological functions such as 'metacognition' and 'mentalizing', which broadly refer to understanding the mental states of oneself and others, as well as the comorbidity of axis-I and axis-II disorders, including psychopathy, have been suggested as viable explanatory or mediating factors for the occurrence of aggression observed in schizophrenia (Bo *et al.*, 2011). This view is promoted by findings showing clear links between disrupted social functioning in schizophrenia and the presence of aberrant metacognitive abilities and comorbid personality disorders. In this regard, research reports high comorbidity rates between schizophrenia and various axis-I (McMillan *et al.*, 2009) and axis-II disorders (Lyons *et al.*, 1997; Newton-Howes *et al.*, 2008), and that behavioral outcomes as well as the course and treatment of schizophrenia are highly influenced by such comorbid psychopathology (Lysaker *et al.*, 2003). In fact, it has been suggested that axis-II personality disorders are traceable and co-occur in patients diagnosed with schizophrenia (Donat *et al.*, 1992; Moore *et al.*, 2012), and as such are pertinent to understanding the psychopathology and behavior present in these patients (Camisa *et al.*, 2005). This is particularly important given that the results of one meta-analysis found that the prevalence rate for personality disorders in schizophrenia was as high as 39.5% (Newton-Howes *et al.*, 2008). In addition, a wide range of studies have shown that impoverished metacognitive abilities are present in both individuals with schizophrenia (Lysaker *et al.*, 2012) and various personality disorders (for a review see Bateman and Fonagy (2011)). With respect to schizophrenia, a large body of research now confirms that metacognitive and mentalizing abilities are compromised in schizophrenia (Ang and Pridmore, 2009; Bora *et al.*, 2009; Brune, 2005; Chung *et al.*, 2013; Frith, 2004; Harrington *et al.*, 2005; Lysaker *et al.*, 2011), and it has been suggested that schizophrenia can be understood as a disorder of the representation of mental states. For example, delusions of persecution and ideas of reference can be understood in terms of a breakdown in the ability to monitor the thoughts and intentions of others (Corcoran *et al.*, 1995; Frith, 2004; Pickup and Frith, 2001). In this regard, it is noteworthy that difficulties in understanding the mental states of others may not be reducible to symptomatology associated with disorders within the current classification systems (i.e., *International Statistical Classification of Diseases,* 10th revision (ICD-10) and *Diagnostic and Statistical Manual of Mental Disorders,* Fifth Edition (DSM-V)), or to neurocognitive deficits alone (Hasson-Ohayon *et al.*, 2009), particularly in light of evidence showing that such difficulties appear to affect patients' level of functioning above and beyond the impact of symptomatology and concurrent neurocognitive deficits (Lysaker *et al.*, 2011).

VIOLENCE AND AGGRESSION – A DEFINITION OF CONCEPTS

Aggression is a ubiquitous phenomenon in humans as well as in nonhuman animals, and its underpinnings is considered to be multifactorial, including political, socioeconomic, cultural, neurobiologic, and psychological (WHO, 2007). Aggression per se is not a destructive force, but a naturally and evolutionary developed mechanism that has contributed to the survival of the human race. However, in a pathologic form, aggression refers to any behavior that is hostile, injurious, or destructive and has the potential to inflict injury or damage to people or objects. Violence is subsumed by the broader concept of aggression, specifically encapsulating physical aggression in interpersonal settings (Rippon, 2000). With this in mind, we will use the two concepts interchangeably, due to the lack of specificity in which these terms have been used in the literature (Douglas *et al.*, 2009). However, we do stress the importance for future research to be more specific in defining these concepts since it would aid in developing more precise causal models of the relationship between schizophrenia and aggression vis-à-vis violence (Bo *et al.*, 2011).

The most commonly used and perhaps most heuristically valuable classification of aggression is that of premeditated versus impulsive aggression. The subtype of premeditated aggression, also termed instrumental, proactive, or predatory aggression (Barratt and Felthous, 2003; Meloy, 2006), is characterized by a goal-oriented, planned, and callous pattern of aggressive behavior not driven by autonomic arousal. The impulsive subtype of aggression, also named reactive or affective aggression, is defined as an unplanned and emotionally driven act, accompanied by high levels of autonomic arousal, and is often precipitated by provocation associated with negative emotionality (Barratt et al., 1999; Haden et al., 2008). It is usually understood as a reaction to perceived stress, and becomes pathologic when the response is exaggerated compared with the emotional provocation. Research shows that premeditated aggression predicts future aggressive behavior and is considered a more severe pathologic form of aggression than impulsive aggression (Cornell et al., 1996). The differentiation of distinct subtypes of aggression has been identified among aggressive men, college students (Haden et al., 2008), adolescent offenders (Flight and Forth, 2007), and in forensic patients with severe mental disorders (Felthous et al., 2009), including schizophrenia (Bo et al., 2013).

METACOGNITION AS A FRAMEWORK TO UNDERSTANDING THE OCCURRENCE OF VIOLENCE AND AGGRESSION IN SCHIZOPHRENIA

The ability to represent and attribute mental states to one self and others is often referred to as 'metacognition' or 'mentalizing'. Concepts such as 'Theory of Mind' (ToM) and 'Social Cognition' have also been related to metacognition (Allen et al., 2008). Although often used interchangeably in empirical research (Dimaggio et al., 2011), these concepts have distinct theoretical and developmental origins (Allen et al., 2008), generally referring to the ability to comprehend actions and behaviors in terms of one's own and other mental states. The concept of metacognition was first used by Flavell (1979) to describe the set of mental activities related to thinking about thinking. In this chapter, we use the concept of metacognition, encompassing the capacity to understand the *cognitive* and *affective* mental states of *oneself* and *others* (Semerari et al., 2003). Self versus other mental states and cognitive (i.e., reasoning about knowledge and beliefs) versus affective (i.e., reasoning about emotions) are considered semi-independent components supported by distinct yet overlapping neurobiologic underpinnings (Abu-Akel and Shamay-Tsoory, 2011; Choi-Kain and Gunderson, 2008; Semerari et al., 2007) and will serve as the cornerstones of our metacognitive framework to understanding aggression and violence in schizophrenia.

Together, these components are considered necessary for adequate inter- and intra-relational attunement, including affect regulation and impulsive control (Bateman and Fonagy, 2011; Baumeister and Heatherton, 1996; Weiss et al., 2006). Aberrant metacognitive processing can disrupt awareness of internal mental states, potentially causing the individual to act upon these states as opposed to processing them mentally. Difficulties with mental state attribution and mental state reasoning of others can interfere with the recognition of important information inherent in human interactions (Bora *et al.*, 2006; Bora *et al.*, 2009). Furthermore, impairments in metacognitive abilities could lead to grave difficulties in the representation and construction of complex ideas as well as forming specific theories of the internal states of self and others. These abilities (or the lack thereof) have direct consequences on how people solve interpersonal issues confronted with in daily life (Kean, 2009; Roe and Davidson, 2005) and thus could impact one's propensity to engage in acts of violence and aggression. Specifically, being unable to understand the mind of the others, such as their intentional states, may lead to misunderstandings and, in some cases, the erroneous perceptions of these intentions as threatening or hostile (Salvatore *et al.*, 2012), potentially leading the individual to respond violently.

A growing body of literature provides evidence for the utility of using metacognition as a framework to understanding violence and delinquent behavior (Addy *et al.*, 2007; Blair *et al.*, 2006; Blair *et al.*, 2004; Covell and Scalora, 2002; Levinson and Fonagy, 2004), and particularly by utilizing the distinction between the cognitive and affective dimensions of metacognitive abilities. Indeed, there is evidence demonstrating that emotional mental states understanding can (1) reduce the propensity to engage in violence (e.g., Eisenberg and Fabes, 1990; Miller and Eisenberg, 1988; Tangney, 1991), (2) function as a potent inhibitor of aggression (Fullam and Dolan, 2006), and (3) the lack thereof can be a risk factor for violence (Murphy, 1998; Ward *et al.*, 2000). Moreover, Abu-Akel and Abushua'leh (2004) who investigated the association between violence and metacognitive abilities in patients with schizophrenia showed that while the ability to make empathic inferences (i.e., affective ToM) decreased the likelihood of violence engagement, demonstrating comprehension of cognitive mental states (i.e., cognitive ToM) increased the possibility for violence. In a more recent study, Majorek *et al.* (2009) compared a forensic and nonforensic sample of patients with schizophrenia with a healthy control group, in relation to symptomatology, metacognitive abilities, and executive functioning. Metacognitive skills in this study were assessed using a picture-story-sequencing task followed by a questionnaire that addressed the mental states of the cartoon characters. While the forensic and nonforensic groups did not differ in their overall performance, the forensic outperformed the nonforensic group in the questionnaire part of the task. This difference was not due to differences in premorbid intelligence or executive functioning between the two groups. However, when taking into account differences in the psychopathologic profile of the two patients groups, the overall performance of the forensic group was significantly better than the nonforensic group. Interestingly, both studies report better cognitive metacognitive abilities in the violent than in the nonviolent group. The association of intact cognitive metacognitive abilities with increased risk of violence may appear paradoxical, however. In one respect, this seeming contradiction is not illogical, given that metacognitive abilities are necessary for manipulative and deceptive purposes. For example, it is possible that violence observed among patients with paranoid schizophrenia (Abu-Akel and Abushua'leh, 2004) can be attributed, in addition to deficits in empathic abilities, to the ability to use metacognitive abilities to manipulate and deceive their victims. This is in keeping with studies reporting that patients with schizophrenia can commit premeditated violent crimes (Rice and Harris, 1995), which inherently require metacognitive abilities, as well as with reports indicating that lethal or near lethal acts of violence can be associated with intellectually intact psychotic individuals (Nestor *et al.*, 1995).

However, the studies mentioned above did not differentiate between impulsive and premeditated aggression. This distinction is important since, as we pointed out above, premeditated aggression is considered a more severe form of aggression and a better predictor of future aggressive recidivism (Cornell *et al.*, 1996). Furthermore, these studies did not consider the more nuanced distinction between the various dimensions of metacognition. With the purpose of further elucidating the relationship between aggression and metacognition, we investigated the association of premeditated and impulsive aggression and metacognition (assessed by the Metacognitive Assessment Scale, Abbreviated Version (MAS-A) (Lysaker *et al.*, 2005)) in 108 individuals with schizophrenia (Bo *et al.*, 2013). The results of this study showed that overall diminished metacognitive abilities were more pronounced in patients displaying a pattern of predominantly premeditated aggression, compared with patients who mainly engaged in impulsive aggression. At first sight, this seems to be contradictory to the results reported above (i.e., Abu-Akel and Abushua'leh, 2004; Majorek *et al.*, 2009), where a profile of superior 'cognitive' and decreased 'affective' metacognition was related to general aggression. However, by considering the patients' performance, on both the cognitive and affective components of self and other, we find that the underlying metacognitive profile of patients with schizophrenia displaying predominantly premeditated aggression consists of relatively intact 'cognitive', but severely impaired 'affective' metacognitive abilities. In contrast, patients with predominantly impulsive aggression had difficulties in both cognitive and affective processing of mental states. This finding is in line with other studies associating impulsive aggression with affect dysregulation (e.g., Glenn *et al.*, 2009). In this regard, it has been proposed that difficulties with affective processing could lead the individual to being overwhelmed with emotional material, which, in turn, may raise the risk of overengaging limbic structures at the expense of a more rationale and conscious prefrontal activity. Such limbic–prefrontal imbalance in the processing of emotions is one mechanism that may explain the occurrence of impulsive aggression in these individuals (Bateman and Fonagy, 2011).

Furthermore, a long held view is that there is a strong association between psychopathy and premeditated aggression (Cornell *et al.*, 1996). However, little is known as to why this association exists. In one study, we have shown that metacognition is a substantial mediator between psychopathy and premeditated aggression in a large sample of patients with schizophrenia (Bo *et al.*, 2014). In this study, we found that a specific profile consisting of intact 'cognitive' and impaired 'affective' metacognitive functioning of the others' mind mediates the relationship between psychopathy and premeditated aggression, accounting for 60% of the total effect size. This study found no significant mediating effect for representing and understanding mental states related to the self

Taken together, these results point toward a potential model that can explain the occurrence of different subtypes of aggression and violence in patients with schizophrenia. First, the occurrence of premeditated aggression in schizophrenia appears to be associated with an indifference to others' affective mental states, whereby perpetrators could perceive others as instruments to obtain personal goals notwithstanding the consequences. This impairment coexists with intact cognitive metacognitive processing of the other, which provides the capacity to engage in manipulation in the service of achieving one's own personal goals. In accordance, these studies support a model positing that a combination of *intact cognitive* and *impaired emotional* metacognitive abilities is characteristic of patients with schizophrenia committing premeditated aggression. Within this context, it can be argued that the more premeditated violence patients with schizophrenia display, the more they would be aware of how the mind of the other function, when planning and preparing for their violence. Simultaneously, they would have to be ignorant of, or indifferent to, the emotional states of the other. Some have argued, however, that the lack of affective metacognitive processing, should not be considered a deficiency (Meloy, 2012), but instead an adaptation that enhances predatory success, accomplished by keeping higher cognitive levels of metacognition unaffected by emotional awareness of others.

This view is in concordance with studies advocating that cognitive and emotional metacognitive processing are supported by semi-independent networks (Dimaggio *et al.*, 2009). Interestingly, neuroimaging work provides evidence suggesting that patients who display predominantly premeditated aggression process emotions and affective states along alternative cognitive pathways in the prefrontal cortex as opposed to the traditional limbic areas of the brain (Anderson and Kiehl, 2012; Anderson and Stanford, 2012; Kiehl, 2006). While these findings require replication, they nonetheless provide an alternative to the idea that metacognition is 'defective' or deficient in patients displaying premeditated aggression and suggest that premeditated or predatory aggression can be understood as aspects of an adaptive life strategy, where emotions and the mental understanding of emotions in others is processed in different neurobiologic systems, allowing such individuals to plan their acts of violence strategically without invoking feelings of remorse or guilt.

CONCLUSION

In this chapter, we presented the potential of metacognition as a framework to explaining aggression, and have shown (as illustrated in Fig. 8.1) how different metacognitive profiles are linked to specific patterns of violence and aggression. While general metacognitive impairments are related to enhanced aggression and violence in schizophrenia, our research suggests that it entails unnecessarily a limited view of the specific metacognitive profiles associated with the occurrence of aggression. In one respect, research needs to at least make a distinction between impulsive and premeditated aggression, which appear, as we have shown, to be associated with differing metacognitive profiles. Furthermore, in adopting a metacognitive approach, there is a need to distinguish between self and other as well as the ability to process cognitive and affective mental states. This approach is surely to afford a more nuanced way to conceptualize and understand the severity of violence and aggression displayed by patients with schizophrenia.

There is little evidence that psychopharmacologic treatments, specifically those using antipsychotic drugs, enhance metacognition and the awareness of one's own and others' mental states (Kucharska-Pietura and Mortimer, 2013). However, researchers are now implementing promising psychosocial interventions based on the concept of metacognition, which are designed to aid patients with schizophrenia to reflect on their own symptoms and the state of the mind of others better (Moritz and Woodward, 2007; Salvatore *et al.*, 2012). While, these proposals were not designed to specifically diminish aggression in patients with schizophrenia, they entail the potential of reducing

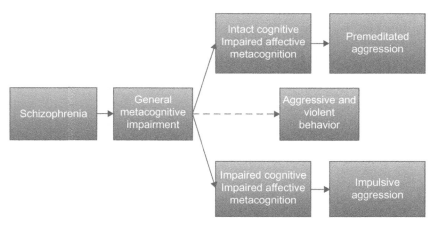

FIGURE 8.1   Metacognitive profiles of impulsive and premeditated aggression.

aggression by way of correcting associated metacognitive abnormalities. In this regard, we suggest that clinical interventions aimed at reducing aggression and violence in patients with schizophrenia would benefit from being sensitive to types of aggression and the metacognitive profiles with which they are associated.

REFERENCES

Aarsland, D., Cummings, J. L., Yenner, G., & Miller, B. (1996). Relationship of aggressive behavior to other neuropsychiatric symptoms in patients with Alzheimer's disease. *American Journal of Psychiatry, 153*(2), 243–247.

Abu-Akel, A., & Abushua'leh, K. (2004). 'Theory of mind' in violent and nonviolent patients with paranoid schizophrenia. *Schizophrenia Research, 69*(1), 45–53.

Abu-Akel, A., & Shamay-Tsoory, S. (2011). Neuroanatomical and neurochemical bases of theory of mind. *Neuropsychologia, 49*(11), 2971–2984.

Addy, K., Shannon, K., & Brookfield, K. (2007). Theory of mind function, motor empathy, emotional empathy and schizophrenia: A single case study. *Journal of Forensic Psychiatry & Psychology, 18*(3), 293–306.

Allen, J. G., Fonagy, P., & Bateman, A. (2008). *Mentalizing in clinical practice*. Arlington: American Psychiatric Publishing.

Anderson, N. E., & Kiehl, K. A. (2012). The psychopath magnetized: Insights from brain imaging. *Trends in Cognitive Sciences, 16*(1), 52–60.

Anderson, N. E., & Stanford, M. S. (2012). Demonstrating emotional processing differences in psychopathy using affective ERP modulation. *Psychophysiology, 49*(6), 792–806.

Ang, G. K., & Pridmore, S. (2009). Theory of mind and psychiatry: An introduction. *Australasian Psychiatry: Bulletin of Royal Australian and New Zealand College of Psychiatrists, 17*(2), 117–122.

Barratt, E. S., & Felthous, A. R. (2003). Impulsive versus premeditated aggression: Implications for mens rea decisions. *Behavioral Sciences & the Law, 21*(5), 619–630.

Barratt, E. S., Stanford, M. S., Dowdy, L., Liebman, M. J., & Kent, T. A. (1999). Impulsive and premeditated aggression: A factor analysis of self-reported acts. *Psychiatry Research, 86*(2), 163–173.

Bateman, A. W., & Fonagy, P. (2011). *Handbook of mentalizing in mental health practice*. Washington, DC: American Psychiatric Publishing, Inc.

Baumeister, R. F., & Heatherton, T. F. (1996). Self-regulation failure: An overview. *Psychological Inquiry, 7*(1), 1–15.

Blair, R. J., Peschardt, K. S., Budhani, S., Mitchell, D. G., & Pine, D. S. (2006). The development of psychopathy. *Journal of Child Psychology and Psychiatry, and Allied Disciplines, 47*(3–4), 262–276.

Blair, R. J. R., Mitchell, D. G. V., Peschardt, K. S., Colledge, E., Leonard, R. A., Shine, J. H., et al. (2004). Reduced sensitivity to others' fearful expressions in psychopathic individuals. *Personality and Individual Differences, 37*(6), 1111–1122.

Bo, S., Abu-Akel, A., Bertelsen, P., Kongerslev, M., & Haahr, U. H. (2013). Attachment, mentalizing and personality pathology severity in premeditated and impulsive aggression in schizophrenia. *International Journal of Forensic Mental Health, 12*(2), 126–138.

Bo, S., Abu-Akel, A., Kongerslev, M., Haahr, U. H., & Simonsen, E. (2011). Risk factors for violence among patients with schizophrenia. *Clinical Psychology Review, 31*(5), 711–726.

Bo, S., Abu-Akel, A., Kongerslev, M., Helt, U. H., & Bateman, A. (2014). Mentalizing mediates the relationship between psychopathy and type of aggression in schizophrenia. *Journal of Nervous and Mental Disease, 202*(1), 55–63.

Bonta, J. (1998). The prediction of criminal and violent recidivism among mentally disordered offenders: A meta-analysis. *Psychological Bulletin, 123*(2), 123–142.

Bora, E., Eryavuz, A., Kayahan, B., Sungu, G., & Veznedaroglu, B. (2006). Social functioning, theory of mind and neurocognition in outpatients with schizophrenia; mental state decoding may be a better predictor of social functioning than mental state reasoning. *Psychiatry Research, 145*(2–3), 95–103.

Bora, E., Yucel, M., & Pantelis, C. (2009). Theory of mind impairment in schizophrenia: Meta-analysis. *Schizophrenia Research, 109*(1–3), 1–9.

Brennan, P. A., Mednick, S. A., & Hodgins, S. (2000). Major mental disorders and criminal violence in a Danish birth cohort. *Archives of General Psychiatry, 57*(5), 494–500.

Brune, M. (2005). "Theory of mind" in schizophrenia: A review of the literature. *Schizophrenia Bulletin, 31*(1), 21–42.

Camisa, K. M., Bockbrader, M. A., Lysaker, P., Rae, L. L., Brenner, C. A., & O'Donnell, B. F. (2005). Personality traits in schizophrenia and related personality disorders. *Psychiatry Research, 133*(1), 23–33.

Choi-Kain, L. W., & Gunderson, J. G. (2008). Mentalization: Ontogeny, assessment, and application in the treatment of borderline personality disorder. *American Journal of Psychiatry, 165*(9), 1127–1135.

Corcoran, R., Mercer, G., & Frith, C. D. (1995). Schizophrenia, symptomatology and social inference: Investigating "theory of mind" in people with schizophrenia. *Schizophrenia Research, 17*(1), 5–13.

Cornell, D. G., Warren, J., Hawk, G., Stafford, E., Oram, G., & Pine, D. (1996). Psychopathy in instrumental and reactive violent offenders. *Journal of Consulting and Clinical Psychology, 64*(4), 783–790.

Covell, C. N., & Scalora, M. J. (2002). Empathic deficits in sexual offenders: An integration of affective, social, and cognitive constructs. *Aggression and Violent Behavior, 7*(3), 251–270.

Dack, C., Ross, J., Papadopoulos, C., Stewart, D., & Bowers, L. (2013). A review and meta-analysis of the patient factors associated with psychiatric in-patient aggression. *Acta Psychiatrica Scandinavica, 127*(4), 255–268.

Dickerson, F., Boronow, J. J., Ringel, N., & Parente, F. (1999). Social functioning and neurocognitive deficits in outpatients with schizophrenia: A 2-year follow-up. *Schizophrenia Research, 37*(1), 13–20.

Dimaggio, G., Nicolò, G., Brüne, M., & Lysaker, P. H. (2011). Mental state understanding in adult psychiatric disorders: Impact on symptoms, social functioning and treatment. *Psychiatry Research, 190*(1), 1–2.

Dimaggio, G., Vanheule, S., Lysaker, P. H., Carcione, A., & Nicolò, G. (2009). Impaired self-reflection in psychiatric disorders among adults: A proposal for the existence of a network of semi independent functions. *Consciousness and Cognition, 18*(3), 653–664.

Donat, D., Geczy, B., & Helmrich, J. (1992). Empirically derived personality subtypes in public psychiatric patients: Effects on self-reported symptoms, coping inclinations and evaluations of expressed emotion in care givers. *Journal of Personality Assessment, 58*, 36–50.

Douglas, K. S., Guy, L. S., & Hart, S. D. (2009). Psychosis as a risk factor for violence to others: A meta-analysis. *Psychological Bulletin, 135*(5), 679–706.

Editorial. (1988). Where next with psychiatric illness? *Nature, 336*(6195), 95–96.

Eisenberg, N., & Fabes, R. A. (1990). Empathy: Conceptualization, measurement, and relation to prosocial behavior. *Motivation and Emotion, 14*(2), 131–149.

Erb, M., Hodgins, S., Freese, R., Müller-Isberner, R., & Jöckel, D. (2001). Homicide and schizophrenia: Maybe treatment does have a preventive effect. *Criminal Behaviour and Mental Health: CBMH, 11*(1), 6–26.

Etherington, R. (1993). Diagnostic and personality differences of juvenile sex offenders, non-sex offenders and non-offenders. *Dissertation Abstracts International, 54(4-B)*, 2195.

Fazel, S., & Grann, M. (2006). The population impact of severe mental illness on violent crime. *American Journal of Psychiatry, 163*(8), 1397–1403.

Fazel, S., Långström, N., Hjern, A., Grann, M., & Lichtenstein, P. (2009). Schizophrenia, substance abuse, and violent crime. *JAMA, 301*(19), 2016–2023.

Felthous, A. R., Weaver, D., Evans, R., Braik, S., Stanford, M. S., Johnson, R., et al. (2009). Assessment of impulsive aggression in patients with severe mental disorders and demonstrated violence: Inter-rater reliability of rating instrument. *Journal of Forensic Sciences, 54*(6), 1470–1474.

Flavell, J. H. (1979). Metacognition and cognitive monitoring: A new area of cognitive-developmental inquiry. *American Psychologist, 34*(10), 906–911.

Flight, J. I., & Forth, A. E. (2007). Instrumentally violent youths. *Criminal Justice and Behavior, 34*(6), 739–751.

Frith, C. D. (2004). Schizophrenia and theory of mind. *Psychological Medicine, 34*(3), 385–389.

Fullam, R., & Dolan, M. (2006). Emotional information processing in violent patients with schizophrenia: Association with psychopathy and symptomatology. *Psychiatry Research, 141*(1), 29–37.

Glenn, A. L., Raine, A., & Schug, R. A. (2009). The neural correlates of moral decision-making in psychopathy. *Molecular Psychiatry, 14*(1), 5–6.

Grann, M., Danesh, J., & Fazel, S. (2008). The association between psychiatric diagnosis and violent re-offending in adult offenders in the community. *BMC Psychiatry, 8*, 92–99.

Haden, S. C., Scarpa, A., & Stanford, M. S. (2008). Validation of the impulsive/premeditated aggression scale in college students. *Journal of Aggression, Maltreatment & Trauma, 17*(3), 352–373.

Harrington, L., Siegert, R. J., & McClure, J. (2005). Theory of mind in schizophrenia: A critical review. *Cognitive Neuropsychiatry, 10*(4), 249–286.

Hasson-Ohayon, I., Kravetz, S., Levy, I., & Roe, D. (2009). Metacognitive and interpersonal interventions for persons with severe mental illness: Theory and practice. *The Israel Journal of Psychiatry and Related Sciences, 46*(2), 141–148.

Hodgins, S. (2008). Violent behaviour among people with schizophrenia: A framework for investigations of causes, and effective treatment, and prevention. *Philosophical Transactions of the Royal Society of London. Series B, Biological Sciences, 363*(1503), 2505–2518.

Hori, H., Richards, M., Kawamoto, Y., & Kunugi, H. (2011). Attitudes toward schizophrenia in the general population, psychiatric staff, physicians, and psychiatrists: A web-based survey in Japan. *Psychiatry Research, 186*(2–3), 183–189.

Jablensky, A., Kirkbride, J. B., & Jones, P. B. (1995). Schizophrenia: The epidemiological horizon. *Schizophrenia*, 185–225.

Kean, C. (2009). Silencing the self: Schizophrenia as a self-disturbance. *Schizophrenia Bulletin, 35*(6), 1034–1036.

Kiehl, K. A. (2006). A cognitive neuroscience perspective on psychopathy: Evidence for paralimbic system dysfunction. *Psychiatry Research, 142*(2–3), 107–128.

Kucharska-Pietura, K., & Mortimer, A. (2013). Can antipsychotics improve social cognition in patients with schizophrenia? *CNS Drugs*, *27*(5), 335–343.

Levinson, A., & Fonagy, P. (2004). Offending and attachment: The relationship between interpersonal awareness and offending in a prison population with psychiatric. *Canadian Journal of Psychoanalysis*, *12*(2), 225–251.

Lyons, M. J., Tyrer, P., Gunderson, J., & Tohen, M. (1997). Special feature: Heuristic models of comorbidity of axis I and axis II disorders. *Journal of Personality Disorders*, *11*(3), 260–269.

Lysaker, P. H., Carcione, A., Dimaggio, G., Johannesen, J. K., Nicolò, G., Procacci, M., et al. (2005). Metacognition amidst narratives of self and illness in schizophrenia: Associations with neurocognition, symptoms, insight and quality of life. *Acta Psychiatrica Scandinavica*, *112*(1), 64–71.

Lysaker, P. H., Dimaggio, G., Buck, K. D., Callaway, S. S., Salvatore, G., Carcione, A., et al. (2011). Poor insight in schizophrenia: Links between different forms of metacognition with awareness of symptoms, treatment need, and consequences of illness. *Comprehensive Psychiatry*, *52*(3), 253–260.

Lysaker, P. H., Ringer, J. M., Buck, K. D., Grant, M., Olesek, K., Leudtke, B. L., et al. (2012). Metacognitive and social cognition deficits in patients with significant psychiatric and medical adversity: A comparison between participants with schizophrenia and a sample of participants who are HIV-positive. *Journal of Nervous and Mental Disease*, *200*(2), 130–134.

Lysaker, P. H., Wilt, M. A., Plascak-Hallberg, C. D., Brenner, C. A., & Clements, C. A. (2003). Personality dimensions in schizophrenia: Associations with symptoms and coping. *Journal of Nervous and Mental Disease*, *191*(2), 80–86.

Majorek, K., Wolfkühler, W., Küper, C., Saimeh, N., Juckel, G., & Brüne, M. (2009). "Theory of mind" and executive functioning in forensic patients with schizophrenia. *Journal of Forensic Sciences*, *54*(2), 469–473.

McMillan, K. A., Enns, M. W., Cox, B. J., & Sareen, J. (2009). Comorbidity of axis I and II mental disorders with schizophrenia and psychotic disorders: Findings from the national epidemiologic survey on alcohol and related conditions. Canadian Journal of Psychiatry. *Revue Canadienne De Psychiatrie*, *54*(7), 477–486.

Meloy, J. R. (2006). Empirical basis and forensic application of affective and predatory violence. *Australian and New Zealand Journal of Psychiatry*, *40*(6–7), 539–547.

Meloy, J. R. (2012). Predatory violence and psychopathy. In H. Häkkänen-Nyholm & J. O. Nyholm (Eds.), *Psychopathy and Law: A Practitioner's Guide*. Wiley-Blackwell, Hoboken, NJ (pp. 159–176).

Miller, P. A., & Eisenberg, N. (1988). The relation of empathy to aggressive and externalizing/antisocial behavior. *Psychological Bulletin*, *103*(3), 324–344.

Moore, E. A., Green, M. J., & Carr, V. J. (2012). Comorbid personality traits in schizophrenia: Prevalence and clinical characteristics. *Journal of Psychiatric Research*, *46*(3), 353–359.

Moritz, S., & Woodward, T. S. (2007). Metacognitive training for schizophrenia patients (MCT): A pilot study on feasibility, treatment adherence, and subjective efficacy. *German Journal of Psychiatry*, *10*(3), 69–78.

Murphy, D. (1998). Theory of mind in a schizophrenia sample of men with schizophrenia detained in a special hospital: Its relationship to symptom profiles and neuropsychological tests. *Criminal Behaviour and Mental Health*, *8*, 13–26.

Nestor, P. G., Haycock, J., Doiron, S., Kelly, J., & Kelly, D. (1995). Lethal violence and psychosis: A clinical profile. *Bulletin of the American Academy of Psychiatry and the Law*, *23*(3), 331–341.

Newton-Howes, G., Tyrer, P., North, B., & Yang, M. (2008). The prevalence of personality disorder in schizophrenia and psychotic disorders: Systematic review of rates and explanatory modelling. *Psychological Medicine*, *38*(8), 1075–1082.

Pickup, G. J., & Frith, C. D. (2001). Theory of mind impairments in schizophrenia: Symptomatology, severity and specificity. *Psychological Medicine, 31*(2), 207–220.

Rice, M. E., & Harris, G. T. (1995). Psychopathy, schizophrenia, alcohol abuse, and violent recidivism. *International Journal of Law and Psychiatry, 18*(3), 333–342.

Rippon, T. J. (2000). Aggression and violence in health care professions. *Journal of Advanced Nursing, 31*(2), 452–460.

Roe, D., & Davidson, L. (2005). Self and narrative in schizophrenia: Time to author a new story. *Medical Humanities, 31*(2), 89–94.

Salvatore, G., Lysaker, P. H., Gumley, A., Popolo, R., Mari, J., & Dimaggio, G. (2012). Out of illness experience: Metacognition-oriented therapy for promoting self-awareness in individuals with psychosis. *American Journal of Psychotherapy, 66*(1), 85–106.

Semerari, A., Carcione, A., Dimaggio, G., Falcone, M., Nicolò, G., Procacci, M., et al. (2003). How to evaluate metacognitive function in psychotherapy? The metacognition assessment scale and its applications. *Clinical Psychology and Psychotherapy, 10*(4), 238–261.

Semerari, A., Carcione, A., Dimaggio, G., Nicolò, G., & Procacci, M. (2007). Understanding minds: Different functions and different disorders? The contribution of psychotherapy research. *Psychotherapy Research, 17*(1), 106–119.

Serafini, G., Pompili, M., Haghighat, R., Pucci, D., Pastina, M., Lester, D., et al. (2011). Stigmatization of schizophrenia as perceived by nurses, medical doctors, medical students and patients. *Journal of Psychiatric and Mental Health Nursing, 18*(7), 576–585.

Soyka, M., Graz, C., Bottlender, R., Dirschedl, P., & Schoech, H. (2007). Clinical correlates of later violence and criminal offences in schizophrenia. *Schizophrenia Research, 94*(1–3), 89–98.

Tangney, J. P. (1991). Moral affect: The good, the bad, and the ugly. *Journal of Personality and Social Psychology, 61*(4), 598–607.

Tiihonen, J., Isohanni, M., Räsänen, P., Koiranen, M., & Moring, J. (1997). Specific major mental disorders and criminality: A 26-year prospective study of the 1966 northern Finland birth cohort. *American Journal of Psychiatry, 154*(6), 840–845.

Vahabzadeh, A., Wittenauer, J., & Carr, E. (2011). Stigma, schizophrenia and the media: Exploring changes in the reporting of schizophrenia in major U.S. newspapers. *Journal of Psychiatric Practice, 17*(6), 439–446.

Volavka, J. (2013). Violence in schizophrenia and bipolar disorder. *Psychiatria Danubina, 25*(1), 24–33.

Walsh, E., Buchanan, A., & Fahy, T. (2002). Violence and schizophrenia: Examining the evidence. *British Journal of Psychiatry, 180*(6), 490–495.

Ward, T., Keenan, T., & Hudson, S. M. (2000). Understanding cognitive, affective, and intimacy deficits in sexual offenders: A developmental perspective. *Aggression and Violent Behavior, 5*(1), 41–62.

Weiss, E. M., Kohler, C. G., Nolan, K. A., Czobor, P., Volavka, J., Platt, M. M., et al. (2006). The relationship between history of violent and criminal behavior and recognition of facial expression of emotions in men with schizophrenia and schizoaffective disorder. *Aggressive Behavior, 32*(3), 187–194.

WHO. (2007). *Third milestones of a global campaign for violence prevention report 2007: Scaling-up.* Geneva, Switzerland: World Health Organization.

Witt, K., Zhang, X. Y., van Dorn, R., & Fazel, S. (2013). Risk factors for violence in psychosis: Systematic review and meta-regression analysis of 110 studies. *PLoS One, 8*(2), e55942.

Chapter 9

Social Cognition and Interaction Training: The Role of Metacognition

João M. Fernandes[1] and David L. Roberts[2]

[1]*Centro Hospitalar de Lisboa Ocidental, EPE, Lisbon, Portugal,* [2]*University of Texas Health Science Center, San Antonio, TX, USA*

Chapter Outline

INTRODUCTION

In this chapter, we present a social cognition intervention program called social cognition and interaction training (SCIT), placing special emphasis on its metacognitive components. The first part of the chapter will describe SCIT, a group-based intervention that is delivered weekly over 6 months and is designed to improve social cognition and social functioning in patients with schizophrenia spectrum disorders. SCIT comprises three phases of increasing difficulty and emotional challenge: (1) introduction and emotion recognition, (2) figuring out situations, and (3) integration and application to daily life. In the second part of the chapter, we will show how SCIT integrates metacognitive processes across two different levels: patient and intervention. On the patient level, SCIT is designed to leverage patients' metacognitive experiences

Social Cognition and Metacognition in Schizophrenia.
DOI: http://dx.doi.org/10.1016/B978-0-12-405172-0.00009-0
© 2014 Elsevier Inc. All rights reserved.

such that it is seen as fun, intrinsically rewarding, and not cognitively demanding. In this way, it helps patients to feel engaged but not overwhelmed. Early sessions of SCIT emphasize easy fictional and impersonal content, whereas later sessions emphasize more complicated and personal content. By gradually increasing emotional and cognitive challenge, SCIT should not feel threatening or intrusive to patients and should provide the necessary time for trust to develop. On the intervention level, SCIT is designed to enhance adaptive integration between automatic cognitive processing, which is more immediate, efficient, unintended and emotion-influenced, and controlled cognitive processing, which is more reflective, effortful, and less vulnerable to emotion-based bias. To accomplish this, SCIT teaches patients techniques for recognizing automatic social cognitive tendencies, evaluating the accuracy of social judgments, and reflecting on how social cognitive processes affect their lives. While the patient level of metacognitive processing promotes adherence to the program and treatment satisfaction, the intervention level teaches skills that help to consolidate and enhance social cognitive improvements. Finally, we summarize SCIT treatment outcome findings and discuss current and future lines of investigation.

SOCIAL COGNITION AND INTERACTION TRAINING

Social cognition has been defined as consisting of 'the mental operations underlying social interactions, which include the human ability to perceive the intentions and dispositions of others' (Brothers, 1990). It has gained importance given its close and strong relation with impaired social functioning in schizophrenia (Couture *et al.*, 2006; Fett *et al.*, 2011). Therefore, it is reasonable to expect that targeting social cognitive impairments in treatment may bring improvements in social functioning. However, treatment interventions targeting social cognition in schizophrenia have generally conceptualized social cognitive dysfunction more as a deficit state and less as involving social cognitive biases (Roberts and Penn, 2009). Social cognition and interaction training (SCIT; Roberts *et al.*, in press) is a manual-based intervention that was developed in part to address this limitation by taking into account the specific active cognitive processes that underlie social cognition (Penn *et al.*, 2007): (1) *need for closure (or intolerance of ambiguity)* is associated with the tendency to bypass explanatory evidence gathering and jump to hasty conclusions in social situations (Bentall and Swarbrick, 2003); (2) *externalizing and personalizing attributional biases* in explaining negative events that refers to the tendency to blame outside factors or people as opposed to situations when dealing with negative events (Kinderman and Bentall, 1997); (3) *theory of mind* (ToM) is the ability to simulate in one's own mind the mental states of people other than oneself. This includes not only the ability to infer the intentions, perspectives, desires, and emotions of other people (i.e., 'to put oneself in another's shoes'), but also includes the ability to imagine oneself in a different situation from the here-and-now, and to evaluate one's current thoughts and emotions nonsubjectively, as if looking at oneself from the outside. This latter aspect of ToM overlaps with the concept of metacognition; and (4) *emotion perception* abnormalities include difficulties identifying facially expressed emotions in others. Abnormalities in emotion perception are thought to exacerbate the above constellation of difficulties as they apply to interpersonal functioning.

By addressing the range of abilities that comprise social cognition, SCIT differs from so-called 'targeted' social cognitive interventions, which focus on improving one specific social cognitive skill (e.g., emotion perception training). Also, as described below, SCIT not only helps patients develop social cognitive skills but also promotes generalization to their personal difficulties in social functioning.

SCIT also differs from more traditional psychotherapeutic approaches to schizophrenia. By focusing on social cognitive processes rather than cognitive content, SCIT distances itself from traditional cognitive behavioral therapy (Beck, 2001). That is, instead of challenging the logic underlying specific overvalued beliefs, SCIT targets distorted interpretive processes that may generate and maintain delusions (Roberts *et al.*, 2010). By focusing on socially related cognitive processes such as attributional style and ToM rather than the relatively independent neurocognitive abilities such as attention or memory, SCIT also differs from cognitive remediation therapy.

SCIT's treatment manual (Roberts *et al.*, in press) comprises the following elements: (1) introduction, which provides an overview of SCIT; explains its rationale; and explains treatment phases, session format, and structure; (2) session content, which describes session organization and procedures, and goals for each treatment phase; and (3) a DVD supplement with clinical vignettes portrayed by hired actors that are viewed and discussed throughout the SCIT protocol. SCIT is delivered in 20 to 24 weekly 45- to 60-minute group sessions by one or two therapists and comprises the following three treatment phases: (1) *introduction and emotions*, which addresses emotion perception dysfunction; (2) *figuring out situations*, which addresses attributional biases and ToM dysfunction; and (3) *integration*, in which participants integrate newly learned skills and practice applying them to interpersonal problems in their own lives.

During *introduction and emotions* training, the initial goal is to introduce SCIT and social cognition to patients, while helping build group alliance. This phase also intends to provide information about emotions and their relationship to thoughts and social contexts, define seven basic emotions, help individuals to distinguish between different facial expressions of emotion via commercially available computer-based programs, and conceptualize paranoia as an emotion. The primary goal during *figuring out situations* is to help patients recognize 'jumping to conclusions' processes and their potential negative social consequences. This phase intends to teach patients the difference between external, internal, and situational causal attributions for negative events, and the difference between social 'facts' and social 'guesses'. Social cognitive strategies used during this phase include promoting discussion of attributions from different perspectives (external, internal, and situational), practicing gathering evidence instead of jumping to conclusions, and tolerating ambiguity in social situations (by shifting from a strict true/false paradigm to a likelihood paradigm). The purpose of the final phase, *integration*, is to consolidate patients' learned skills and help them put these into practice in their own lives. During this phase, patients are encouraged to bring up troubling interpersonal situations and collaboratively assess these situations within the group by identifying underlying emotions of self and others, distinguishing facts from guesses, avoiding jumping to conclusions by gathering as much information as possible (while recognizing that without such information it may not be possible to fully understand a situation), and coming up with a solution or action plan.

METACOGNITION IN SOCIAL COGNITION AND INTERACTION TRAINING: SUBJECT LEVEL

As previously mentioned, an overlap exists between some facets of specific social cognitive processes, such as ToM, and metacognition. Metacognition can generally be conceptualized as 'thinking about thinking' (Lysaker *et al.*, 2011). Metacognition enables patients to evaluate their own thoughts critically and decide on whether ideas and beliefs about themselves and others should be accepted or rejected. Therefore, it integrates closely with SCIT's content and procedures, by serving as a necessary tool to enable more accurate ToM and emotion perception processes and enhance patients' fact-based thinking and tolerance of ambiguity and doubt. Concordantly, deficits in metacognition have been found to play a role in social functioning and interpersonal relations in schizophrenia (Lysaker *et al.*, 2010).

SCIT is also designed to capitalize on patients' *metacognitive experience*. This term refers to the feeling states that accompany cognitive processing (Schwarz, 2004). Continuous with research showing that people sometimes use 'affect as information' in making judgments (Clore *et al.*, 2001), research on *metacognitive experience* shows that the ease or difficulty that people experience when thinking influences the confidence they have in the validity of their judgments. Cognitive content associated with easy or fluid metacognitive experiences is judged to be more valid than content associated with effortful or taxing cognitive experiences. In holding with this, SCIT's phases have been designed to be gradually involving and emotionally challenging to the patient. In this way, they respect the fact that patients may initially have relatively underdeveloped metacognitive capacity and social cognitive skill. If early sessions were excessively emotionally arousing or demanding, this would promote patients' feeling overwhelmed, judging painful experiences or difficult new techniques to be bad, and relying on the more familiar, easy, and fluid techniques associated with social cognitive dysfunction, such as jumping to conclusions.

In order to engage patients comfortably, SCIT's first phase, *introduction and emotions*, spends some time building group alliance and creating a safe and fluid sharing and discussion environment. Interestingly, previous research has found that patients with schizophrenia who have relatively stronger metacognitive abilities are able to form stronger therapeutic relationships with their therapists (Davis *et al.*, 2011). Since some patients will be lacking adequate metacognitive capacity during the first stages of the intervention, developing group trust is particularly important, especially when considering SCIT's relative emphasis on interpersonal problems and paranoia, which are also likely to be exhibited by patients with schizophrenia. Therefore, before group trust develops, the intervention focuses on easy fictional and impersonal content that will not feel intrusive to patients. Also, SCIT facilitators use Socratic questioning to guide patients and reduce their perception that they are being driven to think what others want them to think. SCIT exercises are designed to be fun and intrinsically rewarding, which we expect will help patients adhere to the intervention by recruiting the same intuitive processes that make us evaluate something more favorably when more positive attributes come to mind (Schwarz, 2004). For instance, videotaped vignettes are used because besides being ecologically valid they are engaging and fun to watch. Similarly, the use of a modified form of the game *20 Questions* has been found to be unusually engaging among participant groups. The strategies learned through SCIT exercises are designed to be easily recalled and applied to patients' daily lives so that they will not be experienced as difficult and the judgments they produce will be seen as more valid (Schwarz, 2004). This latter aspect is particularly relevant if negative symptoms, specifically amotivation, are present, as these correlate not only with metacognitive deficits (Nicolò *et al.*, 2012) and learning potential (Tas *et al.*, 2012a) but also with poorer social functioning (Lysaker *et al.*, 2013).

However, while SCIT's initial tasks are designed to be cognitively and emotionally less demanding, SCIT's effectiveness eventually hinges on the participants' capacity to share their own interpersonal difficulties within the group, and to accept and provide feedback and suggestions from and to other members. To achieve this, SCIT uses different techniques that allow for a safe and gradual increase of its emotional and cognitive demands. First, SCIT promotes the involvement of a 'practice partner' – a specific person in the patient's life outside the group that has agreed to help him/her practice SCIT skills. The practice partner can be a family member, a friend, an individual therapist or case manager, or a close acquaintance. By using a practice partner, patients have an increased opportunity for consolidating concepts, as well as for skill application and integration through social interaction. Moreover, practicing with a familiar other promotes comfort and ease, maximizing positive metacognitive experiences. Supporting this approach, one study found that providing SCIT along with the active participation of close family members or friends was more effective in improving quality of life, social functioning, and social cognition compared with a basic social stimulation approach (Tas *et al.*, 2012b).

Second, the latter half of the intervention, and particularly the *integration* phase, focuses on difficult social situations brought in by patients from their own lives. Equipped with over-learned techniques and increased group alliance, it is expected that patients will now be able to share, analyze, and search for a solution to these problems with decreased vulnerability to biases such as jumping to conclusions. In other words, patients not only have new social cognitive skills, but improved awareness of their own social cognitive vulnerabilities, and an increased feeling of fluidity, confidence, and mastery associated with the deployment of skills.

By using this phased approach, SCIT is expected to promote patient adherence to the program and result in increased treatment satisfaction. It should also be experienced as a natural and effortless learning process by patients, even when complexity and emotional involvement increase, in order to be regarded as a good and valid experience by patients.

METACOGNITION IN SOCIAL COGNITION AND INTERACTION TRAINING: INTERVENTION LEVEL

We have described previously how SCIT attends to patient's metacognitive experiences by adapting to their presumed metacognitive state throughout the intervention. There is a second level of understanding of metacognition in SCIT, which is not related directly to patients' metacognitive skills or experiences but more to the metacognitive basis of the intervention itself. By this we mean that SCIT's exercises and content are designed to promote a more adaptive integration between *automatic* and *controlled* cognitive processes. While the former are more immediate, unintended, and emotion-influenced (and generally distant from typical metacognitive monitoring of mental activity), the latter are more reflective, effortful, and less vulnerable to emotion-based bias, hence closer to what is traditionally defined as metacognition (Bargh, 1994). However, as previously discussed, it is not reasonable to assume patients with schizophrenia will be able to maintain regular metacognitive capacity throughout the intervention, much less so during their regular social lives (David *et al.*, 2012). Additionally, effortful cognitive processing may actually hinder adaptive interpersonal interactions and even reinforce the biased judgments it was intending to minimize because thoughts experienced as difficult and laborious tend to be interpreted as bad, invalid, or incorrect (Roberts and Velligan, 2012). Also, due to the comparative ease with which they are generated, automatic cognitive processes will most frequently be the basis of real-world social judgments (Schwarz, 2004). Therefore, they should not be undervalued but ideally integrated into the treatment approach.

To accomplish this, SCIT first provides patients with a range of techniques for recognizing biases in automatic thinking. For instance, patients are encouraged to challenge automatic *external-personal* attributions by exercising

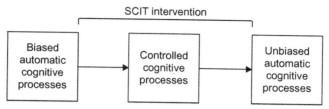

FIGURE 9.1   Integration of automatic and controlled cognitive processes in social cognition and interaction training (SCIT).

attributional flexibility and providing examples of different (i.e., *internal* or *situational*) explanations for the same fictional or real-life event. Patients are also invited to analyze 'acting without thinking' situations from a metacognitive perspective, by reflecting on how emotions affect one's perception of a situation or alter one's behavior. Also, patients are encouraged to suspend hasty judgments by collecting as much evidence as possible and being able to analyze the difference between the facts of a situation and one's guesses about the situation critically. These techniques should help patients to evaluate the accuracy of social judgments better and reflect on how social cognitive processes affect their lives. Once these techniques are learned, patients practice them in order to increase the ease and fluidity with which they can be deployed. The ultimate goal is to automatize these newly learned controlled cognitive strategies so that they can supplant previous biased processes as patients' first-line approach for making social judgments (Fig. 9.1).

RELEVANT RESEARCH USING SOCIAL COGNITION AND INTERACTION TRAINING

SCIT has been investigated in different settings and with different patient populations. SCIT's early testing was conducted in a pilot study with seven patients from an inpatient unit using a modified protocol adapted to this setting (Penn *et al.*, 2005). Significant improvements in ToM performance and trend level benefits in attributional style were observed, suggesting SCIT's feasibility and potential clinical benefits. Because emotion perception capacity did not change significantly in this study, this component was strengthened in a subsequent comparative study with inpatients with schizophrenia spectrum disorders (Combs *et al.*, 2007). Compared with 10 patients who completed a coping skills group, 18 patients who completed SCIT showed improved social cognition, self-reported social relationships, cognitive flexibility, and reduced aggression, independently of changes in clinical symptoms. On 6-month follow-up, the same 18 SCIT participants, now compared with 18 nonpsychiatric community-matched controls, showed generally improved social cognitive scores from baseline, and more importantly, levels of social cognitive functioning were not significantly different from controls (Combs *et al.*, 2009).

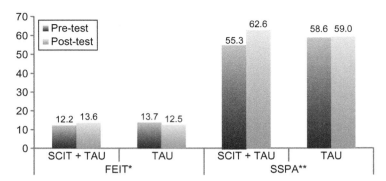

FIGURE 9.2   Pre- and post-test means in the Face Emotion Identification Test (FEIT) and Social Skills Performance Assessment (SSPA). SCIT: social cognition and interaction training; TAU: treatment as usual. *Significant time × group interaction (P = 0.001). **Significant time × group interaction (P = 0.024). *Adapted from Roberts and Penn, 2009.*

Feasibility in an outpatient setting was studied in a quasi-experimental trial comparing SCIT plus treatment as usual (TAU) (n = 20) to TAU (n = 11) in participants with schizophrenia spectrum disorders (Roberts and Penn, 2009). Participants who received SCIT plus TAU showed significant improvements in emotion perception (Fig 9.2), but not on ToM and hostile/aggressive attributional biases measures, although this was probably explained by relatively high ToM performance and low hostile intent at baseline (suggesting ceiling and floor effects, respectively). More importantly, SCIT was associated with improvements in social skills that best reflect SCIT's primary goal of improving social functioning through improved social cognition.

SCIT has also been studied in community settings unaffiliated with its developers (Roberts *et al.*, 2010). This was an open, single-group study that recruited 50 participants with schizophrenia spectrum disorders. Thirty-eight patients completed the SCIT training, yielding a 76% completion rate. Of the 12 drop-outs, 11 occurred either before or during the first three sessions of SCIT treatment. The large majority of patients rated SCIT as either 'helpful' or 'very helpful' in terms of group usefulness and of whether the group helped them in thinking about social situations and in interacting socially. Participants showed statistically significant improvements in emotion perception (Face Emotion Identification Test (FEIT), P = 0.034) and ToM (hinting task, P = 0.003). This study was particularly important in demonstrating the feasible incorporation of SCIT into routine programing in outpatient healthcare centers.

Of particular relevance to the metacognitive levels of SCIT described above, Roberts *et al.* (2012) recruited 24 outpatients with schizophrenia to complete a six-session training on one SCIT technique that particularly emphasizes ease during the learning process and achievement of skill automaticity. The technique, called Mary/Eddie/Bill (MEB), is designed to make the process of generating alternative social interpretations easier, by associating *internal-personal, external-situational,* and *external-personal* attributions with three easy-to-remember characters. Participants are taught that My-fault Mary always blames herself for negative events, Easy Eddie always blames bad luck, and Blaming Bill always blames other people. Colorful imagery, videos, and games are used to practice flexibly interpreting situations from these three characters' perspectives. At post-test, patients exhibited statistically significant within-group increases in ToM and decreases in metacognitive overconfidence. Moreover, two-thirds of participants described the training as 'very easy' to understand, and all participants were able to name the three characters and to identify at least one appropriate behavior, thought, or emotion associated with each. These findings suggest that the intervention created in patients the experience of metacognitive ease and that this translated into patients being able to remember and deploy the MEB strategy after six once-weekly sessions.

In the early phase of psychosis, where no specific interventions targeting social cognition have been developed to date, SCIT's feasibility and effectiveness were studied in an open pilot trial (Bartholomeusz *et al.,* 2013). Twelve participants with first-episode psychosis participated in two SCIT groups modified for youth-appropriateness and cultural relevance. Seventy-five percent of them met predefined completion criteria (attendance for at least 50% of sessions). Participants showed significant improvements in emotion perception and social functioning (measured by the Social and Occupational Functioning Scale and the Global Functioning Scales). This study is particularly important considering social cognitive impairments are common and frequently precede onset of full-blown psychosis (Lecardeur *et al.,* 2013).

On an additional note, SCIT has also been tested with different patient populations, including individuals with schizotypal personality features, autism spectrum disorders (ASD), and bipolar disorder (BD). In a sample of individuals with schizotypal personality features (Chan *et al.,* 2010), the group treated with SCIT (n = 19) showed improvements in the General Health Questionnaire somatic symptoms and social dysfunction dimensions that were maintained at 6-month follow-up, compared with a naturalistic control group (n = 21). In adults with ASD (Turner-Brown *et al.,* 2008), a modified version of SCIT for Autism (SCIT-A) has been shown to be feasible with high attendance rates (92%) and globally positive satisfaction reports. Similar to findings observed with schizophrenia spectrum disorders samples, significant improvements in ToM performance were observed in adults with ASD. One further study (Turner-Brown, personal communication) in a sample of adolescents with ASD also demonstrated significantly larger improvements in social functioning and psychological well-being in people treated with SCIT-A plus services as usual (SAU), compared with those treated with SAU alone. Finally, patients with BD and social cognitive deficits treated with SCIT plus TAU (n = 21) showed significant improvements in emotion perception and ToM measures, compared

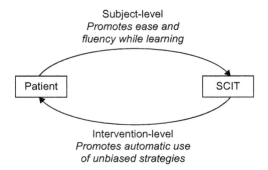

FIGURE 9.3 Levels of metacognitive intervention in social cognition and interaction training (SCIT).

with participants treated with TAU alone (n = 16), in a quasi-experimental trial with independent, treatment-blinded evaluators (Lahera *et al.*, 2013).

CONCLUSION

SCIT is a comprehensive social cognitive intervention designed to target multiple domains of social cognition. From a metacognitive perspective, SCIT aims to enhance patients' use of adaptive social cognitive strategies in the social world by promoting effortless learning during SCIT treatment. This increases the automaticity of adaptive strategies so that when patients think about the process it feels natural to them (schemed in Fig. 9.3). Research involving SCIT confirms good patient adherence and has provided promising results not only in terms of improvement in social cognitive domains such as emotion perception and ToM but also in improved social skill and functioning. Future lines of research should replicate these findings using larger and more representative samples but also explore SCIT's potential with different patient populations such as ASD or personality disorders characterized by dysfunctional social cognition.

REFERENCES

Bargh, J. A. (1994). The four horsemen of automaticity: awareness, intention, efficiency and control in social cognition. In R. Wyer & T. Srull (Eds.), *Handbook of Social Cognition*. New York: Lawrence Erlbaum.

Bartholomeusz, C. F., Allott, K., Killackey, E., Liu, P., Wood, S. J., & Thompson, A. (2013). Social cognition training as an intervention for improving functional outcome in first-episode psychosis: a feasibility study. *Early Intervention in Psychiatry*, 7(4), 421–426.

Beck, J. (2001). *Cognitive Therapy: Basics and Beyond*. New York: Guilford Press.

Bentall, R. P., & Swarbrick, R. (2003). The best laid schemas of paranoid patients: autonomy, sociotropy, and need for closure. *Psychology and Psychotherapy*, 76, 163–171.

Brothers, L. (1990). The social brain: a project for integrating primate behavior and neurophysiology in a new domain. *Concepts in Neuroscience, 1*, 27–61.

Chan, R. C., Gao, X. J., Li, X. Y., Li, H. H., Cui, J. F., Deng, Y. Y., et al. (2010). The social cognition and interaction training (SCIT): an extension to individuals with schizotypal personality features. *Psychiatry Research, 178*(1), 208–210.

Clore, G. L., Gasper, K., & Garvin, E. (2001). Affect as information. In J. P. Forgas (Ed.), *Handbook of Affect and Social Cognition* (pp. 121–144). Mahwah, NJ: Lawrence Erlbaum.

Combs, D. R., Adams, S. D., Penn, D. L., Roberts, D., Tiegreen, J., & Stem, P. (2007). Social cognition and interaction training (SCIT) for inpatients with schizophrenia spectrum disorders: preliminary findings. *Schizophrenia Research, 91*(1–3), 112–116.

Combs, D. R., Elerson, K., Penn, D. L., Tiegreen, J. A., Nelson, A., Ledet, S. N., et al. (2009). Stability and generalization of social cognition and interaction training (SCIT) for schizophrenia: six-month follow-up results. *Schizophrenia Research, 112*(1–3), 196–197.

Couture, S., Penn, D. L., & Roberts, D. L. (2006). The functional significance of social cognition in schizophrenia: a review. *Schizophrenia Bulletin Supplement, 1*, S44–S63.

David, A. S., Bedford, N., Wiffen, B., & Gilleen, J. (2012). Failures of metacognition and lack of insight in neuropsychiatric disorders. *Philosophical Transactions of the Royal Society of London. Series B, Biological Sciences, 367*, 1379–1390.

Davis, L. W., Eicher, A. C., & Lysaker, P. H. (2011). Metacognition as a predictor of therapeutic alliance over 26 weeks of psychotherapy in schizophrenia. *Schizophrenia Research, 129*, 85–90.

Fett, A.-K., Viechtbauer, W., Dominquez, M. G., Penn, D. L., van Os, J., & Krabbendam, L. (2011). The relationship between neurocognition and social cognition with functional outcomes in schizophrenia: a meta-analysis. *Neuroscience and Biobehavioral Reviews, 35*, 573–588.

Kinderman, P., & Bentall, R. P. (1997). Causal attributions in paranoia and depression: internal, personal, and situational attributions for negative events. *Journal of Abnormal Psychology, 106*(2), 341–345.

Lahera, G., Benito, A., Montes, J. M., Fernández-Liria, A., Olbert, C. M., & Penn, D. L. (2013). Social cognition and interaction training (SCIT) for outpatients with bipolar disorder. *Journal of Affective Disorders, 146*(1), 132–136.

Lecardeur, L., Meunier-Cussac, S., & Dollfus, S. (2013). Cognitive deficits in first episode psychosis patients and people at risk for psychosis: from diagnosis to treatment. *Encephale, 39*(Suppl. 1), S64–S71.

Lysaker, P. H., Erickson, M. A., Buck, B., Buck, K. D., Olesek, K., Grant, M. L. A., et al. (2011). Metacognition and social function in schizophrenia: associations over a period of five months. *Cognitive Neuropsychology, 16*(3), 241–255.

Lysaker, P. H., Gumley, A., Luedtke, B., Buck, K. D., Ringer, J. M., Olesek, K., et al. (2013). Social cognition and metacognition in schizophrenia: evidence of their independence and linkage with outcomes. *Acta Psychiatrica Scandinavica, 27*(3), 239–247.

Lysaker, P. H., Shea, A. M., Buck, K. D., Dimaggio, G., Nicolò, G., Procacci, M., et al. (2010). Metacognition as a mediator of the effects of impairments in neurocognition on social function in schizophrenia spectrum disorders. *Acta Psychiatrica Scandinavica, 122*, 405–413.

Nicolò, G., Dimaggio, G., Popolo, R., Carcione, A., Procacci, M., Hamm, J., et al. (2012). Associations of metacognition with symptoms, insight, and neurocognition in clinically stable outpatients with schizophrenia. *Journal of Nervous and Mental Disease, 200*(7), 644–647.

Penn, D., Roberts, D. L., Munt, E. D., Silverstein, E., Jones, N., & Sheitman, B. (2005). A pilot study of social cognition and interaction training (SCIT) for schizophrenia. *Schizophrenia Research, 80*(2–3), 357–359.

Penn, D. L., Roberts, D. L., Combs, D., & Sterne, A. (2007). Best practices: the development of the Social Cognition and Interaction Training program for schizophrenia spectrum disorders. *Psychiatric Services*, *58*(4), 449–451.

Roberts, D. L., Kleinlein, P., & Stevens, B. J. (2012). An alternative to generating alternative interpretations in social cognitive therapy for psychosis. *Behavioural & Cognitive Psychotherapy*, *40*, 491–495.

Roberts, D. L., & Penn, D. L. (2009). Social cognition and interaction training (SCIT) for outpatients with schizophrenia: a preliminary study. *Psychiatry Research*, *166*(2–3), 141–147.

Roberts, D. L., Penn, D. L., & Combs, D. (in press). Social Cognition and Interaction Training: Treatment Manual. Oxford University Press, New York.

Roberts, D. L., Penn, D. L., Labate, D., Margolis, S. A., & Sterne, A. (2010). Transportability and feasibility of social cognition and interaction training (SCIT) in community settings. *Behavioural and Cognitive Psychotherapy*, *38*(1), 35–47.

Roberts, D. L., & Velligan, D. I. (2012). Can social functioning in schizophrenia be improved through targeted social cognitive intervention? *Rehabilitation and Research Practice*, *2012*, 742106.

Schwarz, N. (2004). Metacognitive experiences in consumer judgment and decision making. *Journal of Consumer Psychology*, *14*(4), 332–348.

Tas, C., Brown, E. C., Esen-Danaci, A., Lysaker, P. H., & Brüne, M. (2012a). Intrinsic motivation and metacognition as predictors of learning potential in patients with remitted schizophrenia. *Journal of Psychiatric Research*, *46*, 1086–1092.

Tas, C., Danaci, A. E., Cubukcuoglu, Z., & Brüne, M. (2012b). Impact of family involvement on social cognition training in clinically stable outpatients with schizophrenia – a randomized pilot study. *Psychiatry Research*, *195*(1–2), 32–38.

Turner-Brown, L. M., Perry, T. D., Dichter, G. S., Bodfish, J. W., & Penn, D. L. (2008). Brief report: feasibility of social cognition and interaction training for adults with high functioning autism. *Journal of Autism and Developmental Disorders*, *38*(9), 1777–1784.

Chapter 10

An Overview of Social Cognitive Treatment Interventions

Dennis R. Combs,[1] Emily Drake[1] and Michael R. Basso[2]

[1]*The University of Texas at Tyler, Tyler, TX, USA*, [2]*The University of Tulsa, Tulsa, OK, USA*

Chapter Outline

INTRODUCTION

Since the mid- to late-1990s, the study of social cognition has emerged as a key construct in schizophrenia in terms of developing novel treatment interventions (Roberts and Penn, 2012). Before we discuss various treatment approaches, we must define this area of study, its core domains, and importance in schizophrenia. Broadly, social cognition can be defined as the 'mental operations underlying social interactions, which include the human ability and capacity to perceive the intentions and dispositions of others' (Brothers, 1990). Fiske and Taylor (1991) stated that social cognition is the 'way in which people make sense of other people' (p. 1). Furthermore, Adolphs (2001) added that social cognition is 'the ability to construct representations of the relation between oneself and others and to use those representations flexibly to guide social behavior' (p. 231). All of these definitions emphasize the idea

Social Cognition and Metacognition in Schizophrenia.
DOI: http://dx.doi.org/10.1016/B978-0-12-405172-0.00010-7
© 2014 Elsevier Inc. All rights reserved.

TABLE 10.1 Social Cognition Domains, Descriptions, and Measures.

Domain	Description	Representative Measures
Theory of mind	Ability to represent the mental states of others or make inferences about others' intentions. This includes understanding hints, false beliefs, intentions, irony, metaphor, sarcasm, and faux pas.	• Hinting Task • Brüne Cartoons • Test of Awareness of Social Inference (TASIT)
Attributional style	Assigning causality to positive and negative events; may emphasize ambiguous situations.	• Internal, Personal, and Situational Attributions Questionnaire (IPSAQ) • Ambiguous Intentions Hostility Questionnaire (AIHQ)
Emotion perception	Identification or discrimination of emotional expressions. Emotional expressions reflect positive and negative expressions; emotions may range from subtle to salient.	• Face Emotion Identification Test (FEIT) • Bell-Lysaker Emotion Recognition Test (BLERT) • Ekman Faces
Social perception	Perception or scanning of social details and use of contextual cues to determine emotional states or intentions.	• Profile of Nonverbal Sensitivity • Social Perception Scale

that social cognition is a set of cognitive processes that are related to the perception, interpretation, and understanding of social information (Penn *et al.*, 1997). At both the theoretical and empirical levels, social cognition is linked to social behavior and as applied to schizophrenia may form an avenue to promote recovery and improved social, occupational, and community functioning (Couture *et al.*, 2006).

In the study of social cognition in schizophrenia, four key domains have emerged: (1) emotion perception, (2) social perception, (3) theory of mind (ToM), and (4) attributional style (see Green *et al.*, 2005; Green *et al.*, 2008). An example of each domain is presented in Table 10.1 along with representative assessment measures often used in treatment research.

It should be noted that the concept of emotion perception has been incorporated into the National Institutes of Mental Health (NIMH) Measurement and Treatment Research to Improve Cognition in Schizophrenia (MATRICS) battery as part of the broader concept of emotion regulation, which not only included perceiving emotions, but regulating and understanding emotions as well (Green *et al.*, 2008). There is now consistent evidence that people with schizophrenia show impairment on all four of the key domains compared to normal, healthy controls and even to other psychiatric groups such as people with anxiety and depression (Penn *et al.*, 2006 for a review). There is less evidence on differences between schizophrenia and more severe conditions such as bipolar disorder (Addington and Addington, 1998) or traumatic brain injury (McDonald and Flanagan, 2004).

Why is social cognition an important target in the treatment of schizophrenia? First, research has shown that social cognition appears to be an independent construct that is different from both neurocognition (van Hooren *et al.*, 2008) and psychotic symptoms (Sergi *et al.*, 2007) and has distinct neural structures that underlie these processes. Imaging research has suggested that there is a 'social cognitive neural circuit', which includes the amygdala, fusiform gyrus, superior temporal sulcus, and prefrontal cortices (Pinkham, 2012; Pinkham *et al.*, 2003). This makes the targeting of social cognition different from treating symptoms with antipsychotic medications or engaging in expensive and lengthy cognitive remediation interventions. Unfortunately, antipsychotic medication studies have generally shown minimal or no improvement on social cognitive tasks (Penn *et al.*, 2009). Second, impairments in social cognition are stable across the course of schizophrenia, which makes them an ideal treatment target for interventions (Addington and Addington, 1998; Green *et al.*, 2012; Wölwer *et al.*, 1996). Finally, social cognition has a clear association with social and community functioning (Couture *et al.*, 2006; Fett *et al.*, 2011). In fact, there are now a large number of empirical and meta-analytic studies that demonstrate that social cognition is a direct predictor (Bell *et al.*, 2008; Bora *et al.*, 2006; Brüne, 2005; Pan *et al.*, 2009), mediator (Addington *et al.*, 2006; Vauth *et al.*, 2004), or moderator (Nienow *et al.*, 2006) of social and community functioning (as reviewed in Couture *et al.*, 2006). In addition, some studies have shown that social cognition has a stronger relationship with functional outcome than neurocognition does (Penn *et al.*, 1996; Pinkham and Penn, 2006; Roncone *et al.*, 2006). Whatever the specific mechanism, it is clear that social cognition does affect social and community functioning and, if we can improve social cognition, then social functioning may also improve. The debate is over the best approach to improve social cognition in schizophrenia.

TYPES OF SOCIAL COGNITIVE INTERVENTIONS

Social cognitive interventions are classified into three general types depending on the focus and activities included in the treatments. Interventions can be targeted, comprehensive, or broad-based in scope (see Fizdon 2012; Horan *et al.*, 2009a). Targeted interventions focus on improving a single aspect of social cognition such as emotion perception, ToM, or attributional style. Most early research studies on social cognition were single-session studies (or proof-of-concept studies) that showed that social cognition could be improved and tested different methods for improving a single ability or skill. The main conclusion from this area of research was that social cognition could in fact be improved, which then led the way to the more complex treatments used currently (Wölwer *et al.*, 2010). Comprehensive interventions are often longer in duration (6 months on average) and typically deliver treatment in groups of five to 12 participants. Comprehensive treatments focus on improving several domains of social cognition within a given treatment. For example, social cognition and interaction training (SCIT) targets deficits in emotion perception, ToM, attributional style, and jumping to conclusions in a 24-session treatment package. More recent social cognitive treatments are comprehensive in nature. Finally, broad-based interventions have a long-standing tradition in the treatment of schizophrenia. Broad-based interventions target social cognition and involve in-depth training in neurocognitive remediation, social skills training, cognitive behavioral therapy, or symptom management (Fizdon, 2012; Wölwer *et al.*, 2010). An assumption of this type of intervention is that other areas such as cognition need to be improved before more complex social cognitive domains can be remediated. Classic examples of broad-based interventions include integrated psychological therapy (IPT) and cognitive enhancement therapy (CET).

TARGETED INTERVENTION APPROACHES

Emotion Perception

Most of the targeted intervention studies have focused on improving emotion perception or facial affect perception. The first targeted intervention study to improve emotion perception was conducted by Penn and Combs (2000). In this study, 40 chronic inpatients with schizophrenia were randomly assigned to four different intervention groups: repeated practice, monetary reinforcement, facial feedback, and a combination of reinforcement and facial feedback. Participants completed a single-session intervention with gains assessed at immediate post-test and at a 1-week follow-up. Results showed that all conditions except repeated practice improved, but the gains at 1-week follow-up were not maintained. Although the results were not overly impressive, this research was the impetus for the development of the attention shaping intervention developed by Combs and colleagues. Rooted in neuropsychological studies and eye tracking research, Combs *et al.* (2006; 2008) developed an attention shaping methodology to focus visual attention on the eyes, nose, and mouth areas of the face as a way to improve emotion perception. In this intervention, an attentional prompt (a large cross) appears over the center of the face for 5 seconds and then fades from view. By focusing attention on the face, it is believed that more information about the person's emotional expression can be obtained. At present, there are three published studies showing consistent results using attention shaping to improve emotion perception, including two larger randomized studies (Combs *et al.*, 2006; Combs *et al.*, 2008; Combs *et al.*, 2011). Attention shaping is a computerized training tool, which allows it to be administered repeatedly (showing different expressions each time it is used) and incorporated into other existing treatments. In fact, the most recent study showed that five sessions of attention shaping training (compared to one and three sessions) led to greater improvements on two unrelated tests of emotion perception. More importantly, eye-tracking data showed that participants scanned faces for shorter amounts of time but were more accurate than before the training, which suggested that this process was becoming more automatic (Combs *et al.*, 2011). One drawback from these studies is the weak transfer from emotion perception to larger gains in social and community functioning.

Other studies have used different methods to improve emotion perception, but all have in common the application of repeated practice using computerized training. Russell *et al.* (2006) used the computer-based Micro-Expression Training Tool (METT) as a possible means to improve emotion perception in schizophrenia. METT is based on the work of Paul Ekman and comes from research stating that each emotional expression has unique facial-action coding units specific to that emotion. If a person can recognize and detect these specific facial-coding units, then emotion perception will improve. METT uses microexpressions, which are rapid 15-millisecond 'flashes' of facial affect beginning and ending with a neutral face. For this study, the training started with slow-motion video showing differences between the basic facial affect expressions. Thereafter, participants had to label 28 trials of microexpressions, with feedback provided if incorrect. Incorrect trials led to a repetition of the trial or a still picture display of the emotion in order to correct the response. Participants with schizophrenia exposed to METT showed a significant improvement in performance with post-treatment scores almost reaching the pretreatment performance level of healthy controls. A more recent follow-up study compared METT with a repeated exposure condition and showed improved emotion perception scores and visual scanning behaviors at post-test for the METT group only (Russell *et al.*, 2008). In contrast to attention-shaping research, participants assigned to METT showed more time scanning features of the face at post-test. However, these visual scanning changes attenuated to a trend at a 1-week follow-up.

A final computerized training tool, called the 'Emotion Trainer,' originally developed for use with children with autism, was used by Silver *et al.* (2004) in a sample of 20 chronic schizophrenia participants. Participants completed three 15-minute sessions of the Emotion Trainer, each spaced 2 to 3 days apart, and showed improvement in emotion recognition scores at post-test compared with baseline. However, the findings of this study are quite limited since it was an uncontrolled study.

Moving beyond single-session treatments, Training Affect Recognition (TAR) is a 12-session manualized intervention designed to improve facial affect recognition in schizophrenia (see Wölwer *et al.*, 2010). The intervention consists of three blocks of training sessions that involve computerized images, desk-work, and homework activities to provide the skills to recognize different emotional expressions. TAR is based on training individuals to recognize specific facial features associated with emotions (facial-action coding units) and then apply these to more holistic expressions. Core principles in TAR include error-less learning, repetition, and positive feedback. TAR begins by showing participants specific features of the face, then progresses to degraded images, and finally involves contextual cues to aid in emotion recognition. Along the way, participants work in pairs, verbalize their strategies, and engage in self-instruction to maximize gains. Sessions are delivered twice a week for 1 hour each.

Empirical studies on TAR have been promising (Frommann et al., 2003; Wölwer *et al.*, 2010; as discussed in Fizdon, 2012). Wölwer *et al.* (2005) compared TAR to cognitive remediation and a treatment-as-usual group in 77 participants with schizophrenia. Participants were randomly assigned to one of the three treatment conditions with measurement at pre- and post-intervention. Results showed that TAR led to improved emotion recognition scores, but did not improve cognitive functioning, while the cognitive remediation group showed improved cognitive scores (verbal learning/memory), but did not show improved affect recognition. Wölwer and Frommann (2009) found that the gains following TAR were maintained for 6 weeks in a forensic sample, but the improvements in emotion perception did not transfer to a social skills role-play. The most recent study on TAR randomly assigned 40 participants to either TAR or treatment-as-usual and showed improved affect recognition following TAR, but more importantly improved social relationships on a quality-of-life measure (Sachs *et al.*, 2012). In sum, improvement in facial affect perception has been consistently demonstrated in a number of studies, but far fewer studies have shown that these gains transfer to improved social and community functioning as well (Roberts and Velligan, 2012; Statuka and Walder, 2013; Wölwer *et al.*, 2010).

Theory of Mind

Compared to emotion perception studies, there are fewer interventions that target ToM deficits. Early studies on improving ToM were based on having participants watch short video clips of social interactions or look at cartoons with missing frames (picture completion-type tasks) to determine if ToM could be improved by having participants verbalize their strategies (Kayser *et al.*, 2006; Sarfati *et al.*, 2000). Results showed that involving verbal processes aided and improved ToM abilities, which formed the basis for more recent interventions for ToM. More formal studies on ToM interventions have been conducted with encouraging results, but the methods used in these studies vary considerably. For example, Roncone *et al.* (2004) randomly assigned 20 participants with residual schizophrenia to either an Instrumental Enrichment Program

(IEP) or treatment-as-usual. IEP is described as a 6-month intervention conducted with weekly sessions designed to move the person's cognitive structure from passive to autonomous by exposing participants to a series of novel situations and scenarios (see Fizdon, 2012). Specific activities in IEP are not clearly presented so it is unclear what participants actually do in the group sessions. Following IEP, there were significant improvements on ToM abilities as well as improvement on the recognition of negative emotions such as fear and sadness.

Mazza *et al.* (2010) developed a 12-session ToM intervention called Emotion and ToM Imitation Training (ETIT), which consists of four phases involving observing others' eye direction and gaze, imitating emotional/affective expressions, inferring the intentions of others, and making attributions and social judgments. In the only study of ETIT, Mazza randomly assigned 33 participants with schizophrenia to either ETIT or a problem-solving intervention. At post-test, participants assigned to the ETIT intervention showed significant gains in ToM abilities, affect recognition, empathy, and positive symptoms (see Fizdon, 2012). Gains in social functioning were found, but were based on clinician ratings only. The effect of ToM interventions on symptom improvement has been found in other studies as well (Lecardeur *et al.*, 2009; Roncone *et al.*, 2004). Future research on ToM needs to establish consistent methods to improve ToM skills much in the way that affect recognition studies have done (repeated practice computerized training methods). There is much variability in the ways ToM can be remediated leading to the question as to what is the commonality among these different interventions.

COMPREHENSIVE INTERVENTION APPROACHES

Comprehensive-based approaches have moved beyond targeting a single social cognitive ability to include activities that address deficits and biases in multiple domains such as emotion perception, ToM, and attributional style in the context of a treatment package. Examples of broad-based interventions are SCIT (Roberts *et al.*, personal communication) and social cognitive skill training (SCST; Horan *et al.*, 2009b; Horan *et al.*, 2011), both of which will be briefly discussed below.

SCIT is a 24-week group-based intervention that has demonstrated efficacy in a series of studies with inpatients (Combs *et al.*, 2007; Penn *et al.*, 2005) and outpatients (Roberts and Penn, 2009), and in community agencies (Roberts *et al.*, 2010). SCIT is a 'stand-alone' manual-based intervention that targets the three core social cognitive deficits in schizophrenia: emotion perception, ToM, and attributional style (see Penn *et al.*, 2007). SCIT is comprised of three phases and lasts 20 to 24 weeks. SCIT is built around a 50-minute group therapy session with the recommended group size between five and eight members with two group leaders. SCIT involves the use of didactic instruction, videotape and computerized learning tools, and role-play methods to improve social cognition. SCIT activities are meant to be engaging for participants. Often, lessons are built into games and videotape activities. SCIT includes weekly homework assignments to bolster in-session learning, and each participant is encouraged to identify a 'practice partner' who works with the participant during the week. Each practice partner has information (weekly handouts are provided) about the session, its goals, what the person should have learned, and specific activities to do together. The three phases of SCIT are as follows:

- Phase 1 (sessions 1–7): the primary goals of phase one (emotion training) are to provide information about emotions and their relationship to thoughts and situations, define the basic emotions, improve emotion-perception skills with computerized facial expression training tools, and teach clients to distinguish between justified and unjustified suspiciousness.
- Phase 2 (sessions 8–16): the primary goals of phase two (figuring-out situations) are to teach clients about the potential pitfalls of jumping to conclusions, to improve cognitive flexibility in social situations, to help clients distinguish between personal and situational attributions, and to differentiate social 'facts' from social 'guesses.'
- Phase 3 (sessions 17–24): the primary goals of phase three (integration) are to assess the certainty of facts and guesses surrounding events in clients' personal lives, to recognize that it is sometimes necessary to obtain more information about social situations, and to teach effective social skills for checking out guesses. The purpose of the final phase is to put into practice what clients have learned in SCIT.

Several studies have supported the efficacy of SCIT at improving social cognition (see Fizdon, 2012 for a review). In one of the first clinical studies, Combs *et al.* (2007) compared SCIT to a coping-skills group in a sample of 28 forensic inpatients with schizophrenia. A total of 18 people completed SCIT and 10 completed the coping-skills group. Assignment was not random, but was based on client interest and motivation. Compared to pre-test scores, participants who completed SCIT showed robust improvements (medium-to-large effect sizes) on emotion perception and ToM and made less hostile and blaming attributions. Importantly, there was a significant decrease in behavioral incidents of aggression, and there was improved social functioning in terms of engaging others in conversation and having a larger social network. A follow-up study on this SCIT cohort found that scores on these measures did decrease from post-treatment to the 6-month follow-up, but the gains were still higher than pre-test levels (Combs *et al.*, 2009). At 6-month follow-up, there were no differences between SCIT participants and a nonclinical community sample. Roberts and Penn (2009) examined SCIT in a sample of 31 outpatients with schizophrenia and found that people who completed SCIT (n = 20) showed better scores on emotion perception and social skill ratings than people who received treatment as usual (n = 11). No changes in social functioning were noted, but this may be due to the higher level of functioning found in some outpatients compared to inpatient samples. Since the late 2000s, the original SCIT intervention has been modified to include the use of family members as practice partners (F-SCIT; Tas *et al.*, 2012). It has been examined in samples of people with high functioning autism (SCIT-A; Turner-Brown *et al.*, 2008) and in people with elevated schizotypal traits (Chan *et al.*, 2010). SCIT groups have been conducted all over the world including clinical settings in China, Australia, and Germany. SCIT is becoming recognized as an evidence-based practice for people with schizophrenia (Combs *et al.*, 2012; Penn *et al.*, 2007).

A more recent comprehensive treatment comes from the work of Horan and Green at University of California, Los Angeles (UCLA) on SCST. The original 12-session version of SCST (Horan *et al.*, 2009a; Horan *et al.*, 2009b) has been expanded to a 24-session treatment to maximize gains on ToM, social perception, and attributional style (Horan *et al.*, 2011). SCST adapted some of the activities from SCIT and TAR, but SCST differs in that it has more focus on nonverbal cue recognition and higher-order ToM abilities such as deception and sarcasm (Fizdon, 2012). The 24-session version of SCST includes four modules that address emotional processing, social perception, attributional bias, and mentalizing abilities. SCST is based on breaking down each social cognitive domain into fundamental components, building more complex skills over time, and repeated practice to make skills more automatic in nature. In the end, SCST seeks to apply the skills learned in-group to the real world environment.

Two research studies have supported the efficacy of SCST in clinical trials. In the first study, Horan *et al.* (2009b) at UCLA randomly assigned 34 Veterans Affairs (VA) participants with schizophrenia disorders to either a 12-session social cognitive intervention or a group-based symptom management intervention. Results showed that at post-test, scores on emotion perception significantly improved compared to the symptom management group. However, scores on other measures of social cognition such as attributional style, social perception, and ToM did not improve. This led to the development of the current 24-session version of SCST. Horan *et al.* (2011) compared this 24-session version of SCST to three other treatment conditions: a computerized neurocognitive remediation program, a hybrid SCST and neurocognitive treatment, and an illness management group. Results showed that participants who completed SCST showed significant improvements in emotion perception and emotion management with a trend toward better social skills on a roleplay. Changes were specific to SCST and not related to neurocognition or symptom variables.

BROAD-BASED INTERVENTION APPROACHES

Compared to targeted and comprehensive interventions, broad-based treatments provide training in social cognition AND involve other activities such as neurocognitive remediation, cognitive behavioral therapy, and symptom management skills (Fizdon, 2012; Horan et al., 2009a). This category of interventions results in a large number of activities that usually assume that training on basic neurocognitive activities (attention, memory, executive functions) and social cognition must be conducted before more complex social and interpersonal skills can develop. One of the earliest broad-based treatment approaches is IPT (Roder et al., 2010). IPT is a manualized group-based intervention that generally consists of five related subprograms: neurocognition/cognitive differentiation, social perception, verbal communication, social skills, and social problem solving (Fizdon, 2012; Mueller et al., 2012). The social perception subprogram of IPT (program 2) is directed toward improving social and emotion recognition and emotional expression with later programs aimed at social skill and social problem solving. However, since researchers can select which of the five programs to administer, some studies have not included the social perception program and thus have focused more on cognitive change than social cognitive change (Roder et al., 2006). Despite differences in studies in terms of setting, participant characteristics, and treatment components, IPT has robust evidence that it is effective, based on recent empirical and meta-analytic reviews of IPT studies (Roder et al., 2006; Roder et al., 2011). Gains from IPT are evident up to 6 to 8 months post intervention (Fizdon, 2012) and are not impacted by age (Mueller et al., 2012; Mueller et al., 2013). A modified version of IPT, called integrated neurocognitive therapy (INT; Roder and Mueller, personal communication) has been developed. INT expands on the neurocognition and social perception subprograms from IPT in order to provide more comprehensive training in these areas, with the idea that more training in these areas will translate to improved functional outcomes. Similar to IPT, activities in INT move from fundamental 'bottom-up' type tasks to more 'top-down' complex tasks over time. The social perception program of INT now includes activities for emotion perception, social perception/ToM, social schemas, attributions, and emotion regulation (see Mueller et al., 2012).

CET is another broad-based intervention that targets both the cognitive and social cognitive deficits found in schizophrenia (e.g., Eack et al., 2007). CET involves 60 hours of neurocognitive training and 45 sessions of social cognitive training conducted in small groups (Eack, 2012). In CET, the neurocognitive training is computer-based while the social cognitive training largely occurs in groups (three or four pairs of participants). The social cognitive aspect of CET involves three modules that focus on basic concepts (emotion regulation, stress management, cognitive flexibility, gistful social cognition), social cognition (context interpretation, nonverbal skills, ToM), and applications to real life (applying CET concepts to real-life areas and problems). CET is based on the idea that improving neurocognition is essential to forming a solid foundation for improving social cognition. The main premise of CET is to move social cognition from a serial, effortful process to more of an automatic, gistful process.

CET has shown good efficacy in several clinical studies (Eack, 2012; as reviewed in Fizdon, 2012). Hogarty *et al.* (2004) randomly assigned 121 people with schizophrenia to either CET or supportive therapy with outcomes assessed at 12 and 24 months. Social cognition training was provided in small groups that meet weekly in months 4 to 6 of CET (cognitive training was conducted first in months 0–4). In these groups, members discussed real-life social situations, practiced social skill exercises, conducted emotional expression activities, and discussed how context influences emotional reactions. At 12 months, participants in the CET condition showed improved neurocognition, processing speed, and social adjustment with a trend for improved social cognition ratings (composite scale of 50 items rated by nonblinded clinicians) and cognitive style (approach to completing tasks). At 24 months, social cognition ratings continued to improve. A follow-up report on most of the original sample showed that at 1 year, post-treatment gains on processing speed, cognitive style, social cognition, and adjustment were maintained, but there were no group differences on neurocognition (Hogarty *et al.*, 2006).

CET has expanded to focus on participants with early-course schizophrenia and the effect of CET on brain volume/morphology. In participants with early-course schizophrenia, research has suggested that CET leads to improvement on emotional intelligence measures (Eack *et al.*, 2007) with evidence of long-term functional benefits on social cognition, social adjustment, and symptomatology (Eack *et al.*, 2009; Eack *et al.*, 2010a). In terms of effect on brain structures, Eack *et al.* (2010b) found that CET was linked to a reduction in cortex gray matter cell loss in the temporal lobe in early-stage schizophrenia. Interestingly, Keshavan *et al.* (2011) found that that among CET participants with early-course schizophrenia, those with larger cortical surface areas and a higher volume of gray matter showed more rapid improvement on social cognition tasks. However, those with reduced cortical surface areas and lower gray matter volume did improve, but took about twice as long (1 year versus 2 years).

CONCLUSIONS AND FUTURE DIRECTIONS

As evident from the studies presented in this chapter, social cognition does appear to be a modifiable construct. There are many methods to do so and studies differ in terms of their approach and activities, but overall the evidence is clear that social cognitive training interventions are effective (Kurtz and Richardson, 2012). Targeted interventions have been valuable in developing effective methods for improving a single social cognitive ability, which are often adopted by comprehensive interventions. For example, in improving emotion perception, it appears that repeated practice viewing different expressions, along with teaching individuals how expressions differ, is found in most interventions. The drawback of targeted interventions is the lack of generalization to social and community functioning (Roberts and Velligan, 2012).

In contrast, both comprehensive and broad-based interventions involve a number of different activities, can last for 6 months to 2 years, and are very expensive and time-consuming to conduct. It is unknown which activities are important, and dismantling studies are needed to see if a common core can be derived. The recent trend is to expand treatments and make them more intensive, but there is value in shorter, more focused interventions that are preferred by clients and agencies that struggle with limited budgets and funds. It does not appear that improving neurocognition is a 'necessity,' but a subset of people with schizophrenia may need this component prior to social cognition training. Finding which people may need this additional neurocognitive training would be valuable. Future studies should begin to compare different social cognitive interventions with each other directly in order to generate important efficacy data that could become part of a best-practices list of treatments. In closing, attempting to remediate the social cognitive impairments found in schizophrenia is a worthwhile endeavor. By doing so, it may be possible to promote recovery, improve social and community relationships, and create a better quality of life for individuals with schizophrenia.

REFERENCES

Addington, J., & Addington, D. (1998). Facial affect recognition and information processing in schizophrenia and bipolar disorder. *Schizophrenia Research, 32*, 171–181.

Addington, J., Saeedi, H., & Addington, D. (2006). Facial affect recognition: A mediator between cognitive and social functioning in psychosis? *Schizophrenia Research, 85*, 142–150.

Adolphs, R. (2001). The neurobiology of social cognition. *Current Opinion in Neurobiology, 11*(2), 231–239.

Bell, M. D., Tsang, H. W., Greig, T. C., & Bryson, G. J. (2008). Neurocognition, social cognition, perceived social discomfort, and vocational outcomes in schizophrenia. *Schizophrenia Bulletin, 35*(4), 738–747.

Bora, E., Eryavuz, A., Kayahan, B., Sungu, G., & Veznedaroglu, B. (2006). Social functioning, theory of mind and neurocognition in outpatients with schizophrenia; mental state decoding may be a better predictor of social functioning than mental state reasoning. *Psychiatry Research, 145*, 95–103.

Brothers, L. (1990). The social brain: A project for integrating primate behavior and neurophysiology in a new domain. *Concepts in Neuroscience, 1*, 27–61.

Brüne, M. (2005). Emotion recognition, 'theory of mind,' and social behavior in schizophrenia. *Psychiatry Research, 133*, 135–147.

Chan, R. C. K., Goa, X., Li, X., Li., H., Cui, J., Deng, Y., et al. (2010). The social cognition and interaction training (SCIT): An extension to individuals with schizotypal personality features. *Psychiatry Research, 178*, 208–210.

Combs, D. R., Adams, S. D., Penn, D. L., Roberts, D. L, Tiegreen, J. A., & Stem, P. (2007). Social cognition and interaction training for schizophrenia spectrum disorders: Preliminary findings. *Schizophrenia Research, 91*, 112–116.

Combs, D. R., Chapman, D. C., Waguspack, J., Basso, M. R., & Penn, D. L. (2011). Attention shaping as a means to improve emotion perception deficits in outpatients with schizophrenia and impaired controls. *Schizophrenia Research, 171*, 151–156.

Combs, D. R., Penn, D. L., Ledet, S., Tiegreen, J., Nelson, A., Basso, M. R., et al. (2009). Social cognition and interaction training (SCIT) for schizophrenia: Six month follow-up results. *Schizophrenia Research, 112,* 196–197.

Combs, D. R., Torres, J., & Basso, M. R. (2012). Social cognition and interaction training. In D. Roberts & D. Penn (Eds.), *Social cognition in schizophrenia* (pp. 384–400). New York: Oxford Press.

Combs, D. R., Tosheva, A., Penn, D. L., Basso, M. R., Wanner, J. L., & Laib, K. (2008). Attentional-shaping as a means to improve emotion perception deficits in schizophrenia. *Schizophrenia Research, 105,* 68–77.

Combs, D. R., Tosheva, A., Wanner, J., & Basso, M. R. (2006). Remediation of emotion perception deficits in schizophrenia: The use of attentional prompts. *Schizophrenia Research, 87,* 340–341.

Couture, S., Penn, D. L., & Roberts, D. L. (2006). The functional significance of social cognition in schizophrenia: A review. *Schizophrenia Bulletin, 32,* S44–S63.

Eack, S. M. (2012). Cognitive enhancement therapy. In D. Roberts & D. Penn (Eds.), *Social cognition in schizophrenia* (pp. 335–358). New York: Oxford Press.

Eack, S. M., Greenwald, D. P., Hogarty, S. S., Cooley, S. J., DiBarry, A. L., Montrose, D. M., et al. (2009). Cognitive enhancement therapy for early-course schizophrenia: Effects of a two-year randomized controlled trial. *Psychiatric Services, 60,* 1468–1476.

Eack, S. M., Greenwald, D. P., Hogarty, S. S., & Keshavan, M. S. (2010a). One-year durability of the effects of cognitive enhancement therapy on functional outcome in early schizophrenia. *Schizophrenia Research, 120,* 210–216.

Eack, S. M., Hogarty, G. E., Cho, R. Y., Prasad, K. M., Greenwald, D. P., Hogarty, S. S., et al. (2010b). Neuroprotective effects of cognitive enhancement therapy against grey matter loss in early schizophrenia: Results from a 2-year randomized controlled trial. *Archives of General Psychiatry, 67*(7), 674–682.

Eack, S. M., Hogarty, G. E., Greenwald, D. P., Hogarty, S. S., & Keshavan, M. S. (2007). Cognitive enhancement therapy improves emotional intelligence in early course schizophrenia: Preliminary effects. *Schizophrenia Research, 89,* 308–311.

Fett, A. J., Viechtbauer, W., Dominguez, M., Penn, D. L., van Os, J., & Krabbendam, L. (2011). The relationship between neurocognition and social cognition with functional outcomes in schizophrenia: A meta-analysis. *Neuroscience and Biobehavioral Reviews, 35,* 573–588.

Fiske, S. T., & Taylor, S. (1991). *Social cognition* (2nd ed.). New York: McGraw-Hill.

Fizdon, J. (2012). Introduction to social cognitive treatment approaches for schizophrenia. In D. Roberts & D. Penn (Eds.), *Social cognition in schizophrenia* (pp. 285–310). New York: Oxford Press.

Frommann, N., Streit, M., & Wölwer, W. (2003). Remediation of facial affect recognition impairments in patients with schizophrenia: A new training program. *Psychiatry Research, 117,* 281–284.

Green, M. F., Bearden, C. E., Cannon, T. D., Fiske, A. P., Hellemann, G. S., Horan, W. P., et al. (2012). Social cognition in schizophrenia, part 1: Performance across phase of illness. *Schizophrenia Bulletin, 38*(4), 854–864.

Green, M. F., Olivier, B., Crawley, J. N., Penn, D. L., & Silverstein, S. (2005). Social cognition in schizophrenia: Recommendations from the MATRICS new approaches conference. *Schizophrenia Bulletin, 31,* 882–887.

Green, M. F., Penn, D. L., Bentall, R., Carpenter, W. T., Gaebel, W., Gur, R. C., et al. (2008). Social cognition in schizophrenia: An NIMH workshop on definitions, assessment, and research opportunities. *Schizophrenia Bulletin, 34*(6), 1211–1220.

Hogarty, G. E., Flesher, S., Ulrich, R., Carter, M., Greenwald, D. P., Pogue-Geile, M., et al. (2004). Cognitive enhancement therapy for schizophrenia: Effects of a 2-year randomized trial on cognition and behavior. *Archives of General Psychiatry*, *61*, 866–876.

Hogarty, G. E., Greenwald, D. P., & Eack, S. M. (2006). Durability and mechanism of effects of cognitive enhancement therapy. *Psychiatric Services*, *57*, 1751–1757.

Horan, W. P., Kern, R. S., Green, M. F., & Penn, D. L. (2009a). Social cognition training for individuals with schizophrenia: Emerging evidence. *American Journal of Psychiatric Rehabilitation*, *11*(3), 205–252.

Horan, W. P., Kern, R. S., Shokat-Fadai, K., Sergi, M. J., Wynn, J. K., & Green, M. F. (2009b). Social cognitive skills training in schizophrenia: An initial efficacy study of stabilized outpatients. *Schizophrenia Research*, *107*, 47–54.

Horan, W. P., Kern, R. S., Tripp, C., Hellemann, G., Wynn, J. K., Bell, M., et al. (2011). Efficacy and specificity of social cognitive skills training for outpatients with psychotic disorders. *Journal of Psychiatric Research*, *46*, 1113–1122.

Kayser, N., Sarfati, Y., Besche, C., & Hardy-Bayle, M. C. (2006). Elaboration of a rehabilitation method based on a pathogenetic hypothesis of 'theory of mind' impairment in schizophrenia. *Neuropsychological Rehabilitation*, *16*, 83–95.

Keshavan, M. S., Eack, S. M., Wojtalik, J. A., Prasad, K. M., Francis, A. N., Bhojraj, T. S., et al. (2011). A broad cortical reserve accelerates response to cognitive enhancement therapy in early course schizophrenia. *Schizophrenia Research*, *130*, 123–129.

Kurtz, M. M., & Richardson, C. L. (2012). Social cognitive training for schizophrenia: A meta-analytic investigation of controlled research. *Schizophrenia Bulletin*, *38*, 1092–1104.

Lecardeur, L., Strip, E., Giguere, M., Blouin, G., Rodriguez, J. P., & Champagne-Lavau, M. (2009). Effects of cognitive remediation therapies on psychotic symptoms and cognitive complaints in patients with schizophrenia and related disorders: A randomized study. *Schizophrenia Research*, *111*, 153–158.

Mazza, M., Lucci, G., Pacitti, F., Pino, M. C., Mariano, M., Casacchia, M., et al. (2010). Could schizophrenia subjects improve their social cognition abilities only with observation and imitation of social situations? *Neuropsychological Rehabilitation*, *20*, 675–703.

McDonald, S., & Flanagan, S. (2004). Social perception deficits after traumatic brain injury: Interaction between emotion recognition, mentalizing ability, and social communication. *Neuropsychology*, *18*, 572–579.

Mueller, D. R., Schmidt, S. J., & Roder, V. (2012). Integrated neurocognitive therapy. In D. Roberts & D. Penn (Eds.), *Social cognition in schizophrenia* (pp. 311–334). New York: Oxford Press.

Mueller, D. R., Schmidt, S. J., & Roder, V. (2013). Integrated psychological therapy: Effectiveness in schizophrenia inpatient settings related to patients' age. *American Journal of Geriatric Psychiatry*, *21*, 231–241.

Nienow, T. M., Docherty, N. M., Cohen, A. S., & Dinzeo, T. J. (2006). Attentional dysfunction, social perception, and social competence: What is the nature of the relationship? *Journal of Abnormal Psychology*, *115*, 408–417.

Pan, Y., Chen, S., Chen, W., & Liu, S. (2009). Affect recognition as an independent social function determinant in schizophrenia. *Comprehensive Psychiatry*, *50*(5), 443–452.

Penn, D. L., Addington, J., & Pinkham, A. (2006). Social cognitive impairments. In J. A. Lieberman, T. S. Stroup, & D. O. Perkins (Eds.), *American psychiatric association textbook of schizophrenia* (pp. 261–274). Arlington, VA: American Psychiatric Publishing Press, Inc..

Penn, D. L., & Combs, D. R. (2000). Modification of affect perception deficits in schizophrenia. *Schizophrenia Research*, *46*, 217–229.

Penn, D. L., Corrigan, P. W., Bentall, R., Racenstein, J. M., & Newman, L. (1997). Social cognition in schizophrenia. *Psychological Bulletin, 121,* 114–132.

Penn, D. L., Keefe, R., Davis, D., Meyer, P., Perkins, D., Losardo, D., et al. (2009). The effects of antipsychotic medications on emotion perception in patients with chronic schizophrenia in the CATIE trial. *Schizophrenia Research, 115,* 17–23.

Penn, D. L., Roberts, D., Munt, E. D., Silverstein, E., Jones, N., & Sheitman, B. (2005). A pilot study of social cognition and interaction training (SCIT) for schizophrenia. *Schizophrenia Research, 80,* 357–359.

Penn, D. L., Roberts, D. L., Combs, D. R., & Sterne, A. (2007). The development of the social cognition and interaction training (SCIT) program for schizophrenia spectrum disorders. *Psychiatric Services, 58,* 449–451.

Penn, D. L., Spaulding, W., Reed, D., & Sullivan, M. (1996). The relationship of social cognition to ward behavior in chronic schizophrenia. *Schizophrenia Research, 20,* 327–335.

Pinkham, A. E. (2012). The social cognitive neuroscience of schizophrenia. In D. Roberts & D. Penn (Eds.), *Social cognition in schizophrenia* (pp. 263–284). New York: Oxford Press.

Pinkham, A. E., & Penn, D. L. (2006). Neurocognitive and social cognitive predictors of social skill in schizophrenia. *Psychiatry Research, 143,* 167–178.

Pinkham, A. E., Penn, D. L., Perkins, D. O., & Lieberman, J. (2003). Implications for the neural basis of social cognition for the study of schizophrenia. *American Journal of Psychiatry, 160,* 815–824.

Roberts, D. L., & Penn, D. L. (2009). Social cognition and interaction training (SCIT) for outpatients with schizophrenia: A preliminary study. *Psychiatry Research, 166,* 141–147.

Roberts, D. L., & Penn, D. L. (2012). *Social cognition in schizophrenia: From evidence to treatment.* New York: Oxford Press.

Roberts, D. L., Penn, D. L., Labate, D., Margolis, S. A., & Sterne, A. (2010). Transportability and feasibility of social cognition and interaction training (SCIT) in community settings. *Behavioral and Cognitive Psychotherapy, 38,* 35–47.

Roberts, D. L., & Velligan, D. I. (2012). Can social functioning in schizophrenia be improved through targeted social cognitive intervention? *Rehabilitation Research and Practice, 2012,* 742106.

Roder, V., Mueller, D., Mueser, K. T., & Brenner, H. D. (2006). Integrated psychological therapy for schizophrenia: Is it effective? *Schizophrenia Bulletin, 32,* S81–S93.

Roder, V., Mueller, D., & Schmidt, S. J. (2011). Effectiveness of integrated psychological therapy (IPT) for schizophrenia patients: A research up-date. *Schizophrenia Bulletin, 37,* 71–79.

Roder, V., Mueller, D., Spaulding, W. S., & Brenner, H. D. (2010). *Integrated Psychological Therapy (IPT) for schizophrenia patients 2nd Ed.* Cambridge, MA: Hogrefe Publishing.

Roncone, R., Falloon, I. R., Mazza, M., De Risio, A., Pollice, R., Necozione, S., et al. (2002). Is theory of mind in schizophrenia more strongly associated with clinical and social functioning than with neurocognitive deficits? *Psychopathology, 35,* 280–288.

Roncone, R., Mazza, M., Frangou, I., De Risio, A., Ussorio, D., Tozzini, C., et al. (2004). Rehabilitation of theory of mind deficit in schizophrenia: A pilot study of metacognitive strategies in group treatment. *Neuropsychological Rehabilitation, 14*(4), 421–435.

Russell, T. A., Chu, E., & Phillips, M. L. (2006). A pilot study to investigate the effectiveness of emotion recognition remediation in schizophrenia using the micro-expression training tool. *British Journal of Clinical Psychology, 45,* 579–583.

Russell, T. A., Green, M. J., Simpson, I., & Coltheart, M. (2008). Remediation of facial emotion perception in schizophrenia: Concomitant changes in visual attention. *Schizophrenia Research, 103,* 248–256.

Sachs, G., Winklbaur, B., Jagsch, R., Lasser, I., Kryspin-Exner, I., Frommann, N., et al. (2012). Training of affect recognition (TAR) in schizophrenia – impact on functional outcome. *Schizophrenia Research, 138*, 262–267.

Sarfati, Y., Passerieux, C., & Hardy-Baylé, M. (2000). Can verbalization remedy the theory of mind deficit in schizophrenia? *Psychopathology, 33*, 246–251.

Sergi, M. J., Rassovsky, Y., Widmark, C., Reist, C., Erhart, S., Braff, D. L., et al. (2007). Social cognition in schizophrenia: Relationships with neurocognition and negative symptoms. *Schizophrenia Research, 90*, 316–324.

Silver, H., Goodman, C., Knoll, G., & Isakof, V. (2004). Brief emotion training improves recognition of facial emotions in chronic schizophrenia: A pilot study. *Psychiatry Research, 128*(21), 147–154.

Statuka, M., & Walder, D. J. (2013). Efficacy of social cognition remediation programs targeting facial affect recognition deficits in schizophrenia: A review and consideration of high-risk samples and sex differences. *Psychiatry Research, 206*, 125–139.

Tas, C., Danaci, A. E., Cubukcuoglu, Z., & Brüne, M. (2012). Impact of family involvement on social cognition training in clinically stable outpatients with schizophrenia – a randomized pilot study. *Psychiatry Research, 195*, 32–38.

Turner-Brown, L. M., Perry, T. D., Dichter, G. S., Bodfish, J. W., & Penn, D. L. (2008). Brief report: Feasibility of social cognition and interaction training for adults with high functioning autism. *Journal of Autism and Developmental Disorders, 38*, 1777–1784.

van Hooren, S., Versmissen, D., Janssen, I., Myin-Germeys, I., á Campo, J., Mengelers, R., et al. (2008). Social cognition and neurocognition as independent domains in psychosis. *Schizophrenia Research, 103*, 257–265.

Vauth, R., Rusch, N., Wirtz, M., & Corrigan, P. W. (2004). Does social cognition influence the relation between neurocognitive deficits and vocational functioning in schizophrenia? *Psychiatry Research, 128*, 155–165.

Wölwer, W., Combs, D. R., Frommann, N., & Penn, D. L. (2010). Treatment approaches with a special focus on social cognition: Overview and empirical results. In A. Medalia & V. Roder (Eds.), *Neurocognition and social cognition in schizophrenia patients: Basic concepts and treatment* (pp. 61–78). Switzerland: Karger Publishers, Basel.

Wölwer, W., & Frommann, N. (2009). The training of affect recognition (TAR): Efficacy, functional specificity, and generalization of effects. *Schizophrenia Bulletin, 35*, 351.

Wölwer, W., Frommann, N., Halfmann, S., Piaszek, A., Streit, M., & Gaebel, W. (2005). Remediation of impairments in facial affect recognition in schizophrenia: Efficacy and specificity of a new training program. *Schizophrenia Research, 80*, 295–303.

Wölwer, W., Streit, M., Polzer, U., & Gaebel, W. (1996). Facial affect recognition in the course of schizophrenia. *European Archives of Psychiatry and Clinical Neuroscience, 246*, 165–170.

Chapter 11

Metacognitive Training and Therapy: An Individualized and Group Intervention for Psychosis

Todd S. Woodward,[1,2] Ryan Balzan,[3]
Mahesh Menon[1] and Steffen Moritz[4]

[1]University of British Columbia, Vancouver, BC, Canada,
[2]BC Mental Health and Addictions Research Institute, Vancouver, BC, Canada,
[3]Flinders University, Adelaide, SA, Australia, [4]Universitätsklinikum Hamburg-Eppendorf,
Hamburg, Germany

Chapter Outline

INTRODUCTION

Despite providing relief for many people with schizophrenia, pharmaceutical interventions are often met with symptom relapse, poor compliance, lack of insight, and potentially serious side effects and are not effective for about one-third of patients (Leucht et al., 2009; van Os and Kapur, 2009). This has led to efforts to develop and refine novel treatment methods that may reduce symptom severity over and above that already available through pharmaceutical interventions, an approach that may be more effective than antipsychotic

Social Cognition and Metacognition in Schizophrenia.
DOI: http://dx.doi.org/10.1016/B978-0-12-405172-0.00011-9
© 2014 Elsevier Inc. All rights reserved.

medication treatment alone (Wykes *et al.*, 2008), possibly also increasing adherence to pharmaceutical treatment (van Os and Kapur, 2009).

A number of nonpharmaceutical treatment methods are available that primarily target positive symptoms (Fowler *et al.*, 1995; Waller *et al.*, 2011; Wykes *et al.*, 2008; Zimmermann *et al.*, 2005). One of these was developed by our group and is called metacognitive training (MCT) or metacognitive therapy (MCT+) (Moritz and Woodward, 2007b; Moritz *et al*, 2012a), depending on whether reference is to the group or individualized application, respectively. MCT evolved from the concepts and goals introduced by cognitive behavioral therapy for psychosis (CBTp), which is to identify and change maladaptive beliefs by testing the evidence for and against them, thereby helping patients become aware of alternative explanations and coping strategies (Steel, 2013; Wykes *et al.*, 2008; Zimmermann *et al.*, 2005). CBTp sessions typically involve discussion of the client's own delusions and have been labeled a 'front door' psychotherapeutic approach accordingly. In contrast, MCT can be considered a 'back door' psychotherapeutic program, because it targets psychotic symptoms indirectly by focusing on the underlying cognitive biases underlying delusions in general rather than the idiosyncratic delusions specific to the individual patient. MCT unpacks the elements of biased thinking and reasoning styles that underlie delusions ('cognitive biases') and introduces them experientially (in a wide range of situations) by walking participants through visual displays inspired by over 25 years of research into the cognitive underpinnings of delusions in schizophrenia (Bell *et al.*, 2006; Blackwood *et al.*, 2001; Garety and Freeman, 1999). The goal of MCT is to provide tools promoting self-recognition of these thinking biases, and countering them, a benefit that could (unlike pharmaceutical interventions) persist well past the actual treatment sessions. This awareness of these thinking biases is the first step toward managing symptoms, potentially reducing the clinical impact of delusions.

MCT is both a behavioral intervention and knowledge translation program. Metacognition literally means 'about thinking', can be interpreted as 'thinking about one's own thinking', and this is both the educational goal and therapeutic approach of MCT. The first of three fundamental components of the MCT program is knowledge transfer from researcher to patient through the group facilitator. Specifically, patients are informed of current empirical research that links cognitive biases to delusion formation/maintenance and are provided with illustrative examples demonstrating these cognitive biases. Although knowledge translation is typically conceptualized as information flowing from research teams to clinical care teams, MCT involves knowledge translation from research teams directly to people who experience psychosis, through a group facilitator. In this sense MCT is focused on raising patients' awareness of their illness, because bringing certain thinking disturbances to the attention of patients leads to a new awareness of how schizophrenia can be understood.

The second component of MCT is a demonstration of the negative consequences of these cognitive biases (or unhealthy thinking patterns) via exercises that target each bias individually, and which simultaneously establish the falli-bility of human cognition generally. MCT promotes countering these unhealthy thinking patterns, with the intention of preventing or reducing the severity of relapse. Participants are guided slowly through a sampling of the cognitive tests that were used to identify these thinking patterns, with these thinking patterns being discussed at every step.

The third component of MCT involves offering clients alternative think-ing strategies, which may help them to arrive at more appropriate inferences and thereby avoid the 'cognitive traps' that otherwise lead to delusional beliefs (Moritz and Woodward, 2007b). It is through relating these concepts back to participants' everyday experiences that MCT exerts its effects. MCT is com-prised of eight modules consisting of pdf-converted PowerPoint slides and can be downloaded free of charge via the following link: www.uke.de/mkt. MCT is currently available in 30 languages.

In the original group-based MCT program, we compiled material from a range of researchers studying delusions with cognitive neuropsychology, and arranged these (with other material) into a series of eight instructor-led group intervention sessions. Each MCT module introduces different thinking biases, although there is some overlap between the modules and two prominent prob-lems, jumping to conclusions (JTC) and social cognition, are presented twice with parallel versions. The group-based MCT program consists of eight mod-ules. The modules deal with attributional style (Module 1: participants are conveyed the disadvantages of monocausal inferences; instead, alternative possibilities should be contemplated); JTC (Modules 2 and 7: participants are encouraged to avoid hasty decision making, especially for momentous incidences); changing beliefs (Module 3: participants are taught to stay open-minded for alternative assumptions as evidence/situations may change over time); theory of mind (ToM)/social cognition (Modules 4 and 6: participants are taught to pay attention to multiple social cues before inferring the state of mind of another person); memory/overconfidence (Module 5: participants are taught to withhold strong judgments and to prevent false memories); and mood/self-esteem (Module 8: exercises attempt to lift self-esteem and change negative cognitive schemata). The training is delivered by a healthcare special-ist (facilitator) with groups of three to 10 clients with psychosis.

The individualized MCT+program combines the 'process-oriented' approach of the MCT group training with elements from individual CBTp. The combined approach works by relating information from the original MCT mod-ules to the individual experiences, observations, and symptoms of the individual patient (Moritz et al., 2010). Given that CBTp attempts to shift delusional think-ing by targeting the specific delusional content, while group-based MCT aims to reduce delusions by educating patients about the cognitive biases underlying delusion formation and maintenance, the MCT+ approach may be more effec-tive than either psychological treatment alone. The English version of all MCT+ therapy units can be downloaded free of charge from: www.uke.de/mkt_plus.

COGNITIVE BIASES TARGETED BY METACOGNITIVE TRAINING

The identification of biased cognitive processes that underlie delusional thought has been the topic of a branch of cognitive neuropsychiatry research that spans more than 25 years. The major findings were first summarized by Garety and Freeman (1999) and investigations and summaries continue (Bell et al., 2006; Blackwood et al., 2001; Langdon et al., 2008). A number of biased cognitive processes have now been identified, and attempts to define their nature and degree of correlation with the severity of delusions are ongoing (e.g., So et al., 2010). This empirical research into the thinking biases that underlie delusions has provided the motivation for development of the MCT program. Below we introduce each thinking bias and explain how they are addressed by the MCT modules.

Jumping to Conclusions

It has been noted that schizophrenia patients show a JTC bias, whereby strong conclusions can be reached based on little evidence (starting with Huq et al., 1988). A JTC bias can be detected in delusion-neutral material and is thought to play an important role in the formation and maintenance of delusions. This association between JTC and severity/presence of delusions been demonstrated in a number of studies (Balzan et al., 2012; Garety and Freeman, 1999; Speechley et al., 2010; Woodward et al., 2009), has been confirmed in reviews (Bell et al., 2006; Blackwood et al., 2001; Fine et al., 2007; Garety and Freeman, 1999), and may be more associated with core paranoid beliefs than with general suspiciousness (Moritz et al., 2012b). Our group also demonstrated, in two studies, that when delusions decreased, the JTC bias also decreased (Sanford et al., 2013; Woodward et al., 2009).

Modules 2 and 7 both focus on JTC. In both modules, the group first discusses advantages (e.g., saving time) and especially disadvantages of JTC (less reliable judgment, high probability of errors). Examples are provided for how JTC may cause difficulties in everyday life. Exercises of the first task set of Module 2 show common objects, which are displayed in decreasing degrees of fragmentation: new features are added in eight successive stages, until the entire object is eventually displayed. Participants are asked to rate the plausibility of either self-generated or pre-specified response alternatives. In one example, the image in the first stage of the 'frog' exercise strongly resembles a lemon, because only the contour of the frog is displayed. Thus, a hasty decision results in an error. Another task requires participants to observe 'two-way' pictures, which initially suggest one scenario (e.g., an elderly couple staring at each other), but on closer inspection it is clear that alternative interpretations exist (e.g., the 'elderly couple' actually consist of two seated musicians). In these tasks, it is made clear that hasty decisions do not always lead to errors, but they sometimes only tell half the story. Additionally, arguments for and against common false beliefs in society are discussed. It is made clear to the participants that urban legends have partly arisen due to JTC and are based on very little evidence (e.g., Paul McCartney of Beatles fame died in 1966 in an accident and was replaced by a lookalike double, as 'evidenced' by the Abbey Road album cover). Thus, they can be considered a good miniature model for delusional ideas in general. In Module 7 (JTC II), a number of paintings are shown to the participants. The task is to choose the correct title from four response options. For some paintings the solution is rather obvious, but for others it only becomes clear upon a thorough visual search and group discussion. Again, the learning purpose is that hasty decisions lead to errors, and that careful examination of the evidence is required before reaching a definite decision.

Bias Against Disconfirmatory Evidence

Delusions are defined as fixed false beliefs that are maintained despite counter-evidence and rational counter-argument. Maintenance of delusions despite counter-evidence and rational counter-argument involves explaining away disconfirming evidence by integrating it into the delusional framework, and this process has been described as safety behaviors (e.g., the only reason they did not shoot me yesterday was because I avoided watching television) and incorporation (e.g., the only reason they did not shoot me yesterday was because they want me to suffer another day) (Freeman et al., 2002; Garety et al., 2001). In past work, our group has shown that a cognitive bias against disconfirmatory evidence (BADE) exists in schizophrenia that is observable on delusion-neutral material, tapping into a cognitive process that may underlie the fixed aspect of delusions (i.e., maintained despite counter-evidence and rational counter-argument), presumably resulting in safety behaviors and incorporation. This bias is present in schizophrenia (Moritz and Woodward, 2006b; Woodward et al., 2008) and is particularly enhanced in delusional patients (Speechley et al., 2012; Woodward et al., 2006a; Woodward et al., 2006b).

The BADE effect has been measured on a range of tasks. In a typical BADE task, the subject is confronted with sequentially increasing pieces of information. For BADE trials, the subject is lured into false beliefs that are disconfirmed by subsequent information. Patients are less able to disengage from initially plausible interpretations, which, over the course of three trials, became increasingly implausible. This effect was demonstrated in both first-episode (Woodward et al., 2006a) and predominantly chronic patients (Moritz and Woodward, 2006b) as well as in healthy participants scoring high on delusional symptoms (Buchy et al., 2007). In some studies, this bias was more pronounced in currently deluded patients (Woodward et al., 2006a; Woodward et al., 2006b). The BADE effect has also recently been elucidated using alterative tasks designed to test the confirmation bias (Balzan et al., 2013) and representativeness heuristic (Balzan et al., 2012), suggesting it can be generalized to a number of contexts.

The disadvantages of inflexibility are highlighted at the beginning of Module 3. Historical and case examples are given on how an unwillingness to revise positions promotes problems to the point of disastrous events. The exercises consist of a series of three pictures shown in reversed order. (Some of these were developed in the studies mentioned above.) The sequences of pictures gradually disambiguate a scenario. For each picture, participants are asked to rate the plausibility of four different interpretations. The correct interpretation is highlighted at the end of each trial. One of the four interpretations appears improbable upon the presentation of the first picture, but are eventually shown to be true in most cases. Two of the other interpretations seem plausible upon the presentation of the first picture, but are eventually shown to be implausible. The goal is for participants to learn to search for more information before judging and to correct themselves if disconfirmatory evidence is encountered.

Metamemory and Overconfidence in Errors

Extensive literature suggests that patients with schizophrenia display a decrease in memory functioning (Aleman *et al.*, 1999). These dysfunctions negatively impact functional outcome such as independent living and the patient's work situation and social skills (Green and Phillips, 2004). In addition to the investigation of objective memory functioning, a new line of literature has turned to metamemory, which is the subjective appraisal of one's own memory performance, for example, response confidence (Moritz and Woodward, 2006a). Our research demonstrated that patients with schizophrenia are overconfident in memory errors while at the same time are underconfident in correct responses (for a review see Moritz and Woodward, 2006a). This pattern of results has been demonstrated using false memory paradigms (Moritz and Woodward, 2006c; Moritz *et al.*, 2004; Moritz *et al.*, 2006b) and source memory tasks (Moritz and Woodward, 2002; Moritz and Woodward, 2006a; Moritz *et al.*, 2003; Moritz *et al.*, 2005; Moritz *et al.*, 2006a) for both false-positive and false-negative memory errors. As is the case for the aforementioned biases, overconfidence in errors is not restricted to delusional memories, but is regarded as a risk factor and antecedent rather than a consequence of paranoid symptoms. To highlight this point, more recent work has determined that the metamemory 'overconfidence in errors' effect can be generalized to other domains of cognition outside of memory errors (Köther *et al.*, 2012; Moritz *et al.*, 2012), and, interestingly, there is evidence that decreasing overconfidence in errors is a prominent mechanism of change induced by antipsychotic agents (Andreou *et al.*, 2013).

In Module 5, the group first discusses ways to enhance memory recall through mnemonic strategies. The ubiquity of memory errors is highlighted: no-one can recall a past incident perfectly and humans are not only prone to forgetting, but also to false memories. Then, visual stimuli with strong themes are presented, which are known to elicit false memories (e.g., a beach towel is commonly 'remembered' in beach scenes, even when absent). Group members are instructed to look at the pictures carefully and to memorize each item in order to avoid the false memory effect. Each picture is followed by a recognition task in which participants are required to decide whether an item has been displayed or not. Although in false memory investigations patients with schizophrenia may not differ from controls in accuracy, their conviction for error responses was disproportionately increased (Moritz et al., 2006b). One of the objectives of this module is to teach participants to doubt their memories, if a vivid recollection is not available. In this case, further proof should be collected, particularly for important situations (e.g., interpersonal conflicts).

Attributional Style and Self-Esteem

Patients with schizophrenia display a bias whereby unjustified blame for negative events can be cast on other people (e.g., neighbors) and/or institutions (e.g., police), when in fact unidentified events may be to blame (Bentall, 1994; Diez-Alegria et al., 2006; Kinderman and Bentall, 1997; Kinderman et al., 1992). To a lesser degree, this attributional style is also found in healthy people in everyday life. This attributional style may help protect a deep-rooted low self-esteem (Bentall et al., 2001); however, a review concluded that paranoid delusions do not serve to enhance self-esteem, but that they directly reflect specific negative self-schemas (Kesting and Lincoln, 2013). The literature is in general agreement that paranoid delusions may be associated with externalization of blame to other people (Kinderman and Bentall, 1997; Kinderman et al., 1992; Randall et al., 2003), and we replicated this result for positive and negative material (Moritz et al., 2007). This was also confirmed by a review of the literature (Garety and Freeman, 1999). Relatedly, our group recently found that patients with schizophrenia tend to provide one-sided (monocausal) explanations for complex social events (Randjbar et al., 2011).

In Module 1, participants are first familiarized with the concept of attribution. The social consequences of different attributional styles are highlighted (e.g., blaming others for failure may lead to interpersonal tensions). Following this, participants are asked to find reasons for briefly described incidents. Situational as well as personal factors should be taken into account. There is always a number of different possible explanations that should be considered even if only one explanation seems valid at first, 'A friend is talking behind your back'; possible explanation: 'The person is planning a conspiracy against you'; alternative interpretations: 'That person asked other people whether you were ill as you look quite stressed out. He did not want to ask you directly since you could be upset or insulted'; 'This is normal, we all gossip from time to time.'

Module 8 (mood and self-esteem) deals less with attributional style, but more with depression and self-esteem, because many patients with schizophrenia show affective disturbances and low self-esteem. It has been estimated that at least 50% of the schizophrenia population suffers from depression (Buckley *et al.*, 2009). These exercises target depressive cognitive biases such as overgeneralization and selective abstraction. The facilitator explains how distorted cognitive schemata can be replaced by more realistic and helpful ones. In addition, the module targets dysfunctional coping strategies often adopted by people with psychological problems. Finally, some techniques are provided, which, when used regularly, help to alter low self-esteem and to raise depressed mood.

Theory of Mind

ToM is a commonly investigated aspect of social cognition in schizophrenia, for which consideration of situational variables is required in order to determine the thoughts and perspectives of other people. This is of interest for the study of delusions because delusions can involve a misunderstanding of what is on the mind of others (e.g., paranoid delusions). The most commonly used measures of ToM are referred to as first- and second-order false belief tasks. In these tasks, a protagonist in a story holds a belief that the observer should know is false, based on the context of the situation. In first-order tasks the protagonist's false belief is about a situation, and in second-order tasks the protagonist's false belief is about the intentions of another protagonist. These tasks also include reality questions that determine whether or not the person understood the situation well enough to properly respond to the ToM query. Impairments are more consistently reported on second-order ToM tasks (Doody *et al.*, 1998; Frith and Corcoran, 1996; Pickup and Frith, 2001), but also in first-order ToM tasks (Mazza *et al.*, 2001).

The Hinting task (Corcoran *et al.*, 1995) is another consistently used ToM task (Couture *et al.*, 2006). The hinting task tests the ability of subjects to infer the real intentions behind indirect speech (e.g., what did the child really mean when he or she said 'Mom I'm hungry' when passing the candy aisle). Reviews of the literature concluded that evidence for a correspondence between ToM and delusions is considered weak/rare (Blackwood *et al.*, 2001; Garety and Freeman, 1999), and that they are instead associated with negative symptoms (Brune, 2005; Harrington *et al.*, 2005), which continues to be empirically replicated (Langdon *et al.*, 2001; Mizrahi *et al.*, 2006). Cognitive biases such as JTC and BADE may become most problematic in combination with problems in social reasoning, especially if there is a tendency to interpret the facial expressions and actions of others as hostile.

In Module 4 the group first discusses different cues for social cognition (e.g., appearance, language) and their validity. It is stressed that each cue is fallible and that social cognition is best when a set of different cues is considered. Participants are then asked to identify basic human emotions and assign them to facial expressions. This module conveys the message that although facial expressions are very important for the understanding of inner feelings of a person, they can lead to false conclusions.

In Module 6, comic sequences are presented, for which participants are required to take the perspective of one of the protagonists, and to deduce what the character may think about another person or certain event. In the 'BADE-ized' administration mode, most slides are presented in reverse sequential order, with the final picture within the comic sequence being displayed first. In other words, the last picture(s) is (are) presented first, while the first pictures of the comic sequence remain covered. As each picture is revealed, more context information is revealed about the storyline. For the majority of items in the standard as well as in the BADE-ized administration, several interpretations remain possible until the end. In this case, participants should propose what additional information is required for a reliable judgment. Even if a sequence remains ambiguous, it should be discussed which interpretation is best supported by the available evidence.

ADMINISTRATION OF THE PROGRAM

The original group-based MCT consists of two parallel cycles (A and B), with each being comprised of eight modules (see www.uke.de/mkt). An administration mode of two sessions per week is considered optimal, with one module per session. Thus, inpatients in treatment for four weeks or longer could undergo a full cycle. Outpatients and day patients receiving prolonged treatment could attend both cycles A and B. The parallel A and B versions are identical in terms of their rationale, but show different exercises. The group size ranges from three to 10 participants, whereby an optimal group size comprises around five participants. Trainers should be healthcare professionals, such as psychologists, psychiatrists, psychiatric nurses, social workers, and occupational therapists having long-term experience with schizophrenia spectrum disorder patients. Each session should last between 45 and 60 minutes. The modules are pdf-converted PowerPoint files, which should be projected onto a white wall or screen in the Adobe Acrobat® full-screen mode. Participants can enter at any module within a cycle.

Individualized MCT+ runs over a similar layout to the group-based MCT and consists of 10 therapy units (see: www.uke.de/mkt_plus). Each unit contains a wide range of therapeutic material covering psychoeducational information, exercises, case examples, demonstrations, and worksheets. Six of the therapy units deal with common cognitive errors and problem-solving deviations in schizophrenia (attribution styles, decision-making, belief flexibility, empathy, memory and overconfidence, and self-esteem and mood). In addition, MCT+ helps to establish an individual illness model (Therapy Unit 3). At the beginning of a therapy cycle, a structured interview should be administered to evaluate the medical history as well as to provide an introduction to MCT+ (see Therapy Units 1 and 2). Therapy is completed with a unit on relapse prevention that also conveys stress coping strategies (Therapy Unit 10).

FEASIBILITY, SUBJECTIVE, AND OBJECTIVE EFFECTIVENESS

Several studies have been conducted since the introduction of the MCT in 2005 in order to address the feasibility, safety, and effectiveness of the approach (Moritz et al., 2010; Moritz et al., 2013). In a preliminary study (Moritz and Woodward, 2007a), MCT was rated as superior to a control condition on fun and usefulness to daily life. Efficacy of MCT has now been studied in a number of randomized controlled trials. Three trials have been restricted to examining the safety, feasibility, and efficacy of MCT in the German (Moritz and Woodward, 2007a), French (Favrod et al., 2011), and Polish (Gawęda et al., 2009) versions, and in all studies MCT was considered by participants to be engaging and (subjectively) effective. The earliest study investigating the efficacy of MCT in reducing positive symptoms compared MCT to an active control (Aghotor et al., 2010). The study enrolled 15 patients per group, and reductions in positive symptoms and an MCT targeted, objectively measured thinking bias (JTC measured by an evidence gathering task) were noted at re-test (4 weeks). However, these did not reach statistical significance, likely due to the small sample sizes. A second study allocated 17 patients per group to either a brief 'reasoning training' (Modules 2 and 7 of the MCT) or an attention control group (Ross et al., 2011). Less conviction in delusions was noted in the MCT trials, but again this finding did not reach statistical significance. In a third study using 18 subjects per group (Moritz et al., 2011a), the effectiveness of MCT was compared with treatment as usual (TAU) at baseline and post-treatment assessments at 8 weeks, and in this trial. MCT significantly reduced delusion distress (effect size $d = 0.68$; reported for MCT vs. control condition comparisons here and below), and improved social functioning ($d = 0.77$). In two small-scale studies (between 8 and 14 subjects per group, with MCT compared with TAU groups), MCT was found to significantly decrease delusions (Balzan et al., 2014; Kumar et al., 2010), and JTC-style and BADE-style cognitive biases (Balzan et al., 2014).

Building on these preliminary results, funding was procured for larger studies investigating the efficacy of the MCT. They first recruited 24 subjects per group (Moritz et al., 2011b) and explored the effectiveness of MCT plus individualized MCT+ producing a hybrid of group and individualized MCT. Cognitive remediation therapy (CRT) was used as the control condition, and pre- and post-assessments were separated by 4 weeks. Patients in the MCT/MCT+ arm showed significantly greater improvement on delusion severity ($d = 0.68$), delusion conviction ($d = 0.63$), as well as on a measure of JTC ($d = 0.59$). The most recent and largest randomized controlled trial to date involved sample sizes of 75 per group, and MCT was compared with CRT using 16 sessions each (Moritz et al., personal communication). Assessments were made at baseline, 4 weeks, and 6 months later. Relative to CRT, MCT significantly reduced delusions on multiple scales at both post-treatment time points (4 weeks and 6 months, $d = 0.41$ and 0.51, respectively).

As mentioned above, MCT exerts its effects by helping patients become aware of their own thinking biases, and this is sometimes echoed by those who benefit from the program. For example, the Canadian Alliance on Mental Illness and Mental Health 'Faces of Mental Illness' campaign 2012 representative recipient Sandra MacKay wrote about how MCT contributed to her recovery: *'If I'm walking down the street and I hear a stranger swear, I might think the person is angry at me. However, maybe he's having a bad day, on a cellphone, or talking to himself. Just because he said something, doesn't mean it has anything to do with me but may be more to do with him or the situation or circumstance . . . By questioning myself, I can recognize symptoms more readily and see experiences from different angles rather than seeing only my point of view. MCT may not cure me, but it is a very useful wellness tool'.* (www.peerwork.wordpress.com/ 'How Metacognitive Therapy Helped Me'). Similar anecdotes have been published elsewhere (Kumar *et al.*, personal communication).

CONCLUSION

Since the mid-1990s, increasing support has been accumulating for psychological models of schizophrenia indicating that cognitive biases may play an important role in the formation and maintenance of delusions. The goal of the MCT is to sharpen participants' (metacognitive) awareness of these biases and to carry over the learning aims to their daily life and experiences. There is also increasing support for the effectiveness of MCT as a stand-alone program, but we encourage individual therapy for many patients, and material for this is now available with the MCT+. Given mounting evidence for beneficial effects of cognitive intervention in schizophrenia, and considering the high rates of relapse, there is a strong argument for integration of cognitive interventions into TAU.

ACKNOWLEDGMENTS

TSW is supported by career investigator awards from the Canadian Institutes of Health Research (CIHR) and the Michael Smith Foundation for Health Research (MSFHR). RB was supported by a grant from the BC Psychosis program.

REFERENCES

Aghotor, J., Pfueller, U., Moritz, S., Weisbrod, M., & Roesch-Ely, D. (2010). Metacognitive training for patients with schizophrenia (MCT): Feasibility and preliminary evidence for its efficacy. *Journal of Behavior Therapy and Experimental Psychiatry, 41,* 207–211.

Aleman, A., Hijman, R., de Haan, E. H. F., & Kahn, R. S. (1999). Memory impairment in schizophrenia: A meta-analysis. *American Journal of Psychiatry, 156,* 1358–1366.

Andreou, C., Moritz, S., Veith, K., Veckenstedt, R., & Naber, D. (2013). Dopaminergic modulation of probabilistic reasoning and overconfidence in errors: A double-blind study. *Schizophrenia Bulletin* in press.

Balzan, R. P., Delfabbro, P. H., Galletly, C., & Woodward, T. S. (2012). Reasoning heuristics across the psychosis continuum: The contribution of hypersalient evidence-hypothesis matches. *Cognitive Neuropsychiatry, 17*, 431–450.

Balzan, R. P., Delfabbro, P. H., Galletly, C., & Woodward, T. S. (2013). Confirmation biases across the psychosis continuum: The contribution of hypersalient evidence-hypothesis matches. *British Journal of Clinical Psychology, 52*, 53–69.

Balzan, R. P., Delfabbro, P. H., Galletly, C., & Woodward, T. S. (2014). Metacognitive training for patients with schizophrenia: Preliminary evidence for a targeted single-module program. *Australian and New Zealand Journal of Psychiatry* in press.

Bell, V., Halligan, P. W., & Ellis, H. D. (2006). Explaining delusions: A cognitive perspective. *Trends in Cognitive Sciences, 10*, 219–226.

Bentall, R., Corcoran, R., Howard, R., Blackwood, N., & Kinderman, P. (2001). Persecutory delusions: A review and theoretical integration. *Clinical Psychology Review, 21*, 1143–1192.

Bentall, R. P. (1994). Cognitive biases and abnormal beliefs: Towards a model of persecutory delusions. In A. S. David & J. C. Cutting (Eds.), *The neuropsychology of schizophrenia* (pp. 337–361). Hillside, NJ: Erlbaum.

Blackwood, N. J., Howard, R. J., Bentall, R. P., & Murray, R. M. (2001). Cognitive neuropsychiatric models of persecutory delusions. *American Journal of Psychiatry, 158*, 527–539.

Brune, M. (2005). Emotion recognition, 'theory of mind,' and social behavior in schizophrenia. *Psychiatry Research, 133*(2–3), 135–147.

Buchy, L., Woodward, T. S., & Liotti, M. (2007). A cognitive bias against disconfirmatory evidence (BADE) is associated with schizotypal traits. *Schizophrenia Research, 90*, 334–337.

Buckley, P. F., Miller, B. J., Lehrer, D. S., & Castle, D. J. (2009). Psychiatric comorbidities and schizophrenia. *Schizophrenia Bulletin, 35*, 383–402.

Corcoran, R., Mercer, G., & Frith, C. D. (1995). Schizophrenia, symptomatology and social inference: Investigating "Theory of mind" in people with schizophrenia. *Schizophrenia Research, 17*, 5–13.

Couture, S. M., Penn, D. L., & Roberts, D. L. (2006). The functional significance of social cognition in schizophrenia: A review. *Schizophrenia Bulletin, 32*, S44–S63.

Diez-Alegria, C., Vazquez, C., Nieto-Moreno, M., Valiente, C., & Fuentenebro, F. (2006). Personalizing and externalizing biases in deluded and depressed patients: Are attributional biases a stable and specific characteristic of delusions? *British Journal of Clinical Psychology, 45*, 531–544.

Doody, G. A., Gotz, M., Johnstone, E. C., Frith, C. D., & Owens, D. G. (1998). Theory of mind and psychoses. *Psychological Medicine, 28*, 397–405.

Favrod, J., Maire, A., Bardy, S., Pernier, S., & Bonsack, C. (2011). Improving insight into delusions: A pilot study of metacognitive training for patients with schizophrenia. *Journal of Advanced Nursing, 67*, 401–407.

Fine, C., Gardner, M., Craigie, J., & Gold, I. (2007). Hopping, skipping or jumping to conclusions? Clarifying the role of the JTC bias in delusions. *Cognitive Neuropsychiatry, 12*, 46–77.

Fowler, D., Garety, P., & Kuipers, E. (1995). *Cognitive Behaviour Therapy for Psychosis: Theory and Practice*. Chichester: Wiley.

Freeman, D., Garety, P. A., Kuipers, E., Fowler, D., & Bebbington, P. E. (2002). A cognitive model of persecutory delusions. *British Journal of Clinical Psychology, 41*, 331–347.

Frith, C. D., & Corcoran, R. (1996). Exploring 'theory of mind' in people with schizophrenia. *Psychological Medicine, 26*, 521–530.

Garety, P. A., & Freeman, D. (1999). Cognitive approaches to delusions: A critical review of the evidence. *British Journal of Clinical Psychology, 38*, 113–154.

Garety, P. A., Kuipers, E., Fowler, D., Freeman, D., & Bebbington, P. E. (2001). A cognitive model of the positive symptoms of psychosis. *Psychological Medicine, 31*, 189–195.

Gawęda, Ł., Moritz, S., & Kokoszka, A. (2009). Metacognitive training for schizophrenia patients: Description of method and experiences from clinical practice. *Psychiatria Polska, 43*, 683–692.

Green, M. J., & Phillips, M. L. (2004). Social threat perception and the evolution of paranoia. *Neuroscience and Biobehavioural Reviews, 28*, 333–342.

Huq, S. F., Garety, P. A., & Helmsley, D. R. (1988). Probabilistic judgments in deluded and non-deluded subjects. *Quarterly Journal of Experimental Psychology, 40*, 801–812.

Kesting, M. L., & Lincoln, T. M. (2013). The relevance of self-esteem and self-schemas to persecutory delusions: A systematic review. *Comprehensive Psychiatry, 54*, 766–789.

Kinderman, P., & Bentall, R. P. (1997). Causal attributions in paranoia and depression: Internal, personal, and situational attributions for negative events. *Journal of Abnormal Psychology, 106*, 341–345.

Kinderman, P., Kaney, S., Morley, S., & Bentall, R. P. (1992). Paranoia and the defensive attributional style: Deluded and depressed patients' attributions about their own attributions. *British Journal of Medical Psychology, 65*, 371–383.

Köther, U., Veckenstedt, R., Vitzthum, F., Roesch-Ely, D., Pfueller, U., Scheu, F., et al. (2012). "Don't give me that look" – overconfidence in false mental state perception in schizophrenia. *Psychiatry Research, 196*, 1–8.

Kumar, D., Haq, Zia Ul, Dubey, M., Dotiwala, I., Siddiqui, K., & Abhishek, S. V. (2010). Effect of meta-cognitive training in the reduction of positive symptoms in schizophrenia. *European Journal of Psychotherapy & Counselling, 12*, 149–158.

Langdon, R., Coltheart, M., Ward, P. B., & Catts, S. V. (2001). Mentalising, executive planning and disengagement in schizophrenia. *Cognitive Neuropsychiatry, 6*, 81–108.

Langdon, R., Ward, P. B., & Coltheart, M. (2010). Reasoning anomalies associated with delusions in schizophrenia. *Schizophrenia Bulletin, 36*, 321–330.

Leucht, S., Arbter, D., Engel, R. R., Kissling, W., & Davis, J. M. (2009). How effective are second-generation antipsychotic drugs? A meta-analysis of placebo-controlled trials. *Molecular Psychiatry, 14*(4), 429–447.

Mazza, M., De Risio, A., Surian, L., Roncone, R., & Casacchia, M. (2001). Selective impairments of theory of mind in people with schizophrenia. *Schizophrenia Research, 47*, 299–308.

Mizrahi, R., Korostil, M., Starkstein, S. E., Zipursky, R. B., & Kapur, S. (2006). The effect of antipsychotic treatment on theory of mind. *Psychological Medicine*, 1–7.

Moritz, S., Kerstan, A., Veckenstedt, R., Randjbar, S., Vitzthum, F., Schmidt, C., et al. (2011a). Further evidence for the effectiveness of metacognitive group training in schizophrenia. *Behaviour Research and Therapy, 49*, 151–157.

Moritz, S., Van Quaquebeke, N., & Lincoln, T. M. (2012a). Jumping to conclusions is associated with paranoia but not general suspiciousness: A comparison of two versions of the probabilistic reasoning paradigm. *Schizophrenia Research and Treatment, 2012*, 384039.

Moritz, S., Veckenstedt, R., Randjbar, S., Vitzthum, F., & Woodward, T. S. (2011b). Antipsychotic treatment beyond antipsychotics: Metacognitive intervention for schizophrenia patients improves delusional symptoms in schizophrenia patients. *Psychological Medicine, 41*, 1823–1832.

Moritz, S., Veckenstedt, R., Vitzthum, F., Köther, U., & Woodward, T. S. (2012b). Metacognitive training in schizophrenia. Theoretical rationale and administration. In D. Roberts & D. Penn (Eds.), *Social cognition in schizophrenia: From evidence to treatment* (pp. 358–383). Oxford: Oxford University Press.

Moritz, S., Vitzthuma, F., Randjbara, S., Veckenstedta, R., & Woodward, T. S. (2010). Detecting and defusing cognitive traps: Metacognitive intervention in schizophrenia. *Current Opinion in Psychiatry, 23*, 561–569.

Moritz, S., & Woodward, T. S. (2002). Memory confidence and false memories in schizophrenia. *Journal of Nervous and Mental Disease, 190*, 641–643.

Moritz, S., & Woodward, T. S. (2006a). The contribution of metamemory deficits to schizophrenia. *Journal of Abnormal Psychology, 155*, 15–25.

Moritz, S., & Woodward, T. S. (2006b). A generalized bias against disconfirmatory evidence in schizophrenia. *Psychiatry Research, 142*, 157–165.

Moritz, S., & Woodward, T. S. (2006c). Metacognitive control over false memories: A key determinant of delusional thinking. *Current Psychiatry Reports, 8*, 184–190.

Moritz, S., & Woodward, T. S. (2007a). Metacognitive training for schizophrenia patients (MCT): A pilot study on feasibility, treatment adherence, and subjective efficacy. *German Journal of Psychiatry, 10*, 69–78.

Moritz, S., & Woodward, T. S. (2007b). Metacognitive training in schizophrenia: From basic research to knowledge translation and intervention. *Current Opinion in Psychiatry, 20*, 619–625.

Moritz, S., Woodward, T. S., Burlon, M., Braus, D. F., & Andresen, B. (2007). Attributional style in schizophrenia: Evidence for a decreased sense of self-causation in currently paranoid patients. *Cognitive Therapy and Research, 31*, 371–383.

Moritz, S., Woodward, T. S., & Chen, E. (2006a). Investigation of metamemory dysfunctions in first-episode schizophrenia. *Schizophrenia Research, 81*, 247–252.

Moritz, S., Woodward, T. S., Cuttler, C., Whitman, J., & Watson, J. M. (2004). False memories in schizophrenia. *Neuropsychology, 18*, 276–283.

Moritz, S., Woodward, T. S., & Rodriguez-Raecke, R. (2006b). Patients with schizophrenia do not produce more false memories than controls but are more confident in them. *Psychological Medicine, 36*, 659–667.

Moritz, S., Woodward, T. S., & Ruff, C. C. (2003). Source monitoring and memory confidence in schizophrenia. *Psychological Medicine, 33*, 131–139.

Moritz, S., Woodward, T. S., Whitman, J. C., & Cuttler, C. (2005). Confidence in errors as a possible basis for delusions in schizophrenia. *Journal of Nervous and Mental Disease, 193*, 9–16.

Moritz, S., Woznica, A., Andreou, C., & Köther, U. (2012). Response confidence for emotion perception in schizophrenia using a continuous facial sequence task. *Psychiatry Research, 200*, 202–207.

Pickup, G. J., & Frith, C. D. (2001). Theory of mind impairments in schizophrenia: Symptomatology, severity and specificity. *Psychological Medicine, 31*, 207–220.

Randall, F., Corcoran, R., Day, J. C., & Bentall, R. P. (2003). Attention, theory of mind, and causal attributions in people with persecutory delusions: A preliminary investigation. *Cognitive Neuropsychiatry, 8*, 287–294.

Randjbar, S., Veckenstedt, R., Vitzthum, F., Hottenrott, B., & Moritz, S. (2011). Attributional biases in paranoid schizophrenia: Further evidence for a decreased sense of self-causation in paranoia. *Psychosis, 3*, 74–85.

Ross, K., Freeman, D., Dunn, G., & Garety, P. (2011). A randomized experimental investigation of reasoning training for people with delusions. *Schizophrenia Bulletin, 37*, 324–333.

Sanford, N., Lecomte, T., LeClerc, C., Wykes, T., & Woodward, T. S. (2013). Change in jumping to conclusions linked to change in delusions in early psychosis. *Schizophrenia Research, 147*, 207.

So, S. H., Garety, P. A., Peters, E. R., & Kapur, S. (2010). Do antipsychotics improve reasoning biases? A review. *Psychosomatic Medicine*, *72*, 681–693.

Speechley, W. J., Ngan, E. T. C., Moritz, S., & Woodward, T. S. (2012). Impaired evidence integration and delusions in schizophrenia. *Journal of Experimental Psychopathology*, *3*, 688–701.

Speechley, W. J., Whitman, J. C., & Woodward, T. S. (2010). The contribution of hypersalience to the "jumping to conclusions" bias associated with delusions in schizophrenia. *Journal of Psychiatry and Neuroscience*, *35*, 7–17.

Steel, C. (Ed.). (2013). *CBT for Schizophrenia: Evidence-Based Interventions and Future Directions*. West Sussex, UK: Wiley-Blackwell.

van Os, J., & Kapur, S. (2009). Schizophrenia. *Lancet*, *374*, 635–645.

Waller, H., Freeman, D., Jolley, S., Dunn, G., & Garety, P. (2011). Targeting reasoning biases in delusions: A pilot study of the Maudsley Review Training Programme for individuals with persistent, high conviction delusions. *Journal of Behavior Therapy and Experimental Psychiatry*, *42*, 414–421.

Woodward, T. S., Moritz, S., & Chen, E. Y. H. (2006a). The contribution of a cognitive bias against disconfirmatory evidence (BADE) to delusions: A study in an Asian sample with first episode schizophrenia spectrum disorders. *Schizophrenia Research*, *83*, 297–298.

Woodward, T. S., Moritz, S., Cuttler, C., & Whitman, J. C. (2006b). The contribution of a cognitive bias against disconfirmatory evidence (BADE) to delusions in schizophrenia. *Journal of Clinical and Experimental Neuropsychology*, *28*, 605–617.

Woodward, T. S., Moritz, S., Menon, M., & Klinge, R. (2008). Belief inflexibility in schizophrenia. *Cognitive Neuropsychiatry*, *13*, 267–277.

Woodward, T. S., Munz, M., LeClerc, C., & Lecomte, T. (2009). Change in delusions is associated with change in "jumping to conclusions". *Psychiatry Research*, *170*, 124–127.

Wykes, T., Steel, C., Everitt, B., & Tarrier, N. (2008). Cognitive behavior therapy for schizophrenia: Effect sizes, clinical models, and methodological rigor. *Schizophrenia Bulletin*, *34*, 523–537.

Zimmermann, G., Favrod, J., Trieu, V. H., & Pomini, V. (2005). The effect of cognitive behavioral treatment on the positive symptoms of schizophrenia spectrum disorders: A meta-analysis. *Schizophrenia Research*, *77*, 1–9.

Chapter 12

Metacognitively Focused Psychotherapy for People with Schizophrenia: Eight Core Elements That Define Practice

Paul H. Lysaker,[1,2] Kelly D. Buck,[1] Bethany L. Leonhardt,[3] Benjamin Buck,[4] Jay Hamm[2], Ilanit Hasson-Ohayon,[5] Jenifer L. Vohs,[2] and Giancarlo Dimaggio[6,7]

[1]Richard L. Roudebush VA Medical Center, Indianapolis, IN, USA, [2]Indiana University School of Medicine, Indianapolis, IN, USA, [3]University of Indianapolis, Indianapolis IN, USA, [4]University of North Carolina at Chapel Hill, Chapel Hill, NC, USA, [5]Bar-Ilan University, Ramat-Gan, Israel, [6]Center for Metacognitive Interpersonal Therapy, Rome, Italy, [7]University La Sapienza, Rome, Italy

Chapter Outline

Social Cognition and Metacognition in Schizophrenia.
DOI: http://dx.doi.org/10.1016/B978-0-12-405172-0.00012-0
© 2014 Elsevier Inc. All rights reserved.

INTRODUCTION

A patient recently began a psychotherapy session noting angrily that the therapist (whom he had been seeing for nearly a decade) had ruined his life. After a moment, the therapist asked playfully: 'so you had a good life before you met me and then I shot that all to hell?' The patient replied: 'No . . . before you I spent years with no people anywhere . . . nothing . . . sitting in a hospital . . . no-one noticing . . .' The therapist asked: 'I ruined your life because you were ruined but then I made you aware of ruin?' The patient nodded in affirmation with an air of seriousness and went on: 'I had blasted everyone away . . . there was nothing and why would anyone do that . . . and now my soul has disappeared.' The therapist responded: 'So you've hired me as a kind of private detective to find your soul?' The patient laughed and agreed saying: 'It might be down there but I'll never see it on my own.' Prior to this outpatient treatment, the patient had lived as in inpatient in a largely custodial setting for 15 years.

We present the excerpt since it is clearly one heavy with meaning, pointing to something the patient is seeking. But what is he asking for when he says he is seeking a soul and how could psychotherapy offer any hope for that? Manifestly the patient could be expressing any of a number of wishes. He likely seeks to pursue the recognizable motives of being accepted, autonomous, and a part of a community. He may hope to be noted and valued by himself and others, yet pursuing such activities seems unsafe or threatening to him. His use of the word 'soul' may also express a longing for a greater sense of continuity in his internal experiences that would perhaps make it safe for him to pursue these things and ultimately to be able to love and be loved. While many of these wishes can be discerned and speculated upon, the patient communicates in a manner that reflects a fragmented sense of self with a lack of synthesis of his many psychological experiences into a complex and coherent representation. To begin to think about how psychotherapy could help, we suggest that it is necessary to begin with the question of determining what types of disruptions or barriers stand in the way of his generating this complex and coherent synthesis. In light of the chapters presented across this book, we conceptualize this patient as describing his previous experiences of 'nothing' as resulting from a profound loss of a range of metacognitive functions that occurred across the course of a long custodial hospitalization. During that time, with very limited engagement of his synthetic metacognitive capacities, the patient was without an ability to integrate a range of discrete psychological phenomena (e.g., recognizing emotions, having accurate judgments about one's own experiences) into a complex representation of himself and others, and hence had the experience of being without a viable sense of self as a unique being in the world, one consequently unable to seek out any of the needs noted above. The world was around him, and he was, as he says, nothing. And this could have occurred for any number of reasons. His metacognitive capacity may have declined due to neurocognitive impairment, atrophy resulting from social withdrawal, problematic attachments early in life, or trauma (Gumley, 2010; Lysaker *et al.*, 2013). At the point in time when the excerpt occurred, the patient seems to have developed a limited capacity to name his anguished experiences in the world. In addition, he is not sure he wants that awareness, as it could be a potentially dangerous path to emotional pain. But nevertheless, he is interested in the possibility of again knowing himself and of being known, presumably as a means and part of meeting these other needs. There is a sense that while his grasp of himself is precarious, his conversations with his therapist might help him to become more connected to himself and others.

It has long been hoped that psychotherapy might help patients, like the man in this example, to find a way to form more complex and stable representations of themselves and others, to escape from the nothingness that the patient and others have described, and be able to find ways to meet universal human needs (Lysaker and Lysaker, 2010a; Lysaker *et al.*, 2010b). From a metacognitive perspective, this would *not* initially involve the discovery of a concrete self that was hidden in consciousness or merely the development of a new specific belief about oneself. At issue is something that is well beyond a matter that could be entirely addressed through skill building. There is, instead, a need to help patients synthesize a fragmented series of memories and personal experiences in the moment into complex representations of themselves and others in order to move toward recovery. But exactly what steps are needed for this to occur?

In this chapter, we propose a specific set of activities that should be involved in psychotherapy that seeks to help patients recapture metacognitive capacity. First, we will present the conceptualization of the proposed psychotherapeutic processes. We will next discuss some of the basic assumptions about metacognition with relation to these processes. At the core of the paper, we will discuss the basic preconditions to be considered before providing psychotherapy and then review eight interrelated elements that should be at play in any psychotherapy session focused on metacognition in psychosis. We will finally describe a method for the assessment of therapy process and adherence to these elements.

DEFINING THE CORE ELEMENTS OF A METACOGNITIVE-FOCUSED PSYCHOTHERAPY FOR PSYCHOSIS

We have attempted to describe different types of therapeutic activities that should occur if metacognitive activities are being encouraged and practiced within a session, regardless of the phase of therapy and type of psychotherapy. Of note, we encourage the assimilation of these elements while providing different types of psychotherapy. Similarly, the integration of intersubjective interventions with different cognitive behavioral therapy (CBT)-based protocols has been suggested as a means to increase metacognition among people with psychosis (Hasson-Ohayon, 2012a). The elements are principles to be deployed as driven by the overarching theoretical conceptualization of metacognitive disturbance as a core feature of schizophrenia (cf. Chapter 6; *Metacognition in Schizophrenia Spectrum Disorders: Methods of Assessment and Associations with Psychosocial Function, Neurocognition, Symptoms, and Cognitive Style*). We thus did not articulate a set of activities to be done one after the other. Instead, we sought to identify processes or core elements, which while in some ways are related to one another, could be considered independently. The different elements are not a step-by-step guide, yet should be considered during each psychotherapy session.

To derive these components, the authors, along with several other authors in this volume, Giancarlo Dimaggio, Giampaolo Salvatore, Andrew Gumley, and Suzanne Harder, began a series of long distance discussions in 2009. There was no sponsorship or institution support for this project. In their discussions, individual experiences performing and supervising psychotherapy across many different settings were reflected upon and linked to emerging literature on the nature of metacognitive dysfunction in psychosis. The results of these discussions provoked iterative drafts by the first author describing the core principles, which were then reviewed with different authors. The result is a summary of assumptions about metacognitive capacity in people with psychosis, a set of general principles followed by eight core elements that should be present in a metacognitively focused psychotherapy. Also presented is an adherence scale to the presented guidelines.

ASSUMPTIONS ABOUT METACOGNITION IN SCHIZOPHRENIA FROM A CLINICAL PERSPECTIVE

Regarding metacognitive capacity in people with schizophrenia, we outline five assumptions. First, it is assumed that people possess a certain general capacity to think about themselves and others in more or less complex terms and that this capacity varies between people. Second, metacognitive capacity may vary from situation to situation and can change over time. People may be better able to think in a complex manner about their thinking in one circumstance relative to another. In this sense, metacognitive capacities are considered to function in a manner loosely analogous to blood pressure, which is generally believed to be a relatively stable phenomenon that nevertheless can change in stressful situations. The third assumption is that metacognition involves a range of related but semi-independent functions that include: awareness of oneself, awareness of others, awareness of oneself and others in the larger social context, and the use of that knowledge to respond to psychological challenges. A key implication for later consideration of treatment is that different people can have very different profiles of metacognitive strengths and weaknesses and that these profiles may change over time (Semerari *et al.*, 2003). The fourth assumption is that deficits in metacognition may emerge from different sources. Little is known about the exact causes of deficits in metacognitive capacity but the literature has suggested some aforementioned possible antecedents of these deficits, including the loss of neurocognitive function, atrophy following social withdrawal, deficient attachments to others both in the present and early in life, and trauma (Gumley, 2010; Lysaker *et al.*, 2013).

The final assumption is that acts of metacognition are fundamentally intersubjective phenomena. Broadly used, the term intersubjectivity refers to what is occurring between two minds (Beebe *et al.*, 2005). It may involve the experience of shared states of mind (Trevarthen, 1998) and the mutual understanding of the other's subjective experience (Stern, 2000). As summarized by Cortina and Liotti (2010), intersubjectivity is a type of communication unique to humans, at least in its more developed forms, and is regarded as a precondition for development of self-reflection and the emergence of the narratization of experience. In as much, both complex and less complex understandings of self and others are formed in the context of real or imagined interactions with other people, rather than within isolated minds.

PSYCHOTHERAPY AND METACOGNITION IN SCHIZOPHRENIA: SIX GENERAL PRECONDITIONS

Turning to the issue of what is needed in a therapy that addresses metacognitive capacity, there are certain factors that a therapist must embrace prior to the start of any psychotherapy case. For simplicity, we will suggest there are six such preconditions though we recognize they are to some degree interrelated. The first of these preconditions is therapist acceptance that psychotic experiences can be understood and that people with the most severe forms of mental illness are capable of understanding their thoughts, feelings, intentions, and psychological challenges. The most disorganized utterances have to be seen as potentially meaningful and not only as symptoms, which must be treated before an understanding can be established. As originally suggested by Carl Jung, and as now widely understood, the meaning of symptoms goes well beyond any specific approach to psychotherapy (Hasson-Ohayon, 2012b).

A second precondition for a metacognitively focused psychotherapy is that understanding patients' representations requires consideration of the narrative of their actual life experiences, and not abstractions or conclusions about those experiences (Dimaggio *et al.*, 2007; Salvatore *et al.*, 2004). As Fonagy *et al.* (2011) noted, 'a focus on episodic memory as the most productive material to use in elaborating the patient's self-understanding and understanding of others' (p. 104) is emphasized. Applied to the previous excerpt, this characteristic would lead the therapist to realize and understand some of the patient's specific past experiences in the hospital and in the present. In this case, this would guide the therapist to see that in order to understand the patient's experience of himself, the therapist must realize the patient had been someone previously isolated for days on end receiving forced injections, and how before that he was a victim of childhood sexual abuse.

We suggest that the third general precondition is a therapist's ability to perform an ongoing assessment of the patient's metacognitive capacity in the moment. We recommend using the abbreviated Metacognition Assessment Scale as presented in our earlier chapter (MAS-A; Chapter 6; *Metacognition in Schizophrenia Spectrum Disorders: Methods of Assessment and Associations with Psychosocial Function, Neurocognition, Symptoms, and Cognitive Style*). This precondition, as noted by Fonagy *et al.* (2011), should result in a 'structured, graded approach that holds therapists in check and prevents them from making unwarranted assumptions about the patient's processing capacities' (p. 104). As applied to the previous excerpt, this precondition would guide the therapist to realize that, while the patient has some awareness, he may struggle to integrate affect and thought when thinking about himself and his relationship with the therapist and others.

A fourth general precondition is the therapist's awareness that thinking about oneself and others, especially after a period of psychosis, may be inordinately painful. This will guide therapists to take great care to foster an atmosphere that allows patients to feel safe experiencing and discussing pain in a session. It will enable them to see how emergence from psychosis may leave people aware of painful things that previously were not apparent to them, including loss and trauma (Buck *et al.*, 2013). This will guide therapists to be attentive to affective disturbances in patients and to be willing to actively assist them in managing painful affects by naming and discussing these affects as they emerge. It will orient therapists to foster an atmosphere within the session so that both the therapist and patient can accept the patient's pain without alarm and with the expectation that pain can be understood and endured in the context of a compassionate exchange with others.

A fifth precondition for metacognitive psychotherapy is sensitivity to stigma against people with psychosis. Stigma includes frank assertions that people with mental illness are more prone to be violent and incompetent (Markowitz, 1998), but can also be found in seemingly benign verbalizations in which less than adult expectations are made of patients. Applied to the excerpt above, this precondition enables the therapist to think that the patient is entitled to make sense of his condition as he chooses, that he does not have to be protected against himself or others protected from him, and that a dialogue is potentially possible about the meanings the patient assigns to his condition.

The final general precondition of therapy concerns therapists' understanding of the potential mechanisms of change. There are two related possible processes in psychotherapy that may enhance metacognitive functioning in psychotherapy. First, as patients think about themselves and others in individual therapy, they become more able or capable of performing those cognitive acts. Just as practicing any of a number of things results in better performance over time, so it may be with the ability to think about thinking. The therapist is participating in a dialogue that may enable patients to experience their own subjectivity, as well as that of the therapist (Safran and Muran, 2000), in a way that prompts patients to construct a representation of the other's mind. Second, as patients master emotions they may also be able to bear emotional pain that may come with greater awareness, and so begin to form more complex representations of themselves and others. Applied to the excerpt, this would allow the therapist to see that helping the patient to think about himself might help him become more able to construct a complicated representation of himself and others that allows for a sense of agency, ongoing connection with others as well as the ability to master the pain associated with that.

EIGHT ELEMENTS OF A METACOGNITIVE THERAPY FOR SCHIZOPHRENIA

Turning to the specific therapist activities that we believe are at the heart of promoting metacognition, we believe that there are eight elements that should be considered independent of one another. As previously mentioned, the eight elements are not a step-by-step guide and are not a set of activities to be done one after the other. However, each item is related to the others. Each should nevertheless be considered on its own, and therapists should be expected to be able to keep all eight in mind as the session progresses. The idea is that there will be synergy among these elements. As each is described, it should be apparent how that element should support and be supported by the other elements.

Element 1: The Preeminence of the Patient's Agenda

Therapists must seek to understand patients' agendas or the wishes, hopes, desires, plans, and purposes that patients bring with them to each session and understand that patients should have the primary say in what order and how this content is approached. The understanding of patient agendas is a joint task that calls for reflection with patients and essential information may be found in the words and behaviors of patients as well as therapists' own emotional reactions. Motives and goals are often implicit and can only be inferred from fragments of evidence, requiring a remarkable amount of effort and sustained focus on the part of the therapist. Complicating matters is the fact that there may be multiple agendas, agendas may change, and patients may need time to sort out their thoughts in order to arrive at some idea of what they are intending to communicate in the moment. Understanding patient agendas should involve a process of deciding which utterances are part of the agenda versus those that point to matters to be dealt with before the agenda can emerge. This requires therapist attunement and suspending any predetermined plans. Further, once agendas have been discovered, the patient and therapist should discuss together whether they are a proper subject for reflection and if they are, they should explore them together. Certainly agendas may be discovered (e.g., to harm someone else) that would call for other actions. Notably, as suggested by Gerson (1996), the therapist expresses a fundamental interest in the process of knowing. This enables an intersubjective space for mutual exploration of the agenda. Mutual exploration of the patient's agenda can frame potential psychological problems and allow for the patient to assert his own subjectivity and agency early in session.

Respect for the primacy of the patient agenda is essential for patients to have significant opportunities for the experience of themselves as active agents in the world. Our experience is that this element is the one most often neglected. This may be because of underlying fears that patients cannot determine their own agendas, previous training stressing an immediate focus on symptoms or skill deficits, or a lack of understanding of how long it may take for patients to discover and articulate their agenda. In addition, in the presence of barren or diminished sense of self, therapists often struggle with the impulse to produce a coherent narrative for the patient (Lysaker and Lysaker, 2010a).

Element 2: The Introduction of the Therapist's Thoughts in Ongoing Dialogue

This element holds that therapists must form their own thoughts about the patient's mental states and share those in a way that promotes a dialogue and does not override the patient's agenda. This calls for not just correct or accurate guesses about the patient but the sharing of thoughts about the patient's mental processes in a way that is sensitive to issues in the context of the moment, the degree of trust established, as well as the patient's background. Most importantly, these thoughts should be genuine sharing of the therapist's attempt to understand the patient. This does not call for the abandoning of psychological knowledge. It does require sensitivity that, given the intersubjective nature of metacognition, patients may easily feel threatened or disempowered if therapists' interventions are too forceful. The use of accessible and nontheoretical language is also required. This element combined with the first, which is to understand the patient's agenda and experience in session, should allow for both minds to be present and to intersubjectively explore together the patient's experience.

We have observed multiple barriers to this element including therapists finding themselves in a role in which they want to do more than to understand, which ultimately results in dialogue being imperiled. Therapists may share their thoughts, for instance, mostly in order to *get* the patient to learn something the therapist knows, assert themselves, embrace health, or be comforted, rather than openly understand first what the patient has in mind. Ultimately, the successful performance of this element requires an open stance where knowing about the other takes precedence over trying to change uncomfortable states, and as mentioned in Element 1, a stance of exploring together is essential.

Element 3: Narrative Episodes

The first two elements just presented suggest some of the conditions that would allow the patient and therapist to sit in the same room and try to relate to one another with the ultimate goal of thinking together about the patient and exploring thoughts as a dyad. The next element concerns the types of the things that the dyad should begin to think about together and calls for moving beyond abstractions about the patient and finding an account of a sequence of specific events that the patient has or is experiencing, that is, detailing a narrative episode. Narrative episodes should involve the patient relating a sequence of events involving specific people and places that have occurred for either a clear or unclear reason, have antecedent and consequent events, and have relevance for the patient (Dimaggio *et al.*, 2012a; Dimaggio *et al.*, 2012b). The eliciting of narrative episodes is likely to require action on the therapist's part and has to be pursued with the goal of understanding what has happened. The narratives that are produced, either as individual narrative episodes or as multiple narrative episodes that have been strung together, should be understood by therapists as a universal part of how people make sense of immediate experience in the light of past experience. The creation and consideration of narrative episodes are a common human activity that we all use to lay out ideas about ourselves so they can be shared with others and ultimately adapted and revised in the face of continued participation in the world.

Eliciting narrative episodes is likely to be closely tied to the next element, which is the naming of the psychological problem. Of note, in seeking a narrative episode the ultimate goal is to think with patients about themselves as beings in the world and as such the goal in obtaining a narrative episode is not to collect a history but to think with the patients about the contexts within which they are experiencing certain mental activities.

Common barriers include eliciting narratives in which therapists ask for memories without offering adequate scaffolding when some patients at best can only offer fragments of experience. Therapists may also neglect to explore narrative episodes when those episodes have been previously discussed, thinking nothing new will come from reviewing events in potentially increasing depth, potentially missing a chance for a richer understanding. Conversely, therapists may follow narratives that are not related to the patient's experience and may serve as a diversion from thinking about narratives relevant to the patient's agenda and mental activities.

Element 4: Naming the Psychological Problem

This element concerns pinpointing and discussing with patients a psychological problem with which they are struggling. The problem may be, to varying degrees, intrapersonal or interpersonal. In either case what is a stake is that some relevant goal, need, wish, desire, or concern is perceived and experienced as unmet or frustrated. As a result of this frustration the patient should generally experience either some form of distress or at least the absence of a desirable emotional state. In an ideal session, attention to the patient's agenda, and the insertion of the therapist's thoughts will provoke a narrative episode and then within that narrative episode a psychological problem will emerge.

To detect the psychological problem within a narrative episode, the therapist needs to engage in dialogue with the patient to develop a picture of the actual events that were related to the perceived frustration of the patient's relevant goal, need, wish, or desire. This may involve offering a challenge to patients should they concretely assert that their problem is simply the frustration of need, for instance, that their problems are merely a lack of housing or that someone is angry at them. Therapists should generally seek the psychological problem within the narrative episode of the moment, a possible divergence from other approaches that do not rely so heavily on episode memory. Explicitly, we favor looking at the narrative episode since this is how people construct meaning in regular life. As a narrative is elicited, patients reflect about events that are happening as they remember them and then form new ideas about these events.

It is possible, however, that there may be other paths to the psychological problem. For example, the psychological problem can also be identified as taking place in the process between the patient and the therapist. It may also be impossible to find a narrative episode given the cacophonous nature of the patient's speech or her paranoia in the moment. However, the psychological problem may emerge in the moment as the patient is finding the idea of being known unbearable, that is, threatening her sense of safety. It is also possible that the psychological problem will be manifest within the agenda and then a narrative episode may be elicited in order to understand better what type of psychological problem the patient is confronted with. Regardless, identification of the psychological problem has to be grounded without exception in the material the patient has brought to the session.

Once a psychological problem has been identified, its relationship to other problems discussed should be considered. In particular it should be examined even if just briefly: Does the psychological problem of the session have elements in common with previous psychological problems? If so, to what extent is the psychological problem a natural outgrowth of previous problems or other problems? If the psychological problem is related to previous problems, then is it the next step in a chain of steps needed to move toward health? Or is it part of a previous problem not yet adequately dealt with? Is it something that has to be dealt with before previous psychological problems can be resolved? What elements and what degree is the psychological problem something new? If it is new was it something that has emerged unexpectedly or had been under the surface and neglected until now? Was the discovery of this problem surprising in the moment or something the patient anticipated revealing and discussing? Is it part of a pattern that is slowly being revealed?

While patients may not have answers to all or even any of these questions, asking these questions in a nonpressured and caring manner offers several possibilities. First, it may help evolve a more nuanced picture of what the psychological problem is that the patient is facing. Second, it may offer an opportunity for patients to not only identify something they struggle with, but also to frame the psychological problem as a subject of reflection itself, that is something to be considered beyond of seeking a solution.

Common barriers to performing this element include simply mistaking problems that are indeed problems but that are not psychological in nature (e.g., difficulties with transportation). More complicated are times when problems are posed as psychological in nature but that block or may even be posed in order to avoid opportunities for reflection. For example, expressing wishes to harm a neighbor may pose a problem for the patient and therapist to work on: how to reduce those wishes. In contrast, if the patient's agenda is not to reduce those wishes, this could instead be a distraction or delay from thinking about any number of other matters (e.g., by arousing therapist anxiety or shifting the focus away from something else deeply painful such as a rejection by a friend in the workplace). Simply put, patients may raise issues that can masquerade as concerning psychological problems. This is not to say that these other matters should not be pursued but merely that pursuing them does not satisfy this element. Attention to the overall patterns of the therapy process and attention to the therapeutic relationship can help therapists make these distinctions.

Element 5: Reflecting on Interpersonal Processes Occurring Within the Session

This element holds that sessions should contain a discussion of some of the interpersonal processes occurring within the session between the therapist and patient that support or limit metacognitive activities. We suggest that there are at least four different general aspects of the interpersonal processes occurring within and between sessions that could be discussed within session as they occur. These interpersonal aspects that could be discussed include the possible role or roles the therapist, as an addressee, may be playing in the ongoing dialogue with the patient. Once identified, a second aspect to be potentially addressed concerns why it is important for the therapist to function in these roles and how it may be and/or not be beneficial to the process of psychotherapy for the therapist to function in these roles. The third aspect that can be addressed concerns how well or poorly the therapist is performing his or her role. Finally, the fourth concern is the patient's reaction to the therapist's performance of the role.

The primary purpose in considering the interpersonal processes is not necessarily for the patient or therapist to make more appropriate use of the session. However, that may be one consequence. The therapist subjectivity is addressed in order to promote patients' subjectivity (Safran and Muran, 2000). Thus, thinking about how the patient positions the therapist role and all that follows should be seen as an opportunity for the therapist and patient to understand how the patient is experiencing the therapist as being present and having a mind which could potentially understand him or her and hence to think about the context within which thinking about thinking is being generated. The primary purpose is to utilize the interpersonal, intersubjective context thusly as another subject for reflective activity. It is a set of mental activities occurring that the patient can form ideas about and hence practice metacognitive activities. Performing this element may aid in the generation of a narrative episode, psychological problem and/or elucidation of the agenda.

Common barriers to performing this element include therapists' unawareness of their own thoughts and feelings and hence difficulties intuiting what patients are experiencing. Therapists may also be personally uncomfortable with patients' strong reactions to them including both positive feelings such as love and sexual attraction as well as more negatively toned responses such as anger and jealousy.

Element 6: Reflection on Progress Within the Session

This element is probably the simplest of the elements. It refers to discussing with patients whether they feel they are achieving or getting out of therapy what they want. This could involve eliciting reflections about specific outcomes, something specific in the moment, as well as the overall general progress over the session. It could elicit a reflection, for instance, about progress or lack of progress, feeling less distressed about a certain thing, or just a general sense of whether life is become less confusing. The progress reported or not reported could concern an initial goal or something that had just arisen in the session. It could also refer to ideas initially formed at the beginning of therapy or something that has arisen just in the moment. The overarching purpose of this element is that therapists stimulate metacognition, regarding the patient's experience of therapy as purposive beings who are in search of something. Examples of questions that could elicit this information include: 'What do you think about our conversation so far? This isn't working very well is it? As we talk right now is there tension in your body?'

To distinguish this element from the fifth element, which called for discussion of interpersonal processes, the issue here is not how the therapist is experienced by the patient, but whether the session is what the patient had hoped for, or if not, whether the patient is satisfied with how things are progressing. The appraisal of progress has been made a separate element from the consideration of interpersonal processes, however, as a positive appraisal of one may not always coincide with a positive appraisal of the other. The major barrier to performing this element includes assumptions that therapists already know what the patient thinks or feels or their own discomfort with getting feedback that could make therapists feel vulnerable. Notably, although therapists may feel uncomfortable with patients' expression of anger, frustration, or despair with regard to the progress of therapy, it seems unrealistic that in the process of ongoing change only positive feelings will be experienced by both parties.

Element 7: Stimulating Self-Reflectivity and Awareness of the Other

This element concerns the direct stimulation of patients to think about their own thinking, either about themselves or thinking about others. This requires that therapists first assess the patient's metacognitive level both in terms of self-reflectivity and then in terms of awareness of the other. For this purpose, we recommend the use of the MAS-A, which allows for an assessment of patients' maximum metacognitive capacity in the moment. This instrument has been described in Chapter 6 (*Metacognition in Schizophrenia Spectrum Disorders: Methods of Assessment and Associations with Psychosocial Function, Neurocognition, Symptoms, and Cognitive Style*).

Once therapists have assessed self-reflectivity and awareness of others, therapists should then intervene and ask patients about their thoughts about themselves and others in light of that assessment, asking patients to exercise their maximal level of metacognitive capacity. For instance, if a patient is at best able to notice that they have memories but are unaware of their emotions or subjectivity of thought, it would be best to notice they are having memories rather than asking them to identify an affect or question their thinking. The assumption is that metacognitive capacity will increase with exercise either in a single session or in multiple sessions, hence patients will become able to perform more complex metacognitive acts and therapists will intervene differently over time. Of note, it is possible that metacognitive capacity may also decline within a session as painful material arises, interventions are too taxing, or general levels of life stress increase. In such cases therapists should adjust their interventions accordingly. As a complete discussion of these issues is beyond the scope of this chapter, narrative tasks and interventions per level of the MAS-A Self-Reflectivity and Understanding the Mind of Others are presented in Tables 12.1 and 12.2.

Element 8: Stimulating Mastery

In parallel to the seventh element, this calls for an assessment using the MAS-A of patient's level of Mastery or the ability to use knowledge of oneself and others in order to respond to social or psychological problems. Therapists should then offer interventions appropriate to that level. As in the case of Self-Reflectivity and Understanding the Mind of Others, it is assumed that Mastery scores will change over time in either a positive or negative direction, and therapists should adjust their interventions accordingly.

TABLE 12.1 Characteristic Narrative Tasks, Outcomes, and Interventions Across Nine Levels of Self-Reflectivity (S).

Metacognitive Level	Narrative Tasks	Narrative Outcomes	Examples of Interventions
S1	Noticing subjective experiences of singular perceptions and ideas in the moment.	The person realizes that he has experiences.	'There is a thought that . . .' 'You are seeing . . .'
S2	Noticing that one's subjective experiences are one's own.	The person realizes that her thoughts are her own.	'There is tension in your body' 'There is an idea in your head'
S3	Noticing recent and distal memories and immediate experiences as something the person has uniquely and subjectively experienced.	Individual episodes emerge in the person's life that could be woven into a narrative.	'You are recalling . . .' 'You had a plan to . . . .' 'You chose not to . . .' 'You are imagining . . .'
S4	Imbuing of life events and/or experiences in the moment with different emotions.	The emotional significance of clearly different events becomes distinct.	'Now you are feeling . . .' 'Your feelings have changed.' 'You have two different feelings about . . . .'
S5	Discussing life events and experiences in the moment as matters that are not likely to be instantly understood by others.	A portrait of the narrator emerges as someone who questions his or her own thinking.	'You have changed your mind about . . .' 'You were certain before but now . . .'
S6	Discussing life events as involving realities that frustrate basic needs and have to be accepted.	Frustrations are acknowledged as elements in daily life allowed to exist without the narrator becoming a martyr.	'You wish so much for . . . but it is not so.' 'You have discovered things are different than you needed.'
S7, S8, S9	Discussing the interaction of multiple psychological elements as they interact in singular life episodes, across episodes and the life span, respectively.	There are complete rich descriptions of oneself in single or different events in the short and long term, respectively.	'Your thoughts and feeling were connected when . . .' 'Your thoughts were connected to your feeling both times . . .' 'Across your life your thoughts and feelings have . . .'

TABLE 12.2 Narrative Tasks, Outcomes, and Interventions Across Different Levels of Awareness of the Other.

Metacognitive Level	Narrative Tasks	Narrative Outcomes	Examples of Interventions
01	Noticing subjective experience of singular perceptions and ideas in others in the moment.	The person realizes that others have experiences.	'An idea came to person X' 'You think that person X saw . . .'
02	Noticing that others' subjective experiences are their own.	Other people are referred to more often.	'You saw person X felt tense' 'You noticed that there was an idea in the head of person X'
03	Noticing that others have unique memories, dreams, etc., that they experience subjectively.	A larger number of individual persons begin to appear in the narrative.	'Person X had a plan to . . .' 'Person X had a memory . . . .' 'You noticed that person X chose to . . .' 'So person X imagined . . .'
04	Discussing life events as involving others who themselves have different emotions.	The emotional significance of different events for others becomes distinct.	'You see that person X felt . . .' 'You see that the feelings of person X have changed.' 'You can see that person X has two different feelings about . . .'
05	Discussing life events as involving people whose interacting thoughts and feelings can be intuited.	Making plausible inferences about others knowing their person thoughts and feelings are related.	'You think that when person X says Y they mean Z.' 'You can see how when X feels Y he tends to do Z.'
06, 07	Discussing of the interaction of multiple psychological elements as they interact in others' singular life episodes or multiple life episodes, respectively.	Rich, complete descriptions of others across a discrete or long-term series of events, respectively.	'The thoughts and feelings of person X were connected when . . .' 'Across the life of person X he has . . .'

For example, for patients who are unaware of a plausible problem, it might be reflected that 'You have no sense that anything is wrong with . . .' For patients who have an idea of a problem that is not plausible it might be noted 'You have an idea of what the problem is but it is different than how others see it . . .' For the successively higher levels of Mastery interventions should similarly ask patients to think about their responses to psychological problems at the level they are capable of. For example, for someone only able to passively endure a problem it might be reflected that 'When you face the problem it seems that all you can do sleep and escape . . .' while for someone able to adjust their mental order in response to the problem it might be noted: 'In the face of your problem you are trying to change the thoughts in your head . . .'

Barriers to meeting the seventh and eighth element include excessive focus on the psychology of another person, focus on nonpsychological problems, or therapists solving problems for patients rather than providing them an opportunity to think about themselves. Other barriers include instances when therapists offer interpretations of mental states and problems that are not based on patients' own construction of the issues.

THE EIGHT ELEMENTS SYNTHESIS AND MEASUREMENT OF ADHERENCE

Two final points to be made are that there should be synergy between the elements such that they amplify one another and that therapists and supervisors may assess adherence to these items. To illustrate the issue of synergy among the elements let us return to the patient involved in our initial excerpt. In this case the patient agenda (element 1) was revealed to involve anger at the therapist for linking angry feelings and a wish to protect himself from further pain. The interjection of the therapist's mind (element 2) afforded the possibility that there had been a shift in how the patient was thinking and feeling that might be understood. A narrative episode (element 3) was produced about life during a prolonged hospitalization and about prior childhood sexual abuse. The psychological problem emerged that involved an intolerance for pain and deep self-hatred (element 4). Interpersonal processes were discussed (element 5), which included being jealous of the therapist's success in life and deep fears the therapist would abandon him. The patient noted he found the session helped him to feel somewhat more safe and in control of his emotions (element 6). The patient was assisted to notice his mental activities and the thoughts he was having about himself and the therapist (element 7) and to see himself as an agent who at best could manage pain through angry outbursts at others and the misuse of alcohol (element 8). As a whole, the session thus potentially promoted metacognitive capacity by allowing the patient to spend most of the session considering his thinking in the moment and hence further develop that capacity. He appeared to use the session to discover a view of himself that was more complex and viable in the world with a resulting decrease in anguish.

TABLE 12.3 Therapist Metacognitive Adherence Scale (T-MAS) – Psychosis Rating Form.

Therapist_____   Date_____   Rater_____   Patient ID_____

1. Openness to the patient's agenda at the session outset and throughout the session.

1........2........3.......4.......5

2. Offer of the therapist's thoughts/perceptions regarding the patient's behavior in the session.

1.......2........3.......4.......5

3. Details of a narrative episode are elicited.

1........2........3.......4.......5

4. A psychological problem or dilemma is framed as something to be discussed.

1........2........3.......4.......5

5. Reflection on the interpersonal processes during the session is elicited.

1........2........3.......4.......5

6. Reflection on progress/course of the session is elicited at various times during the session or at session's end.

1........2........3.......4.......5

7. The patient is stimulated to engage in metacognitive acts with interventions that are appropriate to patient's capacity for self-reflectivity and/or awareness of the mind of the other.

1........2........3.......4.......5

8. The patient is stimulated to engage in metacognitive acts with interventions that are appropriate to patients' capacity for metacognitive mastery.

1........2........3.......4.......5

Total score:_____

Key: **1.** absent; **2.** intermittent moments in which basic competency is present; **3.** fully adequate or competent throughout; **4.** fully adequate with some periods of exceptional performance; **5.** consistently exceptional performance.

Regarding adherence, it should be noted that the procedures here could only be studied if they are detectable. To that end we have included in Table 12.3 a form for measuring adherence. It can be rated by clinicians or supervisors, as well as blind raters exposed to a recording or transcript of a session. A more detailed set of anchors for this scale is available from the authors.

LIMITATIONS

Finally there are limitations to be noted. We have described a set of procedures that have yet to be fully tested in a range of settings. It is thus unknown to which types of patients and under what circumstances they might best apply. It may be that these procedures are less applicable, for instance, with acutely ill patients. Also, while we have not addressed the length of treatment, we have described procedures that call for considerable amounts of resources and likely a high degree of therapist competence. It may be that these procedures may be less helpful in settings where there are many patients and few skilled therapists to assist them. Future work is needed to explore these issues systematically across different settings.

REFERENCES

Beebe, B., Knoblauch, S., Rustin, J., & Sorter, D. (2005). *Forms of intersubjectivity in infant research and adult treatment*. New York: Other Press.

Buck, K. D., Roe, D., Yanos, P. T., Buck, B. E., Folgey, R. L., Grant, M. L. A., et al. (2013). Challenges to assisting with the recovery of personal identity and wellness for persons with serious mental illness: Considerations for mental health professionals. *Psychosis, 5,* 127–133.

Cortina, M., & Liotti, G. (2010). The intersubjective and cooperative origins of consciousness: An evolutionary-developmental approach. *Journal of the American Academy of Psychoanalysis and Dynamic Psychiatry, 38,* 291–314.

Dimaggio, G., & Attinà, G. (2012a). Metacognitive interpersonal therapy for narcissistic personality disorder and associated perfectionism. *Journal of Clinical Psychology, 68,* 922–934.

Dimaggio, G., Salvatore, G., Fiore, D., Carcione, A., Nicolò, G., & Semerari, A. (2012b). General principles for treating personality disorder with a prominent inhibitedness trait: Towards an operationalizing integrated technique. *Journal of Personality Disorders, 26,* 63–83.

Dimaggio, G., Semerari, A., Carcione, A., Nicolo, G., & Procacci, M. (2007). *Psychotherapy of personality disorders*. London: Bruner Routledge.

Fonagy, P., Bateman, A., & Bateman, A. (2011). The widening scope of mentalizing: A discussion. *Psychology and Psychotherapy: Theory, Research and Practice, 84,* 98–110.

Gerson, S. (1996). Neutrality, resistance, and self-disclosure in an intersubjective psychoanalysis. *Psychoanalytic Dialogues, 6,* 623–645.

Gumley, A. (2010). The developmental roots of compromised mentalization in complex mental health disturbances in adulthood. In G. Dimaggio & P. H. Lysaker (Eds.), *Metacognition and severe adult mental disorders: From basic research to treatment* (pp. 45–62). London: Bruner Routledge.

Hasson-Ohayon, I. (2012a). Integrating cognitive behavioral-based therapy with an intersubjective approach: Addressing metacognitive deficits among people with schizophrenia. *Journal of Psychotherapy Integration, 22,* 356–374.

Hasson-Ohayon, I. (2012b). Exploring the meaning of visual and auditory hallucinations: A commentary on Pixley's discussion of the difficulties in addressing hallucinations during psychodynamic therapy. *Journal of Psychotherapy Integration, 22,* 393–396.

Lysaker, P. H., Glynn, S. M., Wilkness, S. M., & Silverstein, S. M. (2010b). Psychotherapy and recovery from schizophrenia: A review of potential application and need for future study. *Psychological Services, 7,* 75–91.

Lysaker, P. H., & Lysaker, J. T. (2010a). Schizophrenia and alterations in self-experience: A comparison of six perspectives. *Schizophrenia Bulletin, 36*, 331–340.

Lysaker, P. H., Vohs, J. L., Ballard, R., Fogley, R., Salvatore, G., Popolo, R., et al. (2013). Metacognition, self reflection and recovery in schizophrenia: Review of the literature. *Future Neurology, 8*, 103–115.

Markowitz, F. E. (1998). The effects of stigma on the psychological well-being and life satisfaction of persons with mental illness. *Journal of Health & Social Behavior, 39*, 335–347.

Safran, J. D., & Muran, J. C. (2000). *Negotiating the therapeutic alliance: A relational treatment guide*. New York: Guilford Press.

Salvatore, G., Dimaggio, G., & Semerari, A. (2004). A model of narrative development. Psychopathology and implication for clinical practice. *Psychology and Psychotherapy, 77*, 231–254.

Semerari, A., Carcione, A., Dimaggio, G., Falcone, M., Nicolo, G., Procaci, M., et al. (2003). How to evaluate metacognitive function in psychotherapy? The metacognition assessment scale and its applications. *Clinical Psychology and Psychotherapy, 10*, 238–261.

Stern, D. N. (2000). *The interpersonal world of the infant: A view from psychoanalysis and developmental psychology*. New York: Basic Books.

Trevarthen, C. (1998). The concept and foundations of infant intersubjectivity. In S. Braten (Ed.), *Intersubjective communication and emotion in early ontogeny* (pp. 15–46). Cambridge: Cambridge University Press.

Chapter 13

Adapted-Metacognitive Interpersonal Therapy Applied to Paranoid Schizophrenia: Promoting Higher Levels of Reflection on One's and Others' Minds, Awareness of Interpersonal Schemas, Differentiation, and Mastery of Social Problems

Giampaolo Salvatore,[1] Raffaele Popolo,[1] Paul H. Lysaker,[2,3]
Paolo Ottavi,[1] Nadia Di Sturco[1] and Giancarlo Dimaggio[1,4]

[1]*Center for Metacognitive Interpersonal Therapy, Rome, Italy,*
[2]*Richard L. Roudebush VA Medical Center, Indianapolis, IN, USA,*
[3]*Indiana University School of Medicine, Indianapolis, IN, USA,*
[4]*University La Sapienza, Rome, Italy*

Chapter Outline

Social Cognition and Metacognition in Schizophrenia.
DOI: http://dx.doi.org/10.1016/B978-0-12-405172-0.00013-2
© 2014 Elsevier Inc. All rights reserved.

INTRODUCTION

Research suggests that many people with schizophrenia experience impairments in the ability to make sense of mental states (Brüne *et al.*, 2007; Langdon *et al.*, 2006; Lysaker *et al.*, 2007). As in other chapters in this volume, we use the term metacognition to refer to the ability to make sense of mental states, and conceptualize it as consisting of a range of mental activities which include: (1) thinking about one's own mental states (e.g., one's own thoughts, feelings, memories, wishes, intentions, etc.); (2) thinking about other people's mental states (e.g., their thoughts, feelings, memories, wishes, intentions, etc.); (3) thinking about oneself and other people in the larger social context; and (4) using that knowledge to respond effectively emotionally, cognitively, and behaviorally to challenges and problems (Dimaggio and Lysaker, 2010; Dimaggio *et al.*, 2007; Lysaker *et al.*, 2013; Semerari *et al.*, 2003).

Importantly, impairments in many different kinds of metacognitive functions have been observed. For example, impairments in the ability to describe one's own emotions and thoughts, infer emotions from facial and vocal cues (Kerr and Neale, 1993), and to understand what other people mean from simple hints have been found in patients with schizophrenia (Morrison *et al.*, 1988; Mueser *et al.*, 1996; Pedersen *et al.*, 2012). When patients with schizophrenia are unable to detect what is passing through their own and others' minds correctly and flexibly change perspective on events in line with updated and sensitive psychological information, they lose the ability to understand the nuances of complex social interchanges. The impact of this deficit on functioning becomes a severe problem when patients are faced with situations in which they have to swiftly and skillfully understand what their own and the others' intentions are in order to solve social problems, pursue goals in spite of obstacles, and negotiate meaning (Lysaker *et al.*, 2010; Lysaker *et al.*, 2011; Salvatore *et al.*, 2007).

Beyond this, others have noted that many individuals with schizophrenia often lack the more complex narrative skills that require good underlying metacognition. For example, forming plausible and integrated representations of themselves and others, and synthesizing separate data into a wider understanding of oneself and others (Brüne *et al.*, 2011; Dimaggio *et al.*, 2009; Lysaker *et al.*, 2013). Empirical evidence supports that metacognitive impairment is prominently linked with negative symptoms, and paves the way toward social withdrawal and poor vocational functioning (see Chapter 7; *The Impact of Metacognition on the Development and Maintenance of Negative Symptoms*). Evidence also suggests that many patients with schizophrenia achieve improved levels of social functioning, a subjective sense of recovery, and symptom reduction as a result of recapturing greater levels of metacognition (Dimaggio and Lysaker, 2010; Kukla *et al.*, 2013; Lysaker and Buck, 2008; Lysaker *et al.*, 2005; Lysaker *et al.*, 2007; Lysaker *et al.*, 2013).

A Metacognitive Approach to Schizophrenia Psychotherapy

Given the links between metacognition and wellness, interventions aimed at addressing metacognitive capacity in schizophrenia have thus been devised (Buck and Lysaker, 2010; Lysaker *et al.*, 2011; Lysaker *et al.*, 2013; Salvatore *et al.*, 2012). These interventions seek to progressively help patients acquire the capacity to successfully engage in the simplest elements of the metacognitive system (e.g., being aware one is angry), and then later to be able to perform the more complex elements (e.g., taking a critical distance from rigid schema-driven attributions to self and others or forming a more integrated representation of self and others). In the context of a continuous and tactful regulation of the therapeutic relationship, the aim of these procedures is to foster the recovery of metacognitive capacities, by providing a place where they can be practiced and exercised in increasing complexity, on the basis of the principle that, as in physical therapy, psychotherapy can offer clients the chance to reacquire capacities they had previously held and lost with the onset of illness (Lysaker and Buck, 2010). The intention of these treatments is that the more patients can engage in increasingly complex acts of metacognition, the greater the chances of recovery. For instance, with a broader and more flexible account of one's self and others, relationships are more likely to be repaired after quarrels, confusing symptoms understood, and painful emotional reactions better modulated. Similarly, with a richer sense of oneself and others, one may be more likely to persist at work despite significant frustration and to encounter but not internalize stigma.

To date, the case reports of the application of this metacognitive approach have focused on promoting basic metacognitive capacities, such as ownership of thought and recognizing one's own emotions and thoughts and the causal role they have in generating distress. Some patients have also been reported starting to acquire the ability to differentiate, that is, taking a critical distance from their delusional hypotheses, and forming alternative interpretations (Lysaker and Buck, 2010; Salvatore *et al.*, 2012). Other work has described a sequence of interventions that include: (1) reconstructing episodes in life narratives; (2) helping the patient name distressing emotions appearing in narrative episodes; (3) validating and normalizing the patient's experience; (4) promoting awareness of emotional triggers and the links between affects, contingent emergence of symptoms (e.g., auditory hallucinations, persecutory ideation, or disorganized thought), and social behavior; and (5) eliciting other narrative episodes in which the patient experienced symptoms or social dysfunctions and – always with an aim to validate and help the patient to constantly reformulate problems described in a narrative episode in mentalistic terms (Salvatore *et al.*, 2007; Salvatore *et al.*, 2009; Salvatore *et al.*, 2012).

To date, one limitation in the literature is that procedures for promoting metacognition have been focused on patients with greater levels of metacognition impairment, and therefore the attainment of basic levels (Lysaker *et al.*, 2011). Accordingly, in this chapter we will describe procedures for promoting higher-order metacognitive functions among patients with psychosis. Specifically, we will first describe one specific therapeutic approach and then offer a case illustration.

PROMOTING HIGHER-ORDER METACOGNITIVE FUNCTIONS WITH ADAPTED FOR PSYCHOSIS METACOGNITIVE INTERPERSONAL THERAPY

The psychotherapy operations described in this chapter seek to promote: (1) awareness of disturbed interpersonal schemas and differentiation between them and actual relationships; (2) access to healthy elements of the patient's self; (3) better understanding of others' minds; and (4) adoption of mastery strategies based on a well-nuanced awareness of minds and aimed at coping with symptoms and dealing with social problems. This combination of access to healthy elements of the self and mastery strategies provides a basis for handling social exposure in situations that can bring pleasure, greater contact, and fulfilment of relevant life goals. Patients suited to this stage of treatment must, at least in some sessions, be able to perform the more basic operations described above successfully. Any experience of positive and negative symptoms should something that can be discussed in session.

Metacognitive interpersonal therapy (MIT) was first devised for treating personality disorder (Dimaggio *et al.*, 2007; Dimaggio *et al.*, 2012; Dimaggio *et al.*, 2013), and then adapted for psychosis (A-MIT; Salvatore *et al.*, 2009; Salvatore *et al.*, 2012). A-MIT uses step-by-step procedures for building the metacognitive skills of people with schizophrenia (Lysaker *et al.*, 2011). It aims to promote patients' awareness that they are guided by inflexible and maladaptive interpersonal schemas. This is first done through detailed explorations of narrative episodes (autobiographical memories about social encounters with relevant others) and then through a reconstruction with the patient, often in a written form, of the latter's maladaptive schemas in accordance with the Core Conflictual Relationship Theme (CCRT; Luborsky and Crits-Christoph, 1990).

Therapists should operate as tactful regulators of the therapeutic relationship and work to prevent or repair therapeutic alliance ruptures (Safran and Muran, 2000). If the therapy relationship is good or a rupture has been repaired, and the interpersonal schemas which contribute to patients' worries and malfunctioning behaviors are sufficiently clear, the therapist can validate patients' progress and support the healthy aspects of their minds. At this point, therapy goals are renegotiated and patients are asked to focus on personally relevant goals they would like to pursue in everyday life. Once these goals are set, behavioral experiments aimed at achieving them – in particular social exposure – can be planned. Finally, patients and therapists should agree on potential metacognitive mastery strategies for coping with any anxiety or confusion that might arise during new social encounters.

To illustrate these procedures, we will next describe the treatment of a young woman meeting the criteria for paranoid schizophrenia with A-MIT. After presenting background information and briefly discussing the early phases of therapy, we will turn in depth to the interventions that promoted higher levels of metacognition. We will discuss methods for enhancing awareness of a disturbed interpersonal schema and differentiation between the schema and actual relationships; the promotion of health aspects of the self; and the development of reflection on others' minds and focus on personally relevant goals, social exposure, and metacognitive mastery for symptoms and social problems.

CASE PRESENTATION: BACKGROUND INFORMATION

Angela (a pseudonym) was a 24-year-old woman enrolled as a part-time student and seen in psychotherapy with a range of positive symptoms. Her symptoms had begun to develop 6 months prior after ending a romantic relationship. She began to have difficulty paying attention and concentrating, felt dizzy, and then had auditory hallucinations. One night she woke up full of distress and heard the voice of the boyfriend that had broken up with her 'as if he was on the telephone' giving her orders about the behavior she should adopt with her parents. Angela later developed the fixed belief that her ex-boyfriend was planning with others to rape her. She was also convinced her thoughts were being transmitted to her by this boyfriend. In the face of these symptoms, she withdrew from all but close family. Prior to beginning therapy, her symptoms displayed a good but only partial response to drug therapy (olanzapine, 10 mg). The idea that her thoughts were transmitted disappeared and auditory hallucinations diminished, but did not disappear, as did persecutory delusional ideas. Angela's individual psychotherapy then began in a private outpatient clinic. She initially attended sessions on a weekly basis for a 2-year period and since has been attending on a fortnightly basis. Sessions have lasted 30–40 minutes, and Angela attended more than 80% of the scheduled weekly appointments. The psychotherapist (GS) has 15 years of experience of working with people with severe mental illnesses (psychosis and personality disorders). He has been taking extensive handwritten notes of sessions. After a summary of the most significant aspects dealt with in the first phase of the therapy, we describe the advanced treatment stages, which began after 2 years and are still continuing.

ADAPTED-METACOGNITIVE INTERPERSONAL THERAPY: GENERAL PRINCIPLES AND SUMMARY OF THE FIRST PART OF TREATMENT

As noted above, the main goal of MIT for personality disorders (Dimaggio et al., 2007; Dimaggio et al., 2012; Dimaggio et al., 2013) is to progressively promote metacognition and awareness of problematic forms of subjective experience and of the schemas driving social behavior. When applied to schizophrenia, it has been urged that therapists work within their patients' current metacognitive capacity (Lysaker et al., 2011). In the case of Angela, in the earliest sessions, her therapist displayed interest and respect, listened to her without interrupting, and, in particular, did not attempt to refute her delusional beliefs. In fact, Angela was incapable of considering her representations as being subject to error, given that she did not think that she had her own ideas. The therapist tried, instead, to promote the most basic metacognitive skill, consisting in an awareness of the internal origins of one's thoughts. In one of her first sessions Angela said, 'Marco wants to make me go crazy with these ideas he's putting in my head . . .' The therapist merely replied, 'It looks like today you're thinking very intensely about Marco and about the fact that he sends you thoughts.' When Angela nodded sadly, the therapist said, 'I can imagine how tiring it must be.'

At a more advanced stage of A-MIT, the next intervention a therapist should take consists in helping the patient to recount narrative episodes containing detailed descriptions of situations and of interactions among characters, providing an agreed upon text in which mental states could be detected and discussed (Dimaggio et al., 2012; see Lysaker et al., Chapter 1, this volume). For example, during a session in her third month of therapy, Angela was narrating how she generally felt ill at ease at her university and the therapist asked her to recall a more specific scene. Angela recalled that during one lecture she felt particularly tense in the midst of the crowd and needed to talk with someone who could reassure her. The therapist tried to understand how Angela felt, what thoughts provoked her feelings in that moment, and why. Then they explored whether any symptoms emerged during this event. Shortly after entering the classroom Angela had imagined that everyone was observing that she was 'the ugliest in the class'. At that moment she heard a voice telling her she was 'awkward.' She had sat down at the back without speaking to anyone. At this point Angela, with the therapist's help, managed to grasp that in the university episode she had 'felt different' and 'not up to it,' and that it was precisely at that moment that her sensation of being criticized and the voice telling her she was 'awkward' had appeared.

The next immediate step, after showing comprehension about how stressful this experience must have been, was to elicit other narrative episodes where there had been a similar hallucinatory experience and investigate what the beliefs and emotions were before and during the experience. Angela recalled how she had similarly felt poorly 3 years before and distrusted the person who was at the time her best friend. Angela had failed an important exam and had lost all hope so that she felt the need to confide in this friend. However, while she was speaking with the latter on the telephone, she had the impression that the friend was not being sincere and in reality considered Angela 'lazy and stupid.' After this telephone call Angela did not want to see her friend again.

At this point, Angela was becoming aware that there were thoughts in her own head and that she was sensitive to others' critical judgments and reacted to them by hearing scorning voices. This section of her therapy marked the shift between the first part, that is, promoting an awareness of the more basic aspects of self-reflectivity, including ownership of thoughts, awareness of specific cognitions and emotions, and the ability to establish cause-effect relationships between events, beliefs, cognitions, and both behavior and symptoms, and the more advanced treatment stages, which we are going to describe from now on.

AWARENESS OF A DISTURBED INTERPERSONAL SCHEMA AND DIFFERENTIATION BETWEEN THE SCHEMA AND ACTUAL RELATIONSHIPS

Based on the work conducted during the previous stage, Angela could grasp that her sensation of being threatened and criticized by others, accompanied by voices insulting her, occurred every time she did not feel up to interpersonal situations. She now remembered feeling the same sense of not being up to things when her mother criticized her as a child. She also recalled that her mother's criticisms made her become unmotivated and passive. The following excerpt illustrates the type of intervention the therapist was making at this stage:

Angela: This is a characteristic of me, that I've always had this something that blocks me. I think that in relationships with others I've always been reserved because I always thought that I show I'm not much of a person [. . .] I think that what has been blocking me and making me feel always under observation has been this sense of not being up to it, being inadequate.

Therapist: That sense of inadequacy we saw at the university too, when you felt you were the awkward one in the situation?!

A: Oh, yes, that's right!

T: And so the core of the problem is this not feeling up to it. Do any other examples, including perhaps from further ago in the past when you were a girl, of situations where you had this sense of not being up to it, come to mind?

A: I can remember when I was small and they were all playing cards, it was Christmas, and I wanted to play too and they didn't want to let me play and made me cry my heart out . . . nobody would console me . . . . Then I went crying to my mother and instead of . . . consoling me, she said that I was little and should keep my place and not disturb my older cousins . . . .

T: I see. And at that point what did you do?

A: Nothing. I went into a corner on my own and can't remember what I was doing.

T: So, first you felt the need to be accepted, which is totally normal and healthy in a child, but it didn't get responded to. Then you felt the need to be consoled and understood, to which, instead, you received the reply 'It's you that's wrong,' 'It's you that's not right?!' And at that point you closed in yourself.

A: 'It's you that's not right' precisely! I carried it with me like a sense of being different, even when I was a bit older. I couldn't manage to join in conversations. I remember thinking 'There's something not right with me.'

T: So you can recall this deep suffering from your infancy?

A: Yes and then during all of my adolescence I had this sensation very strongly and I closed up even more.

As noted before, A-MIT schema-reconstruction is based on the CCRT template (Luborsky and Crits-Christoph, 1990). The CCRT reconstructs an interpersonal schema based on the goal – Wish – that a patient pursues and fears will fail because of others' responses. Once the wish is activated, the patient thus expects a Response from the Other, which is followed by the Self's Response to the Other's Response. Thanks to the reconstruction of the schema, it is possible to infer the self-image underlying the wish, that is, in Angela's case, I wish to be appreciated but am not worth anything. In MIT for personality disorders and – in cases where it is possible, based on the level of cognitive and metacognitive functioning – for patients with psychosis, a therapist can at this point formulate the patient's psychological functioning jointly with the latter, often with a resort to written diagrams (Dimaggio *et al.*, 2013; Salvatore et al., in press). When reconstructing with the patient, the therapist should ask for feedback and modify the schema until reaching an agreed formulation, with the patient feeling emotionally that it corresponds to his way of functioning. We would stress that, unlike patients with personality disorder, with whom it is possible to make complex reformulations including links between different schemas, with patients with psychosis it may be necessary to use simpler reformulations, of the 'You wish for approval but see others criticizing you and at that point you feel you're not worth anything and you close up' type.

Using a diagram on a blackboard the therapist reconstructed the following schema with Angela: Angela wished to be comprehended but expected that, instead of comprehending and consoling her, the other would severely criticize her, so that she reacted by feeling profoundly inadequate and closing in on herself, as at university, with her friend 3 years earlier, or when she was small with her mother.

Angela could fully identify herself in this reconstruction and with tears in her eyes she asked the therapist what she could do to not feel so inadequate. He reassured her and told her that the next step in the therapy would be 'becoming ever better at observing Angela in those situations where this schema gets activated,' for example, by monitoring the thoughts and emotions that 'in the heat of the moment' triggered voices. The agreed goal was that Angela should progressively become more aware of the difference between the schema and reality. At the same time, the therapist asked her to take note of situations where the schema was inactive and she felt better, with the aim of putting her in contact with her healthy self facets.

PROMOTING HEALTHY ASPECTS OF THE SELF

Helping patients to make contact with the healthier parts of their self (e.g., a positive self-image, an intact capacity to feel joy) is an operation that should take place immediately after, and in part at the same time as, identifying their pathogenic schemas. When a patient reports an experience where the self-image appears positive, the therapist should pay attention to any adaptive forms of functioning and explicitly validate them. The goal is to make the patient savor healthy, adaptive, and schema-discrepant experiences as long as possible.

The rationale of this intervention is that the experience of positive emotional arousal for a certain period of time can change ideation in a consistent direction and facilitate the storage of positive autobiographical recollections, which will get transformed into self-defining memories (Singer *et al.*, 2013). Once the patient has remained long enough in a positive state, the therapist can carry out a leverage operation, that is, help the patient to use his healthy self as an observing-ego. In short, a patient first needs to identify some good functioning situations and then make contact with the subjective aspects connected to the experiences in question, that is, to perceive that she *feels* satisfied with herself. The therapist should then validate her and ask her to take note that there are these aspects within her. When Angela experienced positive emotion in session, the therapist asked: 'Now that you feel strong and describe yourself as such, what do you think of the Angela who feels awkward? Do you still believe that it's true that you're not worth anything and everybody will notice it?'

At this stage in her therapy, Angela reported experiences where she felt under-rated by her mother and told the therapist how much this made her feel inadequate overall. In one session, however, she said that the afternoon before, her wish to paint had come back. The therapist tried to investigate her love of painting and asked her to show him her old paintings. The next session Angela brought him a DVD containing some of her work. The therapist examined them with interest and was sincerely struck by them. He expressed his appreciation and asked about what sensations Angela experienced while she was creating these works. Angela described her sensation of pleasure and expressed joy. The therapist intervened: 'I'm very struck, because you often tell me how much you don't feel up to it, especially when you feel judged negatively by your mother, and how much this removes every motivation in your life. However, while you were describing yourself painting, I could feel you were full of energy and active. You could hear how much you like it, how confident you were in what you were doing and in the possibility of being appreciated by others too.' Angela paused for a long time and then said she agreed.

In order to anchor Angela to these positive and affectively laden reflections, the therapist then asked: 'Well, but from this adequate and confident position what do you think of the inadequate Angela?' Naturally, as often happens too with patients with personality disorders, the new and positive self-part soon gets overwhelmed by the negative representation, which is the prevalent one and laden with negative affects written during patients' development history. Positive states thus tend by their nature to be short-lived and to reactivate pathologic worries.

In fact, at this point Angela said that this was 'water under the bridge,' that all things considered she was 'an amateur,' as her mother had told her once with a laugh in front of some friends of hers. At this point, however, the therapist has some tools for confronting the negative state, as he can play on the very recent memory of a positive affective state: 'Angela, do you realize that until a few seconds ago you were OK and in particular had confidence in yourself?! Can you see how this tendency of yours to think badly of yourself is a mental automatism, not the truth?' As often happens, Angela benefitted from this observation and stopped completely believing in her negative self-representation for another short period.

PROMOTING REFLECTION ON OTHERS' MINDS

As has been suggested elsewhere, understanding of others' mental states should be stimulated only after promoting patients' understanding of their own minds and of the relation between negative emotions and symptom activation. In fact, awareness of others' minds generally improves only after a significant improvement in awareness of one's own mind (Lysaker *et al.*, 2005; Lysaker *et al.*, 2007; Salvatore *et al.*, 2012). With Angela, the therapist tried to improve her understanding of others' minds only after agreeing with her that her sense of inadequacy in interpersonal situations was a trigger for delusions and hallucinations. It is important to note that not even at this advanced stage does an A-MIT therapist try to use classic cognitive behavioral therapy (CBT) strategies to directly refute delusional beliefs (see Kingdon and Turkington, 2005).

Working together with Angela on various narrative episodes the therapist discussed her delusional beliefs about others and tried to point out the recurrent influence of negative affective states. After focusing on a series of different narrative episodes, a therapist can carry out a more general reformulation like 'I've noticed that what these episodes have in common is that each time you feel vulnerable and anxious when faced with another whom you feel to be strong and dominating, you are very likely to ascribe malicious intentions to the other.' A therapist should, moreover, always remember that the metacognitive progress of patients with psychosis may fluctuate, so that, following improvements there can be losses. Moreover, when patients do not understand others' minds, grasping what is passing through their therapist's mind is very often difficult as well. This is likely to lead patients to construct their therapist in line with pre-existing schemas. A therapist can be seen, for example, as dominating or untrustworthy. For example, in one session with Angela at this stage, her therapist, being confident in her progress and without first measuring the metacognitive level she possessed at that moment, asked her what she thought about taking up regular painting lessons again. Angela showed an irritated expression, replied that she could not see why this was important for him, and started to look down at the floor without saying anything else. The therapist adjusted his interventions by focusing first on the relationship and then on the metacognitive level of awareness of one's own mind. He asked Angela to forgive him for his insistence about the topic of painting, which was probably not the most important for her at that moment. Angela's facial expression became more contented. The therapist then asked her how she felt. With a still slightly sad and diffident expression, she said that she was very sad because of the argument with her mother, occurring the evening before, where the latter had made her again feel 'wrong,' by asking her when she was going to sit her next exam. Now the therapist could fully grasp that he had, with his initial intervention, confirmed Angela's dysfunctional schema. Like her mother, he had embodied the Other in the schema. Instead of tuning in to Angela's priorities, he criticized her. As her mother had made Angela feel 'wrong' by asking her when she would sit the next exam, he had made her feel 'wrong' by pressing her to take up painting again and getting her to think that not taking it up again would disappoint him. The therapist's intervention was as follows: 'It appears I have to beg your pardon twice, because earlier, when I insisted so much with my questions about your painting, I may perhaps, without wanting to, have seemed not so different from how you felt your mother to be yesterday evening.' Angela smiled and confirmed that in fact she had felt a bit 'squashed.' The session atmosphere went back to being very cordial and the therapist told Angela that he could understand this feeling well, because it depended on the fact that, without wanting to, he had confirmed the schema they were working on. He suggested to Angela that in any situation in the future where she got this feeling in her relationship with him she was free to openly tell him (Dimaggio and Lysaker, 2010; Dimaggio et al., 2013; Safran and Muran, 2000). When he saw Angela very relieved, the therapist then formulated an intervention aimed at promoting the understanding of others' minds by using the therapeutic relationship itself as the terrain. He told Angela: 'You know, I think we can nevertheless learn a lot from what just happened between us. Not just the fact that in the relationship between us too there can be moments of incomprehension which, however, can be easily cleared up if we talk about them, but also that all of us can in certain situations have the very clear sensation telling us that the other has evil intentions towards us, whereas in reality that's not the case and at times he has positive intentions.' Angela smiled and said: 'A bit like me with you: I immediately thought the worst. I had also got the suspicion that you'd plotted with my mother.'

FOCUS ON PERSONALLY RELEVANT GOALS, SOCIAL EXPOSURE, AND METACOGNITIVE MASTERY FOR SYMPTOMS AND SOCIAL PROBLEMS

By this point, a patient has been helped to understand his dysfunctional schema, to grasp that it does not necessarily reflect reality, and to see the link by which his hallucinatory voices often surface as a consequence of an activation of the schema. On this basis, a therapist can typically at this point propose reformulating the therapeutic contract and renegotiating the therapy goals.

One essential goal will be the search for activities with which to avoid states involving suffering and better access those involving well-being, adaptation, satisfaction, and pursuit of personal goals. The promotion of states involving well-being in patients with psychosis should be carried out initially with enjoyable activities a patient can cultivate on her own, in order to not be too soon subjected to the pressure of interpersonal transactions. In fact with Angela, we would recall, interpersonal transactions tended to easily activate the inadequacy schema and lead her into an isolation that constituted a fertile terrain for the triggering of delirious beliefs about others' intentions and of hallucinations. The therapist therefore agreed with Angela that it would be very important to first of all stimulate as much as possible her renewed motivation to paint. Angela willingly accepted this. Thanks to this initiative, Angela was able to experience states involving adequacy and personal gratification. Only then did the therapist cautiously propose gradually exposing herself to social exchanges (see Dimaggio *et al.*, 2013, for similar procedures with personality disorders). For example, he advised her to, at least once, accept an invitation to have coffee with a colleague who was being very nice to her.

Moreover, Angela grasped how important it was to not adopt a surly and hostile facial expression when attending lectures. In this connection the therapist said: 'Even if they're gradual, these little experiments will probably cause you a bit of anxiety. However we're now capable of seeing that it's a problem that's possible to tackle; the therapy will provide you with valid tools for doing this.' On this basis, the therapist prepared with Angela a set of tools for mastering her anxiety and, potentially, the voices. One of these was a memo about the inadequacy schema, which Angela was to carry with her and refer to in exposure situations where her anxiety might appear. With this she would be able to recall the session and the therapist in difficult situations. This strategy achieved a positive outcome. After about 1 month, Angela managed to have a coffee with the colleague, who contacted her the next day on a social network.

Therapy Outcome

After 3 years of psychotherapy, there have been several objective indicators of recovery. Positive symptoms have been reduced to a minimal level and Angela has re-engaged in a number of healthy friendships. She has entered a stepdown phase with one session every 2 weeks for 6 months and then one session every 3 weeks for a further 6 months. Fourteen months after the start of the stepdown phase, sessions are now monthly. Many of these sessions are focused on helping her develop strategies for continuing her university courses.

CONCLUSIONS

In summary, the initial steps in A-MIT involve promoting patients' awareness of their own thoughts and understanding of their emotions and factors eliciting them. The advanced steps described in this chapter are: (1) helping patients understand that voices and delusional beliefs are often triggered by distressing interpersonal encounters feeding negative interpretations of self and others; (2) making them aware that these interpretations depend on maladaptive interpersonal schemas. With the patient analyzed by us here the more sophisticated understanding of her sense of inadequacy, emerging in particular in interpersonal transactions (e.g., at university), made possible a joint definition of the dysfunctional interpersonal schema; (3) helping patients achieve an ability to question their schemas and understand they do not necessarily mirror reality. The patient here became aware of how biased representations of self and others were an obstacle to a more nuanced and decentered understanding of interpersonal encounters; (4) helping them to make contact with healthy self-aspects and, in their everyday actions, expand the areas in which they apply the healthy self. The patient here became open to the possibility of experiencing a mental state involving efficacy and well-being, first in less anxiety-provoking activities on her own (e.g., taking up painting again) and then in interpersonal relations; (5) promoting mastery strategies for symptoms and social problems, and exposure to social situations. The therapist in Angela's case had expected frequent negative fluctuations in her metacognitive capacities in reaction to stressful interpersonal events but he responded flexibly to the metacognitive problems arising from time to time during sessions.

We trust the procedures outlined here and the supporting case example help make a case for A-MIT being a suitable tool for treating paranoid schizophrenia. A-MIT seems to be effective in stimulating metacognitive skills and reducing symptoms. Nevertheless, we need to point out several important limitations to this study. First, there was no research specifically into the effectiveness of A-MIT and this is the first single case in which we have described the advanced stages in our treatment model. A lack of formal assessment is certainly a limitation and makes it impossible to establish whether both symptoms, social functioning and metacognition, actually improved, apart from the clinical observations. Neither should the impact of medication be overlooked. In this case, long-term treatment with olanzapine appeared useful in resolving some of the patient's positive symptoms (e.g., the idea that her thoughts were transmitted) but did not lead to full remission of her auditory hallucinations and persecutory delusions. Moreover, social withdrawal did not improve with medication (see Chapter 7; *The Impact of Metacognition on the Development and Maintenance of Negative Symptoms*, for the importance of a metacognitive and narrative approach for addressing the negative symptoms of psychosis). Overall, we hope to have provided the reader with a rationale and a set of strategies for promoting higher-order awareness of mental states in people with paranoid schizophrenia and auditory inner voices, together with an increased awareness of their mental functioning, so that they can deal with the social world in more adaptive ways and in the case of formerly socially withdrawn patients, resume social relationships.

REFERENCES

Brüne, M., Abdel-Hamid, M., Lehmkämper, C., & Sonntag, C. (2007). Mental state attribution, neurocognitive functioning, and psychopathology: What predicts poor social competence in schizophrenia best? *Schizophrenia Research, 92*(1–3), 151–159.

Brüne, M., Dimaggio, G., & Lysaker, P. H. (2011). Metacognition and social functioning in schizophrenia: Evidence, mechanisms of influence and treatment implications. *Current Psychiatry Reviews, 7*, 239–247.

Buck, K. D., & Lysaker, P. H. (2010). Addressing metacognitive capacity in the psychotherapy for schizophrenia: A case study. *Clinical Case Studies, 8*(6), 463–472.

Dimaggio, G., & Lysaker, P. H. (Eds.). (2010). *Metacognition and severe adult mental disorders: From basic research to treatment.* London: Routledge.

Dimaggio, G., Montano, A., Popolo, R., & Salvatore, G. (2013). *Terapia Metacognitiva Interpersonale dei Disturbi di Personalità [Metacognitive Interpersonal Therapy of Personality Disorders].* Milan: Raffaello Cortina Editore.

Dimaggio, G., Salvatore, G., Popolo, R., & Lysaker, P. H. (2012). Autobiographical memory and mentalizing impairment in personality disorders and schizophrenia: Clinical and research implications. *Frontiers in Psychology, 3*, 529.

Dimaggio, G., Semerari, A., Carcione, A., Nicolò, G., & Procacci, M. (2007). *Psychotherapy of personality disorders: Metacognition, states of mind and interpersonal cycles.* London: Routledge.

Dimaggio, G., Vanheule, S., Lysaker, P. H., Carcione, A., & Nicolò, G. (2009). Impaired self-reflection in psychiatric disorders among adults: A proposal for the existence of a network of semi-independent functions. *Consciousness and Cognition, 18*, 653–664.

Kerr, S. L., & Neale, J. M. (1993). Emotion perception in schizophrenia: Specific deficit of further evidence of generalized poor performance? *Journal of Abnormal Psychology, 102*(2), 312–318.

Kingdon, D. G., & Turkington, D. (2005). *Cognitive-behavioral therapy of schizophrenia.* New York: Guilford.

Kukla, M., Lysaker, P. H., & Salyers, M. (2013). Do persons with schizophrenia who have better metacognitive capacity also have a stronger subjective experience of recovery? *Psychiatry Research*, *209*(3), 381–385.

Langdon, R., Coltheart, M., & Ward, P. B. (2006). Empathetic perspective taking is impaired in schizophrenia: Evidence from a study of emotion attribution and theory of mind. *Cognitive Neuropsychiatry*, *11*(2), 133–155.

Luborsky, L., & Crits-Christoph, P. (1990). *Understanding transference: The CCRT method*. New York: Basic Books.

Lysaker, P. H., Bob, P., Pec, O., Hamm, J., Kukla, M., Vohs, J., et al. (2013). Metacognition as a link which connects brain to behavior in schizophrenia. *Translational Neuroscience*, *4*(3), 368–377.

Lysaker, P. H., & Buck, K. D. (2008). Insight and schizophrenia: Correlates, etiology and treatment. *Clinical Schizophrenia and Related Psychoses*, *2*(2), 147–155.

Lysaker, P. H., & Buck, K. D. (2010). Metacognitive capacity as a focus of individual psychotherapy in schizophrenia. In G. Dimaggio & P. H. Lysaker (Eds.), *Metacognition and severe adult mental disorders. From research to treatment* (pp. 4–15). London: Routledge.

Lysaker, P. H., Buck, K. D., & Ringer, J. (2007). The recovery of metacognitive capacity in schizophrenia across thirty two months of individual psychotherapy: A case study. *Psychotherapy Research*, *17*, 713–720.

Lysaker, P. H., Davis, L. D., Eckert, G. J., Strasburger, A., Hunter, N., & Buck, K. D. (2005). Changes in narrative structure and content in schizophrenia in long term individual psychotherapy: A single case study. *Clinical Psychology & Psychotherapy*, *12*, 406–416.

Lysaker, P. H., Erickson, M. A., Buck, B., Buck, K. D., Olesek, K., Grant, M., et al. (2011). Metacognition and social function in schizophrenia: Associations over a period of five months. *Cognitive Neuropsychiatry*, *16*, 241–255.

Lysaker, P. H., Shea, A. M., Buck, K. D., Dimaggio, G., Nicolò, G., Procacci, M., et al. (2010). Metacognition as a mediator of the effects of impairments in neurocognition on social function in schizophrenia spectrum disorders. *Acta Psychiatrica Scandinavica*, *122*(5), 405–413.

Morrison, R. L., Bellack, A. S., & Bashore, T. R. (1988). Perception of emotion among schizophrenic patients. *Journal of Psychopathological Behavior Assessment*, *10*(4), 319–322.

Mueser, K. T., Doonan, B., Penn, D. L., Blanchard, J. J., Bellack, A. S., Nishith, P., et al. (1996). Emotion recognition and social competence on chronic schizophrenia. *Journal of Abnormal Psychology*, *105*, 271–275.

Pedersen, A., Koelkebeck, K., Brandt, M., Wee, M., Kueppers, K. A., Kugel, H., et al. (2012). Theory of mind in patients with schizophrenia: Is mentalizing delayed? *Schizophrenia Research*, *137*, 224–229.

Safran, J. D., & Muran, J. C. (2000). *Negotiating the therapeutic alliance: A relational treatment guide*. New York: Guilford.

Salvatore, G., Dimaggio, G., & Lysaker, P. H. (2007). An intersubjective perspective on negative symptoms of schizophrenia: Implications of simulation theory. *Cognitive Neuropsychiatry*, *12*, 144–164.

Salvatore, G., Dimaggio, G., Popolo, R., Procacci, M., Nicolò, G., & Carcione, A. (2009). Adapted metacognitive interpersonal therapy for improving adherence to intersubjective contexts in a person with schizophrenia. *Clinical Case Studies*, *8*, 473–488.

Salvatore, G., Lysaker, P. H., Gumley, A., Popolo, R., Mari, J., & Dimaggio, G. (2012). Out of illness experience: Metacognition-oriented therapy for promoting self-awareness in psychosis sufferers. *American Journal of Psychotherapy*, *66*, 85–106.

Salvatore, G., Popolo, R., & Dimaggio, G. (in press). Promoting integration between different self-states through ongoing reformulation. In: W. J. Livesley, G. Dimaggio, & J. F. Clarkin (Eds.), *Integrated modular treatment for personality disorders*. New York: Guilford.

Semerari, A., Carcione, A., Dimaggio, G., Falcone, M., Nicolò, G., Procacci, M., et al. (2003). How to evaluate metacognitive functioning in psychotherapy? The Metacognition Assessment Scale and its applications. *Clinical Psychology and Psychotherapy, 10*, 238–261.

Singer, J. A., Blagov, P., Berry, M., & Oost, K. M. (2013). Self-defining memories, scripts, and the life story: Narrative identity in personality and psychotherapy. *Journal of Personality. Special Issue: Personality Psychology and Psychotherapy, 81*, 569–582.

Chapter 14

Triumphs and Tribulations in the Psychotherapy of Schizophrenia: Reflections from a Pilot Study of Metacognitive Narrative Psychotherapy

Rebecca Bargenquast and Robert D. Schweitzer

Queensland University of Technology, Brisbane, QLD, Australia

Chapter Outline

INTRODUCTION

'Schizophrenia is an I am illness – one that may overtake and redefine the identity of the person' (Estroff, 1989, p. 189).

Social Cognition and Metacognition in Schizophrenia.
DOI: http://dx.doi.org/10.1016/B978-0-12-405172-0.00014-4
© 2014 Elsevier Inc. All rights reserved.

The role of psychotherapy in the treatment of people presenting with symptoms of schizophrenia has been the subject of controversy, with more recent evidence supporting the role of psychological interventions. A growing body of evidence from research-based clinical settings suggests that interventions drawing upon cognitive behavioral, psychodynamic, narrative, and humanistic approaches to psychotherapy help people with schizophrenia achieve meaningful degrees of recovery (Gottdiener and Haslam, 2002; Lysaker *et al.*, 2011; Seikkula *et al.*, 2011; Wykes *et al.*, 2008).

Despite these findings, many services continue to rely almost exclusively upon treatment approaches that are rooted in a biomedical paradigm. In spite of good evidence supporting the effectiveness of a range of psychological interventions, few resources are dedicated to such interventions, with many clinicians avoiding psychotherapeutic engagement with patients who meet criteria for schizophrenia. The reasons for this are complex and operate at both a 'global' or paradigmatic level and at the 'experience-near' level of clinician–patient interaction. The innate challenges associated with psychotherapy with people with schizophrenia are confounded by the obstacles associated with translating research findings into clinical practice. Despite a strong push toward evidence-based psychotherapeutic practice, clinicians are often left feeling that rigorously designed research studies lack a 'real-world' quality, reporting findings that seem irrelevant to the settings clinicians are working in and the patients they are treating on a day-to-day basis. Studies suggest that it takes about 20 years for research findings to find their way into clinical practice (Brekke *et al.*, 2007). This is made all the worse in the treatment of people with symptoms of schizophrenia where the same authors report that less than 30% of patients receive any recommended psychosocial support. The percentage receiving any psychotherapeutic benefit is considerably less.

Many therapists from varying theoretical backgrounds continue to persevere and present promising evidence of the viability and effectiveness of psychotherapy in the treatment of schizophrenia. In the midst of disconnection and fear, therapeutic conversations help people with schizophrenia establish internal and interpersonal connections, construct meaning around experiences, master symptoms, and develop a sense of purpose and hope. In this chapter, we wish to provide a description of a project in which we developed and successfully implemented a research-based psychotherapy model for the treatment of people with schizophrenia. We then reflect on the implementation phase of the project. Following this, we describe some of the reasons for, or blocks to, the seemingly slow translation of such interventions into clinical practice. Finally, we offer some suggestions for promoting the translation of clinical research findings into clinical practice.

A DIALOGICAL MODEL OF IMPOVERISHED SELF-EXPERIENCE IN SCHIZOPHRENIA

We wish to articulate a number of ideas that have informed our approach to developing an intervention to assist people presenting with symptoms of schizophrenia. We drew upon the seminal work of Lysaker and colleagues, which provided a theoretical grounding for our treatment model as well as some evidence for the effectiveness of the approach in enhancing recovery in people with symptoms of schizophrenia (e.g., Lysaker *et al.*, 2005b; Lysaker *et al.*, 2011). The approach to be described was informed by a set of assumptions, which privilege sense of personhood over a purely biologic model of schizophrenia. Our approach is not novel. Disturbed sense-of-self and 'extreme perplexity about one's own identity and the meaning of existence' has long been recognized as a central feature of schizophrenia (American Psychiatric Association, 1987, p. 189). While notions of self have seemingly disappeared from current diagnostic criteria, many continue to conceive of disturbed self-experience as a core feature of schizophrenia (Davidson, 2003; Lysaker and Lysaker, 2008; Sass and Parnas, 2003).

We are all storytellers by nature, and it is through the narration of our experiences that we make sense of our lives and develop and maintain a coherent sense-of-self (Hermans, 2004; McAdams and Janis, 2004). Aligned with these ideas is the notion of the dialogical self, in which psychosocial functioning is understood to be the product of continual, flexible conversations both within an individual and between an individual and others (Hermans, 1996). The dialogical self is not a 'core self'; it is relational, ever-changing, and multivoiced. The dialogical self is a '. . . dynamic multiplicity of (voiced) positions in the landscape of the mind, intertwined as this mind is intertwined with the minds of other people' (Hermans, 2004, p. 176). Each voiced position, or self-position, is a unique and identifiable aspect of an individual that entertains dialogical relationships with other self-positions. Coherent self-experience requires (1) a sufficient number of self-positions, (2) the ability to be aware of a variety of self-positions, (3) the capacity for meaningful dialogue among different self-positions, and (4) the capacity to create meta-positions or for metacognitive integration. Metacognition is thus essential in the development and maintenance of the dialogical self (Dimaggio *et al.*, 2010; Lysaker and Lysaker, 2008).

Our approach is based on the premise that people diagnosed with schizophrenia experience interdependent deficits in capacities for metacognition and meaningful dialogue among self-positions (Frith, 1992; Hamm *et al.*, 2012; Lysaker *et al.*, 2010). These deficits culminate in a collapse of the dialogical self and subsequent impoverished self-experience and poor psychosocial functioning. In particular, impaired metacognition and self-experience in people with schizophrenia has been linked to increased symptom severity, neurocognitive impairment, poor insight, poor quality of life, social cognitive deficits, poor work performance, and impaired social functioning (Brune *et al.*, 2011; Harrington *et al.*, 2005; Lysaker *et al.*, 2005a; Lysaker *et al.*, 2009; Lysaker and Lysaker, 2004; Nicolo *et al.*, 2012; Roncone *et al.*, 2002). These findings point to the need for treatment models that target metacognitive deficits, and more broadly self-disturbance, in people diagnosed with schizophrenia.

TREATMENT MODEL AND MANUAL

The trial to be described utilized a form of therapy, termed metacognitive narrative psychotherapy. The therapy was developed to address the needs of people with schizophrenia and targets deficits in capacities for metacognition and coherent storytelling. The treatment model draws upon theory and principles of practice from postmodern, humanistic, and psychodynamic approaches and integrates dialogical narrative principles of psychotherapy (e.g., Anderson, 1997; Angus and McLeod, 2004; Hermans and Dimaggio, 2004), general principles for the psychotherapy of schizophrenia (e.g., Fenton, 2000; Horowitz, 2002), and recent research investigating the therapeutic processes of metacognitive narrative approaches to the treatment of severe psychopathology (e.g., Lysaker *et al.*, 2011; Lysaker and Lysaker, 2006; Salvatore *et al.*, 2009). The theory underpinning metacognitive narrative psychotherapy formed the basis for the development of a manualized treatment program. The manual covered five phases of treatment: (1) developing a therapeutic relationship, (2) eliciting narratives, (3) enhancing metacognitive capacity, (4) enriching narratives, and (5) living enriched narratives (see Table 14.1). The treatment manual was designed to balance the tensions between clinical practice and research implementation (Bargenquast and Schweitzer, 2013).

The therapeutic process and progression through treatment phases are typically nonlinear. Sessions are not conducted in a prescriptive or rigid manner, but rather therapist–patient collaboration is prioritized. The approach described is, in our view, particularly helpful in promoting a subjective sense of recovery in people diagnosed with schizophrenia. We believe this is because the approach directly addresses core deficits associated with impaired sense-of-self and impaired capacity for knowing one's own experience and that of others. This approach does not place the therapist in the position of 'expert,' which is often characteristic of approaches such as cognitive behavioral therapy (CBT) and social skills training, but rather, it works through a collaborative relationship.

IMPLEMENTATION OF THE INTERVENTION

The treatment described above was implemented in a pilot project that treated 11 people diagnosed with schizophrenia. Participants had not been hospitalized or had their medication changed in the 2 months prior to commencing therapy. Their mean age was 45.5 years. The majority of participants were male (82%), single (91%), and unemployed (54%). All but one participant was taking antipsychotic medication. People were excluded from the study if they were intellectually disabled or at high risk of suicide or harming others. The therapists in the study were seven female, postgraduate intern psychologists enrolled in a postgraduate clinical psychology program. They were all white and their ages ranged from 25 to 30 years. All therapists participated in

TABLE 14.1 Phases of Treatment in Metacognitive Narrative Psychotherapy for Schizophrenia.

Phase 1	**Developing a Therapeutic Relationship** Nonauthoritarian therapeutic stance Developing a shared partnership between therapist and patient Focusing on the here-and-now, therapeutic relationship Prioritizing empathic attunement over 'fixing' the patient's difficulties Managing countertransference and relationship ruptures
Phase 2	**Eliciting Narratives** Listening to the patient's stories with curiosity and an open mind Establishing and sustaining dialogue with supportive interventions Managing emotional intensity in-session
Phase 3	**Enhancing Metacognitive Capacity** Modeling a reflective, questioning stance Enhancing self-reflectivity – e.g., learning to recognize and distinguish different cognitive operations and emotional states Enhancing understanding of others' mental states
Phase 4	**Enriching Narratives** Promoting the patient as an agent-protagonist Exploring stories outside of illness Exploring stories that remain untold Envisioning the future
Phase 5	**Living Enriched Narratives** Encouraging the patient to live their enriched life-narrative Generalizing gains made in the therapeutic relationship to relationships outside of therapy Managing termination
Proscribed Practices	Do not hold an authoritarian or mysterious therapeutic stance Do not tell the patient's story for them Do not facilitate too much or rapid patient self-disclosure Do not encourage use of free association Do not encourage overly intense interpersonal engagement

a supervised training program comprising an initial 2-day training program, which focused on the implementation of the treatment model and manual. This was followed by ongoing supervision in the therapeutic modality. Therapy sessions were conducted face-to-face once per week at a university-based training psychology clinic. Participants were seen for a mean of 49 sessions (range 25–88 sessions). The mean length of treatment was 16 months and ranged from 11 to 26 months.

To achieve our evaluation objectives, five variables were measured at pre-, mid-, and post-treatment: subjective recovery, symptom severity, narrative coherence, narrative complexity, and metacognitive capacity. The following scales were used to assess each of these areas respectively: Recovery Assessment Scale (RAS; Corrigan *et al.*, 1999); Brief Psychiatric Rating Scale, extended version (BPRS; Lukoff *et al.*, 1986); Narrative Coherence Rating Scale (NCRS; Lysaker *et al.*, 2002); Scale to Assess Narrative Development (STAND; Lysaker *et al.*, 2003); and Metacognitive Assessment Scale – Self-Reflectivity subscale (MAS-SR; Lysaker *et al.*, 2005a; Semerari *et al.*, 2003).

TREATMENT OUTCOME

Treatment was implemented on a regular basis with minimal dropout. The outcomes of the intervention were positive, with significantly increased scores (medium-to-large effect sizes) on the RAS and MAS-SR (Bargenquast and Schweitzer, in press). All but one patient displayed positive changes on one or more of the outcome measures. Results demonstrated the practicability and value of implementing psychological interventions with people with schizophrenia within a postgraduate training setting. Although the generalizability of our results was limited by the small sample size and lack of a control group, the methodology employed indicated the viability of a larger, controlled trial.

IMPEDIMENTS IN DEVELOPING AND IMPLEMENTING NEW INTERVENTIONS

Implementing a psychotherapy research program that is based upon divergent philosophical positions is not without its challenges. Based upon our experience, we have identified four potential barriers to the implementation and translation of research projects investigating innovative psychological interventions: service and clinician resistance to new paradigms for understanding human distress; the gate-keeping role of established mental health services; difficulties translating research findings into everyday practice; and issues resulting from the nature of the intervention and the skill-base of practitioners. These issues assume prominence in a field where only a minority of people with the symptoms of schizophrenia receive evidence-based psychosocial intervention that targets their functional impairments (Brekke *et al.*, 2007).

PARADIGMS, PREJUDICE, AND EVIDENCE-BASED PRACTICE

Perhaps the most subtle and also stringent barrier to the implementation of new interventions comes from implicit assumptions that we and fellow clinicians hold in relation to the 'management' of people with symptoms of schizophrenia. At its most fundamental, the dominant paradigm, the biomedical model, envisages schizophrenia as a brain disease that needs to be understood as any other disease and treated accordingly. This assumption results in medication being the principal and often sole treatment offered to people diagnosed with schizophrenia. Allowances are certainly made for psychosocial interventions, but these are often construed as addressing the 'manifestations' of the disease. The approach described challenges preconceived notions of schizophrenia by privileging the subjective experience of the person diagnosed with the disorder. This posed challenges for the implementation of our project, in that clinicians struggled to entertain an alternative stance to treatment. However, we suggest that a clinician's interest in innovative interventions can be facilitated by gradual and respectful exposure to 'new' ideas and opportunities to experiment with alternative approaches.

THE GATE-KEEPING ROLE OF ESTABLISHED HEALTH SERVICES

A significant difficulty we had in setting up the study was trying to recruit participants through formal health services. There was a strong view within state mental health services that they were not able to support studies utilizing psychological approaches, especially if they were not mainstream. The fact that we were able to provide evidence for the effectiveness of the interventions based upon previous case studies did not seem to matter; the 'gate-keepers' had very defined views of the nature of the illness and the treatments that should be provided. These were well ensconced in a biologic conception of schizophrenia, and there was an ethos of protecting patients from any intervention that diverged from the dominant way of doing things. By contrast, nongovernment services showed a willingness to participate in our project and reported high levels of staff and consumer interest.

TRANSLATING RESULTS FROM RESEARCH SETTINGS INTO EVERYDAY PRACTICE

A number of authors have identified the difficulties inherent in translating results from clinical studies into everyday clinical practice and into health decision-making (Brekke et al., 2007). A large proportion of psychotherapy research to date has occurred within academic institutions or tertiary hospitals set up for research. There is always the question of whether the findings from such clinical trials will translate into real-world settings, which are often characterized by organizational inertia, infrastructure and resource constraints, and an inability to control variables (Woolf, 2008). For research to make a difference to clinical practice and benefit consumers of such services, it is essential to assess the benefits of treatments within a broader community. There are two dimensions to transferring the findings outlined in this chapter to clinical settings; the first relates to the training and skill development of practitioners in the field, and the second relates to fees for services.

Practitioners can be trained to develop new skills and are often adept at developing new skills. They are also able, with the right education and support, to reconceptualize preconceived notions of mental disorders such as schizophrenia. As an example, we have seen a huge uptake of the recovery movement since the early to mid-2000s, with consumers, practitioners, and the nongovernment sector establishing services to better meet the needs of people with mental health difficulties. With a supportive infrastructure, we suggest that it is possible to develop and disseminate new ideas, up-skill clinicians, and develop appropriate services.

The fee for service issue is more complex. Within the Australian context, services for people with mental health problems are provided in the community through psychiatrists and psychologists. The workload demands upon psychiatrists are such that there is an overwhelming focus upon more seriously disturbed individuals with acute difficulties where medication is often the first line of treatment. Follow-up treatment is often focused upon the adjustment of medication and some psychotherapeutic support. Psychological interventions have increasingly become the domain of clinical psychologists who have extensive training in such approaches. However, clinical psychologists are largely funded within the public sector for short-term interventions, being allocated 10 individual and 10 group sessions per annum for any patient. Such limited funding restricts the types of treatment people with mental health problems can access within the public sector. The treatment model we described does not lend itself to such a brief intervention, but requires longer-term support to bring about the changes identified. Unless such constraints are addressed, the only individuals who will be able to benefit from longer-term interventions are participants in state-funded programs or research programs, which is clearly not satisfactory.

THE NATURE OF THE INTERVENTION

Health practitioners today are encouraged by the availability of an array of manuals that describe step-by-step treatment programs for specific *Diagnostic and Statistical Manual of Mental Disorders*, Fifth Edition (DSM-5) disorders. However, it is notable that little is written about the nature of human suffering and the obligation to treat the person as opposed to the condition. Metacognitive narrative psychotherapy requires the therapist to enter into a dialogue with the person in which both parties work toward making meaning of the person's experience within the context of their life. The process requires the therapist to be present to the 'other' and together address the concerns of the person. It also requires some degree of faith that the process entered into will, over time, be beneficial for a significant proportion of people who engage in the treatment. In addition to developing skills in disorder-specific treatments, therapists also need to be encouraged to appreciate the subjective aspects of mental health disorders and the intersubjective nature of psychotherapy.

FACILITATING THE DEVELOPMENT AND IMPLEMENTATION OF NEW INTERVENTIONS

We endeavored to address the needs of people with symptoms of schizophrenia in a naturalistic, real-world setting and conduct research that had clinical utility. The before-mentioned challenges meant that this was far from a straightforward task. We learned very quickly that we needed to be flexible, open-minded, and tolerant of others' prejudice and resistance if the project was to get off the ground. We also needed to adjust our views of the 'perfect' research project and take into account the limitations of the setting, patients, therapists, and treatment model. Based upon published case studies, we believed a project that supported a longer-term treatment program would likely provide patients with enough therapy to achieve positive gains and also produce unique insights into psychotherapeutic work with people with schizophrenia in a naturalistic setting. Upon reflection, we identified some important factors that addressed identified challenges and contributed to the successful implementation of a demanding clinical research program: the qualities of the therapists involved in the provision of the intervention, the quality of support provided to the therapists involved, the use of a principle-based treatment manual, and partnerships between researchers and clinicians.

THERAPIST QUALITIES

Certain therapist qualities emerged as paramount in the successful implementation of our project and the transferability of research-derived constructs into clinical practice. It has been said that a therapist working with people with schizophrenia should possess '. . . an interest in and a capacity to tolerate intense affect, dependency, and ambiguous communication . . . [and] be flexible, creative, and willing to admit when he or she is wrong' (Fenton, 2000, p. 49). Our experience supports this notion. Psychotherapy with a person with schizophrenia is often challenging, emotionally demanding, and slow to the point of being tedious. We have come to see the therapeutic process as more akin to a marathon than a sprint. Powerful feelings of dependence, rage, terror, and loneliness are evoked; self-other boundaries are confused; and a sense of interpersonal disconnection and mistrust is torturously ever-present. Therapist–patient dynamics are often intense and confusing. Therapists contributed most effectively to the therapeutic process when they were supported in being able to tolerate long periods of 'nothingness' in which progress seemed unlikely. As difficult as this was, we found that when tolerated successfully these periods were often precursors to patients' developing their capacity to reflect upon and narrate their own experiences.

We believe that this type of work may not be suitable for every therapist. With this in mind, we aimed to recruit therapists who were mindful and reflective in their practice, open to new ways of working with patients, able to sit with confusion and uncertainty without 'doing' or 'fixing,' comfortable with using the therapeutic relationship in their work, and able to tolerate slow and nonlinear therapeutic progress.

In an ideal research world, we may have also recruited experienced therapists, as they tend to produce better treatment outcomes. However, this proved difficult with many experienced therapists seemingly not having the time or motivation to learn and implement a new therapeutic approach. It can also be said that the use of experienced therapists tends to create research conditions that do not emulate real-world clinical settings, with staff in public institutions often including a significant cohort of novice clinicians. Because of this, the development and investigation of treatment approaches that can be easily taught to less experienced clinicians is essential. Given these reasons we recruited psychologists completing their postgraduate training. While this came with its challenges, what we discovered was important. Novice clinicians can be trained in the approach described, and with appropriate support they can successfully implement the approach with patients with schizophrenia.

THERAPIST SUPPORT

It is well established that supervision improves clinical practice, especially when working with complex presentations. For the therapists in our project it seemed that supervision represented a parallel process to their therapeutic work with patients. Supervision provided therapists with a space to think curiously about therapist–patient interactions, enhance self-awareness, and make meaning out of confusion. We cannot overstate the importance of having a space to *think with* a reflective other when working with people with schizophrenia. The very nature of psychosis induces a breakdown in reflective capacity, which subsequently makes affective experiences overwhelming. Therapists working with this patient group often experience a similar loss of the ability to think coupled with intense countertransference reactions of anger, despair, boredom, hopelessness, and frustration. Without an opportunity to reflect on these experiences, therapists are left feeling isolated, uncontained, emotionally drained, and sometimes even 'crazy.' Potentially, they may also be more likely to act out with patients and provide iatrogenic interventions.

We provided therapists with regular group and individual supervision throughout the project. The supervision sessions consisted largely of discussing therapist–patient interactions, exploring countertransference issues, and formulating cases using metacognitive narrative principles. We suggest that supervision forms an integral part of the administration of the approach described in both research and clinical settings.

USE OF A PRINCIPLE-BASED TREATMENT MANUAL

Treatment manuals have become an important component of psychotherapy research and practice. They serve to guide therapist training and adherence to the intended approach. However, treatment manuals can also be experienced as therapeutic 'straitjackets' that restrict therapists' natural style and clinical intuition. With this in mind, we did not want to produce a treatment 'cookbook' that describes the specific nature of the intervention in a step-by-step fashion. Instead, we developed a principle-based manual for the approach that describes specific treatment principles and broad therapy processes for each of the phases of treatment. Therapists are provided with both guidance and flexibility in their practice. The approach as described values clinical acumen and therapist intuition in the practice of psychotherapy and therefore leaves room for the therapists' own contribution to the treatment.

PARTNERSHIPS BETWEEN RESEARCHERS AND CLINICIANS

Translating research into practice can be compromised if the project is poorly implemented and, similarly, if the practitioners lack the skills to implement the practice. Poor implementation may lead to negative views of the intervention within real-world settings. It is thus imperative to ensure that the implementation phase is overseen sensitively and preferably within a collaborative context to support the long-term nature of the treatment model as described. Collaboration is important on a number of levels from the therapist–patient and therapist–supervisor relationships to the relationship between researchers and the broader community. We are of the view that one way to achieve these objectives is by developing partnerships between researchers and clinicians involved in the provision of services. A key element in the successful translation of research into practice is good communication between all stakeholders involved based upon a common language and understanding of the issues. This is particularly important in responding to the needs of people with symptoms of schizophrenia, which is considered to be the costliest of mental disorders in terms of treatment and service expenditure.

CONCLUSIONS

We have described a novel intervention. Our experience in a pilot implementation of this intervention revealed some barriers likely to be encountered when providing psychotherapeutic treatment for people with symptoms of schizophrenia. The most effective way of bringing the benefits of such research to the community is through engaging community organizations that collaborate most closely with people with mental health concerns and fostering collaborative research relationships with a view to enhancing public trust in the approaches being developed. In our own experience, individuals who have participated in programs, initially in a research capacity, are the first to espouse the benefits of the program and are enthusiastic to continue to be involved in ongoing support programs aimed at enhancing the capacities outlined in this chapter. However, it would be even more encouraging to involve state mental health services in the provision of such services, preferably within the context of ongoing research aimed at reducing the gap between researchers and practitioners. The process is never simple and will, no doubt, be facilitated by a greater body of supportive evidence for new interventions based upon randomized clinical trials, systematic literature reviews, adaptations of the approach at the delivery level, and practice-based research.

REFERENCES

American Psychiatric Association, (1987). *Diagnostic and statistical manual of mental disorders, third edition, revised (DSM-III-R)*. Washington, DC: American Psychiatric Association.

Anderson, H. (1997). *Conversation, language, and possibilities: A postmodern approach to therapy*. New York: Basic Book.

Angus, L. E., & McLeod, J. (2004). Self-multiplicity and narrative expression in psychotherapy. In H. J. M. Hermans & G. Dimaggio (Eds.), *The dialogical self in psychotherapy* (pp. 77–90). East Sussex, UK: Brunner-Routledge.

Bargenquast, R., & Schweitzer, R. (2013). Metacognitive narrative psychotherapy for people diagnosed with schizophrenia: An outline of a principle-based treatment manual. *Psychosis*, 1–11.

Bargenquast, R., & Schweitzer, R. D. (in press). Enhancing sense of recovery and self-reflectivity in people with schizophrenia: A pilot study of metacognitive narrative psychotherapy. *Psychology and Psychotherapy*.

Brekke, J. S., Ell, K., & Palinkas, L. A. (2007). Translational science at the National Institute of Mental Health: Can social work take its rightful place? *Research on Social Work Practice, 17*(1), 123–133.

Brune, M., Dimaggio, G., & Lysaker, P. H. (2011). Metacognition and social functioning in schizophrenia: Evidence, mechanisms of influence and treatment implications. *Current Psychiatry Reviews, 7*(3), 239–247.

Corrigan, P. W., Giffort, D., Rashid, F., Leary, M., & Okeke, I. (1999). Recovery as a psychological construct. *Community Mental Health Journal, 35*(3), 231–239.

Davidson, L. (2003). *Living outside mental illness: Qualitative studies of recovery in schizophrenia*. New York: New York University Press.

Dimaggio, G., Hermans, H. J. M., & Lysaker, P. H. (2010). Health and adaptation in a multiple self: The role of absence of dialogue and poor metacognition in clinical populations. *Theory & Psychology, 20*(3), 379–399.

Estroff, S. E. (1989). Self, identity, and subjective experiences of schizophrenia: In search of the subject. *Schizophrenia Bulletin, 15*(2), 189–196.

Fenton, W. S. (2000). Evolving perspectives on individual psychotherapy for schizophrenia. *Schizophrenia Bulletin, 26*(1), 47–72.

Frith, C. D. (1992). *The cognitive neuropsychology of schizophrenia*. Sussex, UK: Lawrence Erlbaum Associates.

Gottdiener, W. H., & Haslam, N. (2002). The benefits of individual psychotherapy for people diagnosed with schizophrenia: A meta-analytic review. *Ethical Human Sciences and Services, 4*(3), 163–187.

Hamm, J. A., Renard, S. B., Fogley, R. L., Leonhardt, B. L., Dimaggio, G., Buck, K. D., et al. (2012). Metacognition and social cognition in schizophrenia: Stability and relationship to concurrent and prospective symptom assessments. *Journal of Clinical Psychology, 68*(12), 1303–1312.

Harrington, L., Langdon, R., Siegert, R., & McClure, J. (2005). Schizophrenia, theory of mind, and persecutory delusions. *Cognitive Neuropsychiatry, 10*(2), 87–104.

Hermans, H. J. M. (1996). Voicing the self: From information processing to dialogical inter-change. *Psychological Bulletin, 119*, 31–50.

Hermans, H. J. M. (2004). The innovation of self-narratives: A dialogical approach. In L. E. Angus & J. McLeod (Eds.), *The handbook of narrative and psychotherapy: Practice, theory, and research.* (pp. 175–192). Thousand Oaks, CA: Sage Publications, Inc.

Hermans, H. J. M., & Dimaggio, G. (2004). The dialogical self in psychotherapy: Introduction. In H. J. M. Hermans & G. Dimaggio (Eds.), *The dialogical self in psychotherapy* (pp. 1–10). East Sussex: Brunner-Routledge.

Horowitz, R. (2002). Psychotherapy and schizophrenia: The mirror of countertransference. *Clinical Social Work Journal, 30*, 235–244.

Lukoff, D., Liberman, R. P., & Nuechterlein, K. H. (1986). Symptom monitoring in the rehabilita-tion of schizophrenic patients. *Schizophrenia Bulletin, 12*(4), 578–603.

Lysaker, P. H., Buck, K. D., Carcione, A., Procacci, M., Salvatore, G., Nicolò, G., et al. (2011). Addressing metacognitive capacity for self reflection in the psychotherapy for schizophrenia: A conceptual model of the key tasks and processes. *Psychology and Psychotherapy: Theory, Research and Practice, 84*(1), 58–69.

Lysaker, P. H., Carcione, A., Dimaggio, G., Johannesen, J. K., Nicolò, G., Procacci, M., et al. (2005a). Metacognition amidst narratives of self and illness in schizophrenia: Associations with neurocog-nition, symptoms, insight and quality of life. *Acta Psychiatrica Scandinavica, 112*(1), 64–71.

Lysaker, P. H., Clements, C. A., Plascak-Hallberg, C. D., Knipscheer, S. J., & Wright, D. E. (2002). Insight and personal narratives of illness in schizophrenia. *Psychiatry, 65*(3), 197–206.

Lysaker, P. H., Davis, L. W., Eckert, G. J., Strasburger, A. M., Hunter, N. L., & Buck, K. D. (2005b). Changes in narrative structure and content in schizophrenia in long term individual psychotherapy: A single case study. *Clinical Psychology & Psychotherapy, 12*(5), 406–416.

Lysaker, P. H., Dimaggio, G., Carcione, A., Procacci, M., Buck, K. D., Davis, L. W., et al. (2009). Metacognition and schizophrenia: The capacity for self-reflectivity as a predictor for prospec-tive assessments of work performance over six months. *Schizophrenia Research, 122*(1–3), 124–130.

Lysaker, P. H., Glynn, S. M., Wilkniss, S. M., & Silverstein, S. M. (2010). Psychotherapy and recovery from schizophrenia: A review of potential applications and need for future study. *Psychological Services, 7*(2), 75–91.

Lysaker, P. H., & Lysaker, J. T. (2004). Schizophrenia as dialogue at the ends of its tether: The relationship of disruptions in identity with positive and negative symptoms. *Journal of Constructivist Psychology, 17*(2), 105–119.

Lysaker, P. H., & Lysaker, J. T. (2006). Psychotherapy and schizophrenia: An analysis of require-ments of an individual psychotherapy for persons with profoundly disorganized selves. *Journal of Constructivist Psychology, 19*(2), 171–189.

Lysaker, P. H., & Lysaker, J. T. (2008). *Schizophrenia and the fate of the self.* Oxford: Oxford University Press.

Lysaker, P. H., Wickett, A. M., Campbell, K., & Buck, K. D. (2003). Movement towards coher-ence in the psychotherapy of schizophrenia: A method for assessing narrative transformation. *Journal of Nervous and Mental Disease, 191*(8), 538–541.

McAdams, D. P., & Janis, L. (2004). Narrative identity and narrative therapy. In L. E. Angus & J. McLeod (Eds.), *The handbook of narrative and psychotherapy.* (pp. 159–173). Thousand Oaks, CA: Sage Publications, Inc.

Nicolo, G., Dimaggio, G., Popolo, R., Carcione, A., Procacci, M., Hamm, J., et al. (2012). Associations of metacognition with symptoms, insight, and neurocognition in clinically stable outpatients with schizophrenia. *Journal of Nervous and Mental Disease, 200*(7), 644–647.

Roncone, R., Falloon, I. R. H., Mazza, M., De Risio, A., Pollice, R., Necozione, S., et al. (2002). Is theory of mind in schizophrenia more strongly associated with clinical and social functioning than with neurocognitive deficits? *Psychopathology, 35*(2), 280–288.

Salvatore, G., Procacci, M., Popolo, R., Nicola, G., Carcione, A., Semerari, A., et al. (2009). Adapted metacognitive interpersonal therapy for improving adherence to intersubjective contexts in a person with schizophrenia. *Clinical Case Studies, 8*(6), 473–488.

Sass, L. A., & Parnas, J. (2003). Schizophrenia, consciousness, and the self. *Schizophrenia Bulletin, 29*(3), 427–444.

Seikkula, J., Alakare, B., & Aaltonen, J. (2011). The comprehensive open-dialogue approach in Western Lapland: II. Long-term stability of acute psychosis outcomes in advanced community care. *Psychosis, 3*(3), 192–204.

Semerari, A., Carcione, A., Dimaggio, G., Falcone, M., Nicolò, G., Procacci, M., et al. (2003). How to evaluate metacognitive functioning in psychotherapy? The metacognition assessment scale and its applications. *Clinical Psychology & Psychotherapy, 10*(4), 238–261.

Woolf, S. H. (2008). The meaning of translational research and why it matters. *JAMA, 299*(2), 211–213.

Wykes, T., Steel, C., Everitt, B., & Tarrier, N. (2008). Cognitive behavior therapy for schizophrenia: Effect sizes, clinical models, and methodological rigor. *Schizophrenia Bulletin, 34*(3), 523–537.

Chapter 15

A Mentalization-Based Treatment Approach to Disturbances of Social Understanding in Schizophrenia

Benjamin K. Brent[1,2,3] and Peter Fonagy[4]

[1]*Beth Israel Deaconess Medical Center and Massachusetts Mental Health Center, Boston, MA, USA,*
[2]*Massachusetts General Hospital, Harvard Medical School, Boston, MA, USA,*
[3]*Harvard Medical School, Boston, MA, USA,* [4]*University College London, London, UK*

INTRODUCTION

Mentalization (i.e., the ability to think about states of mind (e.g., thoughts, feelings, intentions) in the self and other people) and metacognition ('thinking about thinking') have increasingly been linked both theoretically and empirically, as both constructs involve the capacity for meta-representation within social contexts (Lysaker *et al.*, 2011; Papeleontiou-Louca, 2008). Promising evidence is emerging for the value of metacognitive psychotherapy in the treatment of people with schizophrenia (see Chapter 6: *Metacognition in Schizophrenia Spectrum Disorders: Methods of Assessment and Associations*

Social Cognition and Metacognition in Schizophrenia.
DOI: http://dx.doi.org/10.1016/B978-0-12-405172-0.00015-6
© 2014 Elsevier Inc. All rights reserved.

with Psychosocial Function, Neurocognition, Symptoms, and Cognitive Style).
In this chapter, we present the rationale for adapting a mentalization-based treatment (MBT) approach to the recovery of mental state understanding in schizophrenia.

Consistent evidence shows that mentalization is significantly impaired in schizophrenia and may be a trait marker for the illness (Sprong *et al.*, 2007). For example, meta-analyses have shown that mentalization (typically measured via theory of mind (ToM) tasks) is abnormal: (1) among patients with schizophrenia in the absence of acute psychotic symptoms (Bora *et al.*, 2008); (2) in genetic high-risk (i.e., first-degree) relatives of patients (Bora and Pantelis, 2013); (3) in people meeting criteria for the schizophrenia prodrome (i.e., individuals with attenuated psychotic symptoms who are thought to be at increased risk of transitioning to schizophrenia) (Bora and Pantelis, 2013). The importance of mentalization deficits in the psychopathology of schizophrenia is further suggested by studies linking disturbances of mentalization with key psychotic symptoms (e.g., delusions and hallucinations) (Harrington *et al.*, 2005), poorer insight into illness (Bora *et al.*, 2007), and greater social dysfunction (Fett *et al.*, 2011) in people with the illness.

The mechanism coupling mentalization deficits with the symptoms and social impairment of schizophrenia, however, remains incompletely understood. Since acute psychotic symptoms commonly arise in the context of misunderstanding social situations (e.g., persecutory delusions and hallucinations), or as a result of aberrant self-appraisal with respect to other people (e.g., grandiose delusions), one hypothesis is that the breakdown of mental state understanding during stressful social settings may contribute to the disruption of reality testing (i.e., the ability to differentiate between internal and external stimuli) and, thus, to the emergence of psychosis in vulnerable individuals (Brent *et al.*, personal communication; van Os *et al.*, 2010). Fostering the capacity to mentalize within stressful social contexts, therefore, may be an important part of the mechanism of change for people with schizophrenia.

Previously, we have proposed that by facilitating social understanding, particularly within attachment relationships, MBT could play an important role in the recovery of the ability to mentalize and the capacity for interpersonal relatedness in people with schizophrenia (Brent, 2009; Brent *et al.*, 2014). Although MBT was initially developed to address the core symptoms of borderline personality disorder (e.g., affect dysregulation, poor impulse control, and self-harm behaviors) (Bateman and Fonagy, 2004), there is growing recognition that mentalization impairments occur across all severe psychological disorders (Fonagy *et al.*, 2012). We begin our discussion of the grounds for taking an MBT approach to psychosis by first outlining the attachment-based perspective regarding mentalization that is central to the MBT model. Next, we elaborate a developmentally informed neuropsychological model that links impairments of mentalization within attachment contexts to the emergence of psychosis in schizophrenia. This is followed by a description of the key features and basic clinical interventions of an MBT approach to the rehabilitation of self and other understanding in people with schizophrenia.

ATTACHMENT AND MENTALIZATION

From an MBT perspective, mentalization is crucially connected with the quality of attachment relationships (Fonagy et al., 2002). It is thought that because attachment relationships provide the context in which the ability to mentalize initially develops, relationships with attachment figures may constitute a social setting that is especially well adapted to facilitate curiosity about minds and the acquisition of mental state understanding (Fonagy et al., 2012). The developmental model of Fonagy and colleagues supporting the relationship between attachment and mentalization has been elaborated in detail elsewhere (Fonagy and Luyten, 2009; Fonagy et al., 2002). In what follows, we highlight some of the key aspects of the model.

During the first year of life, a child and a caregiver form an emotional bond (attachment), which results from the caregiver's repeated responses to the infant's early attachment-seeking behavior (e.g., clinging, smiling, crying) (Bowlby, 1969). It is thought that the quality of the attachment relationship ultimately provides an indication of the child's sense of safety in proximity to the caregiver and reflects the child's expectations of receiving comfort when turning to the caregiver during periods of emotional distress (Bowlby, 1969). In a secure attachment relationship, it is hypothesized that a caregiver's appropriately contingent responses to infantile distress ('marked mirroring'), which both acknowledge and modulate the child's affect, facilitate the child's ability to internalize self-states (Fonagy and Target, 1997). Eventually, these internalized, modulated representations of experiences of distress build up the child's capacity for affect regulation and lead to genuine relatedness with caregivers that include a sense of appropriate self-sufficiency and independence.

Alternatively, in insecure, or disorganized attachment relationships, misattunement of a caregiver to a child's experiences of distress (e.g., inaccurate, nonmentalizing, or unmodulated caregiver responses) may interfere with the child's capacity to take in representations of self-states during periods of affective arousal (Fonagy et al., 2012). A deficient ability to make use of accurate, internalized self-representations of distressing emotions may, in turn, create a vulnerability to deficits of mentalization particularly during subsequent moments of high affective arousal, undermining the development of a sense of agency, or self-efficacy (Fonagy et al., 2012). Among children experiencing trauma in attachment relationships, this vulnerability may be particularly marked, as thinking about the caregiver's mind can itself become associated with danger. By inhibiting the child's evolving curiosity about the mental states of others, maltreatment can undermine the child's sense of safety in linking states of mind with actions (Fonagy et al., 2002). As a result, insecurity may be expressed as a continued need for physical proximity to caregivers, or through exaggerated expressions of a sense of self-sufficiency, or independence from other people. Further, one of the consequences of impaired mentalization from an MBT standpoint is the likelihood that early, 'pre-mentalistic' forms of thinking may emerge during stress; including: (1) psychic equivalence thinking, in which the ability to consider outside perspectives on one's inner experience becomes lost and one's own thoughts and/or feelings are taken as unequivocally real; (2) pretend mode thinking, in which one's mental life is decoupled from any meaningful relationship to external reality, lacking genuine connectedness to actual experiences involving other people; (3) teleological thinking, in which the intentions and behaviors of others can be understood only in terms of physical actions (e.g., when 'genuine' caring is thought to be indicated only by physical displays of affection, such as hugging or touching) (Fonagy *et al.*, 2012).

Accumulating evidence supports the view that the child's ability to link mental states with behavior is closely associated with the quality of attachment relationships (Sharp and Fonagy, 2008). For example, security of attachment, as well as intercorrelated aspects of the caregiving environment that are indicative of a caregiver taking an interest in the child's mind, or of the caregiver's general capacity to think about behavior in terms of states of mind (e.g., parental 'mind-mindedness' and parental discourse about emotions), have been associated with precocious mentalizing in children, as evidenced by the early passing of ToM tasks (Sharp and Fonagy, 2008). By comparison, maltreated children have shown delays in the successful completion of ToM measures (Cicchetti *et al.*, 2003; Pears and Fisher, 2005). On the basis of the foregoing theory and evidence linking mentalization to the quality of attachment, from an MBT perspective, caregiving relationships very likely exert an important moderating influence on the individual's capacity for interpersonal understanding (Fonagy and Luyten, 2009).

ATTACHMENT, MENTALIZATION, AND PSYCHOSIS

The extent to which mentalization impairments that emerge in the setting of insecure attachment relationships play a role in the development of the symptoms and functional disability among people with schizophrenia is incompletely understood. Clearly, there are a multitude of pathways to deficits of mental state understanding that are unrelated to the nature of the childhood attachment environment – for example, chronic substance misuse or head injury, as well as experiences of trauma occurring outside of relationships with caregivers. We propose, however, that the evidence reviewed above regarding the relationship between mentalization impairments and attachment dysfunction may help advance current understanding of the links between aberrant social understanding and the symptoms and social impairment of schizophrenia. In particular, we hypothesize that aberrant mental state understanding arising in the context of attachment disturbances, especially in the context of trauma, may potentiate dysregulation of the stress-response system and

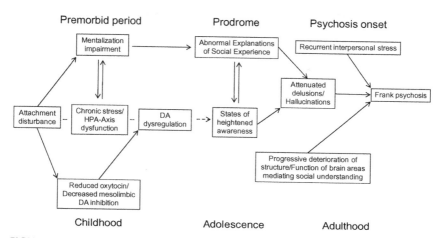

FIGURE 15.1 Developmental model linking mentalization impairments arising in attachment contexts and psychosis. In genetically predisposed individuals, attachment disturbances may contribute to: (1) impaired social understanding (mentalization disturbances) and (2) dopamine dysregulation during childhood resulting from the effects of chronic stress/HPA-axis dysfunction, combined with reduced oxytocin/mesocorticolimbic dopamine inhibition (premorbid period). This is followed in adolescence by the emergence of heightened states of awareness, which become maintained and reinforced owing to ongoing dopamine dysregulation, leading to the elaboration of abnormal explanations of social experience (prodromal symptoms). Recurrent stress in interpersonal, attachment-related contexts in conjunction with progressive deterioration of the structure and function of brain areas underpinning mental state understanding lead to further impairment in reality testing and the onset of frank psychosis in early adulthood. *DA: dopamine; HPA: hypothalamic-pituitary-adrenal.*

mesolimbic dopamine, leading to a heightened risk for developing psychosis among genetically vulnerable individuals (see Figure 15.1).

There is growing recognition that early childhood adversity, such as aberrant relationships with caregivers (Howes *et al.*, 2004) and other experiences of trauma (Varese *et al.*, 2012), represent an important environmental risk factor for schizophrenia. For example, in a comprehensive review, Varese and colleagues have shown that trauma during childhood (e.g., physical or sexual abuse, bullying, or neglect) is linked with a substantially greater risk for later psychosis, with an odds ratio of 2.8 (Varese *et al.*, 2012). Additionally, several studies have shown that dysfunction within the child–caregiver relationship that is plausibly related to attachment disturbance (e.g., poor caregiver sensitivity or attunement) is accompanied by an increased risk for psychosis. For example, two large prospective birth-cohort studies have found that children whose caregivers were less skilled in understanding their needs, or exhibited harsh or negative attitudes toward them, were at significantly greater risk of developing psychosis by adulthood (Cannon *et al.*, 2002; Jones *et al.*, 1994). Further, in the Finnish Adoption Study, it was shown that in adopted-away children of mothers with schizophrenia, the development of psychosis was significantly associated with having adoptive caregivers with higher levels of communication deviance – that is, problems establishing or maintaining a shared focus of attention with their adopted child (Wahlberg *et al.*, 1997).

It is thought that chronic stressors, such as insecure attachment relationships and the experience of adverse childhood events, increase the risk for psychosis through their effect on the hypothalamic-pituitary-adrenal (HPA) axis stress response system (Phillips *et al.*, 2006). Since the HPA-axis system triggers dopamine synthesis and release, chronic stressors that cause HPA-axis overactivity may result in the dysregulation of prefrontal and corticolimbic dopamine that has been linked with psychosis (Phillips *et al.*, 2006). We suggest, however, that in the setting of aberrant attachment relationships, dopamine dysfunction could become further heightened as a result of deficient levels of oxytocin – the key neurohormone associated with attachment and prosocial behavior. Studies have found, for example, that oxytocin is reduced in insecurely attached and emotionally neglected children (Strathearn, 2011; Wismer Fries *et al.*, 2005). Because oxytocin has been shown to have an inhibitory effect on mesocorticolimbic dopamine (Baskerville and Douglas, 2010), lower oxytocin levels may interact with HPA-axis dysfunction to amplify the extent of dopamine dysregulation among people at risk for schizophrenia who have aberrant relationships with caregivers.

According to aberrant salience models of psychosis (Kapur, 2003), dopamine dysregulation may result in 'heightened states of awareness', creating a biologic vulnerability to impairments in differentiating between representations of internal and external stimuli. People at risk for psychosis who develop mentalization impairments in the context of aberrant attachment relationships, therefore, may be particularly susceptible to forming abnormal explanatory models of their social experience (i.e., 'prodromal' symptoms) during acute stress. For such individuals, impaired self-appraisal, or difficulties discerning others' intentions, could lead to the emergence of mild grandiose or paranoid beliefs. By the same token, experiences of a compromised sense of agency associated with an impaired capacity to differentiate between internal and external stimuli could result in an increased risk for aberrant perceptual experiences. Over time, these attenuated delusional beliefs and perceptual abnormalities could become reinforced and perpetuated as a result of ongoing dopamine dysregulation, leading to anomalous self and social experience and, in some cases, to frank psychosis.

Although speculative, several lines of evidence support the view that premorbid and/or prodromal mentalization-mediated deficits of self and other understanding, as well as of other social anomalies, precede psychosis. For example, alterations of the sense of self (e.g., self–other boundary discrimination impairments) are among the earliest reported symptoms in children who go on to develop schizophrenia (Klosterkotter *et al.*, 2001; Poulton *et al.*, 2000). Further, social dysfunction (Amminger *et al.*, 1999; Tarbox and Pogue-Geile, 2008) and aberrant perspective-taking abilities (Schiffman *et al.*, 2004) are significantly greater during the prepsychosis development of people with schizophrenia. Since deficits of mental state understanding have been linked with impaired social function (Fett *et al.*, 2011) and other forms of social cognition (e.g., self-face recognition (Irani *et al.*, 2006)) in schizophrenia, these findings support the possibility that mentalization deficits associated with disruptions in early attachment relationships occur in 'preschizophrenia children'.

MENTALIZATION-BASED TREATMENT FOR PSYCHOSIS

Psychoeducation, Case Formulation, and the Assessment of Mentalization

Central goals of the MBT approach include fostering the ability to mentalize about the self and other people and enhancing understanding of how mentalization is affected by specific relational contexts (Bateman and Fonagy, 2012). During the initial treatment of people with schizophrenia, psychoeducation, case formulation, and the assessment of mentalization in conjunction with structured clinical management (e.g., pharmacotherapy, crisis planning, and active patient follow-up for missed sessions) are provided to facilitate a mentalizing discourse that serves to help patients organize and navigate what can often be a very confusing and dispiriting social world. These structuring aspects of an MBT-based approach to deficits of mentalization in schizophrenia are thought to be particularly important in reducing the potentially disruptive effects of stress that are intrinsic to the social interaction within the therapeutic setting itself, particularly for people with significant impairments conceptualizing the experience of self and other (Bateman and Krawitz, 2013). For example, by providing explicit information about mentalization, patient psychoeducation at the outset of treatment helps facilitate a collaborative treatment process (Tobias, Haslam-Hopwood, Allen, Stein, & Bleiberg, 2006). This includes: briefly and succinctly defining what mentalization is (e.g., thinking about mental states); illustrating mentalization with simple examples (e.g., asking patients what they would think if they saw a man caught in a rainstorm without an umbrella running under a storefront awning); explaining how mentalizing is related to the quality of interpersonal relationships/attachment contexts and emotional states; discussing how the loss of the ability to mentalize (particularly during emotional distress) can contribute to psychosis; and, explaining that the goal of treatment is to help reduce psychosis (or prevent relapses) and to improve social function by promoting the patient's ability to mentalize.

Developing a case formulation and assessing the patient's capacity to mentalize further help to establish a treatment focus, as they serve to identify the specific social and attachment contexts within which disruptions of mental state understanding are most likely linked with psychosis. As an example, Federico's initial case formulation illustrates how attempting to understand a patient's difficulties from a mentalizing perspective can help bring the initial goals of treatment into focus (Box 15.1).

BOX 15.1   Personal History

Federico is a 27-year-old, single, college-educated man, with one prior psychiatric hospitalization for persecutory delusions and hallucinations. He has one younger sister and describes his father as demanding and critical, and his mother as deferential and emotionally reserved. Federico experienced early parental maltreatment and neglect, including having been repeatedly locked in closets for long periods of time as a punishment for episodes of misbehavior during childhood. In high school, Federico felt chronically worthless. He became increasingly socially withdrawn, preoccupied with his inner fantasy life and philosophical questions about whether his life was only a dream. He did well academically, however, and received a scholarship to go to college. While in his second year of college, Federico became progressively socially isolated and had his first episode of psychosis. After being stabilized on antipsychotic medication, he was able to complete his B.A. Since then, he has lived with his parents while working as a cashier at a convenience store. Although his acute psychotic symptoms have abated, he describes increasing paranoia and preoccupation with self-criticism during visits with his extended family. Although wanting to feel more connected with other people, Federico mostly keeps to himself and is reluctant to pursue friendships, owing to his conviction that others will see him as 'damaged'.

Engagement in Therapy

Federico is likely to have misgivings about staying in therapy because of his possible expectation of criticism, or being perceived as 'damaged' by his therapist if he opens up. For example, if he comes to perceive his therapist as critical, Federico may be apt to become paranoid and then withdraw from treatment.

Relationship Difficulties

Federico has difficulties communicating his interests in greater connectedness with other people. He assumes that others see him in a negative light and shows an impaired capacity to be curious about why other people would see him that way. To manage his social anxiety, Federico tends to withdraw from social situations, which then intensifies his sense of anomy.

Psychosis

Both the initial emergence of Federico's 'prodromal' symptoms (e.g., preoccupation with fantasy and existential concerns) and his episode of frank psychosis were associated with experiences of significant disturbances involving, or separations from, attachment figures. Since college, Federico has lived at home, which may indicate, at least in part, his need to maintain physical proximity to caregivers as a way to help manage underlying difficulties with affect regulation and coherent self-experience during stress. Federico may be most susceptible to recurrent psychosis in the context of perceived threats to attachment relationships – e.g., during family gatherings, when he often assumes that his family members are harboring critical judgments about him.

Mentalizing

Concrete mentalizing: Federico often presumes to know how other people think and feel about him based on his interpretation of other people's body language and facial expressions. He also shows a limited ability to test his assumptions by trying to find out more about the way other people actually think or feel.

Sensitive mentalizing: Federico recognizes feeling self-critical because he fears that he has been a disappointment to his parents. He also demonstrates curiosity about his sister's thoughts and feelings about him, which he relates to his sense that she is not typically critical of him. Although commonly retreating from social contact, Federico also acknowledges wanting to have relationships with greater possibilities for openness and for sharing thoughts and emotions.

Initial Focus

For Federico, disruptions of mentalization and a heightened vulnerability to paranoia and psychosis seem to be closely linked with experiences of criticism, particularly in attachment contexts. Two goals of initial treatment, therefore, are to foster Federico's capacity for curiosity about other people's minds and to help him understand more about how the loss of the ability to mentalize may be related to the experience of criticism within interpersonal settings.

During the initial assessment and case formulation, mentalization is assessed through the exploration of the patient's capacity for mental state understanding within specific interpersonal and attachment contexts. In the MBT model, mentalization is conceptualized as a multidimensional construct that includes four functional polarities: automatic (spontaneous, automatic) versus controlled (explicit); internally focused (psychological interior) versus externally focused (physical/visible); self-oriented versus other-oriented; and cognitive versus affective (Fonagy and Luyten, 2009). Patients commonly show impairment within some but not all aspects of mentalization (Fonagy and Luyten, 2009). Thus, the assessment of mentalization helps alert the therapist to the specific domains of mentalization that are impaired and should be addressed during treatment. Questions that are used to explore mentalization within relational and attachment contexts include: 'Why do you think your parents or partner act the way that they do?' 'How do you think you have changed since childhood?' 'Have you ever felt unwanted?' 'Do you remember what you were feeling at that time?' (Bateman and Fonagy, 2012).

Therapeutic Stance

In MBT, the therapist's focus on the patient's mind is crucial to developing a collaborative mentalizing process. Toward this end, maintaining an inquisitive, 'not-knowing' therapeutic stance with respect to a patient's thoughts and feelings is considered a key part of the process of stimulating the patient's curiosity about his or her own mind and facilitating the patient's ability to generate 'second-order representations' of self-states (Bateman and Fonagy, 2012). Active questioning about the patient's state of mind and detailed exploration of how the patient's mental states are related to particular interpersonal contexts are employed to help patients continue to mentalize when stressed, or to recover the capacity to mentalize when it has been lost, or stopped. In the following vignette, we illustrate the use of a 'not-knowing' therapeutic stance in the case of a patient with schizophrenia (Box 15.2).

As highlighted in Box 15.2, by taking a not-knowing stance with respect to James's behavior (i.e., by expressing his own uncertainty about the meaning of James's actions), the therapist hoped to initiate a process in which James could begin to feel curious about how his behavior might be connected to a state of mind (e.g., wanting to feel close to another person), as opposed to simply being about the physical relationship between the objects in the consulting room (e.g., the briefcase, the chair, and the desk).

Basic Interventions

A key MBT principle is that therapeutic interventions need to be tailored to a patient's capacity to mentalize during any given psychotherapy session (Bateman and Fonagy, 2012). Of particular importance, because heightened affective arousal is likely to have a disruptive impact on the ability to mentalize, less complex interventions may be called for during sessions when intense emotions are expressed, in order to foster a sense of safety and avoid breakdowns in mentalizing function (Bateman and Fonagy, 2012). Because patients

---

BOX 15.2

James was a man in his 20s with schizophrenia and an extensive history of childhood maltreatment. During the initial phase of treatment, James exhibited a pattern of behavior that was confusing to his therapist: on several occasions James entered the consultation room, sat down in the therapist's chair by his desk, and then began to talk as though nothing notable or unusual had happened. Rather than telling James where to sit, the therapist attempted to initiate a mentalizing process around James' behavior. He began by noting his observation that James sat in a different chair during different sessions, but that he did not understand why. The therapist then wondered if James had any thoughts about it. James replied that when he sat in the chair at the desk, he could see that the therapist's briefcase and notebook were located close enough to him that he could touch them. The therapist thought that given James' history of maltreatment in caregiving relationships sitting in his chair could reflect a behavioral (nonmentalizing) way of trying to communicate something about his fears and wishes about proximity to him (e.g., being close enough to touch, or to be touched). The therapist then asked James if when sitting in the chair by the desk, he [James] felt closer to him. James said that he did. James's therapist then said that he felt that what was important was not where James sat during their sessions, but that the two of them could talk about, and try to understand, all the things that were on James's mind together.

with schizophrenia frequently have difficulty with basic aspects of mental state understanding (e.g., labeling thoughts and feelings), complex interpretations of 'deep' unconscious motivations and of the relationship between the distant past and the present are generally avoided. Core MBT interventions and principles that can be applied to the psychotherapy of patients with schizophrenia include: 'soundbite' observations (i.e., short and simple); focusing on the patient's mind (particularly affective states), as opposed to his/her behavior or external circumstances; active, nonjudgmental listening; questioning to provoke curiosity about the mentalistic motivations related to behavior in the self and other people; using the therapist's mind as a model; praising positive mentalization; stopping, 'rewinding', and exploring moments when mentalization has become derailed, to enhance reflective ability; and an overall determination to try to understand things from the patient's perspective (Bateman and Fonagy, 2012). We highlight the use of some of these basic MBT techniques in a psychotherapy session with a patient, Nadia, in Box 15.3.

BOX 15.3

Nadia, a 38-year-old woman with schizophrenia, had been talking about how her mother seemed unenthusiastic about her interest in applying for a new job. She spoke in great detail about her conversation, but with limited affect and without cluing her therapist in to what she might want help understanding about her experience. The therapist noticed that he was finding it hard to pay attention to Nadia's narrative. As Nadia went on, the therapist stopped listening to Nadia. He remembered that he had forgotten to move his car, and that he would have to do so after the therapy session to avoid getting a parking ticket. He then began thinking about the possibility of having engine failure while moving his car later on, and nearly having a traffic accident as a result. In the midst of his musings, the therapist began to wonder why he was thinking about having engine failure and a traffic accident when attempting to move his car, while Nadia was talking about changing jobs. Were the therapist's inability to focus on Nadia's story and Nadia's own constricted affect and vagueness perhaps both ways of avoiding anxiety that each of them were experiencing about the possibility that the stress of managing a transition at work could precipitate another breakdown for Nadia?

THERAPIST: I'm sorry to interrupt you, Nadia, but I'm noticing that I'm having trouble following you today, and I'm not sure why that is. Maybe we could try to understand it together?
PATIENT: Well, I really didn't know what to talk about today when I came in.
THERAPIST: I have to say, while you were talking about your conversation with your mom, it was hard for me to tell how you were feeling about it. Do you remember what you were feeling at the time of your conversation?
PATIENT: I think I was feeling a little worried that she was going to tell me that changing jobs might not be a good idea, that I couldn't do it. The last time I made a big change, I wound up in the hospital again.

> THERAPIST: You know, as I think about your situation, I find myself also feeling a bit anxious, and maybe that made it hard for me to pay attention today.
> PATIENT: Well, I'm not sure myself if I can handle a job with more responsibility. I don't know if I'm ready yet . . . But, I'm worried that if I don't do it, my parents will be disappointed in me.

In this example, the therapist uses his experience of what might be termed 'concordant countertransference' (Bateman and Fonagy, 2012) (i.e., emotional responses in the therapist that may resonate with the patient's underlying affect) to try to initiate a mentalizing process at a moment when he noted that his own mentalizing function (and perhaps also that of the patient) had become disrupted. This involved turning back ('rewinding') to a break in mentalizing, exploring the affective experience of both patient and therapist, and talking with the patient about her experience in a nonjudgmental way and at a conceptual level that the patient seemed able to grasp.

CONCLUSION

There is mounting evidence that treatments that target deficits of mental state understanding within social contexts, such as metacognitive psychotherapy, contribute to significant improvement in the social functioning of people with schizophrenia (Lysaker *et al.*, 2007; Lysaker *et al.*, 2010; Lysaker *et al.*, 2011; Salvatore *et al.*, 2012). Further, avatar therapy for refractory auditory hallucinations, which implicitly initiates a mentalizing process as patients create a dialogue with an externalized avatar based on voices that have previously been experienced as 'other', and about which the person could not mentalize, has proven effective in reducing both the intensity and frequency of persistent auditory hallucinations (Leff *et al.*, 2013). Additionally, psychosocial interventions that focus on enhancing self-reflective and/or perspective-taking abilities have been associated with better real-world functional outcomes in schizophrenia (Eack *et al.*, 2009; Subramaniam *et al.*, 2012). Taken together, these findings support the idea that by fostering social understanding, MBT-based interventions could constitute a valuable additional approach to the recovery of the ability to mentalize, and interpersonal relatedness among people with schizophrenia.

We wish to emphasize that although MBT focuses on the links between mentalization and attachment, this is in no way intended to blame caregivers as the cause of these deficits in schizophrenia. First, in the absence of an underlying genetic vulnerability, attachment dysfunction would be highly unlikely to contribute to the emergence of psychosis. In our view, the reason for considering the possibility that the capacity for social understanding may be linked to the quality of attachment relationships in people who develop schizophrenia is motivated by the need to take a compassionate stance to the internal experience of persons with psychosis. It is also consonant with the evidence supporting the beneficial impact of family-based interventions for schizophrenia on clinical course and functional outcomes (McFarlane *et al.*, 2003), which suggests that relationships with caregivers exert an important influence on the lives of people suffering from the illness (McFarlane and Lukens, 1998). Future empirical research is needed, however, to test whether MBT techniques will ultimately prove useful in the recovery of people with schizophrenia.

REFERENCES

Amminger, G. P., Pape, S., Rock, D., Roberts, S. A., Ott, S. L., Squires-Wheeler, E., et al. (1999). Relationship between childhood behavioral disturbance and later schizophrenia in the New York High-Risk Project. *American Journal of Psychiatry*, *156*(4), 525–530.

Baskerville, T. A., & Douglas, A. J. (2010). Dopamine and oxytocin interactions underlying behaviors: Potential contributions to behavioral disorders. *CNS Neuroscience & Therapeutics*, *16*(3), e92–e123.

Bateman, A. W., & Fonagy, P. (2004). Mentalization-based treatment of BPD. *Journal of Personality Disorders*, *18*(1), 36–51.

Bateman, A. W., & Fonagy, P. (2012). Individual techniques of the basic model. In A. W. Bateman & P. Fonagy (Eds.), *Handbook of mentalizing in mental health practice* (pp. 67–80). Washington, DC: American Psychiatric Publishing, Inc.

Bateman, A. W., & Krawitz, R. (2013). *Borderline personality disorder: An evidence-based guide for generalist mental health professionals*. Oxford: Oxford University Press.

Bora, E., Gokcen, S., Kayahan, B., & Veznedaroglu, B. (2008). Deficits of social-cognitive and social-perceptual aspects of theory of mind in remitted patients with schizophrenia: Effect of residual symptoms. *Journal of Nervous and Mental Disease*, *196*(2), 95–99.

Bora, E., & Pantelis, C. (2013). Theory of mind impairments in first-episode psychosis, individuals at ultra-high risk for psychosis and in first-degree relatives of schizophrenia: Systematic review and meta-analysis. *Schizophrenia Research*, *144*(1–3), 31–36.

Bora, E., Sehitoglu, G., Aslier, M., Atabay, I., & Veznedaroglu, B. (2007). Theory of mind and unawareness of illness in schizophrenia: Is poor insight a mentalizing deficit? *European Archives of Psychiatry and Clinical Neuroscience*, *257*(2), 104–111.

Bowlby, J. (1969). *Attachment and loss*. London: Hogarth Press and the Institute of Psycho-Analysis.

Brent, B. (2009). Mentalization-based psychodynamic psychotherapy for psychosis. *Journal of Clinical Psychology*, *65*(8), 803–814.

Brent, B. K., Holt, D. J., Keshavan, M. S., Seidman, L. J., Fonagy, P. (2014). Mentalization-based treatment for psychosis: linking an attachment-based model to the psychotherapy for impaired mental state understanding in people with psychotic disorders. *Israel Journal of Psychiatry and Related Sciences*, *50*(4), 239–246.

Cannon, M., Caspi, A., Moffitt, T. E., Harrington, H., Taylor, A., Murray, R. M., et al. (2002). Evidence for early-childhood, pan-developmental impairment specific to schizophreniform disorder: Results from a longitudinal birth cohort. *Archives of General Psychiatry*, *59*(5), 449–456.

Cicchetti, D., Rogosch, F. A., Maughan, A., Toth, S. L., & Bruce, J. (2003). False belief understanding in maltreated children. *Development and Psychopathology*, *15*(4), 1067–1091.

Eack, S., Greenwald, D. P., Hogarty, S. S., Cooley, S. J., DiBarry, A. L., Montrose, D. M., et al. (2009). Cognitive enhancement therapy for early-course schizophrenia: Effects of a two-year randomized controlled trial. *Psychiatric Services*, *60*, 1468–1476.

Fett, A. K., Viechtbauer, W., Dominguez, M. D., Penn, D. L., van Os, J., & Krabbendam, L. (2011). The relationship between neurocognition and social cognition with functional outcomes in schizophrenia: A meta-analysis. *Neuroscience and Biobehavioral Reviews*, *35*(3), 573–588.

Fonagy, P., Bateman, A. W., & Luyten, P. (2012). Introduction and overview. In A. W. Bateman & P. Fonagy (Eds.), *Handbook of mentalization in mental health practice* (pp. 3–42). Washington, DC: American Psychiatric Publishing, Inc.

Fonagy, P., Gergely, G., Jurist, E., & Target, M. (2002). *Affect Regulation, Mentalization, and the development of the self*. New York: Other Press.

Fonagy, P., & Luyten, P. (2009). A developmental, mentalization-based approach to the understanding and treatment of borderline personality disorder. *Development and Psychopathology*, *21*(4), 1355–1381.

Fonagy, P., & Target, M. (1997). Attachment and reflective function: Their role in self-organization. *Development and Psychopathology*, *9*(4), 679–700.

Harrington, L., Siegert, R. J., & McClure, J. (2005). Theory of mind in schizophrenia: A critical review. *Cognitive Neuropsychiatry*, *10*(4), 249–286.

Howes, O. D., McDonald, C., Cannon, M., Arseneault, L., Boydell, J., & Murray, R. M. (2004). Pathways to schizophrenia: The impact of environmental factors. *International Journal of Neuropsychopharmacology*, *7*(Suppl 1), S7–S13.

Irani, F., Platek, S. M., Panyavin, I. S., Calkins, M. E., Kohler, C., Seigel, S. J., et al. (2006). Self-face recognition and theory of mind in patients with schizophrenia and first-degree relatives. *Schizophrenia Research*, *88*(1–3), 151–160.

Jones, P., Rodgers, B., Murray, R., & Marmot, M. (1994). Child development risk factors for adult schizophrenia in the British 1946 birth cohort. *Lancet*, *344*(8934), 1398–1402.

Kapur, S. (2003). Psychosis as a state of aberrant salience: A framework linking biology, phenomenology, and pharmacology in schizophrenia. *American Journal of Psychiatry*, *160*(1), 13–23.

Klosterkotter, J., Hellmich, M., Steinmeyer, E. M., & Schultze-Lutter, F. (2001). Diagnosing schizophrenia in the initial prodromal phase. *Archives of General Psychiatry*, *58*(2), 158–164.

Leff, J., Williams, G., Huckvale, M. A., Arbuthnot, M., & Leff, A. P. (2013). Computer-assisted therapy for medication-resistant auditory hallucinations: Proof-of-concept study. *British Journal of Psychiatry*, *202*, 428–433.

Lysaker, P. H., Buck, K. D., Carcione, A., Procacci, M., Salvatore, G., Nicolo, G., et al. (2010). Addressing metacognitive capacity for self-reflection in the psychotherapy for schizophrenia: A conceptual model of the key tasks and processes. *Psychology and Psychotherapy: Theory, Research, and Practice*, *84*, 58–69.

Lysaker, P. H., Buck, K. D., & Ringer, J. (2007). The recovery of metacognitive capacity in schizophrenia across 32 months of individual psychotherapy: A case study. *Psychotherapy Research*, *17*(6), 713–720.

Lysaker, P. H., Gumley, A., & Dimaggio, G. (2011). Metacognitive disturbances in persons with severe illness: Theory, correlates with psychopathology and models of psychotherapy. *Psychology and Psychotherapy: Theory, Research, and Practice*, *84*, 1–8.

McFarlane, W. R., Dixon, L., Lukens, E., & Lucksted, A. (2003). Family psychoeducation and schizophrenia: A review of the literature. *Journal of Marital and Family Therapy*, *29*(2), 223–245.

McFarlane, W. R., & Lukens, E. P. (1998). Insight, families, and education: An exploration of the role of attribution in clinical outcome. In X. F. Amador & A. S. David (Eds.), *Insight and psychosis: Awareness of illness in schizophrenia and related disorders* (pp. 317–331). New York: Oxford University Press.

Papeleontiou-Louca, E. (2008). *Metacognition and theory of mind.* Newcastle, UK: Cambridge Scholars Publishing.

Pears, K. C., & Fisher, P. A. (2005). Emotion understanding and theory of mind among maltreated children in foster care: Evidence of deficits. *Development and Psychopathology, 17*(1), 47–65.

Phillips, L. J., McGorry, P. D., Garner, B., Thompson, K. N., Pantelis, C., Wood, S. J., et al. (2006). Stress, the hippocampus and the hypothalamic-pituitary-adrenal axis: Implications for the development of psychotic disorders. *Australian and New Zealand Journal of Psychiatry, 40*(9), 725–741.

Poulton, R., Caspi, A., Moffitt, T. E., Cannon, M., Murray, R., & Harrington, H. (2000). Children's self-reported psychotic symptoms and adult schizophreniform disorder: A 15-year longitudinal study. *Archives of General Psychiatry, 57*(11), 1053–1058.

Salvatore, G., Lysaker, P. H., Gumley, A., Popolo, R., Mari, J., & Dimaggio, G. (2012). Out of illness experience: Metacognition-oriented therapy for promoting self-awareness in individuals with psychosis. *American Journal of Psychotherapy, 66*, 85–106.

Schiffman, J., Lam, C. W., Jiwatram, T., Ekstrom, M., Sorensen, H., & Mednick, S. (2004). Perspective-taking deficits in people with schizophrenia spectrum disorders: A prospective investigation. *Psychological Medicine, 34*(8), 1581–1586.

Sharp, C., & Fonagy, P. (2008). Social cognition and attachment-related disorders. In Sharp, C., Fonagy, P., and Goodyer, I. (Eds.), *Social cognition and developmental psychology* (pp. 271–302). Oxford: Oxford University Press.

Sprong, M., Schothorst, P., Vos, E., Hox, J., & van Engeland, H. (2007). Theory of mind in schizophrenia: Meta-analysis. *British Journal of Psychiatry, 191*, 5–13.

Strathearn, L. (2011). Maternal neglect: Oxytocin, dopamine and the neurobiology of attachment. *Journal of Neuroendocrinology, 23*(11), 1054–1065.

Subramaniam, K., Luks, T. L., Fisher, M., Simpson, G. V., Nagarajan, S., & Vinogradov, S. (2012). Computerized cognitive training restores neural activity within the reality monitoring network in schizophrenia. *Neuron, 73*, 842–853.

Tarbox, S. I., & Pogue-Geile, M. F. (2008). Development of social functioning in preschizophrenia children and adolescents: A systematic review. *Psychological Bulletin, 134*(4), 561–583.

Tobias, G., Haslam-Hopwood, G., Allen, J. G., Stein, A., & Bleiberg, E. (2006). Enhancing mentalizing through psycho-education. In J. G. A. P. Fonagy (Ed.), *Handbook of mentalization-based treatment* (pp. 249–267). Chichester, UK: John Wiley & Sons Ltd.

van Os, J., Kenis, G., & Rutten, B. P. (2010). The environment and schizophrenia. *Nature, 468*(7321), 203–212.

Varese, F., Smeets, F., Drukker, M., Lieverse, R., Lataster, T., Viechtbauer, W., et al. (2012). Childhood adversities increase the risk of psychosis: A meta-analysis of patient-control, prospective- and cross-sectional cohort studies. *Schizophrenia Bulletin, 38*(4), 661–671.

Wahlberg, K. E., Wynne, L. C., Oja, H., Keskitalo, P., Pykalainen, L., Lahti, I., et al. (1997). Gene-environment interaction in vulnerability to schizophrenia: Findings from the Finnish Adoptive Family Study of Schizophrenia. *American Journal of Psychiatry, 154*(3), 355–362.

Wismer Fries, A. B., Ziegler, T. E., Kurian, J. R., Jacoris, S., & Pollak, S. D. (2005). Early experience in humans is associated with changes in neuropeptides critical for regulating social behavior. *Proceedings of the National Academy of Sciences of the United States of America, 102*(47), 17237–17240.

The Relationship Between Metacognitive Profile, Attachment Pattern, and Intersubjective Process in Psychotherapy of a Person Recovering from First-Episode Schizophrenia

Susanne Harder and Sarah Daniel
University of Copenhagen, Copenhagen, Denmark

INTRODUCTION

There is increasing evidence for a compromised metacognitive capacity in individuals diagnosed with schizophrenia (Lysaker *et al.*, 2012). Impaired metacognitive functions have been linked to negative and disorganized symptoms (Lysaker *et al.*, 2011) but especially to different aspects of social

Social Cognition and Metacognition in Schizophrenia.
DOI: http://dx.doi.org/10.1016/B978-0-12-405172-0.00016-8
© 2014 Elsevier Inc. All rights reserved.

functioning such as poor social skills, lower capacity for intimacy, as well as reduced likelihood of returning to gainful employment (Brüne *et al.* 2011; Lysaker *et al.*, 2010). The developmental roots of impaired metacognition in schizophrenia are not well understood. One model proposes that insecure and disorganized infant attachment patterns play an important part in the compromised metacognition found in schizophrenia (Liotti and Gumley, 2008). Insecure attachment and compromised metacognition, however, are also found in other diagnoses, such as bipolar disorder (BPD) and post-traumatic stress disorder (PTSD), and the specific relationship between insecure attachment and metacognitive problems in psychosis is not well described. Furthermore, little is known about how these deficits could be addressed psychotherapeutically in psychosis.

In this chapter, we aim to explore these issues by analyzing the manifestations and changes of metacognitive capacity, attachment, and social functioning across 2.5 years of psychotherapy with a single client diagnosed with first-episode psychosis (FEP). The client, Camellia, who was treated by the first author (Susanne Harder), was also interviewed with the Adult Attachment Interview (AAI) to assess her current state of mind with respect to attachment. In our analysis of the case, we will put particular emphasis on how an understanding of attachment-related dynamics may inform our conceptualization of the metacognitive problems and psychotic symptoms of the client. We will end by considering the change experienced by Camellia after 2.5 years of therapy, and how this change may be understood in relation to the work with intersubjective and metacognitive processes in the context of treatment.

Metacognition

The term metacognition and related terms from various traditions such as theory of mind, social cognition, and mentalization refer to very similar processes concerning a person's general capacity to make sense of their own mental processes and states, as well as the mental processes and states of others. Metacognition is proposed as an umbrella concept for these related concepts and refers to a broad spectrum of activities from how people monitor their own and other's behavior to the extent to which they can create complex and integrated ideas about themselves and others and utilize this information to respond to psychological and interpersonal challenges (Dimaggio and Lysaker, 2010; Lysaker *et al.*, 2005; Semerari *et al.*, 2003). It is hypothesized that metacognition consists of an array of subfunctions such as (1) understanding of self, (2) understanding of others, and (3) mastery, that is, the capacity to use the understanding of self and others to actively find solutions when faced with conflicting emotions or interpersonal challenges. These subfunctions may be semi-independent and may give rise to different profiles of compromised metacognition, which are characteristic of different mental disorders. Attachment research provides a promising approach to understanding the development of specific forms of metacognitive deficit, including those that may be characteristic of schizophrenia.

The Roots of Metacognition in Attachment Relationships

Developmentally, the capacity to mentalize is tied to experiences in attachment relationships and is enhanced by attachment security (Fonagy *et al.*, 2002). Conversely, negative interpersonal experiences and insecure attachment relationships reduce an individual's opportunities to develop mentalization skills, compromising his or her understanding of mental states. An important function of the attachment system is regulation of negative affect. The attachment system is activated in situations of distress – in infants typically in the presence of strangers, in unfamiliar surroundings, when feeling ill, or during separation from caregivers. The activation of the attachment system elicits a need for protection and comfort. When the caregiver provides emotional and/or physical closeness, the attachment system is deactivated and the infant calms down. It is the successful dyadic coregulation of emotional states – the infant signaling distress and seeking proximity and the caregiver providing comfort in a sensitive and consistent manner – that defines the secure attachment relationship.

An important developmental product of childhood attachment-related experiences is the so-called 'state of mind with respect to attachment', which can be assessed from early adulthood using the AAI (Main *et al.*, 2008). Attachment states of mind are related to specific styles of affect regulation, to defensive processes, and to characteristic ways of engaging in close interpersonal relationships. A *secure* attachment state of mind is characterized by coherent and balanced mental representations of attachment relationships, by an ability to mentalize in relation to attachment issues, by adaptive affect regulation, and by an open and trusting approach to close interpersonal relationships in which the person is able to be emotionally close to others and yet autonomous. Two 'organized' insecure attachment states of mind represent deviations from the secure state and are the result of caregiving experiences in which the caregiver was either consistently rejecting of open expressions of distress or was inconsistently responsive in ways that served to heighten the child's attention to the caregiver. A *dismissing* state of mind is developed in response to consistent rejection and is characterized by defensively idealized representations of caregivers that serve to prevent contact with feelings of sadness, hurt, or anger. Emotions are minimized or denied, attention to the mental states of self and others is limited, and the person keeps others at a distance and prefers to remain independent. A *preoccupied* state of mind is developed in response to inconsistent caregiver availability and is characterized by enmeshment in attachment relationships, which are often marked by feelings of anger, resentment, or anxiety. Emotions are exaggerated, and boundaries between self and other are weak or unclear, which leads to inaccurate and overly 'authoritative' attributions of mental states to others.

Some individuals develop more complex attachment states of mind that are associated with increasingly pronounced difficulties with affect regulation and metacognition. An *unresolved/disorganized* state of mind is characterized by dissociative reactions in which the person's reasoning or discourse becomes odd when thinking about traumatic events. Finally, the AAI has a *cannot classify* category for states of mind that are more globally incoherent, for instance, as a result of sudden shifts between dismissing and preoccupied states of mind. These more complex attachment states of mind have been linked to malevolent experiences in childhood in the form of frightening or frightened behavior and other forms of atypical communicative behavior by the caregiver during interaction with the infant, such as affective communication errors, role confusion, negative intrusive behavior, disorientation, or withdrawal (Hesse, 1996; Hesse and Main, 2006; Lyons-Ruth and Jacobvitz, 2008). When caregivers simultaneously serve as the providers of security and as a source of distress, the child is unable to organize a coherent strategy for dealing with the activation of the attachment system, leading to local or more global breakdowns in behavioral organization. Most children with disorganized attachment in infancy later establish *controlling* strategies, in which they attempt to 'manage' their caregivers by adopting a caregiving role themselves or by punitively controlling the caregiver. However, this strategy is prone to break down under increased pressure, which activates the suppressed attachment system, reveals the underlying disorganization, and challenges the ability to mentalize.

Attachment, Metacognition, and Psychosis

Unresolved/disorganized and unclassifiable attachment states of mind are more frequent among people with serious psychopathology, including schizophrenia (Dozier *et al.*, 2008). A study of attachment in FEP found a higher proportion of dismissing attachment in psychosis and a lower proportion of secure attachment. In addition, they found that people with FEP with secure attachment classifications displayed significantly better mentalization than individuals with dismissing attachment classifications did (Macbeth *et al.*, 2011). The study did not assess disorganization. In accordance with these findings, recent theoretical papers use attachment theory as a psychodevelopmentally informed framework for understanding pathways to compromised affect regulation, impaired metacognitive capacity, and experience of psychotic symptoms in psychosis (Gumley, 2010; Harder and Folke, 2012).

As described above, the level of mentalization is found to be generally lower in insecure and disorganized states of mind with respect to attachment. Studies suggest that difficulties in understanding others' minds may be prominent and related to the experience of negative symptoms in FEP (Macbeth *et al.*, 2014; Vohs *et al.*, 2014). In addition to this more stable, trait-like level of mentalization, fluctuations of a more state-like nature linked to degree of distress that activates the attachment system are also likely to occur (Liotti and

Gumley, 2008). This will typically occur in situations that normally activate the attachment system, such as presence of strangers, unfamiliar surroundings, feeling ill, or during separations from people who can provide a feeling of safety. In case of severe forms of disorganized attachment in serious mental illness, a more chronically decompensated state of mind with regard to the capacity to be able to mentalize may be expected.

Besides resulting in a compromised metacognition as seen in psychosis, this enduring or chronic state of distress is also seen as contributing to the development of psychotic symptoms. This hypothesis has gained empirical support from two sources: (1) the findings of an association between childhood disorganized attachment and later development of dissociative symptoms, which establishes a link between attachment and dissociation (Carlson, 1998) and (2) findings linking stress, dissociation, and development of psychotic symptoms in people with psychosis (Varese *et al.*, 2011). A broader approach studies hallucinations and delusions within a group of diagnoses that might share risk factors and pathways to psychopathology. This approach gives increasing support for a link between subtle or overt traumatic experiences, emotional dysregulation, and development of hallucinations and delusions. The disease mechanisms involved have been proposed to be changes in physiologic stress-sensitivity and physiologic response mechanisms in relation to stressful events (Myin-Germeys and van Os, 2007) and deficits in source monitoring (Bentall *et al.*, 2007).

The Therapeutic Framework

The therapy offered to this client had an integrative approach focusing on intersubjective process, affect regulation, and metacognition within an attachment-oriented psychodynamic framework. The focus on affect-regulation and metacognition was derived from the understanding laid out above of compromised strategies for regulation of negative affect and impaired metacognition in disorganized forms of attachment. The intersubjective approach contributes importantly to the understanding of microprocesses in interaction during interpersonal encounters. It has been successful in laying out a framework for studying the nonverbal microprocesses in the developing attachment relationship between mother and infant, which can inform the study of the developing therapeutic relationship.

The term intersubjectivity broadly refers to what is happening between two minds. At the core of intersubjectivity is the experience of shared states of mind and the process of mutual regulation of both interpersonal and inner emotional states during interaction. Here a flexible pattern, where both partners exhibit a symmetrically balanced agency to influence the other as well as being influenced by the other, is regarded as optimal (Beebe *et al.*, 2005). This pattern has been linked to the development of secure attachment. With the development of the symbolic mind at the end of the first year, a sharing of thoughts and thinking form a new level of intersubjectivity built upon the continuously important process of affective intersubjectivity. It is hypothesized that only the inner states and experiences that are successfully shared emotionally are transformed to symbolic thoughts that may be subject to a mutual meaning making process (Stern, 2000). Based on these conceptualizations, the therapy aims: (1) to decrease the client's level of distress and dissociation, (2) to support a shift from disorganized representations of attachment toward more integrated attachment representations and an ability to form secure relationships, and (3) to improve metacognitive capacities.

The basic principle for the therapy is to work nonverbally with the intersubjective balance to install an intersubjective process in which negative emotions and distress can be resolved and a symmetrically balanced agency to contribute to the dialogue is gradually established. Through the therapist's monitoring of the therapeutic relationship in which the contributions from the client are acknowledged, the client will gradually learn how to engage without emotions getting out of control and without having to give up his or her own agency and affect regulation strategies. This will eventually lead toward development of a secure attachment representation, including an inner working model of how emotions, wishes, and needs can be expressed and modulated within a relationship. Metacognition is stimulated through a therapeutic effort at mutual meaning making and understanding of interpersonal encounters within and outside the therapeutic relationship, adapted to the client's actual level of metacognitive functioning. In addition to these therapeutic techniques, the therapy included techniques from supportive psychodynamic psychotherapy: confirmation and validation of the client's experiences, proposing alternative views, and elaboration, differentiation, and integration of subjective experiences in space and time.

THE CASE OF CAMELLIA

Camellia had passed 20 years of age when she first sought help for psychotic symptoms, and her condition was diagnosed as schizophrenia. She was referred to case management services and additional psychodynamic psychotherapy. She was a good-looking, smiling, and likeable person. In the months before seeking help, she had begun studies at a university, but felt she was unable to cope. She developed symptoms – first anxiety related to travelling, then paranoid ideation and fears of being attacked by strangers and additional increase in painful ruminations and lack of agency. All this culminated in an event with visual hallucinatory experiences of merging with an advertisement board above a metro station, feeling that she was falling down into the metro when the board was rolling to display a new advertisement. Following that experience, she felt depressed, lost her capacity to concentrate, and became unable to read books and to manage her life on her own. She dropped out of her studies and moved home to live with her father.

During the initial assessment sessions, a case formulation stating goals and tasks of the therapy was developed and discussed with Camellia. At the core of this formulation were the problems, which caused most distress and suffering to her. Camellia's goal for the therapy was to be helped to get rid of her symptoms, to be able to start studying again, and to understand herself better. She felt she was unaware of her own inner states and needs and felt that she often completely lost track of herself in interpersonal relationships. Besides various hallucinatory experiences, she also presented an almost chronic state of acute distress, an experience of being trapped in interpersonal relationships and severe anxiety related to being exposed to strangers on the street and especially in trains and busses, where she felt she could not escape possible danger. An agreement was reached that the initial foci for therapy were her lack of contact with her own needs and her experience of being trapped in interpersonal relationships combined with a more supportive therapeutic focus on her management of daily life. Initially she was prescribed antipsychotic medication from her psychiatrist but due to severe side effects, she was taken off medication after 1 year in treatment.

Analytical Method

Camellia was interviewed using the AAI (Main *et al.*, 2008) when she had been in therapy for a little less than 2 years. The AAI was coded by a certified coder, who was unaware of the details of Camellia's symptomatology. The coding was checked by the authors, who were both certified AAI coders. For the intensive case analysis, we utilized the AAI as well as a selection of 10 transcribed therapy sessions dispersed across 2.5 years of treatment, approximately one session for every 3 months of therapy. The AAI and the sessions were coded for metacognitive process with the Metacognition Assessment Scale (MAS), coding for Self-reflectivity (S, nine levels), Understanding others' minds (O, seven levels), and Mastery (M, nine levels), (Lysaker, 2010). Both authors, who have received initial training in MAS, independently read the transcripts of the 10 selected therapy sessions, noting the quality of metacognitive processes as well as attachment-related interpersonal dynamics described by Camellia and enacted by Camellia in relation to the therapist. Finally, situations were noted where symptoms and general well-being were discussed in the sessions.

To evaluate the degree to which Camellia contributed to and involved herself in the therapy sessions, that is, the intersubjective balance of agency, we also counted the words uttered by her and by the therapist in the selected sessions and calculated the percentage of the session words uttered by Camellia as well as the mean number of words in Camellia's speaking turns.

Adult Attachment Interview

Camellia grew up with her mother, father, and older sister. In the AAI, she initially presents the childhood relationship to both parents as close and her mother as very loving and physically affectionate. This picture of idyllic family life stands in stark contrast to the subsequent description of a family strongly influenced by the alcohol abuse of Camellia's mother. Camellia claims that it was not until she was 12 years old, that she realized that her mother was alcoholic – her father kept things together, saying that her mother was away on business, when she left the family for days to drink.

The initial positive description of the relationship to her mother gives way to the description of a relationship that was also characterized by 'intensity', 'distance', 'absence', and by her mother 'changing personalities'. She describes instances in which she was clearly frightened by her mother's behavior under the influence of alcohol, and how her mother would switch between being completely absent, for instance on birthdays or on Christmas Eve, and being intensely present but focused on her own needs in ways that could be invading and abusive.

Camellia describes the relationship to her father in positive general terms, but many of the episodes described to illustrate terms such as 'loving' amount to sensory impressions and details of everyday life, such as sharing a love for the same foods. Still, some episodes of real support are recounted and one gets the impression of an affectionate relationship, in which the father at least to some degree attended to Camellia's emotional needs. The father is portrayed as somewhat moody and preoccupied with the difficult relationship to the mother, and as being paradoxically very strong, but also fragile. Camellia describes the parents' relationship as characterized by an 'unhealthy' connection of uniting 'against the rest of the world'.

At one point, Camellia herself comments that she finds it odd that her memories of childhood are always characterized by idyllic family scenes with sunshine and summer. In the AAI it is as if these vague, idyllic memories are kept separate from the memories of traumatic experiences such as violence between the parents, and Camellia does not go on to formulate a more general, overall picture that integrates or evaluates these impressions in relation to each other. While describing difficult childhood experiences, Camellia sometimes keeps emotional distance by grinning or taking a 'professional', analytic attitude towards them – for instance claiming her mother's behavior to be 'interesting'. At other times, she engages in angry accusations, or becomes vague and caught up by small details. Ultimately, she seems unable to integrate the different impressions of her parents, and she shifts frequently between a dismissing stance, minimizing vulnerability and asserting independence, and a preoccupied stance indicating continued emotional enmeshment.

In terms of AAI coding (Main et al., personal communication), the interview is characterized by relatively high levels of both dismissing and preoccupied tendencies, which means that the interview as a whole qualifies for placement in the 'cannot classify' category. There are several instances of switching to the present tense when recounting scary or traumatic experiences, as if these experiences become very much alive in Camellia's mind. A series of losses in her early teenage years are described in a confusing, intermingled way, and while discussing the loss of her grandmother, Camellia is suddenly disturbed by the thought that her father might die soon, which makes her lose track of the conversation. These different indices suggest an unresolved/disorganized state of mind in relation to loss and trauma.

In summary, the AAI suggests that Camellia has been unable to organize a coherent strategy for dealing with attachment-related stress. No episodes are described in which Camellia's attachment system was activated by fear or sadness, and where a sense of protection and comfort was achieved through contact with either parent. A recurring theme in the AAI is also the sense that appearances cannot necessarily be trusted, and that the information that Camellia has been given about the extended family may not be accurate. This lurking feeling of unreality may be related to the psychotic symptoms that Camellia appears to have experienced to some degree already in childhood in the form of voices and other hallucinatory experiences.

With regard to metacognitive effort to understand other people's minds, Camellia uses many words to describe the parents and other family members and in that sense seems occupied with reading the other. However, her level of understanding of their minds is rather low. Most of the time she only describes the actions of the other and she often finds others' behavior strange or weird without further reflections about underlying motivations. She sometimes includes descriptions of others' emotions, mostly in the form of negative emotions. On a few occasions, Camellia gives more narratively coherent descriptions linking behavior, emotions, and interpersonal context. For example, she describes how sad her father would get when he realized that her mother was turning mentally absent and would soon leave the home and embark on another round of drinking, and how that caused him to be less able to manage things at home. This level of understanding others on an action level, only seldom referring to a few emotional states of the other, is judged as a low level of metacognitive understanding of the other on the MAS.

In terms of metacognitive understanding of her own mind, she mentions emotional states such as her irritation towards others, things she liked about her parents, and things that made her happy. She is generally able to doubt herself, and she realizes that her opinions have changed: 'he [her father] could make mistakes, but I did not acknowledge that back then'. She is also able to see her own opinions as being subjective, for example, she doubts her own memories: is it her own memory or is it because she has seen a home video from her childhood? She sometimes links her emotions to interpersonal situations, for example when she explains that her father was very sensitive and might cry if you gave him a little present, and then stating that she gets emotional during the interview, talking about this, because she likes him so much.

In terms of the metacognitive dimension of mastery, Camellia describes how she has now chosen not to see her abusive mother, which is still very difficult for her. She also mentions starting in therapy, where she has actively worked with her difficulties and feels that she is changing because of that. At the Mastery subscale on MAS she is at a medium level in the AAI because of her ability to use relational context, that is, therapy to solve relational and emotional problems.

Therapy Sessions

In the first therapy sessions, Camellia is able to pay attention to the therapist only briefly, often losing contact, with periods of not listening or contributing. She answers questions, but does seldom raise topics of her own. She occasionally reacts by suddenly getting very sleepy. Initially, she is sometimes unable to remain in the therapy session for more than 20 minutes because she feels too tense and starts experiencing hallucinations, for example, of the table in the room moving. Slowly, a more trusting therapeutic relationship develops. The gradual increase in Camellia's participation and contribution to the intersubjective process in therapy is illustrated by the way, in which she takes up more and more 'talking time' in the sessions. At the beginning of therapy, about 40% of all words in sessions are uttered by Camellia, and the therapist takes a very active role in structuring the sessions. After 2.5 years of therapy, Camellia speaks around 70% of the words in each session, and the mean length of her speaking turns has almost tripled. The initial more active structuring by the therapist is done by close and explicit monitoring of the client's actual emotional state/level of stress, taking a more active role in defining a focus from the client's short and not very coherent utterances, linking actual foci to agreed-upon foci for the therapy, wrapping up the session at the end, creating some coherence and meaning, asking what the client thinks is achieved and securing that the client is emotionally ready to leave the session. Gradually the client becomes more coherent and more able to contribute to focusing and structuring the therapy process with the therapist (Fig. 16.1).

First Year in Therapy

The sessions included in our analysis from this phase of the therapy are session number 1, 12, and 25. In the first therapy session, Camellia mostly focuses on her relationship to friends, stating that she often gets annoyed when she spends a lot of time with them. She prefers to know the time frame for different activities, which makes spontaneous time with friends tiring and difficult, but she does not feel good about planned activities with friends either, because she feels unable to predict if she will be in the right mood when the time for the appointment comes up. She seems to express a need for interpersonal contact to be predictable while at the same time being unable to organize a strategy for dealing with this.

Camellia describes an episode where a friend behaved in a way she did not expect, but does not reflect on the mental state behind the friend's behavior.

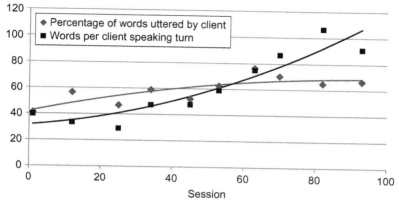

FIGURE 16.1   Client's verbal participation in sessions.

She describes how she silently got more and more irritated at her friend resulting in a very unpleasant feeling, which made her interrupt the friend in a rude manner that only made things worse. She expresses how she felt trapped in an interpersonal context that she really did not want to stay in, because she felt unable to change it or to escape, since withdrawing to be alone would also be very unpleasant.

The therapist invites Camellia to explore this dilemma more together to better understand how these situations emerged and what feelings are involved. During the elaboration, it become clearer that one important problem involved is that she feels unable to manipulate or predict her own state of mind, which may shift abruptly between a wish for interpersonal closeness and an impulse to avoid contact, changing in an instant for her unpredictable and uncontrollable way, preventing her from understanding her needs here and now and taking an active role in any shared or solitude activities.

Three months later, in session 12, Camellia also speaks about a situation in which she feels trapped. She has said yes to a visit from a friend, who is romantically interested in her, but does not really want to spend time with him and worries about his intentions, how she can avoid being alone with him, and how she can monitor his behavior and her own signals in the situation.

Again the therapist invites her to explore this dilemma more together to better understand how this situation has emerged and what feelings are involved. Again her rapidly changing state of mind becomes present, as well as her very mixed feelings containing both attraction and fear of submitting to his needs for physical closeness, which threatens to disintegrate her further. The therapist introduces the possibility of her taking action to protect herself from further disintegration, saying that it is as if she feels she is not allowed to say no to his romantic invitations. Camellia appears overwhelmed by the thought of saying no but the 'permission' to say no implicit in the therapist's question helps her to start thinking about possibilities for doing that. She does not consider openly communicating with the friend about the situation a viable option. She dismisses the possibility of explaining her feelings as being too difficult and awkward. In the end, she decides to tell the friend that he cannot visit after all, because she is not feeling well – a decision that is accompanied by a strong sense of relief but also by guilty feelings since she thinks that she is perhaps responsible for his romantic interest in her. During the whole session, Camellia abruptly oscillates between different positions, for instance between an initial dismissing-like statement that she has 'a few issues of minor concern' and a more preoccupied description of how completely overwhelmed she feels by the upcoming visit, or between saying that her friend's romantic interest in her has absolutely nothing to do with her although she 'accidentally' kissed him, and stating that she often feels that she is responsible for 'controlling every little aspect of her surroundings.' She realizes the futility in her attempts to control others.

In session 25, Camellia tells how her view of her relationship to a friend is changing. She is better able to see him as a person whose behavior might be in conflict with her own wishes and needs – 'I do not want to be together only when we are drunk' – and she wants to discuss the relationship and this change in her opinion with the therapist. Even though Camellia has a clear sense that she wants the relationship to change, she is hesitant about the consequences of expressing this wish to the friend; she is afraid that trying to change the 'unwritten rules' will make him disengage from the relationship, which she appreciates in many respects. Again, Camellia's discussion of the relationship is marked by a high degree of ambivalence, where she shifts between thinking that it is important to listen to her own needs and wishes and backing away from the possible conflict by dismissing her own feelings. In several instances in the selected sessions from the first year of therapy, Camellia explicitly addresses the relationship to the therapist and the process of therapy. This takes place within a therapeutic dialogue, which we will illustrate with an extended description from session 1. After initially securing that Camellia feels comfortable, the therapist offers to inform her of the results of the two previous assessment sessions, inviting her to discuss the goal and tasks of the therapy. Looking together at a figure illustrating Camellia's experience of her relation to self and others (Harder, 2006), the therapist points out that she has rated herself as having a positive self-image at best, but when feeling worst she either loses contact with herself entirely or turns to a very negative control, blaming herself. She seems unable to support herself, when facing difficulties in interpersonal encounters. Camellia agrees with this interpretation. The therapist proposes that therapy could focus on understanding what happens in these difficult situations and why she loses contact with herself when distressed. Together they can try to find ways for her to change that, finding other ways to deal with difficult interpersonal encounters. Camellia agrees again. A couple of other issues are pointed out as well and the therapist then explains that she works therapeutically by inviting the client to talk about experiences and episodes, which she will then try to understand and help the client think and understand more about and find new ways of dealing with. Camellia agrees again. She then tells several episodes of difficult interpersonal encounters, where she felt trapped, and lost contact with herself and the whole situation, not sure what was expected of her or what would be best for her in the situation. She then includes the here and now and expresses strong confusion as to 'what we are doing' in the therapy sessions, how the therapist works and what is expected from her. The therapist acknowledges Camellia's direct question, trying to illustrate how she works by letting her know what she has been thinking while Camellia was telling episodes, for example trying to understand better how she felt trapped, how stressful the situations were for her, wondering about possible alternative ways to deal with these situations. The therapist then asks Camellia if that makes sense to her. She likes the idea of thinking about alternatives, she does not do that by herself, but she finds it difficult to imagine how change could possible take place. The therapist wonders if it is still too vague for her how the therapy works. Camellia replies that as long as she feels that she gains from coming to the sessions, it is not too vague for her. It is difficult for her, which is why she prefers the therapist asks her questions – answering them makes her think and understand. She feels that the therapist is keeping the connecting thread, where she cannot see it herself.

During this dialogue the therapist felt on a knife's edge, feeling that the clients confusion as to 'what they were doing' besides a reasonable doubt about how this therapy works also may be connected to her fear of danger when exposed to strangers, and her pattern of feeling trapped in interpersonal relationships. Thus a feeling of a very fragile therapeutic alliance was present. The therapist wondered how to strengthen the alliance by balancing between the client's expressed need for others to take control by scaffolding, 'keeping the connecting thread', and her fear of being controlled by others, like 'what do they want from me (intrusively imposing their needs), which I cannot escape'. The therapist understood this as an expression of a typical disorganized attachment representation with simultaneous comforting and frightening experience of a potential attachment person. The therapist tried to diminish the frightening part by (1) not being too warm stirring too strong attachment feelings, (2) not asking potential intrusive questions, solely scaffolding the client's agenda, and (3) making the therapist's mind and motives as little opaque for the client as possible, telling her thoughts, serving to counterbalance the client's fear of 'what the therapist wants'. At the end of the session, Camellia finds it very strange that she always feels dead tired in the sessions and in appointments with a psychiatrist and wonders whether this is a physical reaction to her feeling of unease in these situations, which she only later is able to sense and understand with her mind.

Camellia's level of metacognitive functioning within these sessions from the first year can be identified as low on the subscale of understanding others, because she describes actions of others, not thoughts, motives, or emotions. Her level of mastery is low as well. She can define her problems in a plausible way, but use mainly passive strategies, if any, to deal with the problems she faces. Her self-reflectivity is higher than the other subscales of metacognition, most of the time at a medium level, where one can identify some differentiation of her own feelings. When elaborating on events during the therapeutic dialogue she can reach a high level of self-reflectivity, where she is able to integrate and see patterns as in the example above, where she identifies her pattern of becoming sleepy as a reaction to uneasiness in therapeutic encounters. During the first year, there are no clear signs that her general well-being improved significantly, even though she noted a feeling of change in the last session.

Second Year in Therapy

The sessions included in our analysis from this phase of the therapy are session numbers 34, 45, 53, and 63. In session 34, Camellia mostly focuses on her relationship to a girlfriend. She explains that the friend is mad at her because they have not seen each other for a while, and that she feels she has to make an appointment with her now, even though she does not want to. She talks at length in a preoccupied manner about aspects of the relationship and traits in her friend that she finds annoying, with limited understanding of her friend's perspective on the relationship except from the sense that the friend is mad, because Camellia does not show initiative. Camellia again appears to feel trapped in an unpleasant interaction – she is pessimistic with regard to the possibility of talking things over with the friend and does not want to see her; at the same time, she feels obliged to do so.

In session 45, which is the first session after a summer holiday, Camellia talks about being away for a couple of days with the same girlfriend that she discussed in session 34 and another friend. She describes feeling very pressured by her friends who wanted to do things together all the time and made her feel guilty about wanting time to herself, to the point where Camellia got extremely annoyed by small things, such as the sound of one of the friends chewing, and where she developed constipation which she explicitly links to feeling pressured. At the same time, she more dismissingly states, 'it was kind of funny, because it was all so idyllic and things like that...' Camellia finds one of the friends particularly hard to deal with, because she feels that she copies her and wants all the same things as her, and she asks for the therapist's professional opinion on the behavior of the friend. She states that is helps her to think more about her own wishes and emotions in these situations, even if trying to get time for herself was not successful.

In the next selected session (53), Camellia describes how she feels she is changing. She describes how she distances more in romantic relationships, taking more time-outs for herself to get in contact with her own needs. This is in contrast to her former approach, where she quickly got too close to friends and tended to lose contact with her own needs, being solely occupied with what the other wanted from her. The change results in more positive feelings towards a friend in the session. Session 63 is devoted to the discussion of a recent suicide in Camellia's network, which has affected her a lot, even though she was not close to the person who died. Camellia explains that her friends' reaction to the suicide has made a huge impression on her, because she has been thinking about suicide as well. Her discussion of the suicide is intermingled with the discussion of her relationship to her girlfriend whom she has avoided contact with. Camellia seems emotionally overwhelmed by the whole situation, and her narrative of the occurrences becomes fragmented, highly detailed, and confusing at points, suggesting attachment disorganization. She says that she does not know what she needs or what she wants and that she cannot make any decisions because she cannot really judge whether anything feels more right than anything else does.

In this session, the therapist is overwhelmed by the patient's state of chaos and despair, feeling rather helpless with only a 1-hour session to deal with all this. She focuses on trying to help Camellia repair some of her acute stress and painful feelings, listening to her story, empathizing, trying to introduce small pieces of integration, for example, trying to establish a timeline in the events she describes. She is careful not to enlarge the emotional experience, for example, by too much exploration or empathic comments. Toward the end of the session, the therapist chooses to focus on the client's everyday schedule, the agenda for the next week, the appointments for the next therapy sessions. She is concerned how she might assist the client in not losing track of her normal life while dealing with these disturbing experiences and emotions and to circumscribe the traumatic state and embed it in a larger context.

The second year of therapy also involves explicit discussion of the relationship between Camellia and the therapist. In session 45, Camellia mentions the experience of getting tired every time she shows up for therapy. Later in that session she explains that she is starting to notice that talking to the therapist gives her something that she does not get from talking to her friends. She describes calling upon the thought of the therapist during the holiday, making a mental note of 'this is something that I want to discuss with Susanne', a strategy that enabled her to relax more and let it be for the moment. She talks about feeling depressed lately and having thoughts about suicide and meaninglessness, and explicitly wonders whether her depressed mood and her feeling of ultimate solitude were related to the therapist's holiday. The therapist acknowledged that and explored this context for her depressed mood. They discussed the limits of the therapeutic frame, how Camellia had tried to cope with the therapist's absence and that she should contact her contact person from the psychiatric team in case of severe suicidal thoughts. In session 53, Camellia asks the therapist whether what they do together falls under the rubric of 'psychotherapy' and asks about her theoretical rationale. She clearly seems to be trying to piece together an impression of what is going on in the mind of the therapist while they are talking, and mentions that she might try to put herself in a better light or to convey a certain impression to the therapist. She also wants to know if the therapist's way of working with her will change, if she changes. The therapist revealed her thoughts, how she tried to adapt the therapy to the client, and Camellia engaged in a narration of how she feels she has changed since beginning of therapy.

Her metacognitive functioning in these sessions from the second year of therapy is on the same level as the first year in regard to understanding self and others. Only on the mastery scale is some development identifiable. There is some indication of a shift toward more active strategies. For example, in session 45 she is actively trying to refrain from submitting to others' demands, and she use a representation of the therapist to cope with stressful situations. In the session after a suicide in her social network her metacognitive functioning is generally low.

During the second year, Camellia clearly experiences improvements in general well-being. Her anxiety has diminished to a degree, where she can feel pleasure walking on the streets and enjoy exploring 'what is happening in the real world'. In general, she has 'never been so little filled with confusion' (session 53) and her psychotic symptoms are diminished to a degree where she seldom mentions them in therapy. Still, she has extended periods of depressive symptoms and suicidal thoughts related to an unsuccessful attempt to pick up her university studies and during the summer break, where both the therapist and the case manager were away on holiday (session 45).

Third Year in Therapy

The sessions included in our analysis from this phase of the therapy are session numbers 70, 82, and 93. In session 70, Camellia describes a marked change in her approach to romantic relationships, where she is no longer just passively reacting to the wishes of others. She has taken action by breaking up a relationship because she felt the boy was demanding too much of her and scared her with his frustrations when she did not want to commit to him. This is an emotionally very mixed experience for her, which she can describe in therapy. She says that it is hard to put her own needs more forward because she hurts other people's feelings, although she does not feel that she really understands why the friend felt so hurt by her rejection. At the same time, she feels relief because she has acted in accordance with her own needs. She talks about her fears in relation to too much closeness in relationships, using the same expression that she used in the AAI regarding her parents' relationship, 'the two of us against the rest of the world', which she equals to being a 'two-headed monster' and 'completely covered in slime'. She expresses a wish for being able to be in a fantastic relationship and still be her own person with independent wishes and ideas, suggesting an attempt to orient herself according to a more secure attachment state of mind.

Session 82 is mostly focused on discussing her relationship to another friend that she has had scattered contact with across a long period. She talks about wanting the relationship to remain stably distant and uncommitted, but at the same time, she has the sense that it will not work in the long run, 'because it isn't like relationships are like a rock that can just remain the same, right?' Camellia agrees to the therapist's suggestion that she oscillates between interpersonal distance and extreme closeness, but that everything in between is difficult. She has ended another confusing relationship and taken steps to pick up her university studies.

In Session 93, Camellia talks about a relationship to a friend that she has had a crush on. She has been able to set limits without hurting or breaking up the friendship: 'there is a limit to what I want to hear about [regarding his pregnant girlfriend], and we also sometimes approach that limit, and then I say I don't want to talk more about this, it is too much, and he respects that,' 'I feel the relationship is manageable, and I like it.' In this session, she reflects on how much she has changed during the last years, and how she relates emotionally to others in a different way.

During the third year of therapy, there are several instances where Camellia mentions the relation to the therapist. In session 70, she remarks, 'sometimes I am afraid to tell you all these things, because I am afraid that you will think that I am completely fucked up. Well I know that you really can't think that, but, or well you can but, you know...' In session 82, Camellia asks the therapist whether the things that they talk about are something that the therapist can make use of – referring to the sessions being recorded as part of a research project. Camellia also describes being calm about the therapist's upcoming holiday this year, because she has succeeded in focusing on herself and her own needs – also in relation to her upcoming university studies – instead of on 'relational mess'. In session 93, Camellia mentions calling upon a previous discussion with the therapist about the option of leaving unpleasant situations instead of feeling trapped, showing that she takes the therapeutic dialogues with her and uses them when coping with difficult situations. She also wants to write down something that the therapist says in relation to her difficulties with a roommate that she has had trouble pinpointing herself – again signaling that she relies on the conversations and on the therapist's point of view.

The metacognitive functioning in the sessions from the third year is more stable on high level for self-reflectivity, with more integration of feelings, cognitions, and interpersonal experiences, identifying patterns across events. Understanding of others, now also includes more attention to their emotions, not only just their actions raising the metacognitive level more securely into a middle level. Her level of mastery has continued improving. In all selected session she describes an emerging ability to act actively according to her needs, which brings her into the middle to upper level of mastery.

Her general well-being has improved further during the third year. She describes that she is 'not so much in a bubble any more' (session 93), her

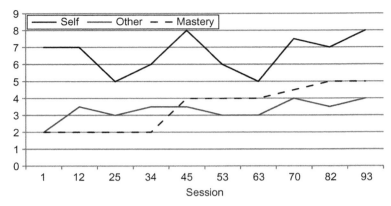

FIGURE 16.2 Metacognition Assessment Scale codes for relational episodes described in sessions.

ruminations are almost gone, and she is able to be more present, have more energy and be less overwhelmed by daily demands. Her experience of psychotic symptoms is now circumscribed to rare episodes of strong distress. Lately she has engaged in a romantic relationship that she describes as calm and safe, which has continued for several months. The relationship is both providing closeness, where they can talk about how they think and feel, and at the same time allowing her to take time out for herself. Furthermore, she has been able to resume her university studies successfully.

The gradual development in the Camellia's metacognitive ability in the relationship to friends as discussed in the sessions is illustrated in Figure 16.2.

DISCUSSION: METACOGNITION, ATTACHMENT, AND PSYCHOTIC SYMPTOMS

In this chapter, we sought to explore the developmental roots of compromised metacognition in psychosis and how these difficulties could be addressed in psychotherapy by studying the relationship between insecure attachment and metacognitive difficulties across 2.5 year of psychotherapy with a single client, whom we have named Camellia.

In the AAI as well as the therapy sessions, Camellia shows a good deal of metacognitive reflection, but of varying quality, especially regarding her understanding of her own mind (S). Sometimes she finds it hard to tell what she feels, wants, or needs, and her descriptions of her own mental and emotional states become very limited or confusing. At other times, she is able to identify recurring patterns in her own thoughts and emotions and link them to interpersonal contexts. This is particularly the case, when she thinks back and reflects upon experiences during the therapy sessions, while her narratives suggest that she often finds it more difficult to think about her own mind when she is engaged in interpersonal episodes outside therapy. During the third year, a more stable high pattern emerged.

Compared to her understanding of her own mind, Camellia's demonstration of understanding of other people's minds (O) is generally more limited. Her descriptions of others often remain at the behavioral level, the inner states motivating their behavior are not given much attention, and when they are, she tends to find them mysterious. Often she states that she does not understand other people's intentions in relation to her. Instead, she seems to be continually monitoring others' behavior and adjusting her own behavior in relation to 'unwritten rules' that she does not really comprehend, but which serve to avoid confrontations or unpleasant situations. For instance, she decides not to openly discuss her wishes of a changed relationship with one friend, because she has a feeling that it might 'rock the boat', even though she does not formulate an understanding of how he would react to such a conversation, or why. During the third year, she becomes more aware of others' emotions.

In terms of the metacognitive dimension of mastery (M), Camellia often resorts to passive reaction or avoidant strategies. This is evident in interpersonal contexts, where she frequently feels trapped and prefers to opt out by avoiding contact rather than communicating about the interpersonal difficulty. However, during the course of the treatment, she increasingly engages in more active problem solving in relation to psychological problems. Thus, she has grown more able to sense her own needs in relationships and to assert them in relation to others without necessarily leading to a complete break-up of the connection. She also mentions actively calling upon different thoughts and understandings derived from therapy, such as for instance that she has the option of leaving a distressing situation.

We want to suggest that Camellia's metacognitive profile can be meaningfully understood in the context of her attachment history. Camellia's narrative in the AAI paints a picture of a mother who would unpredictably shift between being completely inaccessible and being intensely present in an invading and insensitive way that was not attuned to Camellia's needs. Experiences such as these would generally tend to lead to the formation of an avoidant attachment strategy, in which a child would be unable to form a clear sense of his or her own emotions and needs in relation to attachment, and would attempt to suppress activation of the attachment system by asserting strength and independence because of the futility in acting upon attachment needs. This strategy, however, is likely to break down in instances of more severe distress, such as the experience of frightening caregiver behavior. Because of the radical shifts in the mother's behavior from complete neglect to scary presence or sudden strong declarations of love, it must have been next to impossible for Camellia to form an integrated model of the mother's mind. However, it has clearly been of great importance for Camellia to monitor her mother's behavior continually for signs that she might be about to leave or that she was drunk and might behave in scary or unpleasant ways.

It is conceivable that shifts in the quality of Camellia's understanding of her own mind are related to the activation of the attachment system and perhaps especially related to the activation of a trauma-related, disorganized attachment state of mind. Thus in the security provided by the therapeutic relationship, Camellia is able to think coherently about her own mind, but when feeling caught up in invading and unpleasant relational situations or when affected by a recent suicide in the network, Camellia loses sense of herself and becomes unable to evaluate what is going on inside her. This radical loss of a sense of herself naturally leads to impaired metacognitive mastery, characterized by a sense that no viable courses of action are available.

In spite of the difficult aspects of Camellia's childhood, she also seems to have an experience of being loved and cared for, which might be represented by her relationship to her father to whom she today has a mutually rewarding relationship. She wishes for and readily accepts help when offered psychotherapy or case management, even though she finds it difficult to be in the relationship in the beginning. In this sense, she has an image of a secure attachment relationship in which one can feel secure and emotional needs can be met.

During psychotherapy, Camellia improved in reflective awareness of own needs, and improved in her capacity to be alone and to manage her daily living and engage in long-term goals in relation to education. This can be understood as signs of developments toward a better established attachment representation. She is less dependent on being in a relationship to feel secure, but can rely more on an inner representation, which helps her to stay organized when alone. More security also entails a heightened threshold for activation of the attachment system so that fewer situations lead to a breakdown in more organized attachment working models with emergence of disorganized representations. This could explain her feeling of being generally less distressed.

While we have not found clear indications of an improvement of Camellia's understanding of other people's minds in the sessions included in the study, we have noted that she frequently expresses curiosity about the mental states of the therapist and asks directly about the therapist's thoughts and ideas in relation to the therapy process as well as to Camellia's narrative. This curiosity toward the therapist's mind seems to parallel her increasing engagement and agency in the sessions as shown by the gradual establishment of a more balanced intersubjective process in the therapeutic relationship. She is slowly able to speak about herself and her own thoughts, wishes, and needs, instead of the previously dominating theme of monitoring others' unpredictable behavior. In the therapy, she becomes an active part of the relationship exploring both her own mind and that of the therapist and exploring the intersubjective process with the therapist.

Our analysis indicates that a therapeutic focus on monitoring the intersubjective process toward more mutually balanced agency and resolution of distress, combined with mutual meaning making in relation to interpersonal encounters was able to assist the client in her recovery process. Important in this process was the therapist's willingness to disclose her own thoughts and intentions, including the research agenda, as well as the understanding of the client's difficulties that informed her therapeutic approach, in response to the client's growing curiosity toward the therapeutic relationship she had accepted to engage in. The relational development in therapy spread to relationships outside therapy where Camellia became more able to let her needs be known and to have an agenda of her own in relationships. However, while she seemed to explore the therapist's thoughts and motives and developed more awareness of others' emotions, it was still difficult for her to engage in, empathize with, and thus understand the emotional states of others in a more nuanced way. Her exposure to emotionally frightening states of minds in her caregivers may be part of these difficulties.

Camellia's level of metacognitive mastery took a very important step forward as she changed from using passive strategies to using active strategies for solving emotional problems in interpersonal relationships and in preparing for resuming her university studies. In scale scores, her metacognitive improvement was not large, but a more stable capacity for self-reflexivity and a change in mastery from passivity and withdrawal to an ability to take active steps to change had a huge impact on her general well-being. She achieved better social skills, better capacity for emotional closeness and intimacy in relationships, and was able to resume education.

Even though levels of distress and attachment disorganization seem to be related to development and fluctuations in psychotic symptoms, it is evident that other factors might contribute as well. For instance, Camellia experiences that she has a perceptual sensitivity, for example, difficulties with tolerating bright sunshine, that seems to be independent of her state and that she also experiences as involved in the development of hallucinations. Importantly, this chapter only reports on one case with a diagnosis of schizophrenia, and the generalizability of this single case for treatment of metacognitive deficit in psychosis is limited. However, we think that more generally the case supports a detailed analysis of the attachment representations of the client and the activation of these attachment patterns during interpersonal relationships. This may add to our understanding of the developmental roots of clients' compromised metacognitive capacities in a way that will be able to guide psychotherapeutic interventions.

REFERENCES

Beebe, B., Knoblauch, S., Rustin, J., & Sorter, D. (2005). *Forms of intersubjectivity in infant research and adult treatment*. New York: Other Press.

Bentall, R. P., Fernyhough, C., Morrison, A. P, Lewis, S., & Corcoran, R. (2007). Prospects for a cognitive-developmental account of psychotic experiences. *British Journal of Clinical Psychology, 46*, 155–173.

Brüne, M., Dimaggio, G., & Lysaker, P. H. (2011). Metacognition and social functioning in schizophrenia: Evidence, mechanisms of influence and treatment implications. *Current Psychiatric Reviews, 7*, 239–247.

Carlson, E. A. (1998). A prospective longitudinal study of disorganization/disorientation. *Child Development, 69*(4), 1107–1128.

Dimaggio, G., & Lysaker, P. H. (Eds.). (2010). *Metacognition and severe adult mental disorders: From research to treatment.* London: Routledge.

Dozier, M., Stovall-McClough, C., & Albus, K. E. (2008). Attachment and psychopathology in adulthood. In J. Cassidy & P. Shaver (Eds.), *Handbook of attachment. Theory, research, and clinical applications* (pp. 718–744) (2nd ed.). New York: Guilford Press.

Fonagy, P., Gergery, G., Jursit, E., & Target, M. (2002). *Affect regulation, mentalization and the developmental of the self.* London: Karnac.

Gumley, A. (2010). The developmental roots of compromised mentalization in complex mental health disturbances in adulthood: An attachment-based conceptualization. In G. Dimaggio & P. H. Lysaker (Eds.), *Metacognition and severe adult mental disorders: From research to treatment* (pp. 45–63). New York: Routledge.

Harder, S. (2006). Self-image and outcome in first-episode psychosis. *Clinical Psychology and Psychotherapy, 13*, 285–296.

Harder, S., & Folke, S. (2012). Affect regulation and metacognition in psychotherapy of psychosis: An integrative approach. *Journal of Psychotherapy Integration, 22*, 330–343.

Hesse, E. (1996). Discourse, memory, and the Adult Attachment Interview: A note with emphasis on the emerging cannot classify category. *Infant Mental Health Journal, 17*(1), 4–11.

Hesse, E., & Main, M. (2006). Frightened, threatening, and dissociative parental behavior in low-risk samples: Description, discussion, and interpretations. *Development and Psychopathology, 18*(2), 309–343.

Liotti, G., & Gumley, A. (2008). An attachment persepctive on schizophrenia: The role of disorganized attachment, dissociation and mentalization. In A. Moskowitz, I. Schäfer, & J. Doraty (Eds.), *Psychosis, trauma and dissociation* (pp. 117–133). Oxford: Wiley.

Lyons-Ruth, K., & Jacobvitz, D. (2008). Attachment disorganization: Genetic factors, parenting contexts, and developmental transformation from infancy to adulthood. In J. Cassidy & P. Shaver (Eds.), *Handbook of attachment: Theory, research, and clinical applications* (pp. 666–697) (2nd ed.). New York: Guilford Press.

Lysaker, P. H. (2010). Metacognition in schizophrenia spectrum disorders: Methods of assessing metacognition within narrative and links with neurocognition. In G. Dimaggio & P. H. Lysaker (Eds.), *Metacognition and severe adult mental disorders: From research to treatment* (pp. 65–83). New York: Routledge.

Lysaker, P. H., Carcione, A., Dimaggio, G., Johannesen, J. K., Nicolo, G., Procacci, M., et al. (2005). Metacognition amidst narratives of self and illness in schizophrenia: Associations with neurocognition, symptoms, insight and quality of life. *Acta Psychiatrica Scandinavica, 112*(1), 64–71.

Lysaker, P. H., Dimaggio, G., Carcione, A., Procacci, M., Buck, K. D., Davis, L. W, et al. (2010). Metacognition and schizophrenia: The capacity for self-reflectivity as a predictor for prospective assessment of work performance over six months. *Schizophrenia Research, 122*(1–3), 124–130.

Lysaker, P. H., Olesek, K. L., Warman, D. M., Martine, J. M., Salzman, A. K., Nicolo, G., et al. (2011). Metacognition in schizophrenia: Corrrelates and stability of deficits in theory of mind and self-reflectivity. *Psychiatry Research, 190*, 18–22.

Lysaker, P. H., Ringer, J. M., Buck, K. D., Grant, M. A., Olesek, M. A., Leudtke, B. L., et al. (2012). Metacognitive and social cognition deficits in patients with significant psychiatric and medical adversity: A comparison between participats with schizophrenia and a sample of participatns who are HIV-positive. *Journal of Nervous and Mental Disease, 200*(2), 130–134.

MacBeth, A., Gumley, A., Schwannauer, M., Carcione, A., Fisher, R., McLeod, H. J., et al. (2014). Metacognition, symptoms and premorbid functioning in a first episode psychosis sample. *Comprehensive Psychiatry*, *55*(2), 268–273.

MacBeth, A., Gumley, A., Schwannauer, M., & Fisher, R. (2011). Attachment states of mind, mentalization, and their correlates in a first-episode psychosis sample. *Psychology and Psychotherapy: Theory, Research and Practice*, *84*, 42–57.

Main, M., Hesse, E., & Goldwyn, R. (2008). Studying differences in language usage in recounting attachment history: An introduction to the AAI. In H. Steele & M. Steele (Eds.), *Clinical applications of the adult attachment interview* (pp. 31–68). New York: Guilford Press.

Myin-Germeys, I., & van Os, J. (2007). Stress-reactivity in psychosis: Evidence for an affective pathway to psychosis. *Clinical Psychological Review*, *27*, 409–424.

Semerari, A., Carcione, A., Dimaggio, G., Falcone, M., Nicolo, G., Procacci, M., et al. (2003). How to evaluate metacognitive functioning in psychotherapy? The Metacognition Assessment Scale and its applications. *Clinical Psychology and Psychotherapy*, *10*(4), 238–261.

Stern, D. N. (2000). *The interpersonal world of the infant: A view from psychoanalysis and developmental psychology*. New York: Basic Books.

Varese, F., Udachina, A., Myin-Germeys, I., Oorschot, M., & Bentall, R. (2011). The relationship between dissociation and auditory verbal hallucinations in the flow of daily life of patients with psychosis. *Psychosis*, *3*(1), 14–28.

Vohs, J. L., Lysaker, P. H., Francis, M., Hamm, J., Buck, K. D., Olesek, K., et al. (2014). Metacognition, social cognition, and symptoms in patients with first episode and prolonged psychosis. *Schizophrenia Research*, *153*(1–3), 54–59.

Chapter 17

Metacognition-Oriented Social Skills Training

Paolo Ottavi,[1] Manuela Pasinetti,[1] Raffaele Popolo,[1]
Giampaolo Salvatore,[1] Paul H. Lysaker[2,3] and Giancarlo Dimaggio[1]
[1]Center for Metacognitive Interpersonal Therapy, Rome, Italy, [2]Roudebush VA Medical
Center, Indianapolis, IN, USA, [3]Indiana University School of Medicine, Indianapolis, IN, USA

'I can know another person as a person only by entering into personal relation with him. Without this I can know him only by observation and inference; only objectively [. . .]. What we apprehend through these are the intentions, the feelings, the thoughts of another person who is in communication with ourselves.'

John Macmurray (1991. *Persons in relation.* London: Faber and Faber. pp. 28–34)

INTRODUCTION

In this chapter, we describe the theoretical assumptions, methodology, and techniques of Metacognition-Oriented Social Skills Training (MOSST; Ottavi *et al.*, in press), which is a group treatment for patients in both early and later phases of

Social Cognition and Metacognition in Schizophrenia.
DOI: http://dx.doi.org/10.1016/B978-0-12-405172-0.00017-X
© 2014 Elsevier Inc. All rights reserved.

schizophrenia. MOSST is a structured manualized intervention, which employs role-playing exercises that mirror standard Social Skills Training (SST; Bellack *et al.*, 2004). It also seeks to stimulate participants to develop greater capacities to reflect on the thoughts, emotions, and intentions of others. Compared to SST, MOSST offers several innovations: (1) MOSST seeks to promote a rich and articulated understanding of mental states necessary to act more effectively in social situations; (2) MOSST focuses on intersubjectivity, and thus, may promote change through thinking about the relationships in which patients and therapists are emotionally involved and contribute in their own way; (3) MOSST encourages therapists to use metacommunication in a technical way that is to speak openly about the mental states that they themselves experience during role-playing exercises with the patient. To present the intervention we will first describe a range of treatments that focus on social function, and then discuss the basic metacognitive principles and therapeutic requirements for MOSST. Lastly, we will offer a detailed account of the treatment itself with clinical illustrations.

INTERVENTIONS FOR SOCIAL RECOVERY: THE STATE OF THE ART

Currently, specific treatments aiming at a functional recovery of social cognition are divided into two groups: (1) SST, derived from behaviorism; and (2) skills training based on promoting social cognition through specific exercises. SST aims at developing social skills through a systematic training in the production of skillful social behaviors. The SST model is based on theories of behavior modification (Bandura, 1969) and social learning (Bandura, 1977). In this theoretical context, social behavior shares many aspects with other types of behavior: learning occurs through repetition and imitation, is sensitive to reinforcement, and can be decomposed into molecular units of behavior. For example, the social behavior involved in greeting others can be divided into units such as: smiling, opening the eyes widely, reducing the interpersonal space, making greeting gestures (e.g., shaking hands, hugging, and so on), or displaying formal greetings.

In a typical SST session the target skill (e.g., 'greeting others') has been divided into behavioral units; practiced role-plays through modeling; and finally carried out in role-plays using the classical techniques of behavior modification: prompting, shaping, chaining, self-monitoring, self-evaluation, and, of course, differential reinforcement. The effectiveness of SST is controversial: some past meta-analyses confirm its validity (Benton and Schroeder, 1990; Dilk and Bond, 1996), whereas other more recent meta-analyses reveal its limitations and weaknesses (Kurtz and Mueser, 2008; Pilling *et al.*, 2002; Tungpunkom *et al.*, 2012).

In contrast to SST, a number of more recent treatments have sought to address deficits in social behavior from a social cognitive perspective (Penn *et al.*, 2007; Moritz and Woodward, 2007). Social cognition refers to a number of different abilities involved in thinking about social exchanges. In schizophrenia research, these include affect recognition, theory of mind, and attributional style (Brekke and Nakagami, 2010; Kern *et al.*, 2009). To date, one of the most studied social cognition interventions is the Social Cognition and Interaction Training (SCIT). SCIT is a 20–24 weekly group manualized intervention that uses psychoeducation, drill-and-repeat practice, heuristic rehearsal, strategy games, and homework assignments to remediate social cognitive impairments (e.g., emotion perception and theory of mind) and biases (e.g., attributional style) often present in schizophrenia. Further, SCIT offers laboratory-based exercises in which people learn to recognize emotions in faces presented on a computer better (Penn *et al.*, 2007; see Chapter 9; *Social Cognition and Interaction Training: The Role of Metacognition*). Although several studies have shown the efficacy of SCIT and other methods, we suggest that these interventions may not go far enough in two different ways.

First, the skills SCIT targets, such as recognizing a specific emotion or evaluating how a conclusion was reached, are necessary, but not sufficient for social understanding. Beyond identifying others' mental states and reasoning about them, social awareness also requires self-reflectivity, care about others, and the management of emotional arousal that often follows intersubjective experience. To understand another person, one has to do more than recognize emotion in an expression; one has to also think about how one may have been in a similar situation as the other person, empathize with the other person in the sense of caring about him/her beyond just guessing his/her emotion, and then managing any resulting feelings.

Second, computer-based social cognition learning does not bring with it the emotional experiences that real life carries. We suggest that learning about the thoughts and feelings of others has to take place in person in order to be ecologically valid. In order for one to develop his/her abilities to make sense of social situations more effectively, one needs to practice those abilities in complex and stimulating interpersonal situations that can be practically related to the real world. Clinicians may need to help patients with schizophrenia work to recover or develop the abilities to make sense of social interactions through practice in contexts with actual people who have different feelings in the moment, and to adopt new ways of behaving through an understanding of mental states in situations where they are emotionally involved. We emphasize that our approach is not antithetical to other social cognition treatments, but perhaps could complement that approach.

THE CONSTRUCTS OF METACOGNITION AND REGULATION OF THE THERAPY RELATIONSHIP

As noted above, to move treatment that might assist people to make deeper and more adaptive sense of social interactions, we have suggested that programs may also need to incorporate metacognitive interventions and deal with the patient–therapist relationship that exists. Before we describe the intervention itself we will discuss one element of metacognition and also the general idea of how therapeutic relationships are regulated before turning to a concrete description of MOSST.

In the interest of space, we will not offer a full definition of metacognition or discuss its overlap with the related term of social cognition. For these issues we refer the reader to Lysaker and colleagues (Chapter 6; *Metacognition in Schizophrenia Spectrum Disorders: Methods of Assessment and Associations with Psychosocial Function, Neurocognition, Symptoms, and Cognitive Style*). Essential importance for understanding MOSST, is that metacognition does not refer to a monolithic function, but one with at least three separate domains and subfunctions that are at least partially ordered in a hierarchical manner.

The first of these is self-reflectivity. Self-reflectivity involves four related though increasingly complex abilities: (1) recognizing the contents of one's mental states, whether they are thoughts, expectations, evaluations, and/or any other type of propositional attitude; (2) understanding the links between mental contents and the causal relationship tying them to internal or external antecedents, and differentiating different types of representations and appreciating the difference between the quality of representations and that of reality; and (3) synthesizing coherent autobiographical narratives that take into account the role played by the mental states in the moment as well as events across one's life.

The second metacognitive domain involves understanding others' minds. It is that set of skills that makes it possible: (1) to infer the hypothetical mental states underlying others' behavior from explicit signals, especially nonverbal ones, and deduce the motivational role played by beliefs, intentions, propositional attitudes (cognitive identification), and affective states (emotional identification), and the relationship between these mental states and internal/external events (relationship between variables); (2) to take an evaluation and judgment perspective on others' behavior that is independent from one's own point of view, and allowing one to put oneself in the other's shoes (decentering); and (3) to synthesize a complex idea of who another person is taking into account and what is happening in the moment as well as that person's unique history.

A third domain is metacognitive mastery, which is the ability to use mentalistic knowledge in order to manage emotional states in the face of psychological or social challenges. At the lowest levels of Mastery we see patients who are unable to frame problems in a plausible manner. At mid-levels we see patients able to name problems, but respond with passive strategies or at best through seeking social support. At upper levels, we see patients able to take active stances toward difficulties including changing how they think about the problem and ultimately using unique knowledge of themselves, others, and the world at large to accept limitations and respond effectively to complex problems in the moment.

This model allows for treatment to be conceptualized as helping to assist patients to achieve greater levels of metacognitive capacity in terms of them being able to perform increasingly complex metacognitive acts. For example, a patient might be seen to develop greater levels of self-reflectivity by first becoming aware that there are thoughts in his/her head, then distinguishing different mental functions, and then becoming aware of emotions before being able to meaningfully see that his/her conclusions are subjective. The model also naturally suggests that it is necessary to assess the highest level of metacognitive skills that patients are able to master, keeping in mind that interventions should be at that level and if patients fail at a certain step, they will not be able to carry out more complex metacognitive acts (Lysaker *et al.*, 2011). This is, to some extent, similar to working in the therapeutic zone of proximal development (Dimaggio *et al.*, 2012; Dimaggio *et al.*, in press; Leiman and Stiles, 2001; Ribeiro *et al.*, 2013). Turning to the issue of the relationships patients have with each other in the group and with the therapist we emphasize that these have a substantial impact on members' metacognitive functioning. We suggest that this calls for three general conditions. First, the environment should be safe. The location should be adequately protected from incursions by other patients or interruptions. The appointment time should be consistent and negative criticism or provocations should be avoided among group members. Any uncertainty perceived in a treatment environment, in fact, depresses metacognitive functioning (Fonagy and Target, 2001). Second, emotional arousal should be regulated since painful emotional experience can compromise metacognitive function. Third, there should be a playful atmosphere. Contexts involving playfulness among peers with secure one-to-one relationships help individuals to develop metacognitive skills (Dunn and Brown, 1994) by reducing negative emotionality, and stimulating exploration of one's own experience and those of others.

MOSST: THE PROGRAM

Inclusion/Exclusion Criteria

MOSST has been addressed for in- or outpatients affected by schizophrenia and may be fitted for both early and chronic psychosis (Ottavi *et al.*, 2013). Exclusion criteria would include mental retardation, neurologic syndromes (e.g., Alzheimer disease and dementia, epilepsy, multiple sclerosis, Parkinson disease, etc.), affective psychosis, substance dependence, and hallucinations or delusions at severe or extreme levels.

General Criteria

The group can be composed of five to 10 participants in order to be large enough to be stimulating and create an atmosphere of cooperativeness among group members, but not too large as to be chaotic or marginalizing for those more introverted. It should be delivered by two psychotherapists who have been trained or familiarized with metacognition-oriented models of

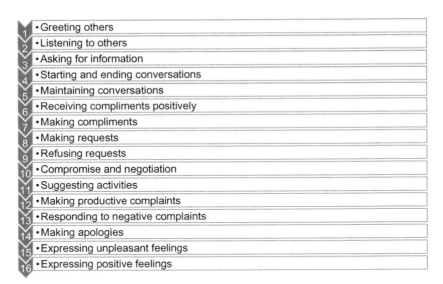

1 • Greeting others
2 • Listening to others
3 • Asking for information
4 • Starting and ending conversations
5 • Maintaining conversations
6 • Receiving compliments positively
7 • Making compliments
8 • Making requests
9 • Refusing requests
10 • Compromise and negotiation
11 • Suggesting activities
12 • Making productive complaints
13 • Responding to negative complaints
14 • Making apologies
15 • Expressing unpleasant feelings
16 • Expressing positive feelings

FIGURE 17.1   List of target social skills used in MOSST.

psychotherapy for psychosis and personality disorders (Dimaggio *et al.*, 2012; Lysaker *et al.*, 2011; Salvatore *et al.*, 2012), and who have a background in conducting groups and SST. Throughout all sessions, a psychologist or psychotherapist who acts as a 'metacognitive facilitator' supports each participant. The metacognitive facilitators are of primary importance in the MOSST, as they help the patient during written tasks, stimulate them in eliciting significant narrative episodes, and reflect on their own and others' mental states. They also have to provide clear and structured feedback using self-disclosures during role-playing exercises.

MOSST consists of 16 sessions lasting 2 hours each, in which several social skills are targeted. The 16 target social skills have been divided into: (1) conversation skills such as listening to others, greeting others, starting and ending conversations, and maintaining conversations; (2) assertiveness skills such as making and refusing requests, making and receiving compliments, asking for information, suggesting activities to other people, and expressing unpleasant and positive feelings; (3) conflict management skills such as compromise and negotiation, making productive complaints, responding to negative complaints, and making apologies. All skills are proposed according to a criterion of increasing difficulty, as shown in Figure 17.1.

Therapists' Tactics

In order to promote metacognition, therapists are instructed to make use of five different general strategies. First, therapists should adopt a validating attitude. An even slightly invalidating, disconfirming, or critical context can trigger defensive and reactive attitudes. An explicitly validating attitude from facilitators can, on the contrary, optimize patients' ability to reflect on mental states (Semerari, 2010). A validating attitude consists of communicating a strong acceptance to patients, being willing to reflect on whatever contents they produce, finding a certain degree of wisdom and correctness in their responses, and believing that they are capable of exiting from their suffering, and creating a life worth living (Linehan, 1997). This represents the minimal prerequisite for exploration of and reflection on mental states.

Therapists are secondly to use communication that is transparent, honest, clear, and simple, as well-structured comments are better at stimulating patients to express to the best of their ability their capacity to understand the other's mind, unlike opaque, figurative, and evocative expressions. Irony should be used cautiously, as it is a notoriously problematic domain for patients with metacognitive dysfunctions (Varga *et al.*, 2010). When therapists resort to humor, timing has to be considered and therapists may at times need to be clear that they are using humor and thus eliminate any ambiguity.

Third, each intervention should be as focused as possible on metacognitive contents. For example, if a patient asks to leave the group to smoke at a point in which other members are making some important disclosures, the therapist can reply: 'I think your mates and I might get offended or upset if you leave the group now. I would like to finish the session with all of us together and I'd like to hear your observations about what X is telling us. I would also feel concern about not being able to keep the group together and motivate you all.' Therapy rules should be explained in mentalistic terms and not as matter of ethics or manners: 'We would ask you to not judge the things said by another participant because he might feel criticized, or ashamed or annoyed, or no longer want to stay in the group.'

Fourth, therapists should normalize patient concerns to create a sense of sharing (Safran and Muran, 2000; Semerari, 2010). Communicating that an emotion or idea are universal, normalizes them. For example, 'I can understand what happened to you: it's one of those situations where we feel terribly embarrassed to ask a stranger for information because we think we're being bothersome or out-of-turn', makes a patient feel more easily accepted and not judged or stigmatized.

Fifth, there should be intensive use of metacommunication. One of the most original aspects of MOSST consists in a structured and strategic use of self-disclosing statements (revealing of personal or biographical aspects by the therapist; Sturges, 2012), self-involving statements, and metacommunications ('the practice of focusing on and communicating about the therapist-patient interaction *as it occurs* in session'; Katzow and Safran, 2007 – italics in original). For example, a therapist can normalize any difficulties met by a patient when receiving compliments by stating how he/she felt embarrassed in a similar situation (*self-disclosing statement*). He/she can demonstrate the effect of a distrustful attitude on the part of a patient by stating that this makes him/her feel ill at ease, tense, and not very inclined to open up, which makes him/herself known (*self-involving statement*). He/she can stress the conflictual relational situation under way with a patient by asserting: 'I feel I'm involved in a tug-of-war where each of us is trying to affirm his/her own point of view at the other's expense' (*metacommunication*).

In MOSST, this type of communication is used to provide metacognitive feedback to patients about their performance in role-play. If therapists are indeed in touch with what patients are experiencing, such interventions strengthen the therapeutic alliance (Safran and Muran, 2000), and increase the sense of security, equality, and cooperativeness in the relationship. This in turn can produce an improvement in patients' reflective skills and give them the chance to understand the flow of the therapist's own mental states and imitate his or her regulation mechanisms.

The Focus on Self-Reflection

MOSST pays first and foremost attention to awareness of self-states, which is the ability to pay attention, name, and communicate the contents of self-experience associated with social interactions. During the first part of MOSST sessions, therapists guide patients to recall personal episodes in which they attempted to perform the target social skills, and then help them explore their thoughts, affects, somatic states, and action tendencies before, during, and after the action. Before the beginning of any role-play, therapists ask patients to identify the state of mind in the moment: 'How do you feel right now? What are you currently thinking?' Moreover, after any role-play the patient is asked for feedback about how he/she perceived the response from the other person: 'How did the way I greeted you made you feel?'

Dyadic-Group Approach

Another original element of MOSST dwells in its hybrid group and dyadic form. Group is the main modality, but very often a facilitator referred to as a 'metacognitive facilitator' replays the most difficult aspects of an ability in a vis-à-vis format. The metacognitive facilitator is a core figure in MOSST and helps patients with written tasks, recalling significant narrative episodes, or reflecting about own and others' mental states. Moreover the metacognitive facilitator gives structured and clear feedback about patients' performance and metacommunicates about the relationship with the therapists and the other patients in the group during the role-play. In order to make the program cost-effective, metacognitive facilitators could be social workers or psychology trainees who have first received a training and are asked to read the most relevant material about metacognition-based psychotherapy programs (Dimaggio and Lysaker, 2010).

The use of this figure originates from a common clinical observation that many patients obtain better metacognition levels in a one-to-one relationship than in groups. This may be because groups can be emotionally overwhelming and also because it may be difficult to form ideas about many people at once. Moreover, since it generally happens that participants have different metacognitive capacities, the presence of a metacognitive facilitator helps achieve a balanced group learning speed by offering more intense coaching to patients with greater cognitive or metacognitive difficulties.

METACOMMUNICATION AND METACOGNITIVE FEEDBACK: THE MATER MODEL

Every session of MOSST is centered around a specific theme and the development of a specific social skill. The first step is for patients to recall a narrative episode in which adopting a certain social skill was needed but difficult. Then there is a social perception task during which patients are asked to observe and analyze a scene performed by the two group leaders centered about the target social skill. These preliminary phases are preparing patients for metacognitive activity by activating the autobiographical memory system, providing the context for the role-play, and stimulating metacognitive functions.

In the second part of the session, patients are involved in the role-play. Here participants perform the needed social skill and interact with the metacognitive facilitators under the guidance of the therapists. Feedback after a role-play is a cornerstone of social skills training programs. In SST, feedback is concerned with overt behaviors. In MOSST, this is still present but marginal. The core element of feedback is about the metacognitive elements and the intersubjective process: the partner in the role-play (usually the metacognitive facilitator) gives the patient a detailed report about his own state of mind during the role-play and how that changed according to the patient behavior. The feedback should be true and include proper metacommunication about the therapy process and some type of therapist self-disclosure. For this to succeed, metacognitive facilitators have to be self-reflective in the moment and have the ability to modulate their own reactions and communicate them to patients in a tactful and nonjudgmental manner.

To make it easier to formulate feedback, metacognitive facilitators are asked to structure and formalize metacognitive feedback using the technique referred to as the MATER model; an acronym which refers to: **M**arker (patient's behavioral marker); **A**utomatic **T**hought (the metacognitive facilitators immediate cognitive-propositional contents coupled with the patient's marker); **E**motion (the metacognitive facilitator's affective state linked to the thought and the marker); **R**esponse (the other's potential response in a real situation). The goal of MATER is to promote awareness of mental states in the midst of an interpersonal interaction, including what is happening in the metacognitive facilitator's mind, to help patients becoming aware of the impact their behavior has on others and to anticipate consequences in the real world.

Examples of Corrective Feedback in Accordance with the MATER Model

A patient (Giorgio) is carrying out the role-play called 'greeting a friend'. In this scene, Giorgio has expressed happiness at this unexpected meeting of an old friend from middle school whom he has not seen for years. He does this, however, while looking up at the ceiling with a serious expression on his face. When the role-play is over the metacognitive facilitator asks Giorgio for feedback about how he felt and what thoughts or feelings his behavior may have triggered in his partner. In response, Giorgio is able to self-reflect: 'I was a bit tense . . . Perhaps I felt embarrassed, because I've never acted before . . .' He struggles though to understand the other's mind: 'Yes, I believe I transmitted to you my joy at meeting you'. At this point it is the metacognitive facilitator's turn to give feedback:

'So, Giorgio, first let me compliment you on how you managed to get through the scene in spite of your tension, totally understandable given that I too felt a certain embarrassment. Here are a few hints about what I saw and what I felt as we were acting and then you can tell me what you think. Bear in mind that what I'm going to say concerns what I would have been likely to think and feel in a real situation, where I was not aware of your tension and your current life situation. While you were expressing your joy to me, I noticed you were looking upwards and had a serious look on your face (Marker). This made me confused, at that moment, because I was expecting you to look me in the eyes and smile at me. I had the thought that you weren't sincere. For one moment it passed through my mind that you were even shocked. You know, like when we have to pretend out of necessity to be cheerful and instead we're irritated (Automatic Thought). Of course, now I know you were tense and not irritated. However, at that moment these thoughts made me feel uneasy, with a bit of anxiety, like when we can't manage to clearly grasp what the other really wants from us (Emotion). Probably, if it was a real situation and I didn't know you, I'd think you weren't interested in seeing me, and I wouldn't feel very motivated to increase our contacts (Response).'

In another session focused on 'paying a compliment' the same patient uses a warmer tone of voice and displays only slight embarrassment, while looking the other person in the eyes. In response the metacognitive facilitator offered validating/reinforcing metacognitive feedback:

'Well, I noticed you had a warm tone of voice and managed to look me in the eyes. Every so often you lowered your gaze a little . . . (Marker) . . . as if you were a bit embarrassed. At least that's how it seemed to me. I thought you sincerely wanted to pay me some compliments and this intimidated you a little (Automatic Thought). I was very pleased with this apparent timidity of yours. I felt appreciated and I in turn felt a bit timid, even if I was gratified. You know, like when someone pays you a nice compliment, so nice that it almost embarrasses you? (Emotion). In real situations this interaction would have induced me to reinforce our relationship, see you in a positive light and pay you compliments in turn (Response).'

Particular caution needs to be used when issuing corrective feedback containing references to strong emotions (e.g., anger, contempt, or fear). Metacognitive facilitators are urged in these cases to mention the automatic thought and immediately follow with a self-regulated thought, put in hypothetical terms, and lastly with a request of the patient for confirmation. An example:

'When you criticized me in the X manner, there and then I thought you wanted to offend me (automatic thought). Then I thought that this perhaps wasn't the case, that perhaps you were just embarrassed or were afraid of hurting me and that consequently it might be difficult for you to express your intentions transparently (self-regulated thought). What, in reality, was your intention at that moment?'

In this way not only are misunderstandings and conflicts avoided, but patients are offered the possibility of observational learning.

Description of a Typical Session

Figure 17.2 illustrates the typical structure of each session of MOSST. Each meeting lasts 2 hours and is divided into two parts, separated by a short break of 15 minutes: a first part, more 'theoretical', about observing and reflecting, and a second part, more 'practical' and intersubjective, focused on the role-play.

Part I is divided into two separate modules that take into account two sub-functions of metacognition: self-reflectivity and understanding others' mind. This first part aims at (1) training and improving the patients' ability to be aware of their mental states, such as thoughts, emotions, desires, expectations, and increasing their ability to understand how the mind of others works; (2) gaining access to patients' autobiographical episodic memories and allowing them to approach the task from more than an intellectual point of view.

In the first module of part I, patients are asked to recall and put into writing an emotionally tinged interpersonal episode that took place in the week prior, which bears on the skill highlighted in that session (see Fig. 17.1 for the list of skills and their order to examination within MOSST). There is then a group discussion about each patient response. Metacognitive facilitators may help patients remember and choose a meaningful narrative episode and elicit mentalistic elements from the narratives. As an illustration, considering the first MOSST topic: greeting others. Here the metacognitive facilitator might ask: 'How did you say hello to the person?' or 'Could you describe your behavior?' When patients are not able to respond to these questions metacognitive facilitators might further guide patients by asking: 'Which among these adjectives is the one that gets closer to your way of greeting others: warm, hurried, shy, cold, arrogant, distrustful.' Depending upon the metacognitive function of the patient they could also ask: 'How did the other person say hello to you and could you describe his/her behavior?'; 'What were your thoughts/ideas in that

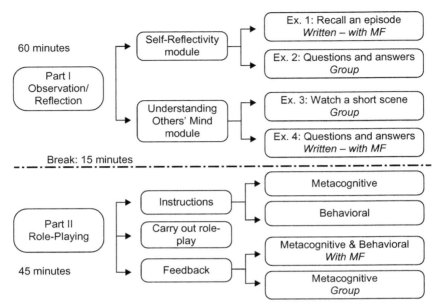

FIGURE 17.2 Typical structure of a session of MOSST. *Ex: example; MF: metacognitive facilitator.*

situation?'; 'How did you feel/what did you experience?'; 'Did that interaction happen the way you expected and if not what might be the reason why it went differently?'; and 'What do you think the other person was feeling?'

The second module of part I focuses on the observation of a role-play performed by the two group leaders, which simulate common life situations in which the protagonist experiences one or more specific mental states followed by discussion and feedback about the experience. During the course of the training, the theme of the skit and the number and complexity of represented emotions are of increasing complexity. Participants are asked to observe and identify these mental states with the metacognitive facilitators helping them and encouraging them to reflect using a worksheet containing some target questions. Next, the exercise is presented again in the group and a table is completed by the therapist on a board in accordance with the answers given by the participants.

The target questions in the worksheet are the following: may you summarize what happened in the role-play you watched? (*reality testing*); what might the protagonist have been thinking? (*cognitive identification*); how might the protagonist have been feeling? (*emotional identification*); what was his/her behavior (facial expressions, tone of voice, posture, eye contact, etc.)? (*behavioral identification*); looking at what you wrote in the table above, do you think the situation, thoughts, emotions, and behaviors are related to each other? (*relationship between variables*); how would you feel in the same situation? What would you think? How would you behave? (*decentering*).

Depending on patients metacognitive capacities, the metacognitive facilitators may ask participants to begin to fill in the worksheet responding only to questions that require lower levels of metacognitive functions (e.g., reality testing and/or behaviors) and then gradually move to those that require more advanced stages (e.g., emotions and thoughts). Questions about the relationship between variables and decentering are always answered last.

Part II revolves around the role-playing exercises. The first module of part II involves giving patients metacognitive and behavioral instructions for running the role-play focused on the target ability. In addition to the classic behavioral indications (e.g., smiling, looking in the eyes, and so on), which do not differ much from those elicited in the SST, participants are encouraged to reflect on those mental states that underlie the behavior to be implemented in certain situations. For each skill, participants are asked to think about four things. First, what is the motivation that drives them to engage in the behavior? For instance the motivation for greeting another person could be to show joy in meeting that person. Second, in what state of mind could they best express the behavior? For example, it might be best to be full of interest or openness when meeting the person. Third, what would they like the other person to feel and think? Fourth, what does the patient feel in the moment before the role play? For some skills, such as listening to others, accepting a compliment, etc., patients could also be asked what the other person might want.

The second module of part II is the execution of the role-play that is performed in a pair with the metacognitive facilitator. Here each dyad carries out two role-plays. In the first role-play the metacognitive facilitator enacts the skill in question, and in the second the patient enacts the skill. Before proceeding with the role-plays, the dyad agrees on the context of the role-play scenario, who they represent, where they are, when the scene takes place, and so. At the end of the first role-plays the metacognitive facilitator provides precise feedback and asks what the patients thought and felt during the role-plays to uncover any discrepancy between their actual emotional state and the optimal emotional states elicited in the metacognitive instructions. They might also ask if patients think the metacognitive facilitator followed the behavioral instructions; how they think the metacognitive facilitator felt and how the behavior of the metacognitive facilitator made them feel.

Following the second role-play in which patients seek to enact the target behavior, metacognitive facilitators should ask patients if they think they followed the behavioral instructions, were in the optimal mental state, and how did they really feel. Patients should also be asked what state they wanted the metacognitive facilitators to experience and whether that happened? Metacognitive facilitators should then express how they felt, if they obtained the hypothetical desired status, and what they thought during the role-play. If corrective feedback is necessary it should always be given in a validating way, and patients should be prompted to try the role-play again. Finally, each session ends in group, where the group leader asks questions about the mental states patients and metacognitive facilitators experienced during role-plays so as to reinforce metacognitive activity a final time.

Sometimes it may happen that participants refuse to proceed with the role-play in which they have to enact the behavior. Especially at the beginning of the training they may feel embarrassed or fear being criticized or overstimulated. Here metacognitive facilitators should avoid jumping to the conclusion that patients are not motivated and accept it as good enough that they are willing to perform the first part. It should be noted that the patients we have treated so far, even the most withdrawn and avoidant, have agreed to engage in the role of enacting the behavior after the first six or seven sessions.

Sequence of Steps During the Role-Play: An Example

In a role-play dedicated to the skill 'expressing positive feelings', the metacognitive facilitator and patient decide to play the roles of two friends. The target subject will express to the other the pleasure of being invited to his birthday party. The metacognitive facilitator starts the role-play and embodies the role of the target subject. The metacognitive facilitator thanks the patient for the invitation, shows gratitude, and tells him that he enjoyed the party a lot and felt comfortable. Then the metacognitive facilitator stops the role-play, and asks the patient for feedback regarding his performance: 'Did I seem to be really happy to have participated in your party?' 'How did my appreciation make you feel?' 'In a real situation, what would my appreciation have led you to do?' After listening to the patient and validating his feedback, the metacognitive facilitator proposes to change roles. Now the patient has to express positive feelings to the metacognitive facilitator for being invited to the party. The metacognitive facilitator starts the role-play and the patient plays his part, and the metacognitive facilitator responds to the communications of the patient with signs of approval, but leaving him the space to drive the scene. Then the metacognitive facilitator concludes the role-play and ask the patient to evaluate himself. Finally, the metacognitive facilitator gives a validating or corrective metacognitive feedback. In the latter case the metacognitive facilitator will propose to repeat the role-play with the appropriate behavioral changes in order to make him hit the desired mental states: 'Would you like to repeat the role-play? This time try to keep a higher tone of voice, as you were slightly excited. In this way you might make me feel even more involved and gratified. Let's see . . .'

CONCLUSIONS

MOSST incorporates many of the principles of SST and seeks to expand their application by stimulating metacognitive activity and discussing the therapeutic relationship as it is occurring in the moment. Role-plays, which simulate the difficult real-world interactions that patients need to master, are a core aspect of MOSST. Another key element is the attention to the regulation of the therapy relationship, which makes MOSST not just a teaching experience, but a social experience in which intersubjectivity is at stake and participants jointly reflect on what is happening when different minds meet with each other during social exchanges. As a result of carrying out these role-plays and thinking about what occurred within them, it is hoped that the program promotes metacognitive capacity, specifically the mental states of the self and the others during social interaction. In this way MOSST may offer a first-line therapeutic intervention focused on self-reflection and understanding the mind of the others.

To date, MOSST has been run on small groups of patients with long-term schizophrenia in regimen of a partial hospital (Ottavi *et al.*, in press) or with first-episode psychosis. Our observations to date are that patients will accept the treatment, and both groups enjoy it and report subjective gains in social skills and observed growth in metacognitive capacity. To date, we are lacking empirical support for these observations. In order to overcome it, we are starting with naturalistic effectiveness study of small groups with patients with both prolonged schizophrenia and first episode psychosis.

REFERENCES

Bandura, A. (1969). *Principles of behavior modification*. New York: Holt, Rinehart and Winston.

Bandura, A. (1977). *Social learning theory*. Englewood Cliffs, NJ: Prentice Hall.

Bellack, A. S., Mueser, K. T., Gingerich, S., & Agresta, J. (2004). *Social skills training for schizophrenia: A step-by-step guide* (2nd ed.). New York: Guilford Press.

Benton, M. K., & Schroeder, H. E. (1990). Social skills training with schizophrenics: A meta-analytic evaluation. *Journal of Consulting and Clinical Psychology, 58*, 741–747.

Brekke, J. S., & Nakagami, E. (2010). The relevance of neurocognition and social cognition for outcome and recovery in schizophrenia. In V. Roder & A. Medalia (Eds.), *Neurocognition and social cognition in schizophrenia patients. Basic concepts and treatment, key issues in mental health* (pp. 23–36). Basel: Karger.

Dilk, M. D., & Bond, G. R. (1996). Meta-analytic evaluation of skills training research for individuals with severe mental illness. *Journal of Consulting and Clinical Psychology, 64*, 1337–1346.

Dimaggio, G., & Lysaker, P. H. (2010). *Metacognition and severe adult mental disorders: From research to treatment*. London: Routledge.

Dimaggio, G., Montano, A., Popolo, R., & Salvatore, G. (in press). *Metacognitive interpersonal therapy for personality disorders: A treatment manual*. London: Routledge.

Dimaggio, G., Salvatore, G., Fiore, D., Carcione, A., Nicolò, G., & Semerari, A. (2012). General principles for treating the overconstricted personality disorder. Toward operationalizing technique. *Journal of Personality Disorders, 26*, 63–83.

Dunn, J., & Brown, J. (1994). Affect expression in the family, children's understanding of emotions, and their interactions with others. *Merrill-Palmer Quarterly, 40*, 120–137.

Fonagy, P., & Target, M. (2001). *Attaccamento e Funzione Riflessiva: Selected Papers of Peter Fonagy and Mary Target*. Milan: Raffaello Cortina.

Katzow, A. W., & Safran, J. D. (2007). Recognizing and resolving ruptures in the therapeutic alliance. In P. Gilbert & R. L. Leahy (Eds.), *The therapeutic relationship in cognitive behavioral psychotherapies* (pp. 190–206). London: Routledge.

Kern, R. S., Glynn, S. M., Horan, W. P., & Marder, S. R. (2009). Psychosocial treatments to promote functional recovery in schizophrenia. *Schizophrenia Bulletin, 35*(2), 347–361.

Kurtz, M. M., & Mueser, K. T. (2008). A meta-analysis of controlled research on social skills training for schizophrenia. *Journal of Consulting and Clinical Psychology, 76*(3), 491–504.

Leiman, M., & Stiles, W. B. (2001). Dialogical sequence analysis and the zone of proximal development as conceptual enhancements to the assimilation model: The case of Jan revisited. *Psychotherapy Research, 11,* 311–330.

Linehan, M. M. (1997). Validation and psychotherapy. In A. C. Bohart & L. S. Greenberg (Eds.), *Empathy reconsidered: New directions in psychotherapy* (pp. 353–392). Washington, DC: American Psychological Association.

Lysaker, P. H., Buck, K. D., Carcione, A., Procacci, M., Salvatore, G., Nicolò, G., et al. (2011). Addressing metacognitive capacity in the psychotherapy for schizophrenia: A conceptual model of the key tasks and processes. *Psychology and Psychotherapy: Theory, Research and Practice, 84,* 58–69.

Moritz, S., & Woodward, T. S. (2007). Metacognitive training in schizophrenia: From basic research to knowledge translation and intervention. *Current Opinion in Psychiatry, 20,* 619–625.

Ottavi, P., D'Alia, D., Lysaker, P. H., Kent, J. S., Popolo, R., Salvatore, G., et al. (in press). Metacognition-oriented social skills training for individuals with long-term schizophrenia: Methodology and clinical illustration. *Clinical Psychology & Psychotherapy.*

Penn, D. L., Roberts, D. L., Combs, D., & Sterne, A. (2007). The development of the social cognition and interaction training program for schizophrenia spectrum disorders. *Psychiatric Services, 58,* 449–451.

Pilling, S., Bebbington, P., Kuipers, E., Garety, P., Geddes, J., Martindale, B., et al. (2002). Psychological treatment in schizophrenia: II. Meta-analyses of randomized controlled trials of social skills training and cognitive remediation. *Psychological Medicine, 32,* 783–791.

Ribeiro, E., Ribeiro, A. P., Gonçalves, M. M., Horvath, A. O., & Stiles, W. B. (2013). How collaboration in therapy becomes therapeutic: The therapeutic collaboration coding system. *Psychology and Psychotherapy: Theory, Research and Practice, 86,* 294–314.

Safran, J. D., & Muran, J. C. (2000). *Negotiating the therapeutic alliance. A relational treatment guide.* New York: Guilford.

Salvatore, G., Russo, B., Russo, M., Popolo, R., & Dimaggio, G. (2012). Metacognition-oriented therapy for psychosis: The case of a woman with delusional disorder and paranoid personality disorder. *Journal of Psychotherapy Integration, 22*(4), 314–329.

Semerari, A. (2010). The impact of metacognitive dysfunctions in personality disorders on the therapeutic relationship and intervention technique. In G. Dimaggio & P. H. Lysaker (Eds.), *Metacognition and severe adult mental disorders: From research to treatment* (pp. 269–284). London: Routledge.

Sturges, J. W. (2012). Use of therapist self-disclosure and self-involving statements. *Behavior Therapist, 35,* 90–93.

Tungpunkom, P., Maayan, N., & Soares-Weiser, K. (2012). Life skills programmes for chronic mental illnesses. *Cochrane Database of Systematic Reviews* (Issue 1).

Varga, E., Hajnal, A., Schnell, Z., Orsi, G., Tényi, T., Fekete, S., et al. (2010). Exploration of irony appreciation in schizophrenia: A functional MRI study. *European Psychiatry, 25*(1), 1572.

Chapter 18

Experimental Usage of Oxytocin to Combat Deficits in Social Cognition in Schizophrenia

Cumhur Tas,[1,2] Elliot C. Brown,[1,3] Cristina Gonzalez[1,2] and Martin Brüne[1]

[1]LWL-University Hospital Bochum, Bochum, Germany, [2]Ruhr-University Bochum, Bochum, Germany, [3]International Graduate School of Neuroscience (IGSN), Ruhr-University Bochum, Bochum, Germany

Chapter Outline

INTRODUCTION

The human brain, as the most complex organ that has ever evolved, gives us tremendous capacities to maintain fruitful social relationships. For many years, the idea of uncovering the magic potion for successful social interaction has received interest from many scientific disciplines, including psychology, psychiatry, philosophy, and neuroscience. Oxytocin, an evolutionarily conserved neuropeptide that has been well known for its role in parturition and lactation, has attracted scientific attention for its function in the regulation of early infant–caregiver relationships and social interaction more generally. It is

Social Cognition and Metacognition in Schizophrenia.
DOI: http://dx.doi.org/10.1016/B978-0-12-405172-0.00018-1
© 2014 Elsevier Inc. All rights reserved.

thus referred to as a 'prosocial hormone' that is relevant for the formation of trustful social bonds through secure attachment (Choleris *et al.*, 2013).

Some of the prosocial effects of the oxytocinergic system have been attributed to its stress-reducing and social 'buffering' effects. According to the social buffering hypothesis, gregarious animals downregulate stress responses through social interaction with genetically related individuals or allies. In essence, when conspecifics are engaged in social interaction, their neuroendocrine stress response gradually decreases, while an increase in social reward-related activity is concurrently observed as a response to the secretion of oxytocin from the paraventricular nucleus (PVN) and the supraoptic nucleus (SON) of the hypothalamus (Neumann and Landgraf, 2008).

In support of these findings, histologic studies have discovered oxytocinergic pathways in higher-order prefrontal structures and other brain areas such as the amygdala that are responsible for the regulation of human social interaction in terms of fight or flight or, more generally speaking, approach and avoidance (Neumann and Landgraf, 2008). Oxytocin, it seems, has the potential to increase approach and decrease avoidance behavior, which may make it an interesting substance for improving social interaction in clinical populations, in which dysregulation of affiliation versus assertiveness coin the clinical picture.

Schizophrenia is a term for a number of heterogeneous syndromes or disorders of which one outstanding commonality is the impairment of patients in social functioning. Poor social functioning is associated with a broad range of negative symptoms such as avolition, apathy, and social withdrawal, as well as with positive symptoms such as delusions and hallucinations. Moreover, social dysfunction in schizophrenia seems to be tightly linked with social cognitive deficits, which statistically act as a mediator of core schizophrenia symptoms and social functioning (Couture *et al.*, 2011). Of note, recent targeted psychosocial interventions have demonstrated that social cognition is a remediable domain, and improvement in social cognitive skills ultimately impacts on the severity of social dysfunction in schizophrenia (e.g., Tas *et al.*, 2012). Since current pharmacologic treatment using antipsychotic drugs has relatively little impact on social cognition in schizophrenia, the hope is that oxytocin may have the potential to enhance patients' social cognitive capacities and helps to ameliorate the core symptoms associated with these disorders, including blunted affect, social withdrawal, suspiciousness, and paranoid ideation, possibly by means of stress reduction, which is why oxytocin has been deemed a 'natural antipsychotic' (Caldwell *et al.*, 2009).

Accordingly, this chapter aims to present an overview of oxytocin studies spanning animal work and experimental use of oxytocin in patients with schizophrenia, to discuss potential mechanisms underlying the effects of oxytocin on symptoms and social cognition in schizophrenia, and to highlight limitations and the prospects of future research in this domain.

TRANSLATIONAL WORK ON THE EFFECT OF OXYTOCIN ON SOCIAL COGNITION

Animal and human studies suggest that oxytocin improves several aspects of social cognition, including the formation of social memories, attachment, fear conditioning, trust, empathy, social and emotion recognition, and theory of mind (Domes *et al.*, 2007; Ferguson *et al.*, 2001; Hurlemann *et al.*, 2010; Kirsch *et al.*, 2005; Kosfeld *et al.*, 2005; Stratharn *et al.*, 2009). The possibility to modify the oxytocinergic system genetically and to carry out pharmacologic intervention studies in animals has produced new insights into the brain mechanisms involved in social cognition. Although the complexity of the human brain cannot be directly compared to a rodent brain, animal models provide valuable information regarding the most basic levels of information processing.

Numerous studies have shown that central administration of oxytocin or oxytocin agonists increases social memory formation in rodents. One widely used test to assess the levels of social memory formation is the social recognition test, in which animals are first presented with a stimulus animal, followed by an interexposure interval (IEI), and finally a re-exposure to the same animal with the addition of a novel one. In the re-exposure part of the experiment, the tested animal spends more time sniffing and investigating the novel animal, if it remembers the first encounter. Administration of oxytocin in the olfactory bulb, the medial preoptic area of the thalamus, and the septum of rats increases the time they spend socially investigating the novel animal after the IEI (Dluzen *et al.*, 1998; Popik and van Ree, 1991; Popik *et al.*, 1992). Interestingly, another study showed a dose-dependent U-curve response of oxytocin on social memory (Benelli *et al.*, 1995). In this study, low doses of oxytocin injected into the cerebral ventricles improved social memory formation while high doses had no beneficial effect. In line with these findings, pretreatment with oxytocin antagonists abolished the improvement by low doses, and increased social memory when high doses of oxytocin were administered. Taken as a whole, these studies suggest that oxytocin in the brain modulates social memory, and that a U-curve dose response might be responsible for the observed effects.

Genetically manipulated animals in which the oxytocin receptor gene (OTR) was knocked out (KO) provide further information relevant to the effects of this neuropeptide on social behavior. For instance, one study in oxytocin KO mice found that they failed to recognize conspecifics after repeated exposures, despite normal behavior in other memory-associated tasks. This effect was fully reversible by oxytocin administration (Ferguson *et al.*, 2001). In line with these findings, intraventricular oxytocin antagonist treatment in wild-type mice produced the same effects seen in oxytocin KO mice (Ferguson *et al.*, 2000). Moreover, intracerebral oxytocin administration in OTR KO mice reduces aggression and improves social and learning deficits (Sala *et al.*, 2011).

More specifically to schizophrenia, studies have found that oxytocin ameliorated social deficits in a mouse model of schizophrenia, in which the animals received the N-methyl-D-aspartate (NMDA) antagonist phencyclidine (PCP), a potent psychotomimetic agent (Lee *et al.*, 2005). Similarly, oxytocin administration in the central amygdala can reverse social impairments in a rat model of schizophrenia that mimicked prenatal stress (Lee *et al.*, 2007). In prenatally stressed animals decreased oxytocin messenger ribonucleic acid (mRNA) was found in the PVN of the thalamus and increased oxytocin binding was observed in the amygdala. Consistent with these experiments, oxytocin KO mice that were treated with psychotomimetic drugs such as amphetamine, apomorphine, or PCP showed altered prepulse inhibition (PPI) responses, which reflects a deviation in the startle response that has also been found in patients with schizophrenia (Caldwell *et al.*, 2009). In rats, the impaired PPI response produced by PCP was normalized by the administration of oxytocin (Feifel and Reza, 1999; Lee *et al.*, 2005). Interestingly, clozapine, but not haloperidol, has the potential to increase the secretion of oxytocin in rats, which may, in part, account for its 'atypicality' (Uvnas-Moberg *et al.*, 1992).

In addition to the effect of oxytocin on social memory and social behavior, other studies have shown oxytocin to be implicated in modulating the response to stressful stimuli. For instance, Windle and colleagues (1997) demonstrated that ovariectomized rats that were given oxytocin injections into the cerebral ventricles had reduced plasma corticosterone responses to white noise stress. Another study reported decreased adrenocorticotropic hormone (ACTH) and corticosterone release in rats treated with oxytocin, in addition to decreased c-Fos mRNA expression in the PVN, the ventrolateral septum, and some subregions of the dorsal hippocampus in response to stress (Windle *et al.*, 2004). Finally, one study in sheep showed that infusion of oxytocin in the posterior pituitary and the PVN reduced the cortisol response to a stressful event (a barking dog), and that lactating sheep had a lower cortisol response (Cook, 1997). This suggests that oxytocin attenuates stress-induced physiologic and behavioral responses by modulating the hypothalamic-pituitary-adrenal (HPA) axis.

To sum up, animal studies demonstrate that oxytocin impacts social behavior and social cognition, partly due to its stress-reducing properties. However, evidence from research in rodents and pigs also suggest some caution in investigating oxytocin as a therapeutic agent in humans, because the administration of low-dose oxytocin over a 10- to 12-week period produced increased aggressiveness and dysfunctional HPA axis in these animals (Bales *et al.*, 2012; Rault *et al.*, 2013).

OXYTOCIN IN HUMAN SOCIAL COGNITION

Intranasal oxytocin administration exerts measurable effects on a broad range of social cognitive abilities. For example, oxytocin increases trust, trustworthiness and attractiveness, cooperation, defensive (but not offensive) aggression toward out-group, generosity, socially reinforced learning, and empathy, among others (De Dreu *et al.*, 2010; Hurlemann *et al.*, 2010; Kirsch *et al.*, 2005; Kosfeld *et al.*, 2005; Theodoridou *et al.*, 2009; Zak *et al.*, 2007). Furthermore, intranasal oxytocin has also been found to improve the ability to recognize emotions from an image showing the eye region of a face only (Domes *et al.*, 2007). Interestingly, the positive effects of oxytocin were more pronounced for difficult expressions, suggesting that this neuropeptide may increase emotional salience.

With regard to the interaction of oxytocin with the HPA axis in humans, it was shown that both social support and oxytocin independently attenuated the cortisol responses induced by a social stress test (Heinrichs *et al.*, 2003), whereby the combination of social support and oxytocin yielded the lowest cortisol response. Compatible with these findings, Pierrehumbert *et al.* (2012) demonstrated that subjects' attachment style can predict cortisol response to stress and oxytocin levels, where high cortisol reactivity and low oxytocin levels were related to more insecure attachment representations. These findings seem to be encouraging with respect to the rationale of utilizing oxytocin for treating symptoms associated with schizophrenia.

OXYTOCIN IN SCHIZOPHRENIA

To examine the role of oxytocin in relation to social cognition and symptomatology, one needs to distinguish between studies measuring the association of peripheral oxytocin with cognition and symptom profile from research into the experimental administration of oxytocin adjunct to antipsychotic medication.

In the 1980s, a few studies produced conflicting results regarding differences in blood or central nervous system (CNS) levels of neuropeptides between schizophrenia and other clinical populations. Linkowski *et al.* (1984), for example, reported lower levels of neurophysins (carrier proteins of oxytocin) in the CNS of patients with schizophrenia compared with patients with major depression or bipolar disorder, and healthy controls (Linkowski *et al.*, 1984). Conversely, another study demonstrated higher CNS levels of oxytocin, but not vasopressin, in patients with schizophrenia compared with healthy controls (Beckmann *et al.*, 1985), a finding that could not be reproduced in a later study (Glovinsky *et al.*, 1994).

More recent studies demonstrated reduced oxytocin serum levels in patients with schizophrenia, which predicted their ability to correctly identify facial emotions (Goldman *et al.*, 2008). In trust-dependent interactions, healthy controls showed increased plasma levels of oxytocin, whereas this effect was absent in patients with schizophrenia (Kéri *et al.*, 2009).

With regard to the symptomatology, one study found that higher oxytocin serum levels in patients with schizophrenia were associated with reduced symptom severity compared with patients with lower oxytocin serum levels (Rubin *et al.*, 2010). In addition, the same study group found that women with schizophrenia who had higher plasma levels of oxytocin evaluated emotions as more positive, although there were no differences in terms of plasma oxytocin levels between men and women (Rubin *et al.*, 2011). One study by Walss-Bass *et al.* (2013) examined the association of plasma oxytocin levels with theory of mind and emotion perception in schizophrenia. The authors created a so-called 'waiting room task' consisting of 26 videos of people in a room who were looking at a camera with varying duration, gaze direction (direct or indirect), and facial expression. It turned out that social cognitive task performance correlated only in patients with delusional beliefs, but not in patients without delusions. Notably, similar correlations were also present in healthy participants in this study, hence these findings do not appear to be specific for paranoid schizophrenia (Walss-Bass *et al.*, 2013).

As regards the experimental administration of oxytocin for treating patients with schizophrenia, the first systematic study was conducted by Bujanow who, back in 1974, already envisioned a role of oxytocin in the treatment of schizophrenia when stating "the neurophysiological matrix of schizophrenia is a central functional organizational scheme related to reduced stress and drives and the biochemistry of pineal gland is closely related to that". In this early study, oxytocin was randomly given (versus placebo) to acute and chronic patients with schizophrenia, and was found to lead to symptomatic improvement and reduce hospitalization rates (Bujanow, 1974). Following this ground-breaking – though at that time under-recognized – research, later studies have focused on the question whether or not intranasal administration of oxytocin can ameliorate symptoms and/or improve social cognition.

With respect to schizophrenia symptoms, Feifel and colleagues (2010) found that oxytocin administration over a 3-week period twice daily improved both positive and negative symptoms in schizophrenia and also reduced the Clinical Global Impression score significantly. Similarly, Pedersen *et al.* (2011) reported a reduction in the Positive and Negative Syndrome Scale score after a 2-week treatment with oxytocin given adjunct to antipsychotics, where, in addition, the ability to appreciate the mental states of others (theory of mind) improved. With regard to emotion recognition, Averbeck *et al.* (2011) found an improved recognition of emotions upon intranasal oxytocin administration in schizophrenia patients. Notably, the effect of oxytocin on emotion recognition was more pronounced when the stimuli were particularly difficult to interpret and negative in content (i.e., anger and fear). Along similar lines, MacDonald *et al.* (2013) found that patients receiving oxytocin were more accurate in determining the emotional mental states of people whose faces were cropped in a way that only the eyes remained in view. Likewise, Davis *et al.* (2013) studied patients' performance on simpler compared with more difficult social cognitive tasks under oxytocin versus placebo, whereby oxytocin improved accuracy only in the more advanced tasks comprising the detection of sarcasm and empathetic perspective-taking.

Lastly, social perception has been proposed to be another subdomain of social cognition in which oxytocin administration has shown some effects.

Fischer-Shofty *et al.* (2013) found that, following the administration of oxytocin, patients with schizophrenia improved their ability to recognize kinship in video clips that were presented to participants as part of the Interpersonal Perception Task (Costanzo and Archer, 1989). Interestingly, healthy controls did not show any improvements following the administration of oxytocin, which may suggest that the effect of oxytocin is more prominent in participants with deficits in social cognitive skills relative to healthy populations.

POTENTIAL PATHWAYS TO IMPROVE SOCIAL COGNITIVE DEFICITS IN SCHIZOPHRENIA BY OXYTOCIN

Despite these encouraging findings of oxytocin administration on social cognition and behavior, most effect sizes in the above-mentioned studies were moderate to small. Previous factor analyses and studies using model-based statistical approaches based on behavioral tests successfully identified the interindependency of subdomains of social cognition. General principles of prefrontal cortex activity, for example, suggest that bottom-up processes such as emotion perception impact on top-down cognitive processes such as theory of mind and metacognition. In support of this assumption, evidence suggests that oxytocin acts as a neuromodulator that primarily targets subcortical structures, which in turn may affect the high cortical areas that are responsible for social decision-making, empathy, theory of mind, and metacognition (Meyer-Lindenberg *et al.*, 2011; Sofroniew, 1980).

The amygdala appears to be one of the brain regions that are most sensitive to oxytocin manipulation (Hurlemann *et al.*, 2010). Several functional magnetic resonance imaging (fMRI) studies reported correlations between amygdala activity and the accurate identification of emotions, which was modifiable by oxytocin administration (Domes *et al.*, 2007; Gamer *et al.*, 2010). In addition, several studies in healthy populations found that the misinterpretation of sensory input at the level of the amygdala might negatively influence higher-order theory of mind skills (Corden *et al.*, 2006; Kreifelts *et al.*, 2010; Mier *et al.*, 2010).

Rosenfeld and his colleagues (2011) proposed an emotional model in which oxytocin and amygdala activity played a central role to understanding social behavior and social cognition in schizophrenia. In brief, they put forth the idea that, while the core features of schizophrenia rely heavily on dysfunctions in the dopaminergic circuits, the network activity involved in the fine-tuning of social behavior, which is centrally controlled by the amygdala via oxytocinergic pathways, could further impact on social impairments in schizophrenia. Specifically, they hypothesized that the impairments in the dopaminergic reward system, the amygdala and oxytocinergic neurons engender a neural milieu that improperly assigns emotional salience to environmental stimuli and hence causes misinterpretations that lead to inappropriate social approach and avoidance responses. Such misinterpretations concerning the salience and intensity of emotional stimuli often lead to an aberrant activation of the amygdala, which leads to a stimulus being appraised as threatening. Consequently, such threatening stimuli activate the autonomic nervous system and the HPA axis as an initial alarm system. Conversely, the oxytocinergic system can dampen the activation of the amygdala, the autonomic nervous system, and HPA axis and can thus contribute to the prevention of false alarm biases. Critically, such oxytocinergic activity occurs more often when the stimuli is appraised as socially rewarding and prosocial. In the absence of this activity, an aberrant activation in amygdala would affect the functionally interconnected prefrontal areas that are responsible for theory of mind and social perception and hence distort social cognitive capacities.

Taken as a whole, it seems parsimonious to assign oxytocin a role in the modulation and expression of social cognitive skills and the symptomatology in patients with schizophrenia. Therefore, more research into the clinical use of oxytocin for improving social cognitive deficits and psychotic symptoms in schizophrenia is warranted.

LIMITATIONS AND FUTURE DIRECTIONS

Schizophrenia is a group of heterogeneous disorders with multiple clinical expressions. Negative findings of current pharmacologic studies propose that there may not be one 'magic bullet' to cure schizophrenia. Focusing on social cognition as a treatment strategy has been found to be one potential strategy for improving social functioning in this disorder. Studies have found beneficial effects of oxytocin on symptom severity and social cognitive skills in schizophrenia. However, clinical studies in schizophrenia have limited the use of oxytocin to at best several weeks. For example, Modabbernia et al. (2013) found in an 8-week randomized trial superior improvement in positive, negative, and general symptoms in schizophrenia when oxytocin was given in addition to risperidone, as compared with risperidone alone. To date, there is no information about follow-up examination after the termination of oxytocin treatment. Another limitation pertains to the lack of knowledge about long-term effects of oxytocin. Moreover, the short half-life of oxytocin makes it difficult to produce stable serum (or CNS) levels (McCullough et al., 2013). In addition, it is far from being clear which patient profiles would respond to oxytocin treatment and which would not. Along similar lines, a general consensus has also not yet been reached for the most effective dose titration of oxytocin, although no severe side effects have been observed following oxytocin administration in humans (MacDonald et al., 2011). Another important point that needs to be clarified is the influence of endogenous oxytocin faculties on the effects of external administration. For instance, patients with lower basal oxytocin levels may benefit more from oxytocin administration. Conversely, patients with normal peripheral levels of oxytocin may benefit less from such treatment strategies. Finally, genetic research has found associations of autism with polymorphic variation of the OTR, and a few studies have pointed to the possibility that the genetics of oxytocin are also related to schizophrenia (Montag *et al.*, 2012; Teltsh *et al.*, 2012).

It is evident that oxytocin studies will expand our understanding of schizophrenia and underline the importance of the social dimension of schizophrenia. The current state of the art may suggest the use of oxytocin administration as an augmentation therapy for treating social cognitive deficits, and perhaps to increase patients' potential to benefit from social cognitive training. Considering the limited effects of current antidopaminergic pharmacologic agents on social cognition and functioning, oxytocin may provide new hope for improving the social capabilities of our patients.

REFERENCES

Averbeck, B. B., Bobin, T., Evans, S., & Shergill, S. S. (2011). Emotion recognition and oxytocin in patients with schizophrenia. *Psychological Medicine*, 1–8.

Bales, K. L., Perkeybile, A. M., Conley, O. G., Lee, M. H., Guoynes, C. D., Downing, G. M., et al. (2012). Chronic intranasal oxytocin causes long-term impairments in partner preference formation in male prairie voles. *Biological Psychiatry*, 74(3), 180–188.

Beckmann, H., Lang, R. E., & Gattaz, W. F. (1985). Vasopressin – oxytocin in cerebrospinal fluid of schizophrenic patients and normal controls. *Psychoneuroendocrinology*, 10(2), 187–191.

Benelli, A., Bertolini, A., Poggioli, R., Menozzi, B., Basaglia, R., & Arletti, R. (1995). Polymodal dose–response curve for oxytocin in the social recognition test. *Neuropeptides*, 28(4), 251–255.

Bujanow, W. (1974). Letter: Is oxytocin an anti-schizophrenic hormone? *Canadian Psychiatric Association Journal*, 19(3), 323.

Caldwell, H. K., Stephens, S. L., & Young, W. S. (2009). Oxytocin as a natural antipsychotic: A study using oxytocin knockout mice. *Molecular Psychiatry*, 14, 190–196.

Choleris, E., Pfaff, D. W., & Kavaliers, M. (2013). *Oxytocin, vasopressin and related peptides in the regulation of behavior*. Cambridge: Cambridge University Press.

Cook, C. J. (1997). Oxytocin and prolactin suppress cortisol responses to acute stress in both lactating and non-lactating sheep. *Journal of Dairy Research*, 64(3), 327–339.

Corden, B., Critchley, H. D., Skuse, D., & Dolan, R. J. (2006). Fear recognition ability predicts differences in social cognitive and neural functioning in men. *Journal of Cognitive Neuroscience*, 18(6), 889–897.

Costanzo, M., & Archer, D. (1989). Interpreting the expressive behavior of others: The Interpersonal Perception Task. *Journal of Nonverbal Behavior*, 13(4), 225–245.

Couture, S. M., Granholm, E. L., & Fish, S. C. (2011). A path model investigation of neurocognition, theory of mind, social competence, negative symptoms and real-world functioning in schizophrenia. *Schizophrenia Research*, 125, 152–160.

Davis, M. C., Lee, J., Horan, W. P., Clarke, A. D., McGee, M. R., Green, M. F., et al. (2013). Effects of single dose intranasal oxytocin on social cognition in schizophrenia. *Schizophrenia Research*, 147(2–3), 393–397.

De Dreu, C. K. W., Greer, L. L., Handgraaf, M. J. J., Shalvi, S., Van Kleef, G. A., Baas, M., Ten Velden, F. S., et al. (2010). The neuropeptide oxytocin regulates parochial altruism in intergroup conflict among humans. *Science (New York, N.Y.)*, 328(5984), 1408–1411.

Dluzen, D. E., Muraoka, S., Engelmann, M., & Landgraf, R. (1998). The effects of infusion of arginine vasopressin, oxytocin, or their antagonists into the olfactory bulb upon social recognition responses in male rats. *Peptides*, *19*(6), 999–1005.

Domes, G., Heinrichs, M., Michel, A., Berger, C., & Herpertz, S. C. (2007). Oxytocin improves "mind-reading" in humans. *Biological Psychiatry*, *61*(6), 731–733.

Feifel, D., MacDonald, K., Nguyen, A., Cobb, P., Warlan, H., Galangue, B., et al. (2010). Adjunctive intranasal oxytocin reduces symptoms in schizophrenia patients. *Biological Psychiatry*, *68*(7), 678–680.

Feifel, D., & Reza, T. (1999). Oxytocin modulates psychotomimetic-induced deficits in sensorimotor gating. *Psychopharmacology (Berlin)*, *141*(1), 93–98.

Ferguson, J. N., Aldag, J. M., Insel, T. R., & Young, L. J. (2001). Oxytocin in the medial amygdala is essential for social recognition in the mouse. *Journal of Neuroscience*, *21*(20), 8278–8285.

Ferguson, J. N., Young, L. J., Hearn, E. F., Matzuk, M. M., Insel, T. R., & Winslow, J. T. (2000). Social amnesia in mice lacking the oxytocin gene. *Nature Genetics*, *25*(3), 284–288.

Fischer-Shofty, M., Brune, M., Ebert, A., Shefet, D., Levkovitz, Y., & Shamay-Tsoory, S. G. (2013). Improving social perception in schizophrenia: The role of oxytocin. *Schizophrenia Research*, *146*(1–3), 357–362.

Gamer, M., Zurowski, B., & Büchel, C. (2010). Different amygdala subregions mediate valence-related and attentional effects of oxytocin in humans. *Proceedings of the National Academy of Sciences of the United States of America*, *107*(20), 9400–9405.

Glovinsky, D., Kalogeras, K. T., Kirch, D. G., Suddath, R., & Wyatt, R. J. (1994). Cerebrospinal fluid oxytocin concentration in schizophrenic patients does not differ from control subjects and is not changed by neuroleptic medication. *Schizophrenia Research*, *11*(3), 273–276.

Goldman, M., Marlow-O'Connor, M., Torres, I., & Carter, C. S. (2008). Diminished plasma oxytocin in schizophrenic patients with neuroendocrine dysfunction and emotional deficits. *Schizophrenia Research*, *98*(1–3), 247–255.

Heinrichs, M., Baumgartner, T., Kirschbaum, C., & Ehlert, U. (2003). Social support and oxytocin interact to suppress cortisol and subjective responses to psychosocial stress. *Biological Psychiatry*, *54*(12), 1389–1398.

Hurlemann, R., Patin, A., Onur, O. A., Cohen, M. X., Baumgartner, T., Metzler, S., et al. (2010). Oxytocin enhances amygdala-dependent, socially reinforced learning and emotional empathy in humans. *Journal of Neuroscience*, *30*(14), 4999–5007.

Kéri, S., Kiss, I., & Kelemen, O. (2009). Sharing secrets: Oxytocin and trust in schizophrenia. *Social Neuroscience*, *4*, 287–293.

Kirsch, P., Esslinger, C., Chen, Q., Mier, D., Lis, S., Siddhanti, S., et al. (2005). Oxytocin modulates neural circuitry for social cognition and fear in humans. *Journal of Neuroscience*, *25*(49), 11489–11493.

Kosfeld, M., Heinrichs, M., Zak, P. J., Fischbacher, U., & Fehr, E. (2005). Oxytocin increases trust in humans. *Nature*, *435*(7042), 673–676.

Kreifelts, B., Ethofer, T., Huberle, E., Grodd, W., & Wildgruber, D. (2010). Association of trait emotional intelligence and individual fMRI-activation patterns during the perception of social signals from voice and face. *Human Brain Mapping*, *31*(7), 979–991.

Lee, P. R., Brady, D. L., Shapiro, R. A., Dorsa, D. M., & Koenig, J. I. (2005). Social interaction deficits caused by chronic phencyclidine administration are reversed by oxytocin. *Neuropsychopharmacology*, *30*(10), 1883–1894.

Lee, P. R., Brady, D. L., Shapiro, R. A., Dorsa, D. M., & Koenig, J. I. (2007). Prenatal stress generates deficits in rat social behavior: Reversal by oxytocin. *Brain Research*, *1156*, 152–167.

Linkowski, P., Geenen, V., Kerkhofs, M., Mendlewicz, J., & Legros, J. J. (1984). Cerebrospinal fluid neurophysins in affective illness and in schizophrenia. *European Archives of Psychiatry and Neurological Science, 234*(3), 162–165.

MacDonald, E., Dadds, M. R., Brennan, J. L., Williams, K., Levy, F., & Cauchi, A. J. (2011). A review of safety, side-effects and subjective reactions to intranasal oxytocin in human research. *Psychoneuroendocrinology, 36*(8), 1114–1126.

MacDonald, K., MacDonald, T. M., Brune, M., Lamb, K., Wilson, M. P., Golshan, S., et al. (2013). Oxytocin and psychotherapy: A pilot study of its physiological, behavioral and subjective effects in males with depression. *Psychoneuroendocrinology, 38*(12), 2831–2843.

McCullough, M. E., Churchland, P. S., & Mendez, A. J. (2013). Problems with measuring peripheral oxytocin: Can the data on oxytocin and human behavior be trusted? *Neuroscience and Biobehavoral Reviews, 37*(8), 1485–1492.

Meyer-Lindenberg, A., Domes, G., Kirsch, P., & Heinrichs, M. (2011). Oxytocin and vasopressin in the human brain: Social neuropeptides for translational medicine. *Nature Reviews. Neuroscience, 12*(9), 524–538.

Mier, D., Sauer, C., Lis, S., Esslinger, C., Wilhelm, J., Gallhofer, B., et al. (2010). Neuronal correlates of affective theory of mind in schizophrenia out-patients: Evidence for a baseline deficit. *Psychological Medicine, 40*(10), 1607–1617.

Modabbernia, A., Rezaei, F., Salehi, B., Jafarinia, M., Ashrafi, M., Tabrizi, M., et al. (2013). Intranasal oxytocin as an adjunct to risperidone in patients with schizophrenia: An 8-week, randomized, double-blind, placebo-controlled study. *CNS Drugs, 27*(1), 57–65.

Montag, C., Brockmann, E. -M., Bayerl, M., Rujescu, D., Müller, D., & Gallinat, J. (2012). Oxytocin and oxytocin receptor gene polymorphisms and risk for schizophrenia: A case-control study. *World Journal of Biological Psychiatry, 14*(7), 500–508.

Neumann, I. D., & Landgraf, R. (2008). *Advances in vasopressin and oxytocin: From genes to behaviour to disease.* Amsterdam: Elsevier.

Pedersen, C. A., Gibson, C. M., Rau, S. W., Salimi, K., Smedley, K. L., Casey, R. L., et al. (2011). Intranasal oxytocin reduces psychotic symptoms and improves theory of mind and social perception in schizophrenia. *Schizophrenia Research, 132*(1), 50–53.

Pierrehumbert, B., Torrisi, R., Ansermet, F., Borghini, A., & Halfon, O. (2012). Adult attachment representations predict cortisol and oxytocin responses to stress. *Attachment & Human Development, 14*, 453–476.

Popik, P., & Van Ree, J. M. (1991). Oxytocin but not vasopressin facilities social recognition following injection into the medial preoptic area of the rat brain. *European Neuropsychopharmacology, 1*(4), 555–560.

Popik, P., Vos, P. E., & Van Ree, J. M. (1992). Neurohypophyseal hormone receptors in the septum are implicated in social recognition in the rat. *Behavioural Pharmacology, 3*(4), 351–358.

Rault, J. L., Carter, C. S., Garner, J. P., Marchant-Forde, J. N., Richert, B. T., & Lay, D. C., Jr. (2013). Repeated intranasal oxytocin administration in early life dysregulates the HPA axis and alters social behavior. *Physiology & Behavior, 112–113*, 40–48.

Rosenfeld, A. J., Lieberman, J. A., & Jarskog, L. F. (2011). Oxytocin, dopamine, and the amygdala: A neurofunctional model of social cognitive deficits in schizophrenia. *Schizophrenia Bulletin, 37*(5), 1077–1087.

Rubin, L. H., Carter, C. S., Drogos, L., Jamadar, R., Pournajafi-Nazarloo, H., Sweeney, J. A., et al. (2011). Sex-specific associations between peripheral oxytocin and emotion perception in schizophrenia. *Schizophrenia Research, 130*(1–3), 266–270.

Rubin, L. H., Carter, C. S., Drogos, L., Pournajafi-Nazarloo, H., Sweeney, J. A., & Maki, P. M. (2010). Peripheral oxytocin is associated with reduced symptom severity in schizophrenia. *Schizophrenia Research, 124*, 13–21.

Sala, M., Braida, D., Lentini, D., Busnelli, M., Bulgheroni, E., Capurro, V., et al. (2011). Pharmacologic rescue of impaired cognitive flexibility, social deficits, increased aggression, and seizure susceptibility in oxytocin receptor null mice: A neurobehavioral model of autism. *Biological Psychiatry, 69*(9), 875–882.

Sofroniew, M. V. (1980). Projections from vasopressin, oxytocin, and neurophysin neurons to neural targets in the rat and human. *Journal of Histochemistry Cytochemistry, 28*(5), 475–478.

Strathearn, L., Fonagy, P., Amico, J., & Montague, P. R. (2009). Adult attachment predicts maternal brain and oxytocin response to infant cues. *Neuropsychopharmacology, 34*(13), 2655–2666.

Tas, C., Danaci, A. E., Cubukcuoglu, Z., & Brüne, M. (2012). Impact of family involvement on social cognition training in clinically stable outpatients with schizophrenia – a randomized pilot study. *Psychiatry Research, 195*(1), 32–38.

Teltsh, O., Kanyas-Sarner, K., Rigbi, A., Greenbaum, L., Lerer, B., & Kohn, Y. (2012). Oxytocin and vasopressin genes are significantly associated with schizophrenia in a large Arab-Israeli pedigree. *International Journal of Neuropsychopharmacology, 15*, 309–319.

Theodoridou, A., Rowe, A. C., Penton-Voak, I. S., & Rogers, P. J. (2009). Oxytocin and social perception: Oxytocin increases perceived facial trustworthiness and attractiveness. *Hormones and Behavior, 56*(1), 128–132.

Uvnas-Moberg, K., Alster, P., & Svensson, T. H. (1992). Amperozide and clozapine but not haloperidol or raclopride increase the secretion of oxytocin in rats. *Psychopharmacology, 109*, 473–476.

Walss-Bass, C., Fernandes, J. M., Roberts, D. L., Service, H., & Velligan, D. (2013). Differential correlations between plasma oxytocin and social cognitive capacity and bias in schizophrenia. *Schizophrenia Research, 147*(2–3), 387–392.

Windle, R. J., Kershaw, Y. M., Shanks, N., Wood, S. A., Lightman, S. L., & Ingram, C. D. (2004). Oxytocin attenuates stress-induced c-fos mRNA expression in specific forebrain regions associated with modulation of hypothalamo-pituitary-adrenal activity. *Journal of Neuroscience, 24*(12), 2974–2982.

Windle, R. J., Shanks, N., Lightman, S. L., & Ingram, C. D. (1997). Central oxytocin administration reduces stress-induced corticosterone release and anxiety behavior in rats. *Endocrinology, 138*(7), 2829–2834.

Zak, P. J., Stanton, A. A., & Ahmadi, S. (2007). Oxytocin increases generosity in humans. *PLoS One, 2*(11), e1128.

Social Cognition and Metacognition in Schizophrenia: Research to Date and Directions for the Future

Paul H. Lysaker,[1,2] Giancarlo Dimaggio[3,4] and Martin Brüne[5]

[1]*Richard L. Roudebush VA Medical Center Indianapolis, IN, USA,* [2]*Indiana University School of Medicine, Indianapolis, IN, USA,* [3]*Center for Metacognitive Interpersonal Therapy, Rome, Italy,* [4]*University La Sapienza, Rome, Italy,* [5]*LWL-University Hospital Bochum, Bochum, Germany*

Chapter Outline

Social Cognition and Metacognition in Schizophrenia.
DOI: http://dx.doi.org/10.1016/B978-0-12-405172-0.00019-3
© 2014 Elsevier Inc. All rights reserved.

'In concluding this chapter I cannot forbear remarking that in insanity, all questions of the intrinsic nature of the disease put aside, the prognosis is often materially influenced by extraneous circumstances – the behaviour of those relatives and friends of the patient who are most nearly interested in him. It admits of no doubt that in some cases the eager impatience, the restless anxieties, the meddlesome interference, and the quarrels of friends thwart the best efforts of the physician. Sincere and sound advice, founded on experience, is not adopted, or, if adopted, not steadily followed; meanwhile that time in which there is the best hope, and sometimes the only hope, from treatment passes; and the period of recovery is delayed, if the progress of it is not arrested. It is not an unwarrantable assertion to make, that some insane people have owed their lifelong mental affliction to the injudicious conduct of those to whom they were most dear.'

Maudsley, 1867, p. 421.

INTRODUCTION

One of the most remarkable and often neglected features of schizophrenia is the collapse of adaptive goal directed behavior in the presence of many mental functions that have remained intact. Many people with schizophrenia may, for instance, be able to pay bills, cash checks at a bank, take public transportation, prepare meals, attend movies, and remember the birth dates of siblings. Some may also have worked, dated, and married, had hopes and dreams and an envisioned future, and yet now in the midst of the disease, appear to find no sufficiently compelling reasons to persist at a job, keep in touch with friends, or think strategically about their future.

When the term schizophrenia was first coined, Bleuler (1908/1950) noticed these phenomena. He proposed that to understand such a puzzling set of interruptions within a human life, one had to look beyond symptoms, such as hallucinations or delusions, and turn attention to how ideas were put together. Specifically, he suggested that at the core of the disorder was a disturbance in the ability to link together and synthesize complex ideas. These included the ability to form integrated and complex ideas about oneself and others: 'the patient hardly knows how to orient himself either inwardly or outwardly . . . a very intelligent patient needs hours of strenuous inner effort to find her own ego for a few brief moments' (p. 143).

Whereas first person and clinical reports have suggested that many people with schizophrenia experience difficulties in thinking about themselves and others, current models of schizophrenia have de-emphasized this as a core feature of the disorder. Schizophrenia has instead been presented as a collection of discrete and observable symptoms related to neurocognitive and psychobiologic processes. This approach has been suggested to have several advantages. For instance, it seeks to make the condition easier to diagnose. It has explicitly attempted to promote the study of unique features of illness and the factors that contribute to their development and sustenance. It has also guided treatment toward increasingly specific targets.

There are disadvantages of this approach, however. For one, it risks losing sight of the phenomenologic qualities of the condition that were of interest to Bleuler as well as to many others such as Maudsley (1867). An exclusive focus on brain activities and behavioral disorder may importantly fail to consider the subjective experience and suffering of the person whose life has been interrupted (Lysaker and Dimaggio, in press). In addition, this is not a minor danger. People with schizophrenia are not merely beings subject to certain biologic and social challenges. They do not merely experience, for instance, symptoms and stigma. They are beings in the world who have to make meaning out of these challenges and of life itself. In addition, the meanings they form necessarily influence how their lives unfold. The meaning people without psychosis make of a life-altering event deeply influences how they respond to that occurrence and ultimately how well or not well they manage their lives in the face of that event. How people, for instance, understand an injury, a chronic nonpsychiatric medical disease, a death, a job loss, or a significant conflict with a loved one affects how they respond to and live with it.

Returning to schizophrenia, the issue of the meaning people with this condition make of their lives in the midst of the disorder is thus essential to consider in the same sense, as we should consider how anyone makes sense of any challenge. This is especially important, given that, as noted by Bleuler, the processes that allow meaning making within one's life may be disrupted in schizophrenia. In other words, this sense making may be unusually problematic for people with schizophrenia and so potentially not just a necessary generic condition for well-being, but also a specific source of disability in schizophrenia.

Support for the contention that there is more to disability than symptoms and neurocognition comes from a wealth of studies suggesting that symptoms and neurocognitive deficits alone do not fully account for either conversion from a high-risk state to schizophrenia or the emergence or persistence of psychosocial deficits when the disorder is manifest. It is also consistent with observations that current treatments that include many elaborate attempts to treat symptoms and skill deficits are not entirely efficacious.

In response to this problem, researchers and scholars from diverse settings have been exploring over the last 20 years (e.g., Frith, 1992) whether people with schizophrenia experience deficits in the ability to make coherent and useful sense of what is happening in their own minds and in the minds of others. Others have, in parallel, been seeking to devise treatments that might assist people with schizophrenia to form the types of understanding of themselves and others that might offer greater opportunities for recovery. This has included work, including all of the chapters of this book, which refers to these processes as 'social cognition' and others that refer to it as 'metacognition.'

This book has sought to bring together work using both terms in order to offer the most current advances in the field. It also aims to elucidate the general conclusions that can be drawn from this approach, what types of debates are ongoing, and what types of research these conclusions call for. In this final chapter, we will turn to the latter three questions. We will first briefly summarize and then synthesize the preceding information about the biologic and social underpinnings of disturbances in social cognition and metacognition, the more precise nature of social cognitive and metacognitive disturbances in schizophrenia, and the various forms of treatment available. We will next pose four areas of debate: the relationships of the construct of social cognition and metacognition, the factors that cause and sustain these difficulties, the implications for conceptualizing the disorder, and issues at stake when trying to treat disturbances in social cognition and metacognition. Finally, directions for future work are discussed. As with all other chapters in this book, our goal is to stimulate dialogue, advance the study of schizophrenia as an element of the human condition, and promote practices that advance the well-being and quality of life of people with this condition.

THE BIOLOGIC AND SOCIAL UNDERPINNINGS OF DISTURBANCES IN SOCIAL COGNITION AND METACOGNITION IN SCHIZOPHRENIA

This book sets out by considering the question about causal factors involved in disruption of social cognition and metacognition in schizophrenia. Addressing this issue, Brown *et al.* (Chapter 1; *Neurobiologic Underpinnings of Social Cognition and Metacognition in Schizophrenia Spectrum Disorders*) offer a summary of insights from animal studies of sensory gating. From this work, they suggest that deficits in 'filtering' information may contribute to deficits in cognitive domains as well as behavioral consequences. In relation to these findings, Brown *et al.* discuss studies in patients with schizophrenia involving the assessment of event-related potentials elicited by social stimuli. The majority of findings they detail strongly suggest that patients with schizophrenia have altered neurophysiologic response patterns in relation to the processing of social stimuli such as facial emotions. Along similar lines, they point to a growing literature on brain imaging in schizophrenia that suggests the presence of aberrant activation patterns during social cognitive task performance, including tasks addressing metacognitive skills. The activation pattern elicited by social cognitive material suggests an involvement of the mirror neuron system. Consistent with this interpretation, there is evidence to suggest that the mirror neuron system is dysfunctional in schizophrenia, as has been shown in several studies that examined imitation of movements and facial expressions, as well as studies utilizing more classic action-observation paradigms.

Turning to the issue of sociocultural influences, Kölkebeck and Wilhelm (Chapter 2; *Cross-Cultural Aspects of Social Cognitive Abilities in Schizophrenia*) explore the question of whether there are cultural differences in processing social information, and whether this should be considered when reflecting on difficulties in social cognition and metacognition among patients with schizophrenia from different cultures. While little work has been done in this area, especially with patients with schizophrenia, Kölkebeck and Wilhelm observe that people in different cultures attend to different elements of social stimuli and attend to those elements in different ways. For instance, cultures that are more individualized, as opposed to more collectivist, direct people to form different types of concepts of self and others. They also discuss research that has revealed differences in brain activation between Caucasian and Japanese individuals when processing social stimuli. Taken together, results orient us to understand that our knowledge of ourselves and others is constructed in social contexts that cannot be ignored and that likely interact with the kinds of neurobiologic factors discussed by Brown *et al.* (Chapter 1; *Neurobiologic Underpinnings of Social Cognition and Metacognition in Schizophrenia Spectrum Disorders*).

FORMS OF SOCIAL COGNITIVE AND METACOGNITIVE DEFICITS FOUND IN SCHIZOPHRENIA

McCleery *et al.* (Chapter 3; *Social Cognition During the Early Phase of Schizophrenia*) focus on the broad examination of whether there are difficulties in forming ideas about the self and others among people in early phases of schizophrenia as well as people at high risk for developing the disorder. These authors refer solely to the construct of social cognition, which they define as involving at least four major domains: (1) emotion processing, (2) theory of mind, (3) social perception, and (4) attributional style. Focusing on a range of cross-section studies, they note consistent evidence for deficits in emotion processing, theory of mind, and social perception in people in early phases of illness that seem similar to, though less severe than, the deficits observed in more prolonged forms of schizophrenia. They also note that these types of deficits are also found in people at high risk for developing the disorder as well as relatives who have not developed the disorder, though results with these groups have produced less consistent results. Regarding attributional style, it is noted that insufficient research in this area leaves us uncertain whether these types of cognitive biases predate the illness or are present early on. Taken together, results suggest that these core deficits do not appear solely in later stages of the illness, and need to be considered in early interventions.

While McCleery *et al.* (Chapter 3; *Social Cognition During the Early Phase of Schizophrenia*) emphasize the broader phenomenon of social cognition, Derntl and Regenbogen (Chapter 4; *Empathy*) offer a focused consideration of one of the most central aspects of social function, namely empathy. Specifically, they emphasize the necessity to differentiate between cognitive and affective perspective-taking, which represent overlapping, but also distinguishable, domains within the construct of social cognition. With respect to studies in schizophrenia, Derntl and Regenbogen argue for the need to examine empathic responses at the behavioral, physiologic, and neural level simultaneously. They summarize recent research showing that people with schizophrenia have difficulties in inferring another's mental state quickly. Furthermore, in contrast to patients with major depression, the ability of people with schizophrenia to empathize with others deteriorates when speech content is experimentally made incomprehensible, whereas depressed patients rely much more on facial expression of emotions. Such differences at the behavioral level are corroborated by differential responses of the autonomous nervous system, demonstrating that patients with schizophrenia are largely hyporesponsive, whereas depressed patients are hyper-responsive to social emotional cues.

Bacon and Izaute (Chapter 5; *Memory-Related Metacognition in Patients with Schizophrenia*) are concerned exclusively with the construct of metacognition and focus on metamemories, that is, the ability to reflect about memories, which includes being subjectively aware of the capacity for memory and having sense of control over memory-related behavior. They are concerned with the quality of memories, which allows for the formation of coherent representations of self and others, rather than the quantity of memory processes. Their account of the literature is that it suggests that people with schizophrenia do not possess a global monitoring deficit but have a particular pattern of intact and degraded aspects of memory-related metacognitive processes. For example, patients with schizophrenia tend to be overconfident about the accuracy of memories that prove to be inaccurate and demonstrate inefficient strategies for organizing memories and managing memory tasks. Of note, the relationship between memory monitoring and control is complex, such that enhancing monitoring may lead to enhanced abilities for memory control.

At the opposite end of the metacognitive spectrum, Lysaker *et al.* (Chapter 6; *Metacognition in Schizophrenia Spectrum Disorders: Methods of Assessment and Associations with Psychosocial Function, Neurocognition, Symptoms, and Cognitive Style*) tackle the broader question of how well or not people form larger integrated representations of the mental states of the self and of other people and utilize that information to respond to the demands of life. They detail the Metacognition Assessment Scale-Abbreviated, a program of research that involves rating more synthetic aspects of metacognition within personal narratives of patients with schizophrenia. Results are presented that suggest that people with schizophrenia struggle to form complex, integrated ideas about themselves and others in early and later phases of illness and that these forms of metacognitive deficits prospectively predict a range of deficits in psychosocial function, independent of symptom severity and level of neurocognitive compromise.

McLeod and colleagues (Chapter 7; *The Impact of Metacognition on the Development and Maintenance of Negative Symptoms*) build on work linking poor metacognition and negative symptoms noted by Lysaker *et al.* (Chapter 6; *Metacognition in Schizophrenia Spectrum Disorders: Methods of Assessment and Associations with Psychosocial Function, Neurocognition, Symptoms, and Cognitive Style*). They argue that negative symptoms in schizophrenia remain among the most recalcitrant and disabling symptoms in psychiatric illness and that the psychological processes that play a role in their creation and sustenance are poorly understood. They suggest an intuitively appealing model in which difficulties in forming complex ideas of oneself and others interact with premorbid psychosocial impairments, which, in part, promote the development and persistence of negative symptoms. They review psychotherapy and psychopathology research in support of this contention and offer some direct clinical implications. For the sake of speculation, a possible treatment rationale that emerges is that psychotherapy could offer a context in which to reason about the mental states underpinning apathy and avolition and slowly recover contact with emotions, wishes, and motivations that were present before illness onset.

A final chapter that is concerned with forms of metacognitive deficits in schizophrenia is provided by Bo and colleagues (Chapter 8; *Metacognition as a Framework to Understanding the Occurrence of Aggression and Violence in Patients with Schizophrenia*). They focus on a subgroup of people with schizophrenia with history of difficulties negotiating social norms resulting in significant legal problems and incarceration within a forensic institute. They report a series of studies in which they first divided a group of forensic patients into those who manifested premeditated aggression versus impulsive aggression. Using the Metacognition Assessment Scale-Abbreviated, they found that premeditated aggression was predicted by a pattern of relatively intact cognitive but impaired affective metacognition, while impulsive aggression was sustained by both impaired affective and cognitive metacognition. They suggest that the two types of aggression may receive treatments consistent with the profile of impaired metacognition, which is consistent with many of the core treatment principles endorsed by authors in this book who are exclusively focused on clinical implications.

DEVELOPING TREATMENTS FOR SOCIAL COGNITIVE AND METACOGNITIVE DEFICITS FOUND IN SCHIZOPHRENIA

While the literature has advanced rapidly in terms of identifying social cognitive and metacognitive deficits and their links with outcome, work on treatment is still beginning to emerge. Written by Fernandes *et al.*, Chapter 9 (*Social Cognition and Interaction Training: The Role of Metacognition*) is the first chapter to deal with this issue. The authors discuss social cognition and interaction training (SCIT), one of the most carefully developed social cognition intervention programs. They describe how SCIT is structured to engage patients and then assist them to recognize emotions, make sense of social exchanges, and apply that information. They note how SCIT, by presenting material of increasing complexity, seeks to encourage patients to feel engaged. They also explain how the intervention seeks to integrate more immediate automatic cognitive processing with more effortful controlled cognitive processing. Promising results of initial trials are reported, which include information that patients will accept this treatment and that treatment may result in improvements in both social cognition and social functioning.

Combs *et al.* (Chapter 10; *An Overview of Social Cognitive Treatment Interventions*) continue in this thread and provide an overview of therapeutic interventions focusing on social cognitive skills. They differentiate between more broad-based approaches and more comprehensive or targeted intervention strategies, whereby the former include, in addition to specific social cognitive skills, other activities such as neurocognitive remediation, cognitive behavior therapy, and symptom management skills. At present, it seems to be unclear which of these approaches works best for people with schizophrenia. It might well be that not all interventions fit equally well the needs of individual patients. On a larger scale, it appears that the efficacy of targeted intervention is not reflected by improvements at the level of social and community function. Moreover, Combs *et al.* remind us to take into account that both comprehensive and broad-based interventions can last for 6 months to 2 years, which implies that both are expensive and time-consuming. Although Combs *et al.* notice a recent trend to expand and intensify treatments, they also emphasize the value of shorter and more focused interventions, which may better meet the needs of patients and health insurance agencies with limited funds to support such therapeutic approaches.

Woodward *et al.* (Chapter 11; *Metacognitive Training and Therapy: An Individualized and Group Intervention for Psychosis*) shift the focus to work that seeks to improve more discrete forms of metacognitive skills. Their focus is on metacognitive training (MCT) both alone and in combination with other forms of treatment, including cognitive behavior therapy. They note that the primary aim of MCT is to assist people with psychosis to become more aware of how they reason about matters and, in particular, about biases they may possess that could form the basis of delusional beliefs. They describe how MCT in both group and individual formats detangles the elements of biased thinking and reasoning styles that underlie delusions for patients and helps them to be more aware of the thoughts they are forming and how those thoughts impact thinking or cognitive biases leading to misunderstandings of delusional proportion. Results of a range of studies are presented, indicating that patients readily engage in the MCT and tend to experience reductions in positive symptoms. The promising potential to integrate MCT with other treatments is lastly described.

As Woodward *et al.* (Chapter 11; *Metacognitive Training and Therapy: An Individualized and Group Intervention for Psychosis*) and also Fernandes *et al.* (Chapter 9; *Social Cognition and Interaction Training: The Role of Metacognition*) describe engaging programs with creative modules designed to help patients with schizophrenia grasp specific aspects of social cognition and metacognition, Lysaker *et al.* (Chapter 12; *Metacognitively Focused Psychotherapy for People with Schizophrenia: Eight Core Elements That*

Define Practice) offer a set of core principles that could allow for individual psychotherapy to more broadly offer patients on an entirely individualized basis opportunities to make sense of their thoughts and feelings about themselves and ultimately to form more complex and integrated representations of themselves and others, so as to be able to better manage the challenges of schizophrenia and their lives in general. In contrast to previous models, the principles offered in this chapter are processes that should be present in a given session and do not offer a particular curriculum. They are not specific activities to be done one after another, but are processes that could come together in any number of ways to stimulate growth in metacognitive capacity. The proximate goals of the intervention are thus not specifically symptom focused but are the enhancement of the sense of agency necessary for patients with schizophrenia to take charge of their own recovery.

Salvatore *et al.* (Chapter 13; *Adapted-Metacognitive Interpersonal Therapy Applied to Paranoid Schizophrenia: Promoting Higher Levels of Reflection on One's and Others' Minds, Awareness of Interpersonal Schemas, Differentiation, and Mastery of Social Problems*) continue along the lines of Lysaker *et al.* (Chapter 12; *Metacognitively Focused Psychotherapy for People with Schizophrenia: Eight Core Elements That Define Practice*) and focus more specifically on psychotherapy for patients who have achieved higher levels of synthetic metacognitive capacity. While Lysaker *et al.* speak more to helping people with the lowest capacities, this chapter offers a rich case study of the application of these procedures to people with schizophrenia who have begun to form complex and integrated ideas of themselves and others. In doing so, they offer a series of step-by-step procedures that help patients infer the cognitive schemas they employ from their narrative episodes and then to reconstruct these schemas. They note how these procedures can further help patients understand the complex interplay of the thoughts, feelings, and intentions they have about others as they are operating in the moment. Of note, Salvatore and colleagues, in line with general principles of metacognitive interpersonal therapy (Dimaggio *et al.* 2012; in press), warn the therapist against promoting prematurely awareness of the mind of other people until self-awareness and a more solid and healthy sense of self has been achieved.

Consistent with the position of both the last two chapters and that of McLeod *et al.* (Chapter 7; *The Impact of Metacognition on the Development and Maintenance of Negative Symptoms*), Bargenquast and Schweitzer (Chapter 14; *Triumphs and Tribulations in the Psychotherapy of Schizophrenia: Reflections from a Pilot Study of Metacognitive Narrative Psychotherapy*) maintain that the psychotherapy of schizophrenia promises to offer more than symptom improvement, but could help patients move toward recovery through the creation of new meaning. Like Lysaker *et al.* (Chapter 12; *Metacognitively Focused Psychotherapy for People with Schizophrenia: Eight Core Elements That Define Practice*), they propose a treatment manual that contains processes that should be in play within sessions rather than exercises to be followed. A novel aspect of their work is its theoretical richness and use of dialogical theories of self-experience. Their experiences testing this manual are described, and they offer unique insights into both the barriers and prospects of this kind of work. They also raise the important issue that not all therapists may be suited to do this type of work and specifically suggest that therapists must be mindful and reflective about their practice, open to trying to understand before acting, and able to tolerate confusion, uncertainty, and slow and nonlinear progress in order to do this type of work effectively. Overall, the chapter demonstrates that some of the broadest and most subjective constructs in the allied fields of psychiatry can be operationalized and tested systematically in a clinical nonlaboratory setting.

While the treatment approaches of Bargenquast and Schweitzer (Chapter 14; *Triumphs and Tribulations in the Psychotherapy of Schizophrenia: Reflections from a Pilot Study of Metacognitive Narrative Psychotherapy*), Lysaker *et al.* (Chapter 12; *Metacognitively Focused Psychotherapy for People with Schizophrenia: Eight Core Elements That Define Practice*), and Salvatore *et al.* (Chapter 13; *Adapted-Metacognitive Interpersonal Therapy Applied to Paranoid Schizophrenia: Promoting Higher Levels of Reflection on One's and Others' Minds, Awareness of Interpersonal Schemas, Differentiation, and Mastery of Social Problems*) are more integrative in nature and less concerned with the etiology of metacognitive deficits, Brent and Fonagy (Chapter 15; *A Mentalization-Based Treatment Approach to Disturbances of Social Understanding in Schizophrenia*) approach the issue of individual psychotherapy from a mentalization-based approach, which conceptualizes metacognitive processes as deeply tied to the processes of human attachment. This work suggests that the deficits in social cognition and metacognition detailed in the earlier part of this book have to be understood as arising in part within the types of relationships people form with others, including primary caretakers, early in life, though the authors take great care to explain that this is not to blame caretakers. The therapeutic approach described is derived in part from previous work with people with severe personality disorder and calls for education about what mentalizing means, then 'case formulation, and the assessment of mentalization in conjunction with structured clinical management (e.g., pharmacotherapy, crisis planning, and active patient follow-up for missed sessions).' An illustrative case example is offered.

Along similar lines, Harder and Daniel (Chapter 16; *The Relationship Between Metacognitive Profile, Attachment Pattern, and Intersubjective Process in Psychotherapy of a Person Recovering from First-Episode Schizophrenia*) present a formulation of metacognitive deficits and treatment from a more psychoanalytic perspective. This chapter is unique in its very careful case analysis, which includes a description of clinical interventions, assessments of outcome, and discussion of the experiences of the therapist, all of which are essential in order to understand the potential of this treatment to promote metacognitive capacity and wellness among quite ill people.

Following five chapters on individual approaches to psychotherapy, Ottavi *et al.* (Chapter 17; *Metacognition-Oriented Social Skills Training*) propose an integrated form of group treatment that incorporates insights from both individual metacognitively oriented work and more skills-based social cognitive work. Specifically, consistent with the idea that behavioral activation, engagement in social contact, assessment of metacognition, and improvement through practice have beneficial effects on patients' functioning, Ottavi *et al.* present a rehabilitation program that seeks to promote social skills as a result of an enhanced awareness of mental states. Instead of merely teaching social skills, this program includes a manualized curriculum that helps patients to reflect upon specific personal experiences and to practice healthier ways of relating to people. Moreover, the program encourages patients to reflect on their own thoughts and feelings during role-plays and to potentially develop a more enhanced capacity to think about themselves and others. The group setting allows patients to learn from each other further and to support each other's learning. Promising information on the acceptability of these procedures for even relatively more disabled patients is presented.

Tas *et al.* (Chapter 18; *Experimental Usage of Oxytocin to Combat Deficits in Social Cognition in Schizophrenia*) return to experimental procedures for enhancing social cognition and metacognition. Their primary focus is on the use of oxytocin. They review work on oxytocin and human cognition in general and then focus on work from 1974 to the present, which suggests positive, though modest, effects of oxytocin for patients with schizophrenia. This includes studies suggesting that oxytocin may be linked to not only symptom reduction, but also improvements in a range of different aspects of social cognition. Finally, Tas *et al.* suggest that oxytocin may function primarily as a neuromodulator that initially affects subcortical structures, which may indirectly support improvements in social cognitive and metacognitive functions. As a whole, this chapter discusses the potential that the combination of drug treatment with the interventions noted above may offer many with schizophrenia a means to resolve an often hidden and persistent barrier to recovery: deficits in social cognition and metacognition.

AREAS OF DEBATE AND FUTURE DIRECTION

How Do the Constructs of Metacognition and Social Cognition Overlap and Diverge?

In this book, we purposely chose to include work on social cognition and metacognition and to avoid yet another book that keeps such closely related work separate. Nevertheless, the issue of the degree and extent to which they overlap and diverge cannot be avoided. Reflecting on the work in this book, we are struck by several ways in which the constructs could be connected but nonetheless distinguished from one another. First, social cognition is often referred to by researchers interested in the extent to which people are able to make an accurate perception of something fundamentally social in nature. For instance, the majority of social cognition tasks involve getting a specific thing right about someone else. For example, is another person happy, do they harbor an ill intention, are they joking? By contrast, metacognitive assessments seem more concerned with a general sense one has formed of oneself or another. This is manifest in the work presented by Lysaker *et al.* (Chapter 12; *Metacognitively Focused Psychotherapy for People with Schizophrenia: Eight Core Elements That Define Practice*), which tries to measure larger integrated representations of the self and others. It is also present in work that is focused on more discrete aspects of metacognition that nevertheless may culminate in a feeling of knowing (Bacon and Izaute; Chapter 5; *Memory-Related Metacognition in Patients with Schizophrenia*) or a larger sense of the meaning of a complex array of human activities (Woodward *et al.*; Chapter 11; *Metacognitive Training and Therapy: An Individualized and Group Intervention for Psychosis*).

Thus, we would tentatively suggest that the field is heading toward the portrayal of human cognition as a set of dissociable processes that involve the collection of facts and the construction of meaning based on those facts. This holds up the issue of whether we will be able to discuss different types of metacognitive and social cognitive functions meaningfully and create a detailed account of how they support and inform one another. At least intuitively, it would seem that understanding the complex array of internal and social experiences in the moment requires both some means to discern basic facts, as well as arranging and integrating them in some meaningful way. This may not merely be an academic point, but could have clinical importance. If these are different processes, it could be that some patients are more in need of metacognitive interventions, while others need more social cognitive interventions, or potentially more specific forms of each in some kind of unique combination.

Where Do Social Cognitive and Metacognitive Deficits Come from and What Sustains Them?

Across the many types of treatments and different types of basic research paradigms offered in this book, one cannot help but be struck by the different possible causes of deficits in social cognition and metacognition. While we offer no conclusions about which are correct, it seems worth bringing to light some of the possibilities. Brown *et al.* (Chapter 1; *Neurobiologic Underpinnings of Social Cognition and Metacognition in Schizophrenia Spectrum Disorders*) and Lysaker *et al.* (Chapter 12; *Metacognitively Focused Psychotherapy for People with Schizophrenia: Eight Core Elements That Define Practice*) suggest directly that neurocognitive compromise may result in the loss of the ability to take into account basic experience and then form complex and integrated ideas about it. They suggest that a certain level of neurocognitive function is needed for adequate metacognition and social cognition and that the loss of neurocognitive function secondary to schizophrenia could be a direct cause of metacognitive and social cognitive function. In light of the broad phenotype of schizophrenia syndromes, it is also conceivable that in some syndromes the link between neurocognitive impairment and social and metacognitive deficits may be strong, whereas in other syndromes, the connection may be fairly superficial, such that selective deficits in social cognition or metacognition may occur in the absence of other cognitive deficits. Consistent with this, Derntl and Regenbogen (Chapter 4; *Empathy*) and Tas *et al.* (Chapter 18; *Experimental Usage of Oxytocin to Combat Deficits in Social Cognition in Schizophrenia*) also suggest an underlying pathophysiology linked to schizophrenia that could cause deficits in metacognitive and social cognitive abilities. Brent and Fonagy (*Chapter 15; A Mentalization-Based Treatment Approach to Disturbances of Social Understanding in Schizophrenia*) and Harder and Daniel (Chapter 16; *The Relationship Between Metacognitive Profile, Attachment Pattern, and Intersubjective Process in Psychotherapy of a Person Recovering from First-Episode Schizophrenia*) do not rule out the potential role of neurocognitive compromise, but suggest that as metacognitive and social cognitive function emerge within attachment relationships, disruption in those experiences, including those related to trauma, may be a direct cause.

Although not explored directly in this volume, there are also socially related causes of metacognitive and social cognitive deficits. We know schizophrenia is a condition that involves the loss of social connection, often prior to the emergence of symptoms; thus it also stands as possible that these deficits are the result of atrophy. In other words, metacognition and social cognition may decline as connections with others are lost, rather than either having never formed or been eroded earlier in life. Outstanding questions thus posed for future research include whether each of the factors independently contribute to metacognitive and social cognitive deficits and/or whether different kinds of causal factors affect different forms of metacognitive and social cognitive function.

If Metacognitive and Social Cognitive Deficits Arise from Multiple Sources and Take on Different Forms There May Be Further Opportunity for Integrated Treatment

If, as suggested by the totality of this book, deficits in social cognition and metacognition may arise from different sources and have very different forms, then many different forms of treatment may needed. Simply put there is not likely to be a 'one size fits all,' and treatments should be seen as not in competition with one another but with each offering to tackle a different corner of the social cognitive or metacognitive map. Furthermore, different patient preferences may also require different treatments. For instance, people not interested in discussing personal issues may have different needs than people wanting to explore how they understand the world. Indeed, in the work presented in this volume, we can see differing and valid approaches. For example, some take a more educational and structured focus while others are more personally tailored and without a reliance on a specific curriculum. Certainly, it is not difficult to see that there is an untapped potential for differing types of social cognitive and metacognitive treatments to augment one another and be used indeed in an integrative manner. As Woodward *et al.* (Chapter 11; *Metacognitive Training and Therapy: An Individualized and Group Intervention for Psychosis*), for instance, discuss integrating MCT within cognitive behavior treatment, we could imagine a larger treatment program which includes MCT along with SCIT and metacognitively oriented individual psychotherapy.

Research on Social Cognition and Metacognition and Emerging Models of Schizophrenia

The purpose of this book is to offer a view on schizophrenia that integrates neurobiologic with treatment-related issues. We think that such an approach does better justice to the heterogeneity of the syndromes called 'schizophrenia,' including Bleuler's original work highlighting exactly that. While documents such as the *Diagnostic and Statistical Manual of the Mental Disorders*, Fifth Edition (American Psychiatric Association, 2013), make it difficult to see schizophrenia as more than a collection of fragmented symptoms, the work in this book highlights a set of syndromes that fit together as a result of alterations in certain forms of consciousness. Schizophrenia in this book does not emerge as a group of loosely connected deficits in the ability to think, but instead, it appears as in part a profound set of difficulties in thinking about oneself and others. Indeed, it may be that deficits in these kinds of thinking, called social cognition and metacognition throughout this book, represent a type of final common pathway to a life interrupted by schizophrenia, a pathway with many possible beginnings and solutions. At the very least, this work seems to allow us to think about schizophrenia as a complex disorder, one with social and biologic roots, but also as a condition that has a person at the center who is experiencing and thinking about those experiences. We hope this work can help us to not lose sight of that person as our insights into the neurobiologic and social phenomena that surround this disorder grow.

SUMMARY AND FUTURE RESEARCH

Taken together, the 19 chapters of this book point to a set of simple joint conclusions. They offer compelling evidence that people across different phases of schizophrenia struggle to make sense of social and psychological experiences and that these struggles are not the result of symptoms of neurocognitive deficits. These difficulties further may moderate or mediate the impact of other aspects of illness upon daily life and may even represent a unique cause of dysfunction on their own. These deficits may additionally be addressed by a range of different treatments. The further development of those treatments holds out hope for many who have not responded to standard treatments.

However, the work is clearly still developing, and there are many questions that need to be addressed by future research. First, assessment methods need considerable refinement. The study of social cognition and metacognition is new, and our current methods, though promising, are in their infancy. Many of the methods used in the work described in this book are relatively untested, and considerable efforts are needed to continue to examine the validity of these methods as well as to produce more developed and effective instruments. Second, there is a need for longitudinal research. Much of what has been presented here has involved either cross-sectional study or research with a small number of observation points. Clearly needed are assessments of metacognition and social cognition not only across the course of illness but also, if possible, when people are merely at risk. Such work is needed to determine the relationships of these constructs with others as well as their relationship to social function, symptoms, and alterations in brain function. Finally, the many types of promising treatments presented here need to be tested in randomized and open trials in multiple settings in order to establish both their effectiveness as well as which types of patients are most likely to benefit from them.

REFERENCES

American Psychiatric Association. (2013). *Diagnostic and statistical manual of the mental disorders*, Fifth edition. Arlington VA: American Psychiatric Association.

Bleuler, E. (1908). Die prognose der dementia praecox (schizophreniegruppe). Allgemeine zeitschrift für psychiatrie und psychisch gerichtliche. *Medizin, 65*, 436–464.

Dimaggio, G., Montano, A., Popolo, R., & Salvatore, G. (in press). *Metacognitive interpersonal therapy for personality disorders: A treatment manual.* London: Routledge.

Dimaggio, G., Salvatore, G., Fiore, D., Carcione, A., Nicolò, G., & Semerari, A. (2012). General principles for treating the overconstricted personality disorder. Toward operationalizing technique. *Journal of Personality Disorders, 26*, 63–83.

Frith, C. D. (1992). *The cognitive neuropsychology of schizophrenia.* Hove, UK: Erlbaum.

Lysaker, P. H., & Dimaggio, G. (in press). Metacognitive capacities for reflection in schizophrenia: Implications for developing treatments. *Schizophrenia Bulletin.*

Maudsley, H. (1867). *The physiology and pathology of the mind.* New York: D. Appleton and Company.

Index

CPI Antony Rowe
Eastbourne, UK
August 08, 2022